SHORTCAKE CAKE

STORY AND ART BY

suu Morishita

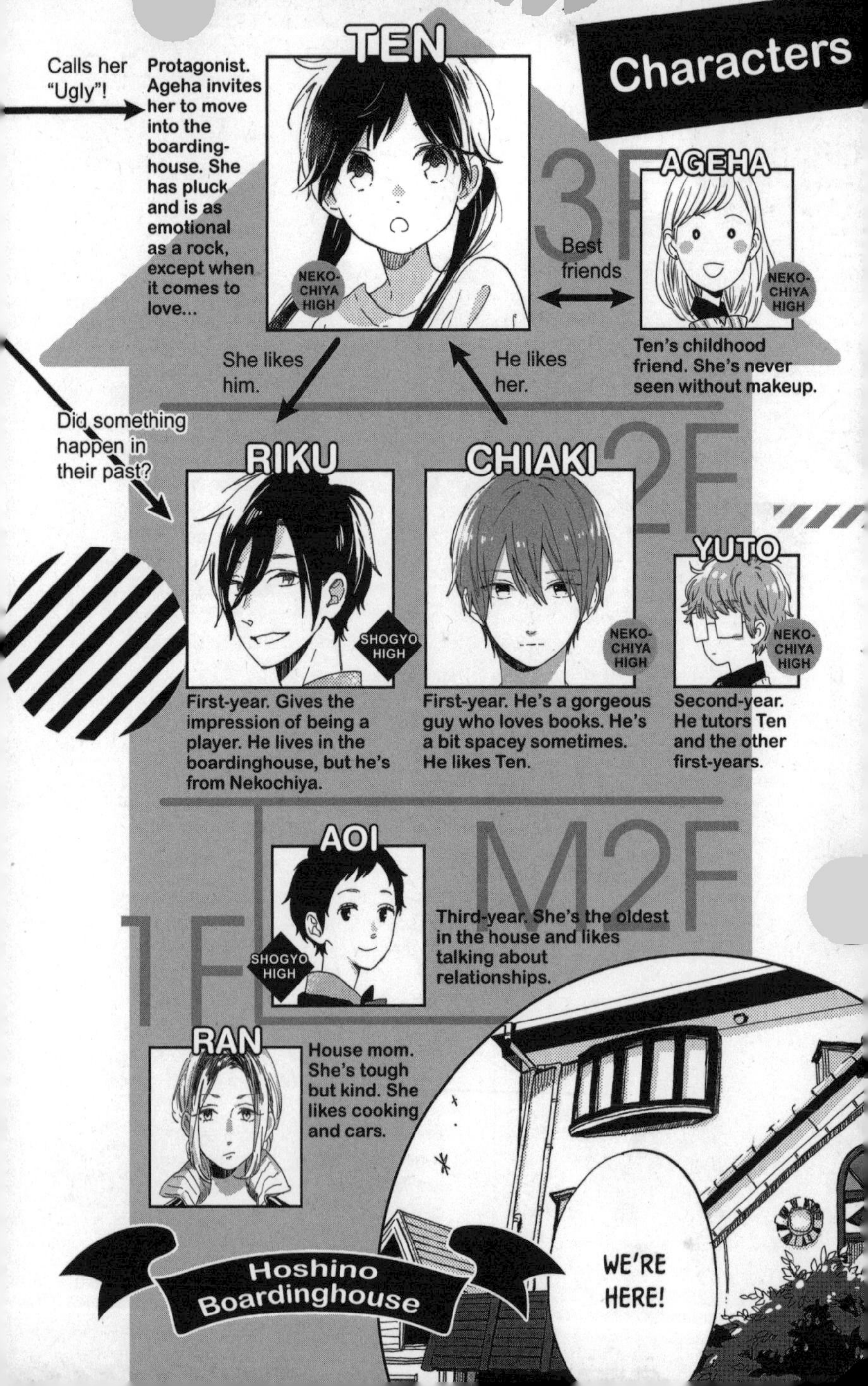

Characters
TEN
Calls her "Ugly"!
Protagonist. Ageha invites her to move into the boardinghouse. She has pluck and is as emotional as a rock, except when it comes to love...
NEKO-CHIYA HIGH
3F
Best friends
AGEHA
NEKO-CHIYA HIGH
Ten's childhood friend. She's never seen without makeup.
She likes him.
He likes her.
Did something happen in their past?
2F
RIKU
SHOGYO HIGH
First-year. Gives the impression of being a player. He lives in the boardinghouse, but he's from Nekochiya.
CHIAKI
NEKO-CHIYA HIGH
First-year. He's a gorgeous guy who loves books. He's a bit spacey sometimes. He likes Ten.
YUTO
NEKO-CHIYA HIGH
Second-year. He tutors Ten and the other first-years.
M2F
AOI
SHOGYO HIGH
Third-year. She's the oldest in the house and likes talking about relationships.
1F
RAN
House mom. She's tough but kind. She likes cooking and cars.
Hoshino Boardinghouse
WE'RE HERE!

Story Thus Far

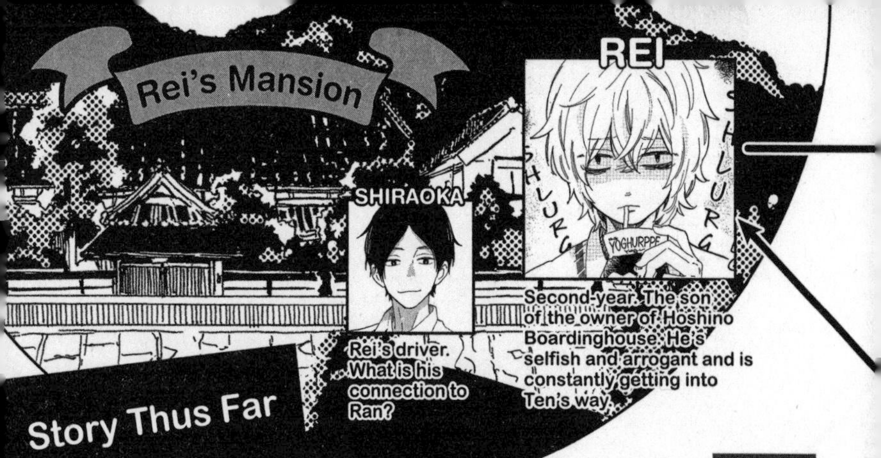
Rei's Mansion
REI
SHLURG SHLURG
YOGHURPPE
SHIRAOKA
Second-year. The son of the owner of Hoshino Boardinghouse. He's selfish and arrogant and is constantly getting into Ten's way.
Rei's driver. What is his connection to Ran?

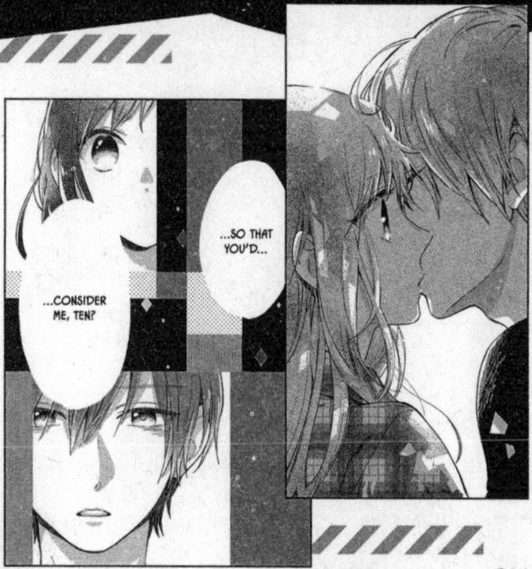
...SO THAT YOU'D...
...CONSIDER ME, TEN?

Ten was commuting two hours each way to school by bus until her friend Ageha invited her to move into the Hoshino Boarding-house. The place is full of characters, and it's there that she meets Riku and Chiaki.

Early on Riku tells Ten that he likes her, but she doesn't take him seriously. She rejects him out of hand. It's only after they spend more time together that Ten realizes she has feelings for him.

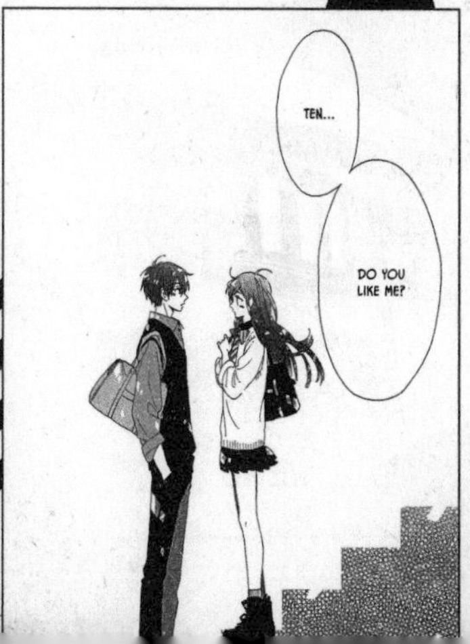
TEN...
DO YOU LIKE ME?

Chiaki can see that Ten likes Riku. He kisses her and asks, "What can I do so that you'd consider me, Ten?"

Ten is flustered and unable to give Chiaki the answer he wants. Knowing her heart is set on Riku, Chiaki lets her know he's rooting for her.

Ten and Riku visit a local shrine together, and she begins to hint at her feelings for him. Riku says she can punch him if he's wrong and then asks her if she likes him.

SHORTCAKE CAKE

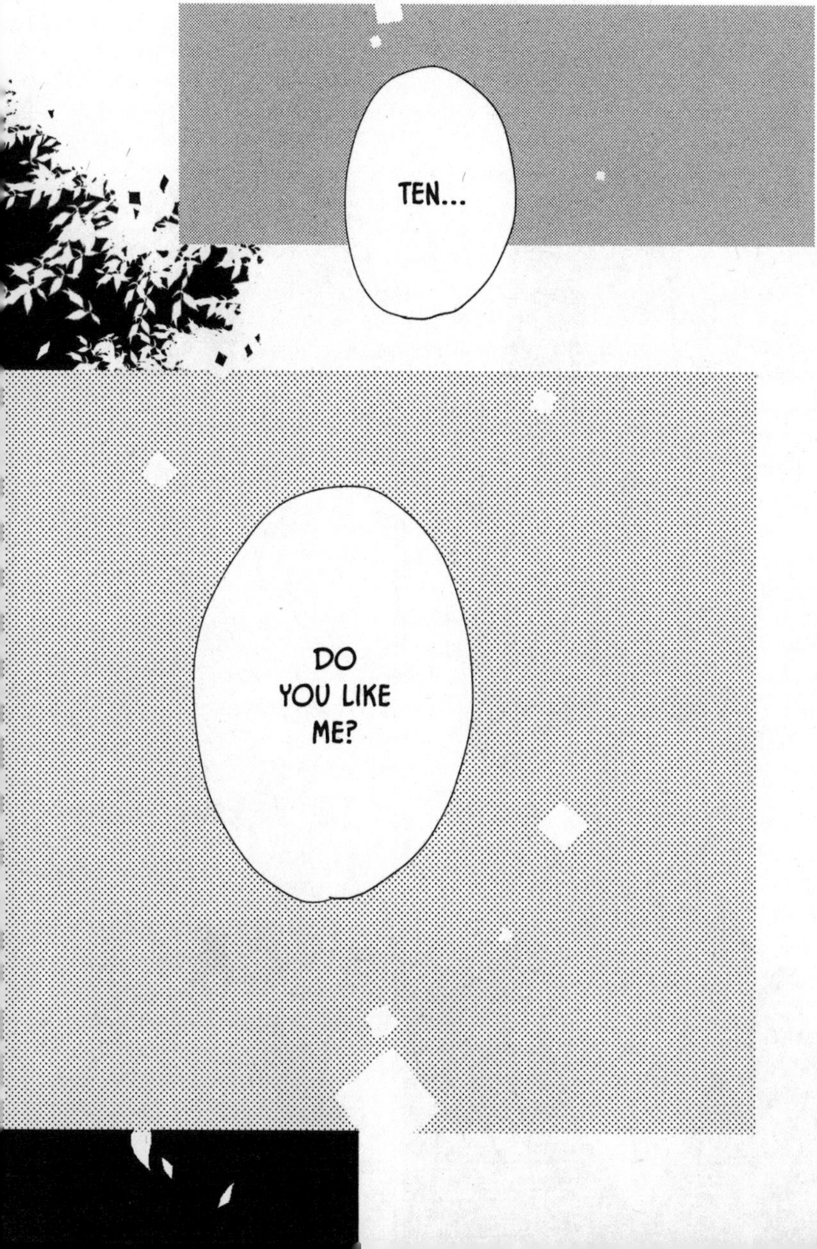
TEN...
DO YOU LIKE ME?

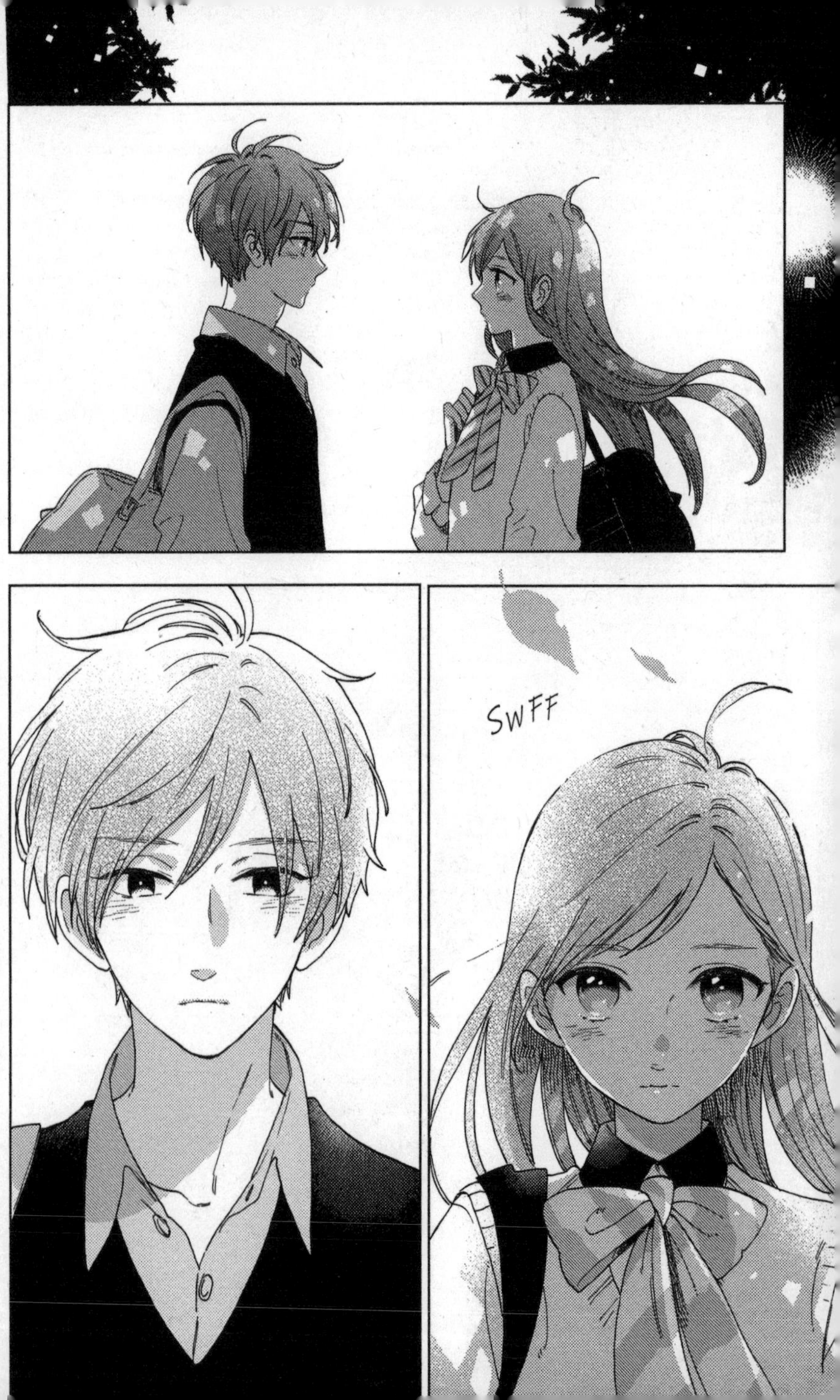
SWFF

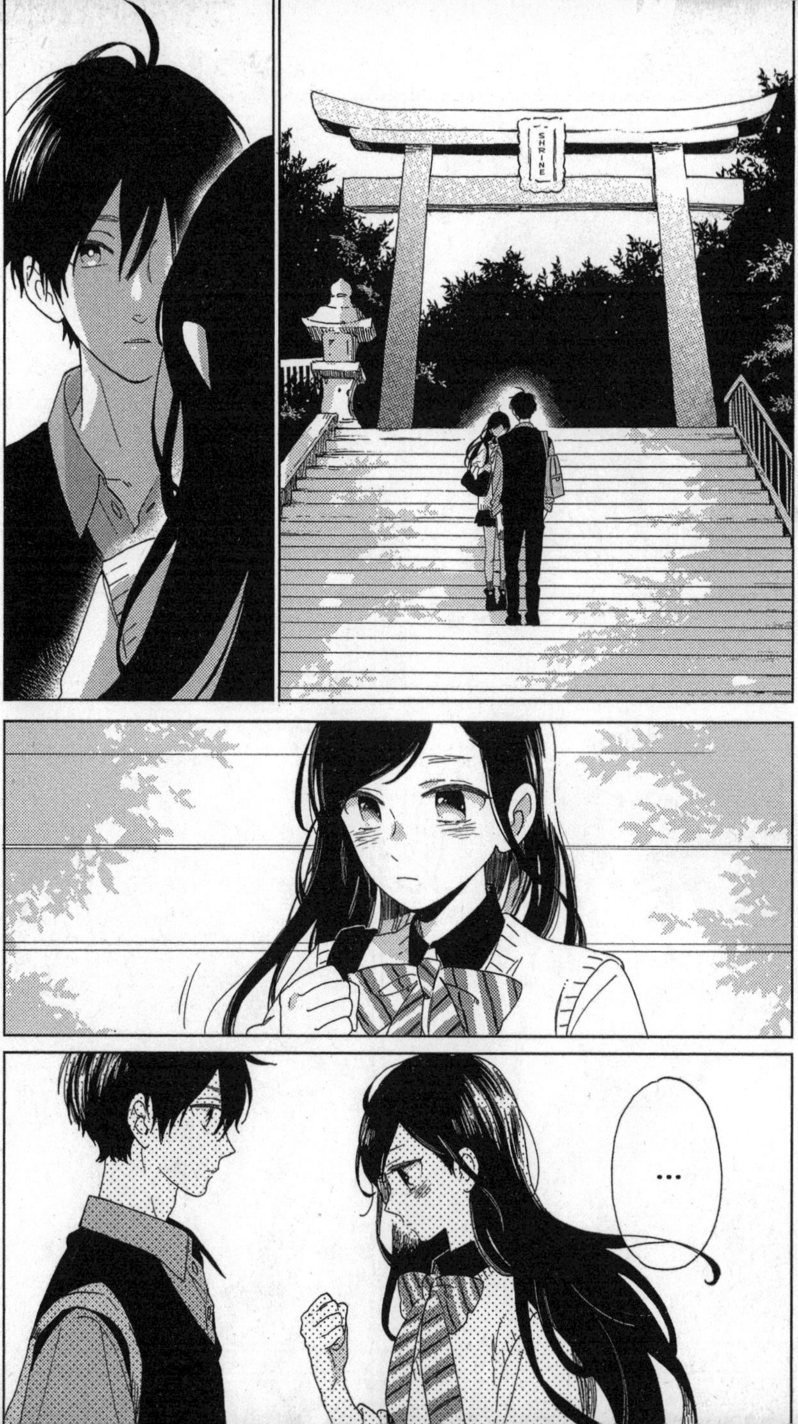
SHRINE
...

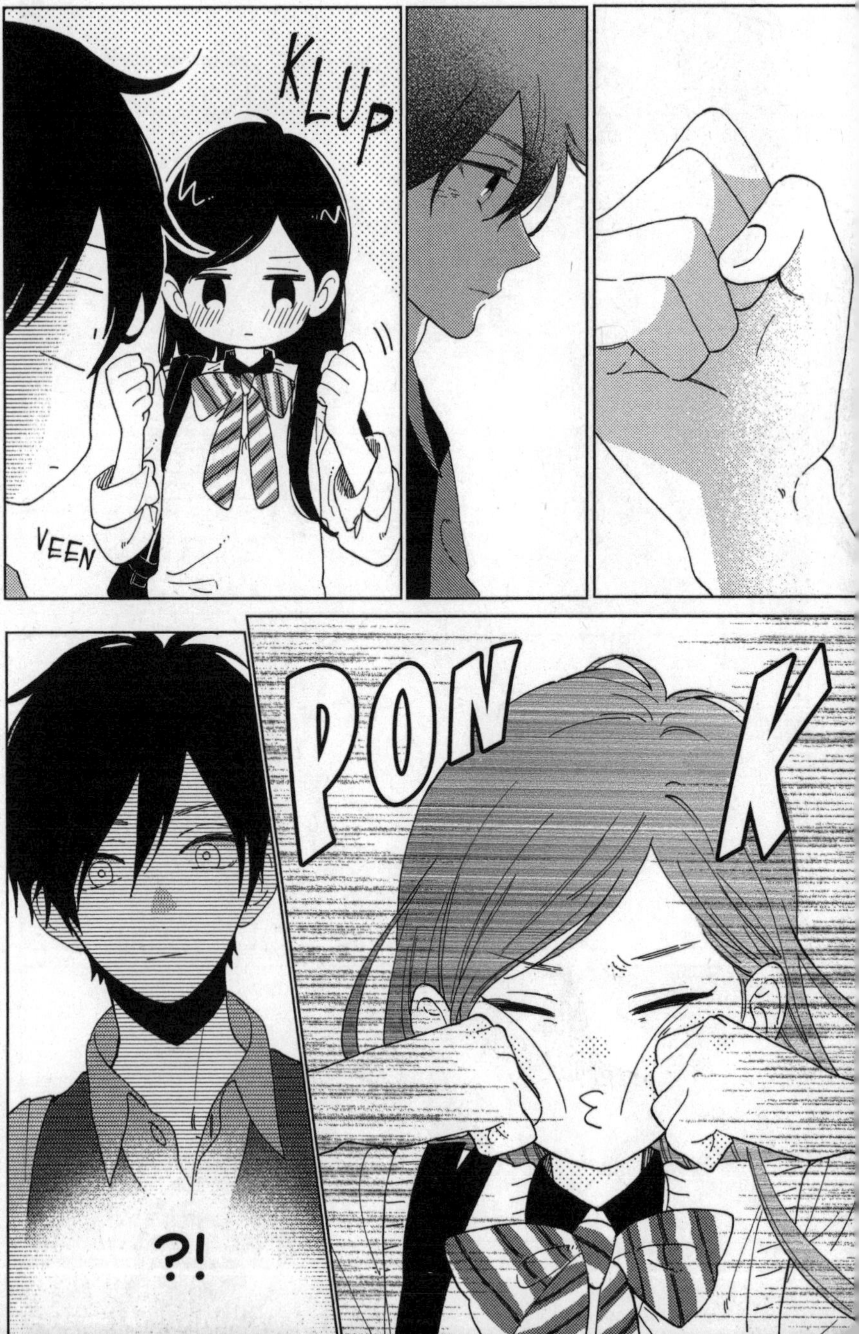
KLUP
VEEN
PONK
?!

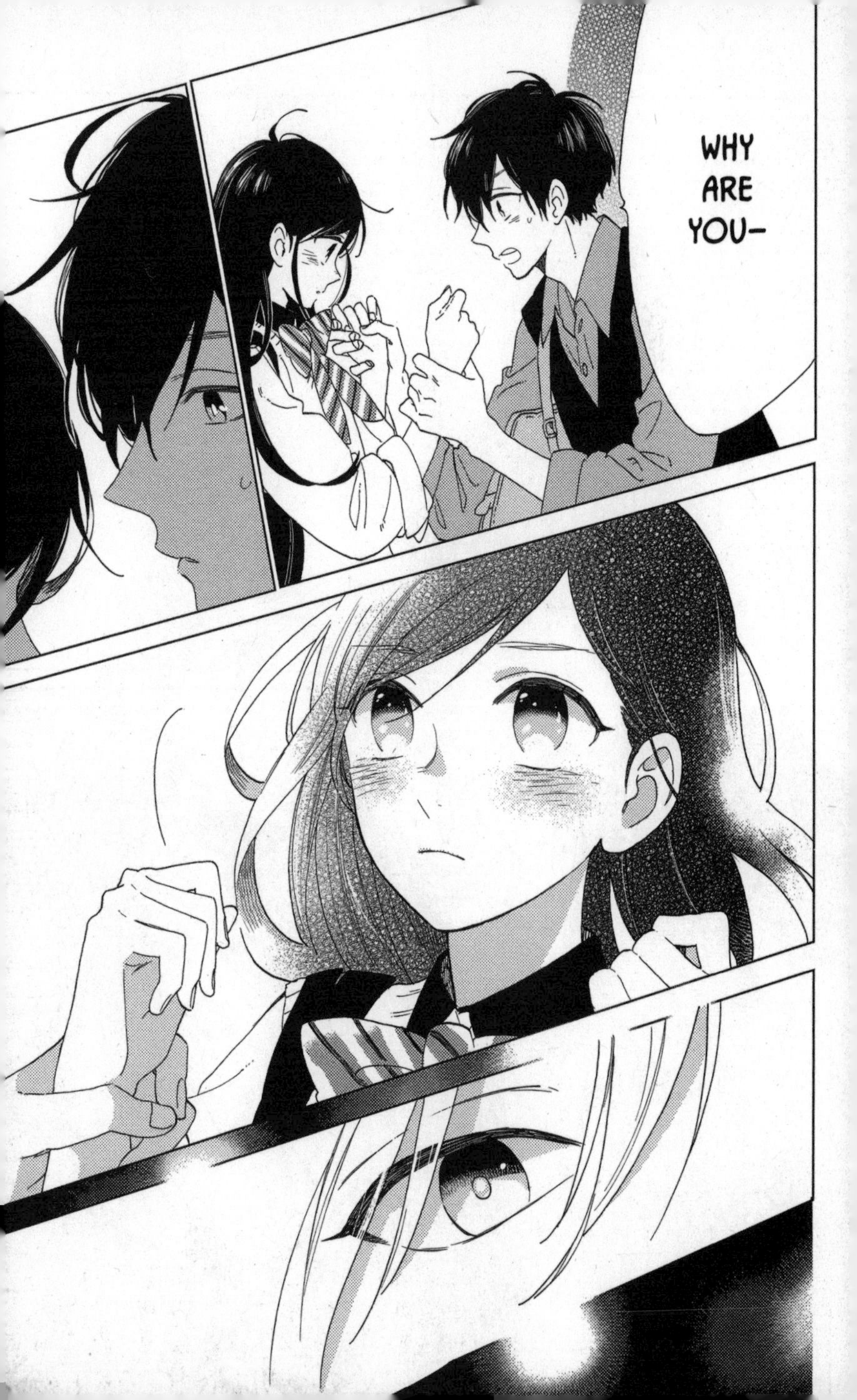
WHY ARE YOU-

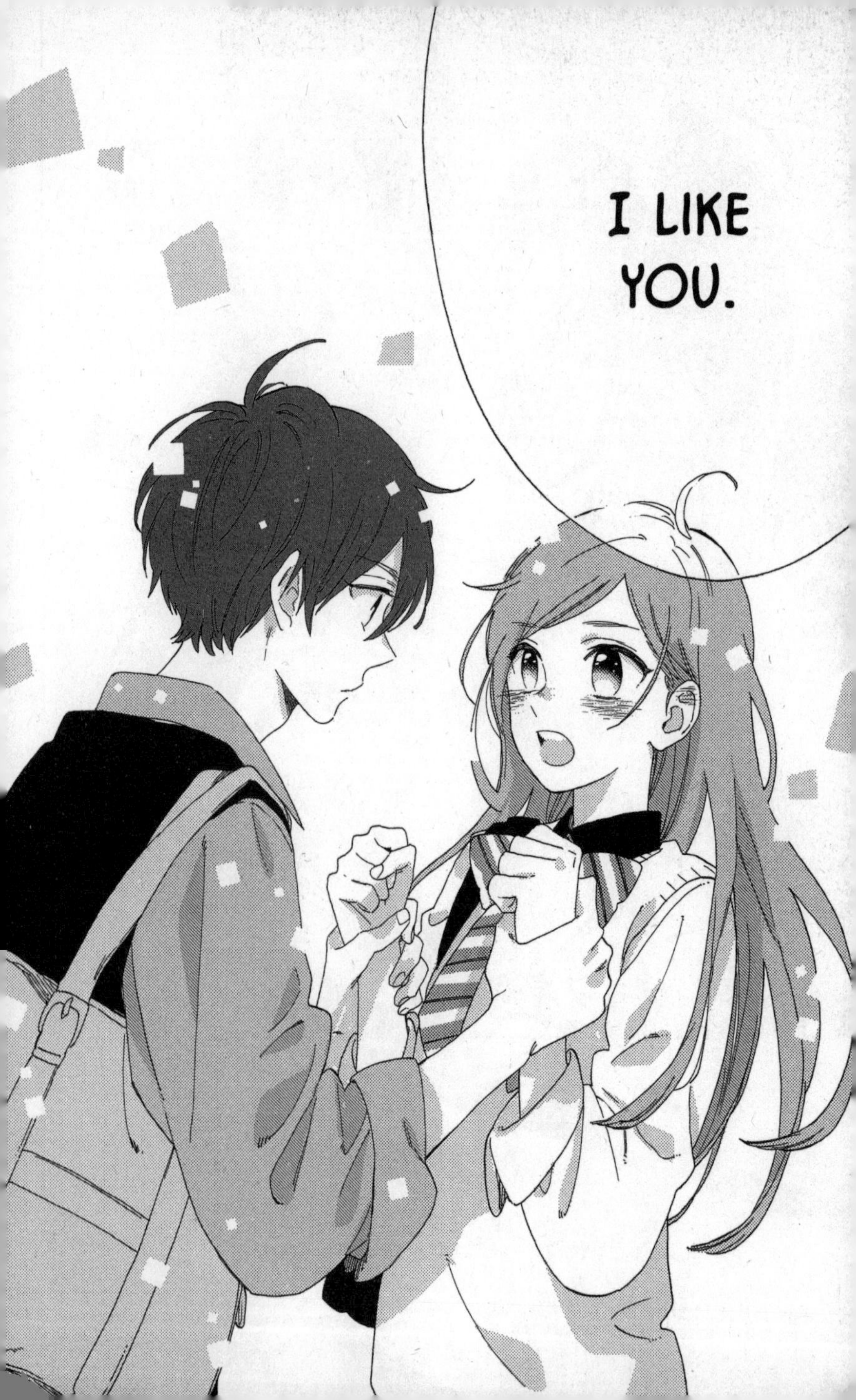
I LIKE YOU.

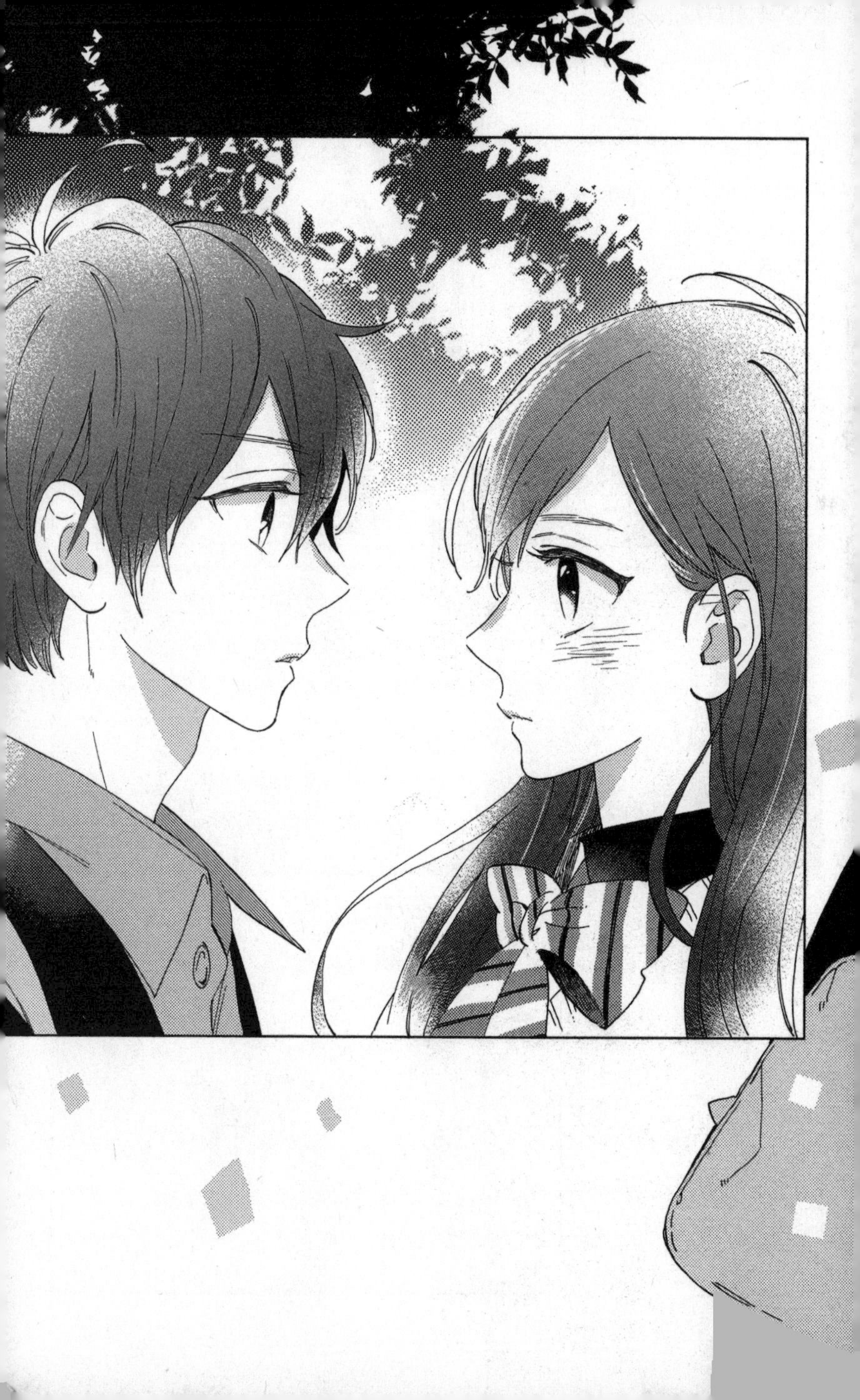

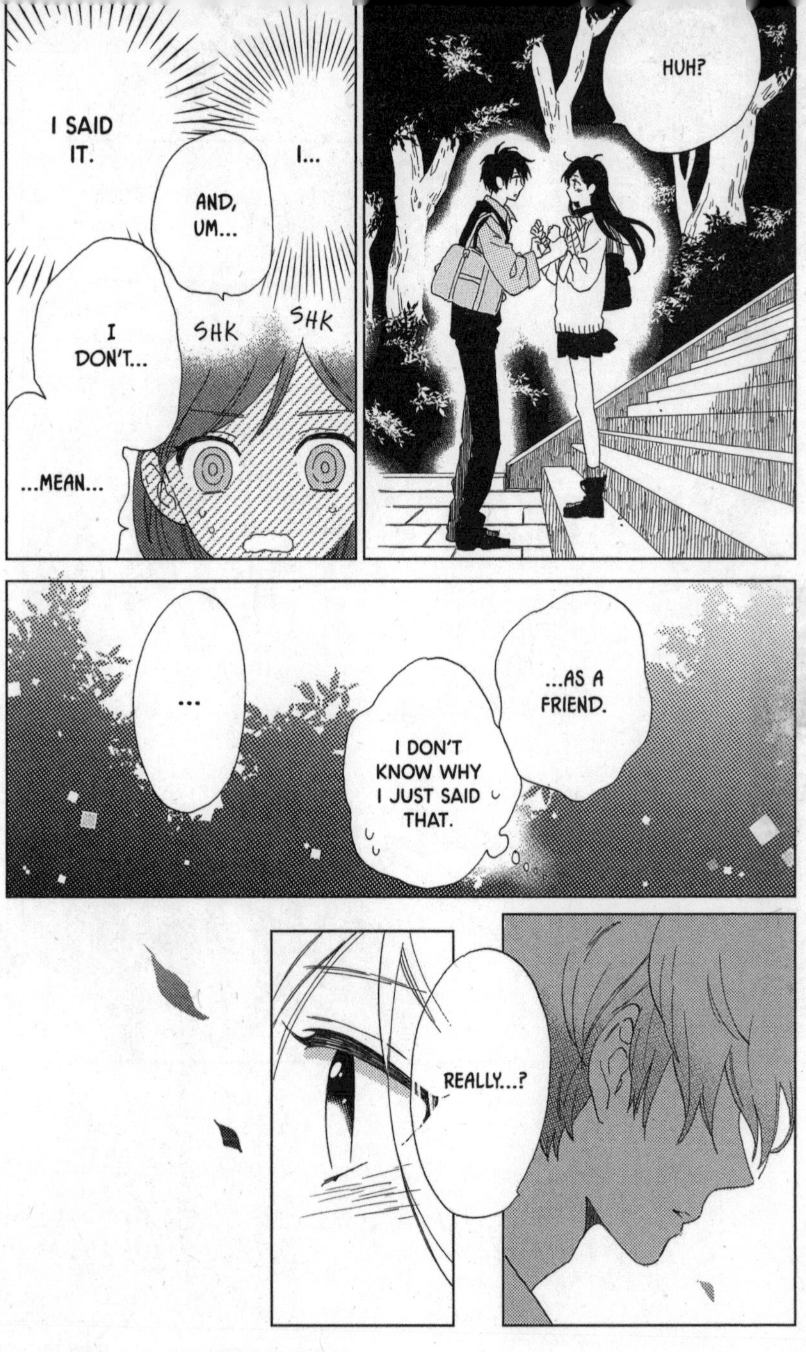
HUH?
I SAID IT.
I...
AND, UM...
SHK
SHK
I DON'T...
...MEAN...
...AS A FRIEND.
I DON'T KNOW WHY I JUST SAID THAT.
...
REALLY...?

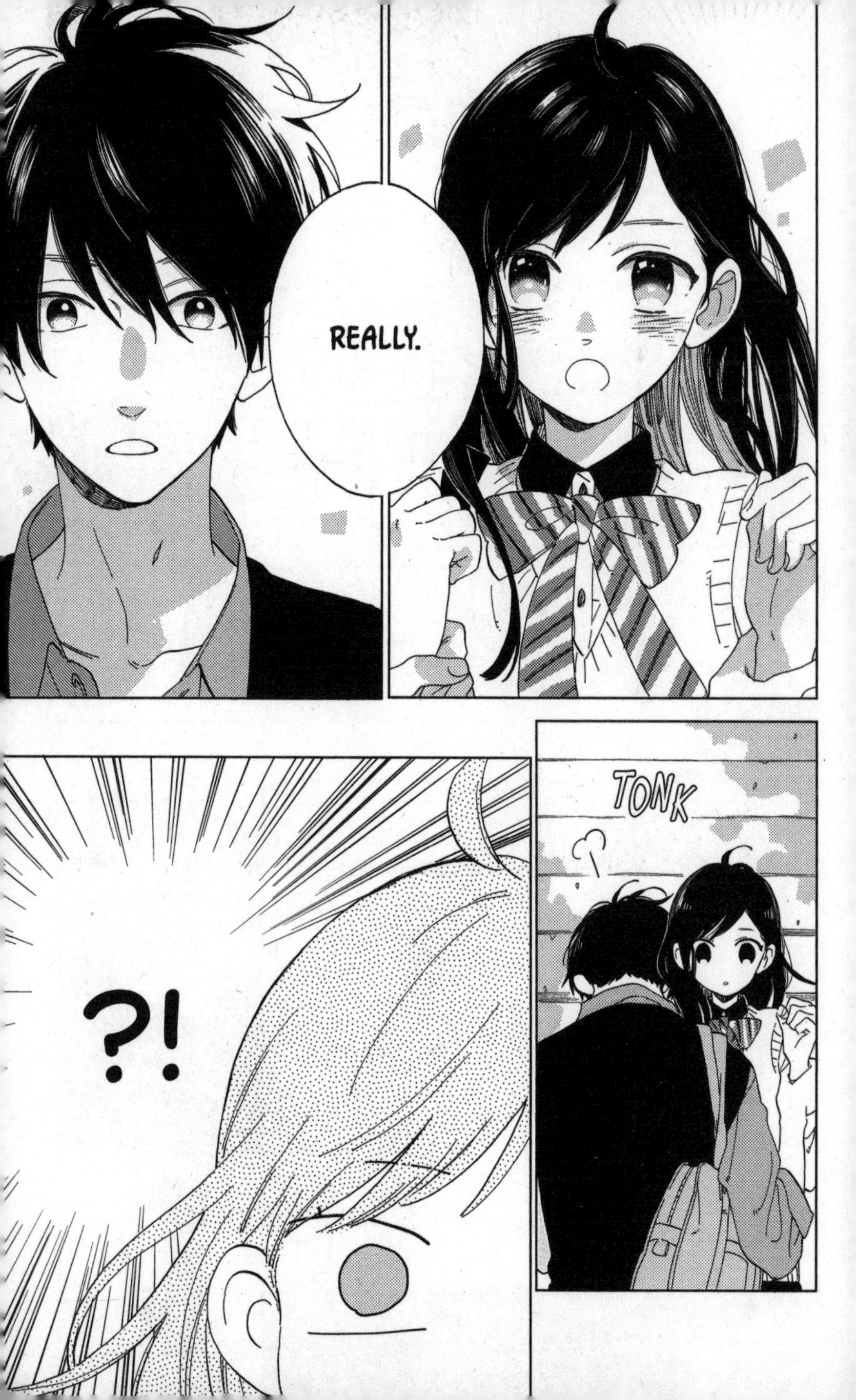
REALLY.
TONK
?!

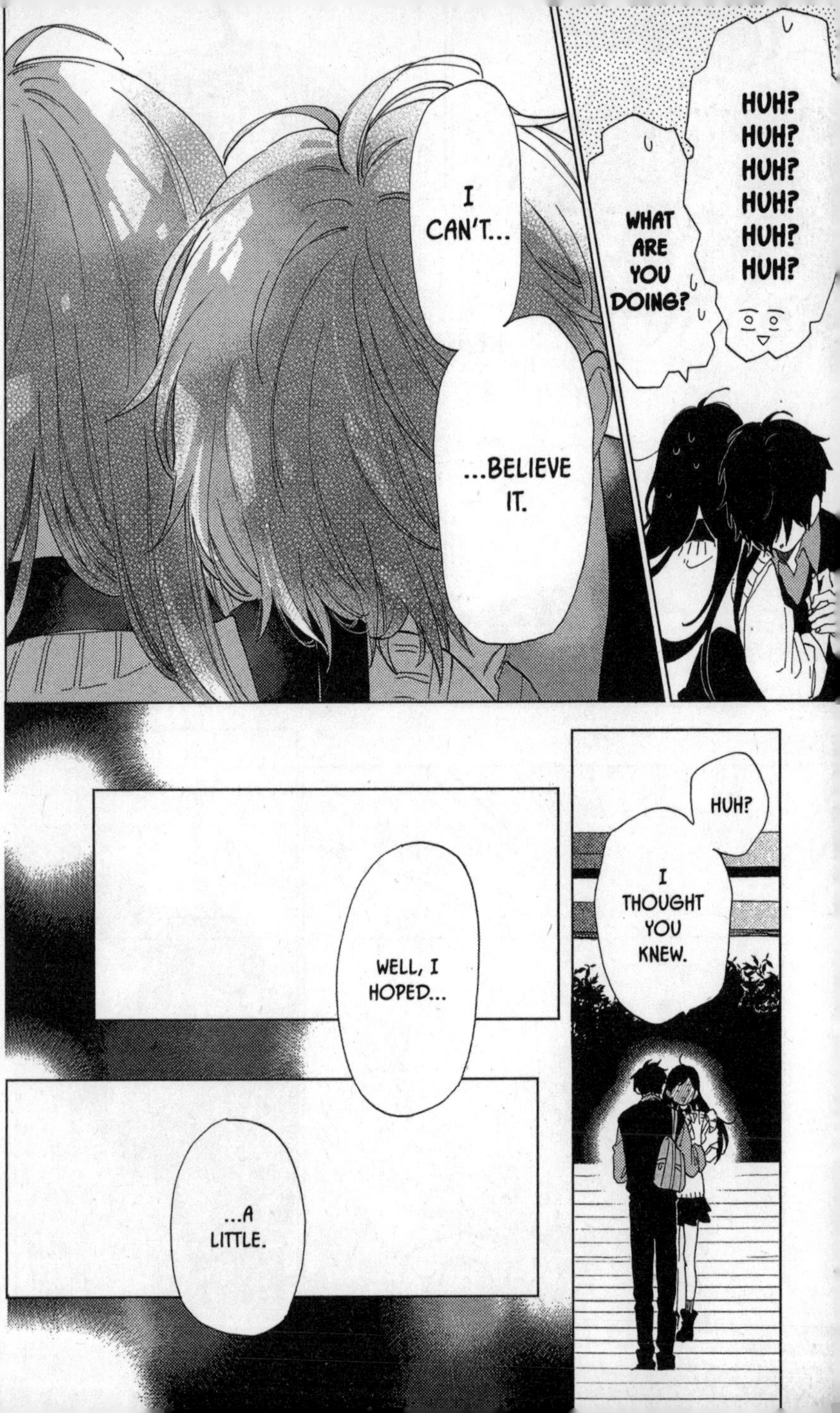
HUH? HUH? HUH? HUH? HUH? HUH?
WHAT ARE YOU DOING?
I CAN'T...
...BELIEVE IT.
HUH?
I THOUGHT YOU KNEW.
WELL, I HOPED...
...A LITTLE.

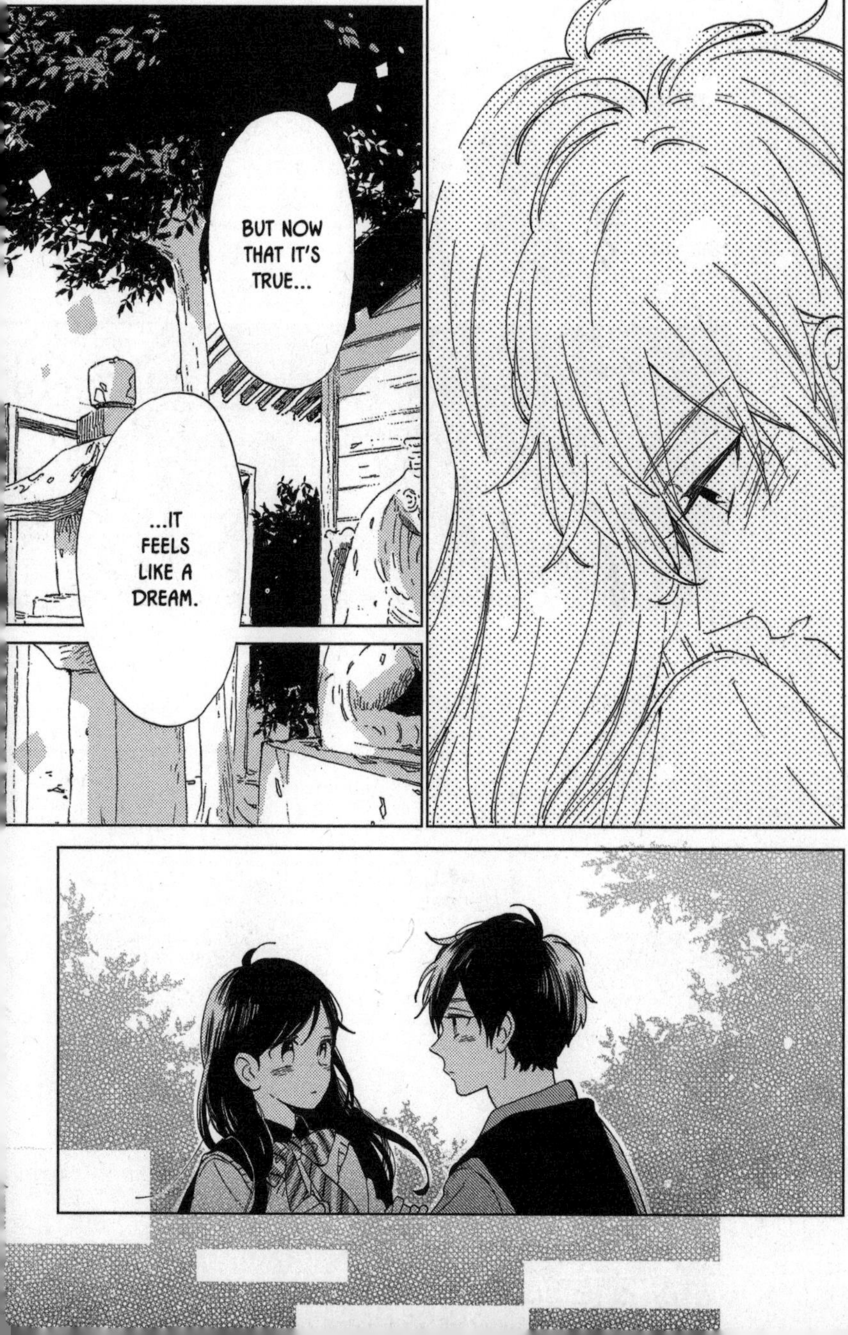
BUT NOW THAT IT'S TRUE...
...IT FEELS LIKE A DREAM.

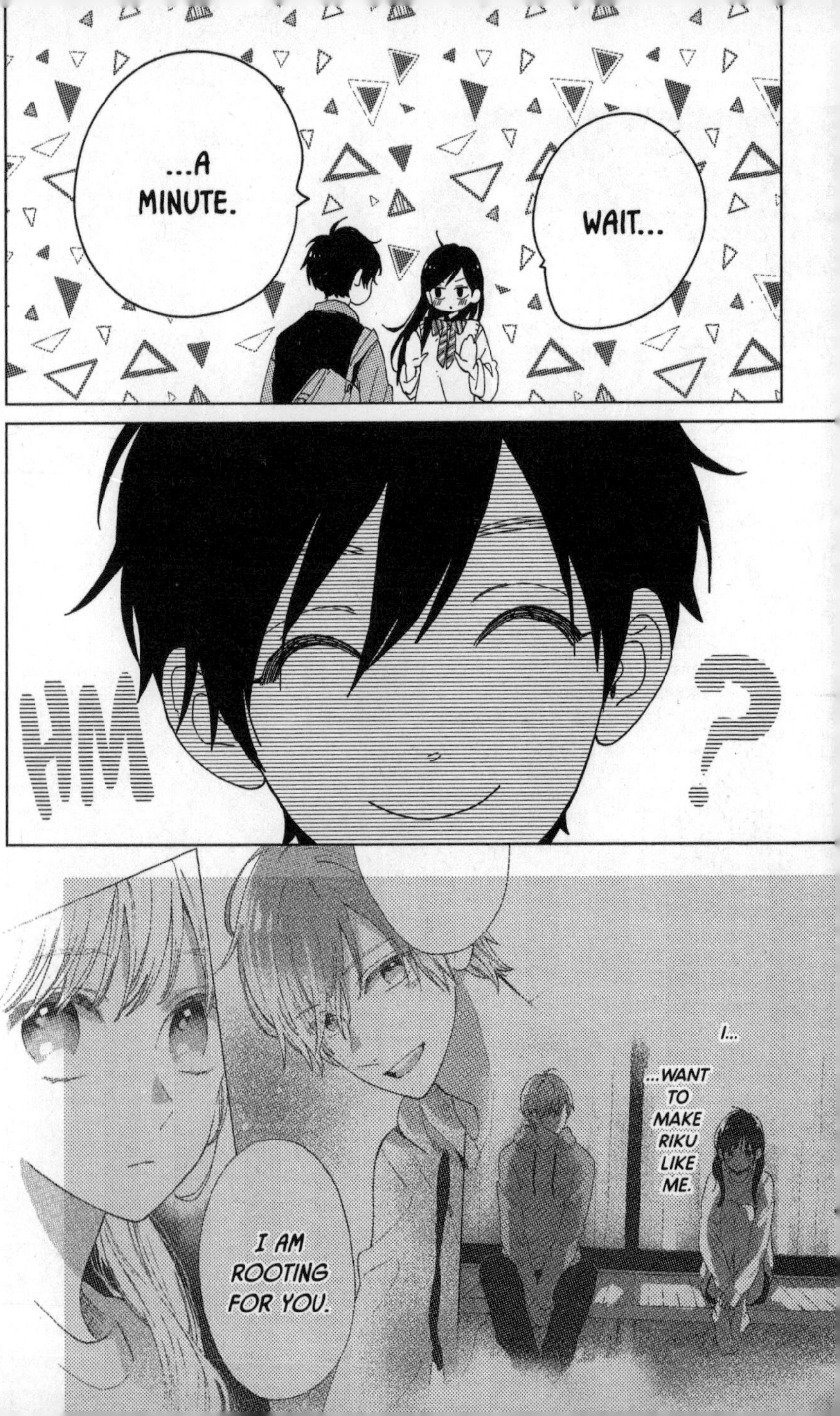
WAIT...
...A MINUTE.
HM?
I...
...WANT TO MAKE RIKU LIKE ME.
I AM ROOTING FOR YOU.

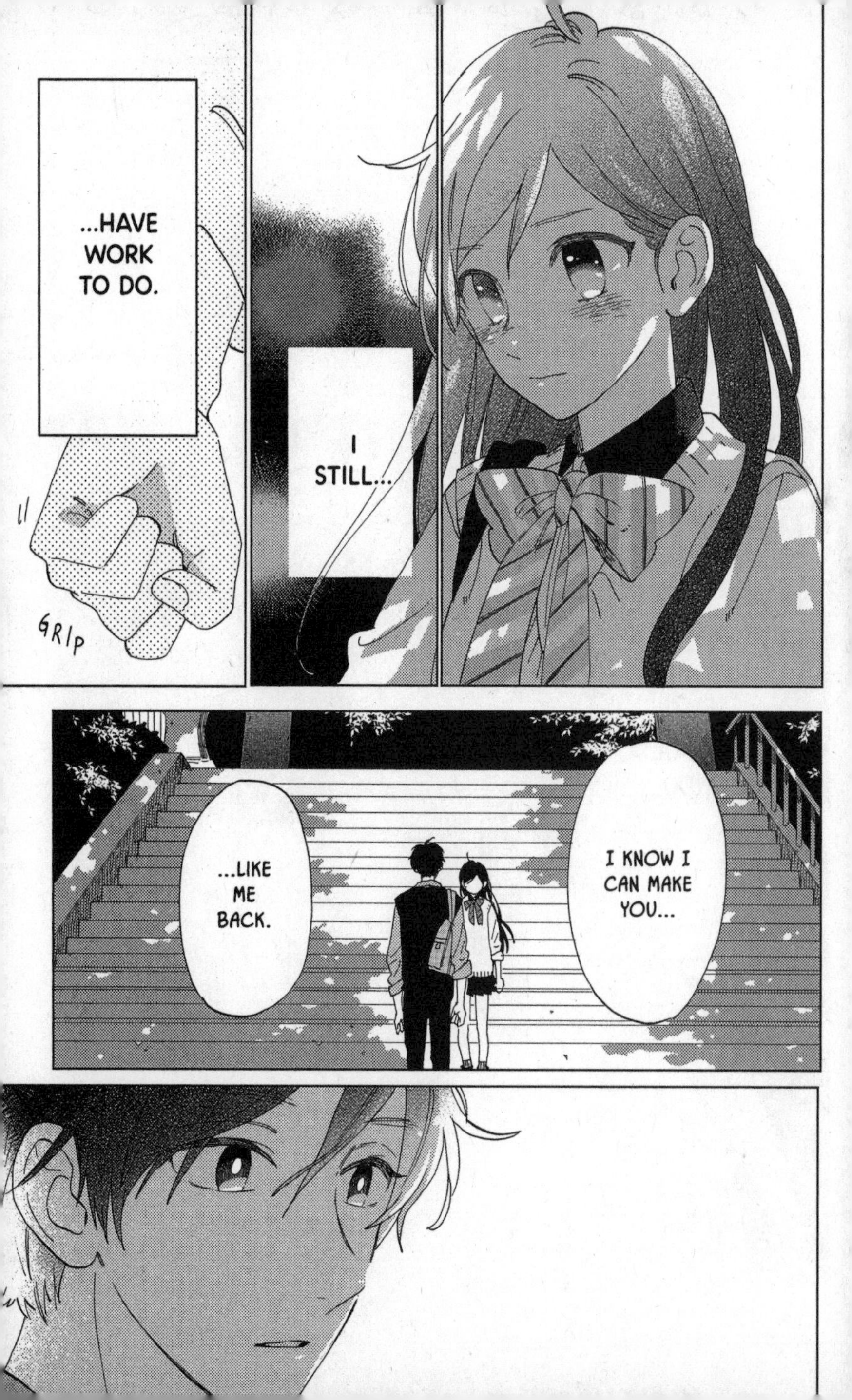
I STILL...
...HAVE WORK TO DO.
GRIP
I KNOW I CAN MAKE YOU...
...LIKE ME BACK.

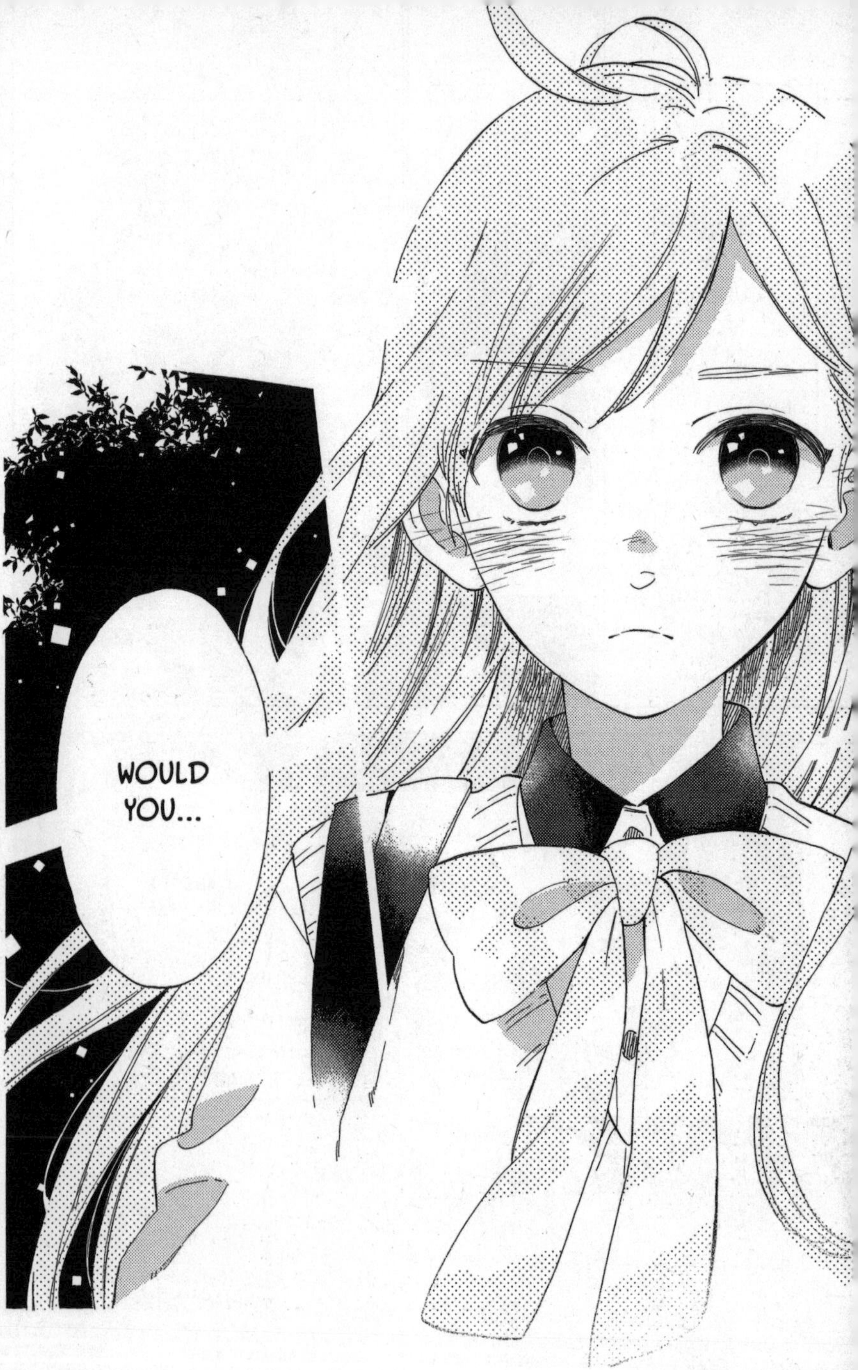
WOULD YOU...

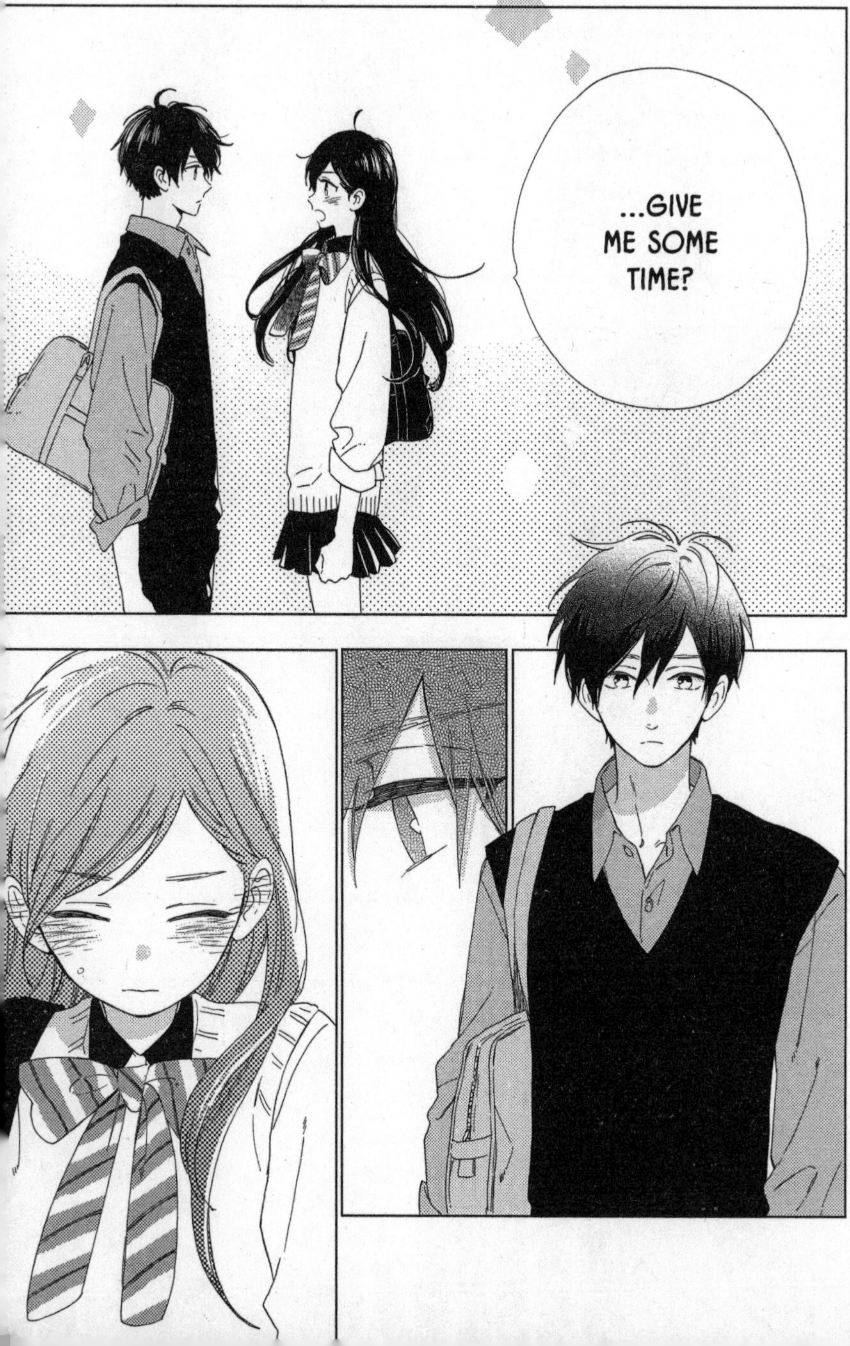
...GIVE ME SOME TIME?

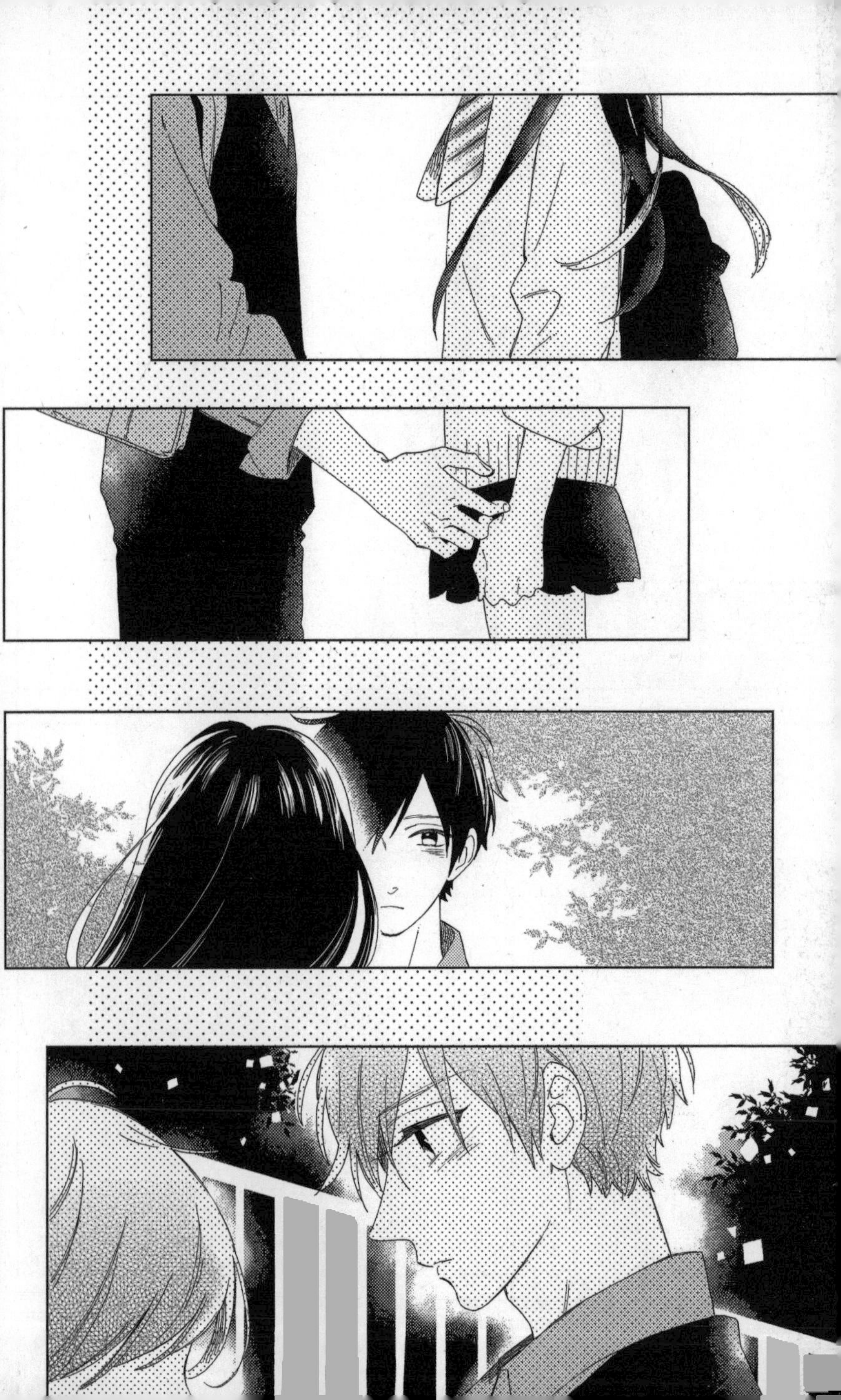

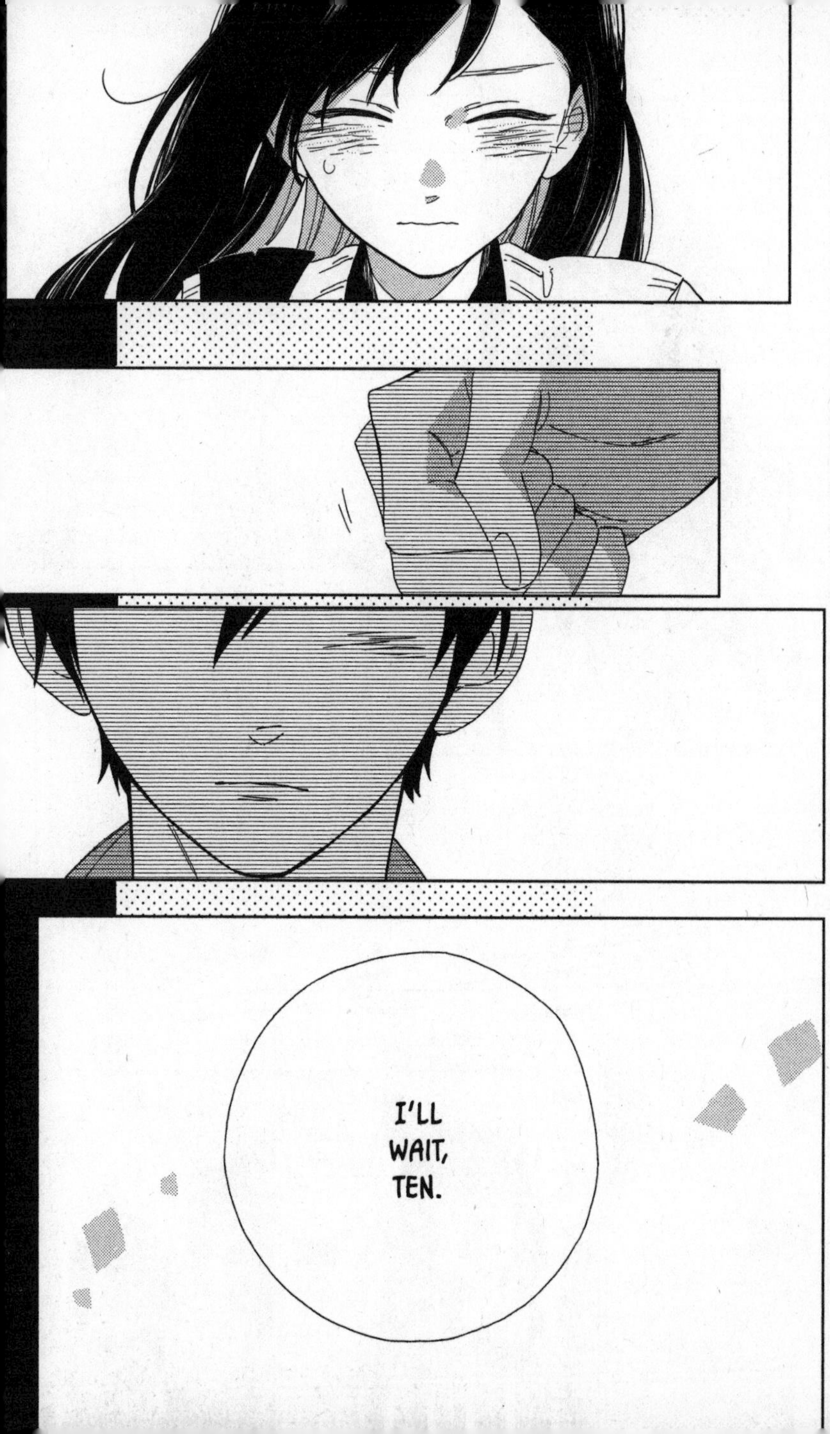
I'LL WAIT, TEN.

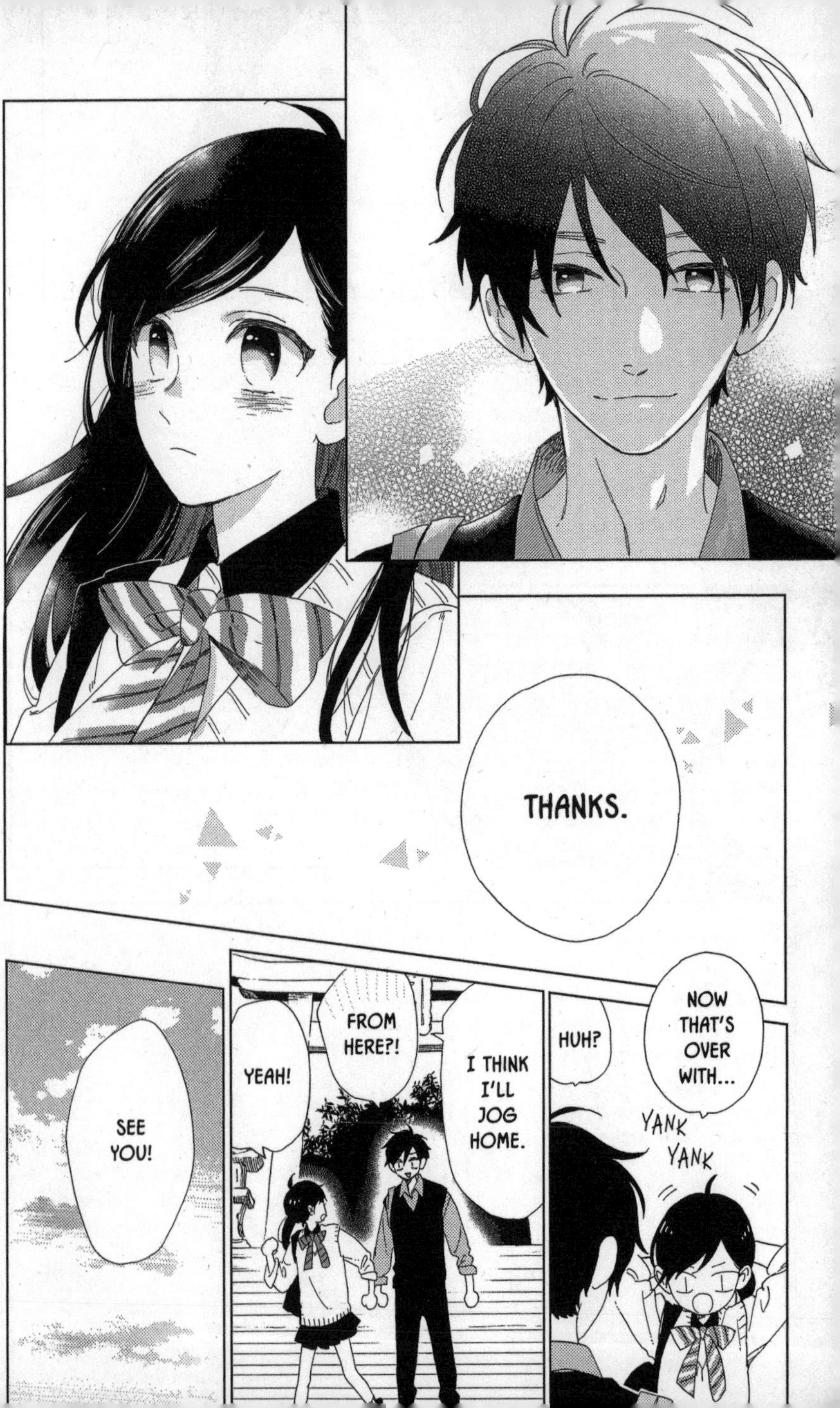
THANKS.
NOW THAT'S OVER WITH...
HUH?
YANK
YANK
I THINK I'LL JOG HOME.
FROM HERE?!
YEAH!
SEE YOU!

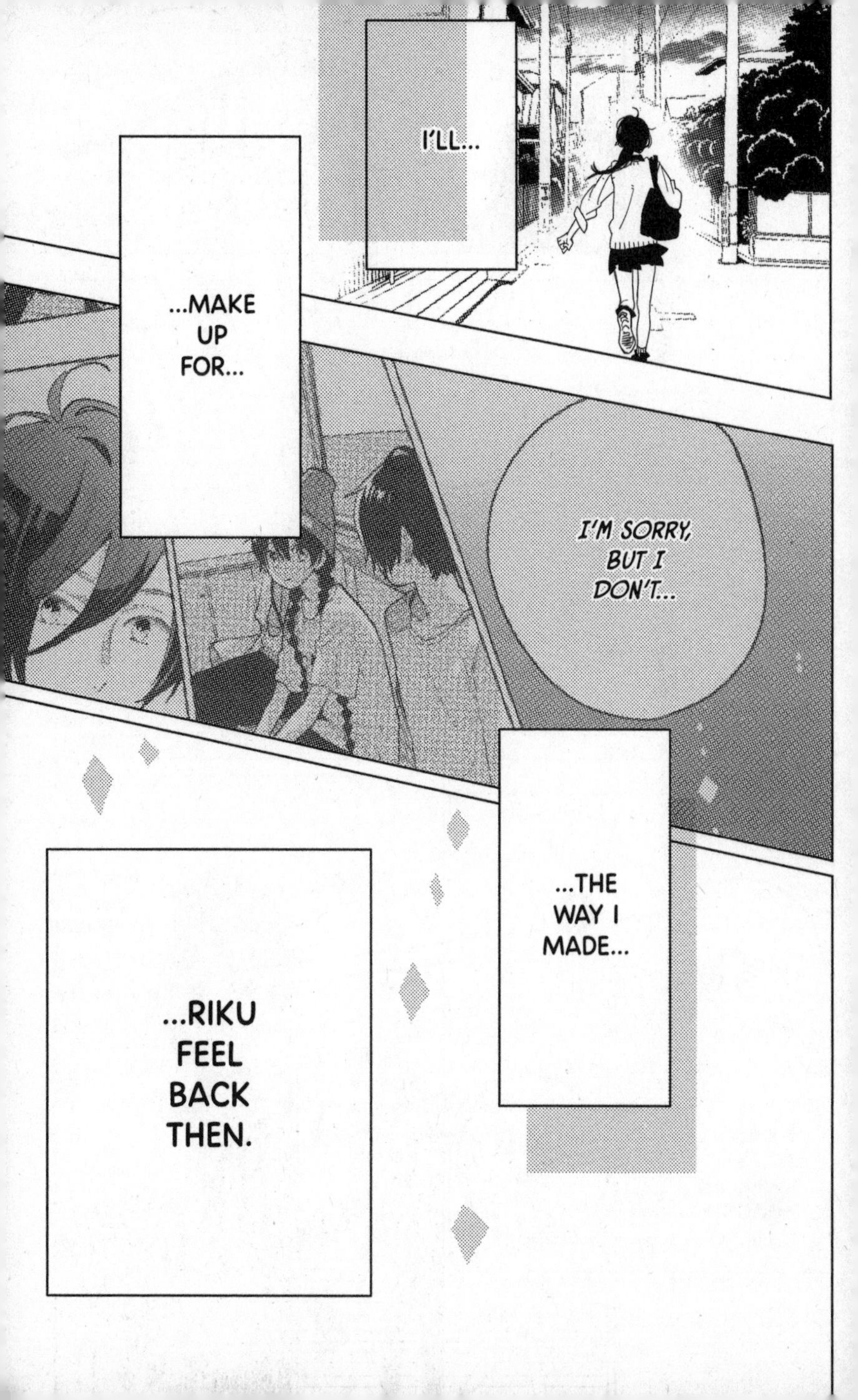
I'LL...
...MAKE UP FOR...
I'M SORRY, BUT I DON'T...
...THE WAY I MADE...
...RIKU FEEL BACK THEN.

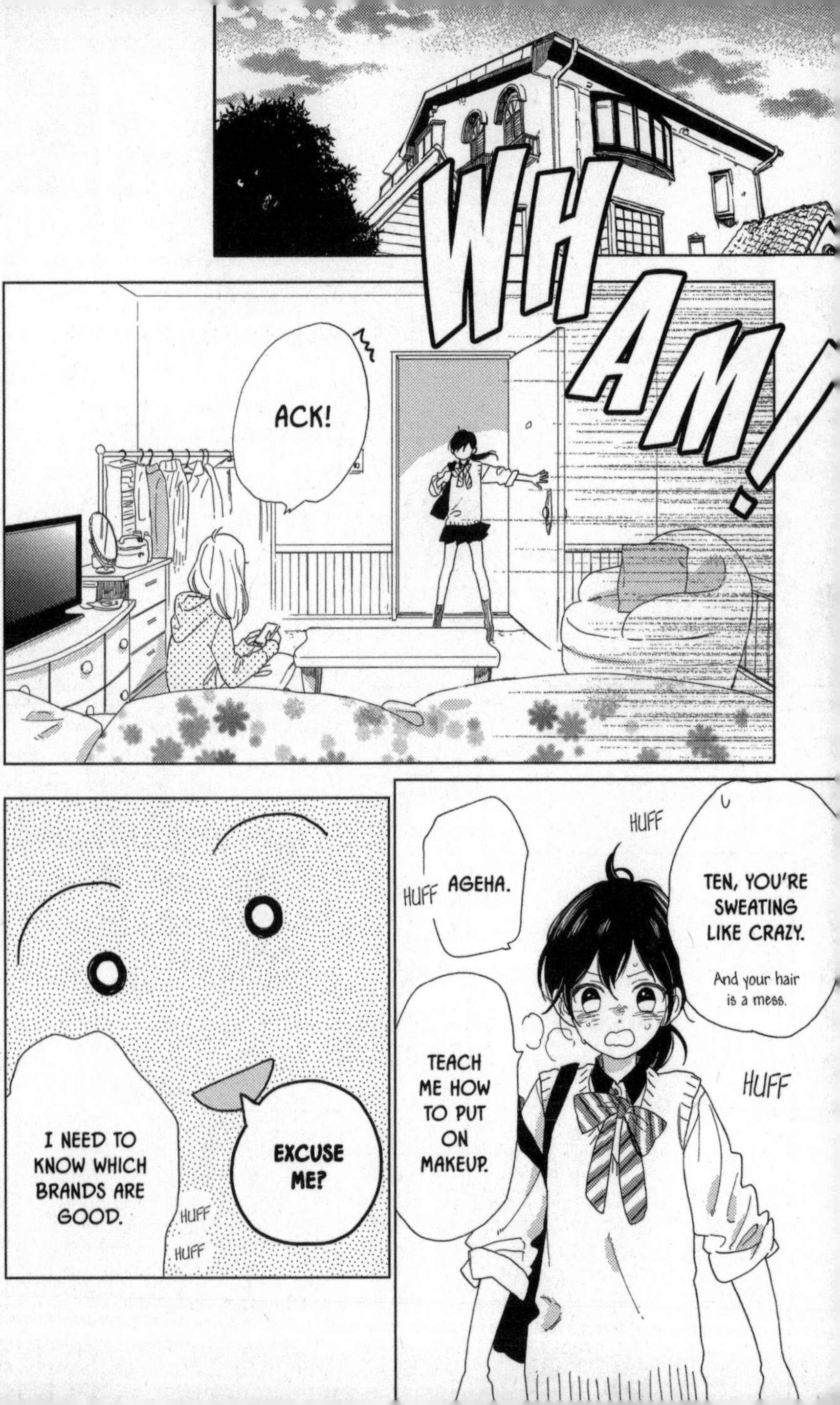
WHAM!
ACK!
HUFF
HUFF
AGEHA.
TEN, YOU'RE SWEATING LIKE CRAZY.
And your hair is a mess.
HUFF
TEACH ME HOW TO PUT ON MAKEUP.
EXCUSE ME?
I NEED TO KNOW WHICH BRANDS ARE GOOD.
HUFF
HUFF

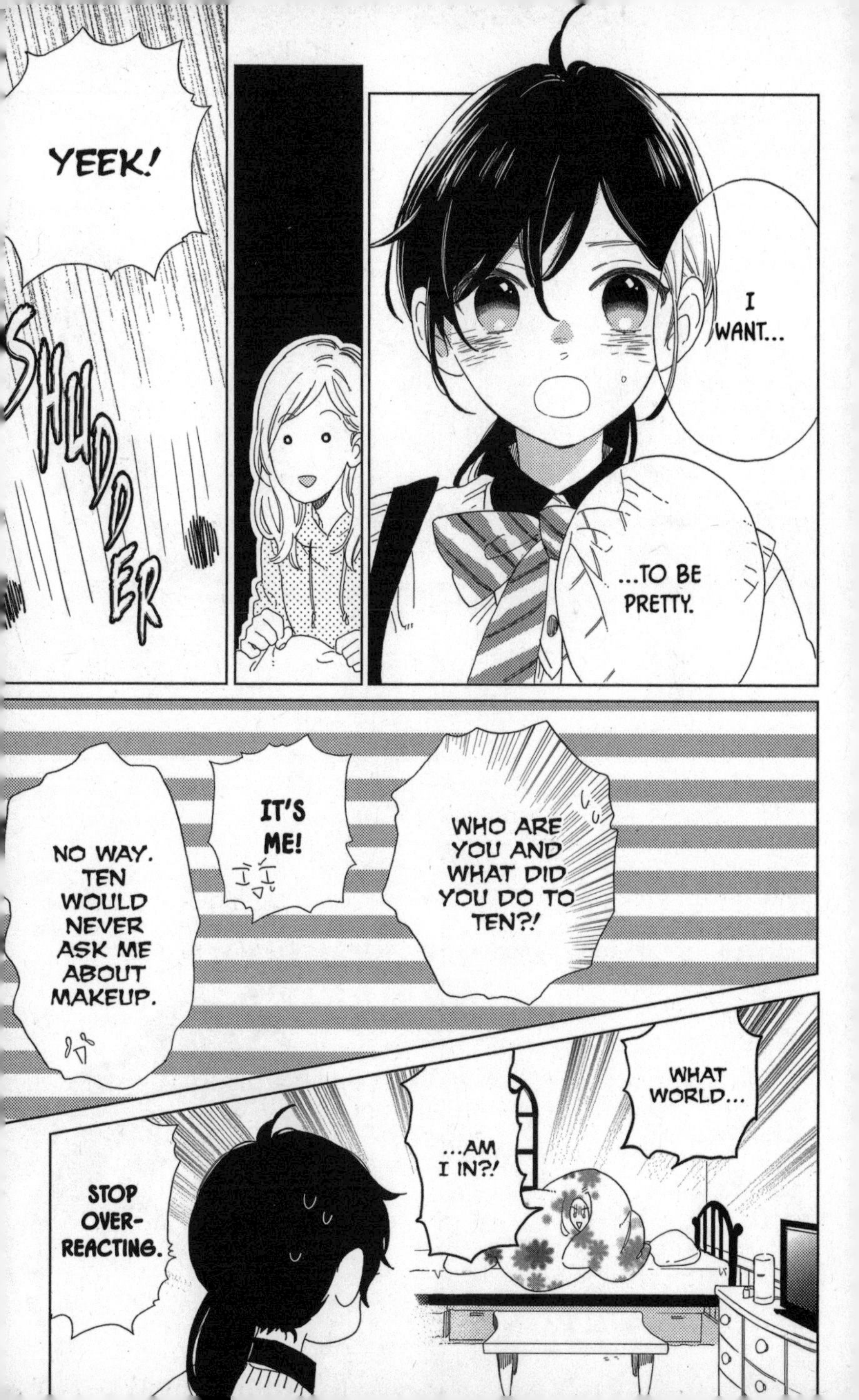
I WANT...
...TO BE PRETTY.
YEEK!
SHUDDER
WHO ARE YOU AND WHAT DID YOU DO TO TEN?!
IT'S ME!
NO WAY. TEN WOULD NEVER ASK ME ABOUT MAKEUP.
WHAT WORLD...
...AM I IN?!
STOP OVER-REACTING.

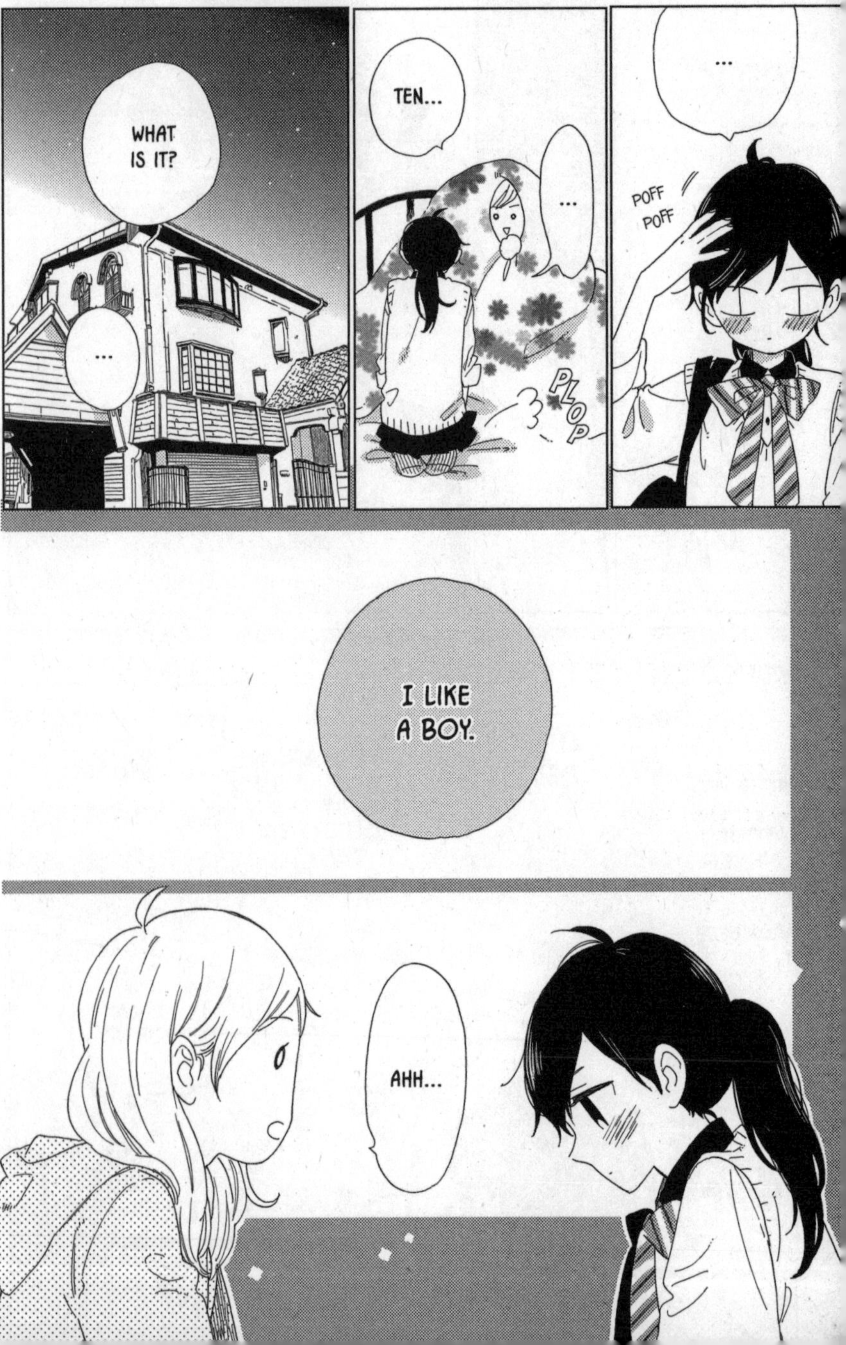
...
POFF POFF
TEN...
...
PLOP
WHAT IS IT?
...
I LIKE A BOY.
AHH...

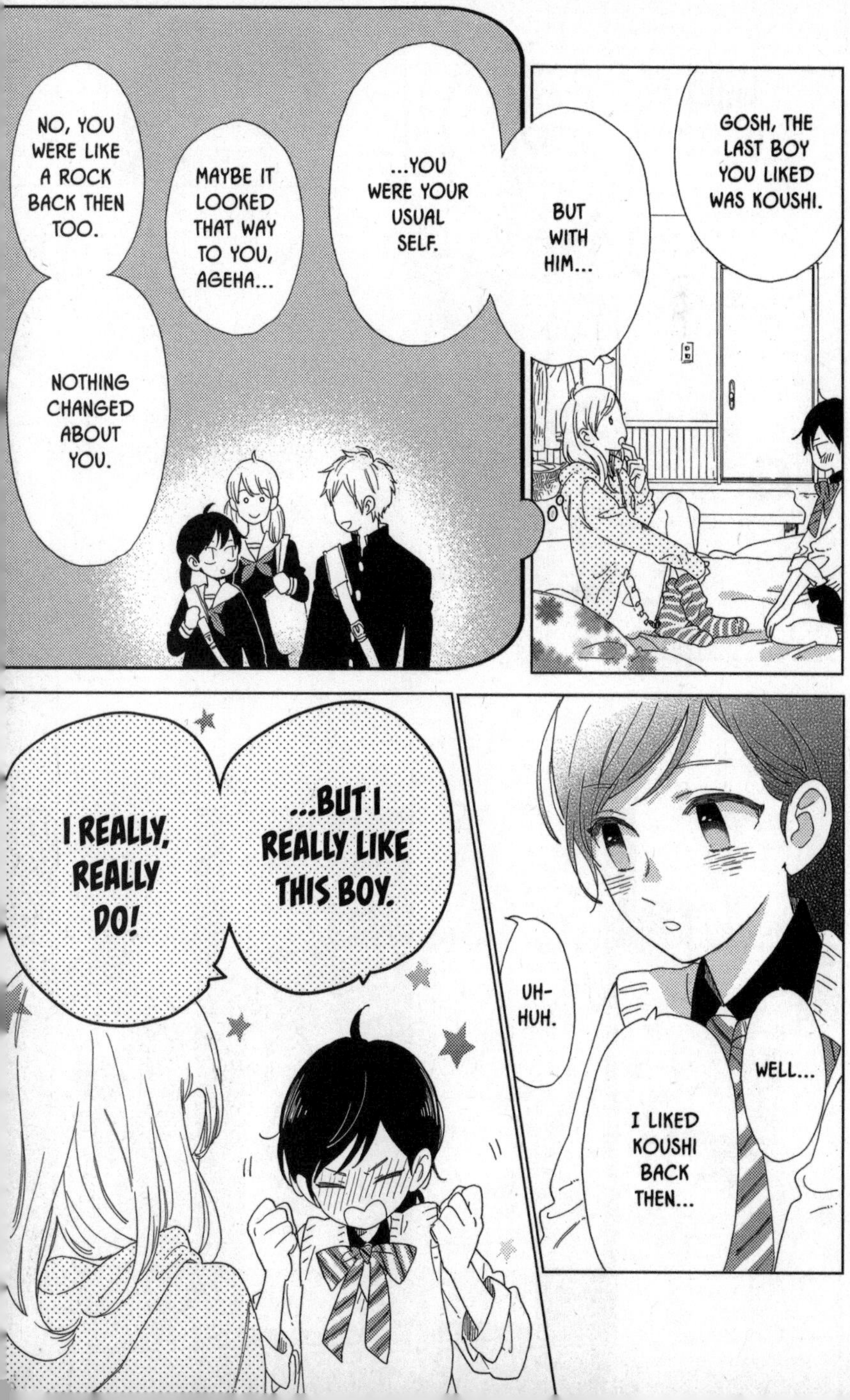
GOSH, THE LAST BOY YOU LIKED WAS KOUSHI.
BUT WITH HIM...
...YOU WERE YOUR USUAL SELF.
MAYBE IT LOOKED THAT WAY TO YOU, AGEHA...
NO, YOU WERE LIKE A ROCK BACK THEN TOO.
NOTHING CHANGED ABOUT YOU.
WELL...
I LIKED KOUSHI BACK THEN...
UH-HUH.
...BUT I REALLY LIKE THIS BOY.
I REALLY, REALLY DO!

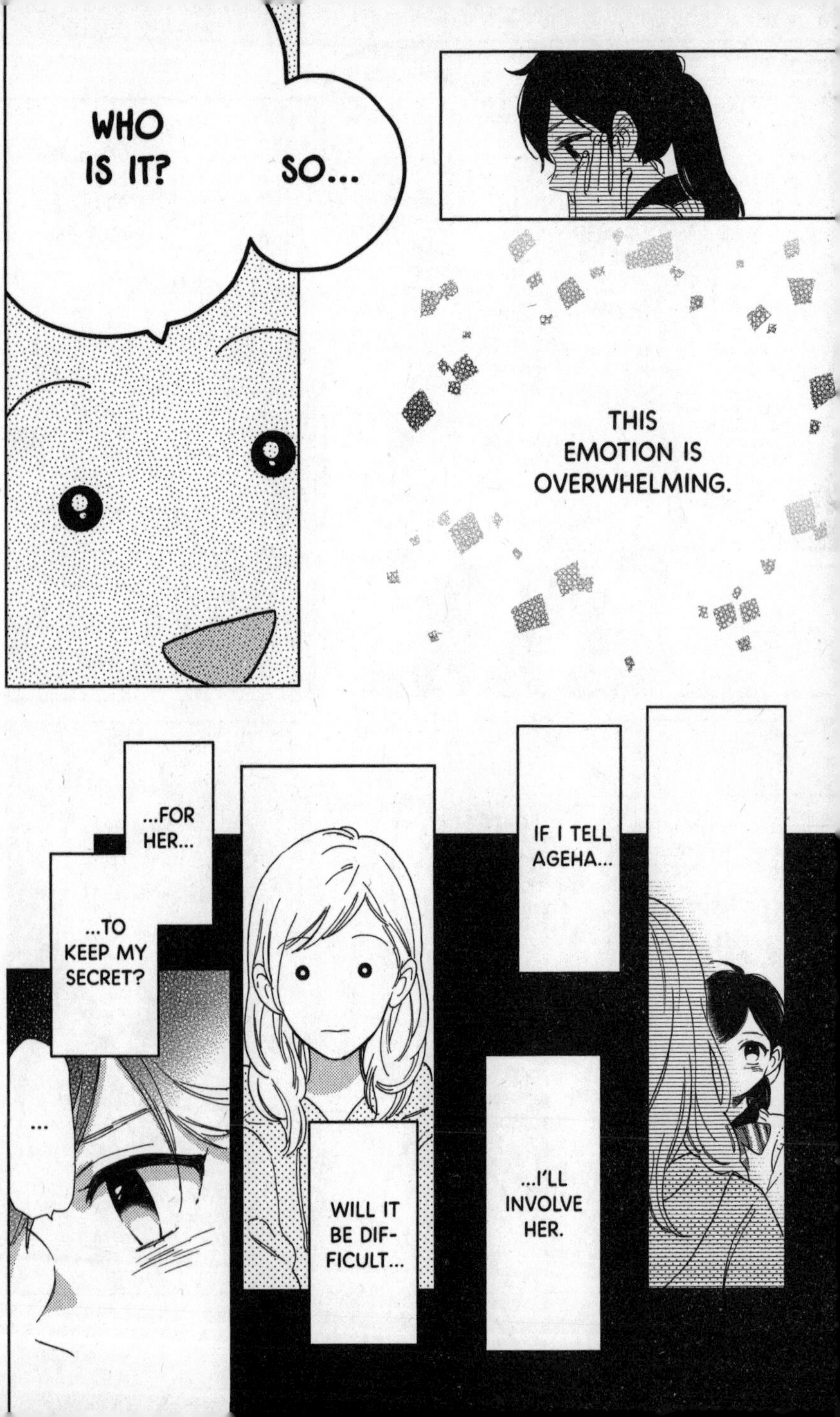
THIS EMOTION IS OVERWHELMING.
SO...
WHO IS IT?
IF I TELL AGEHA...
...I'LL INVOLVE HER.
WILL IT BE DIF-FICULT...
...FOR HER...
...TO KEEP MY SECRET?
...

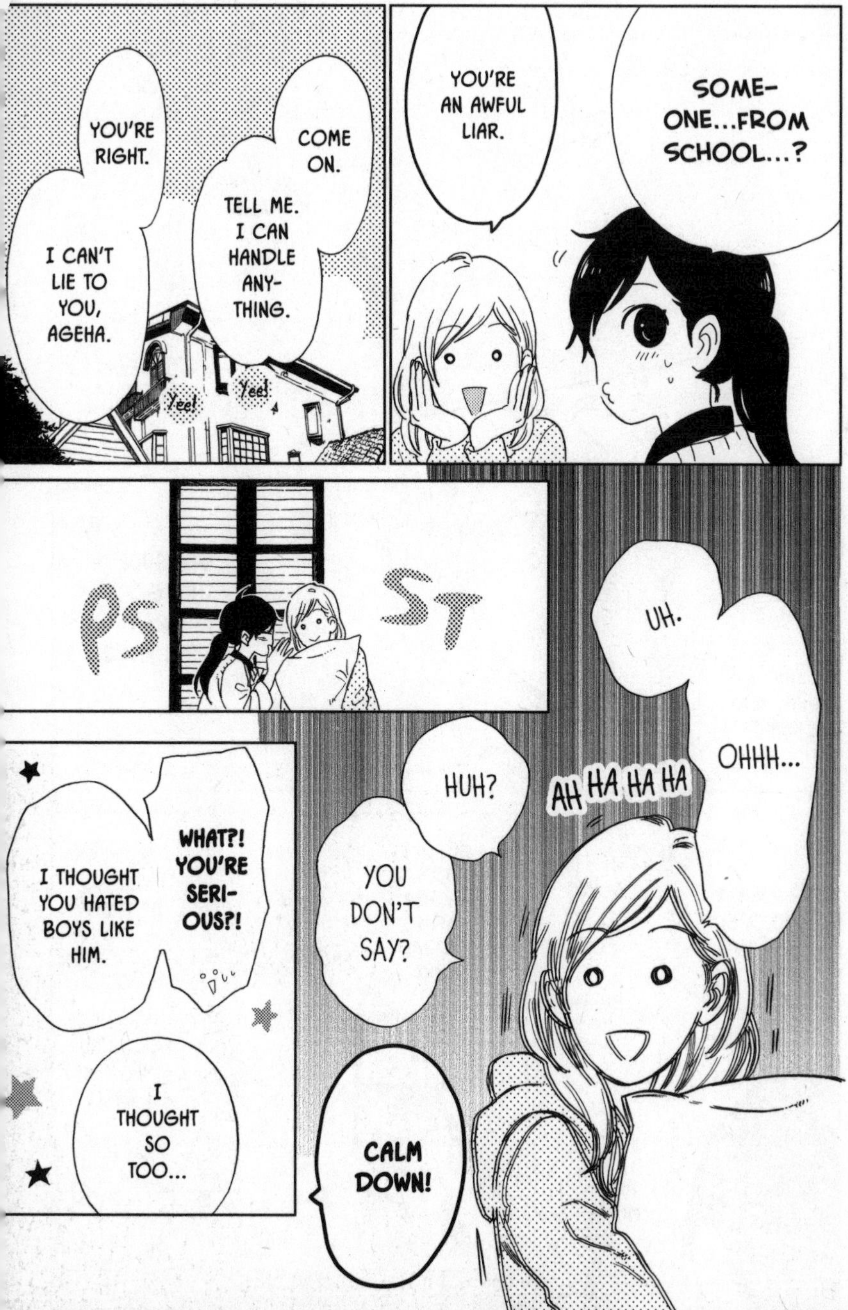
SOME-ONE...FROM SCHOOL...?
YOU'RE AN AWFUL LIAR.
COME ON.
TELL ME. I CAN HANDLE ANY-THING.
Yee!
Yee!
YOU'RE RIGHT.
I CAN'T LIE TO YOU, AGEHA.
PSST
UH.
OHHH...
AH HA HA HA
HUH?
YOU DON'T SAY?
CALM DOWN!
WHAT?! YOU'RE SERI-OUS?!
I THOUGHT YOU HATED BOYS LIKE HIM.
I THOUGHT SO TOO...

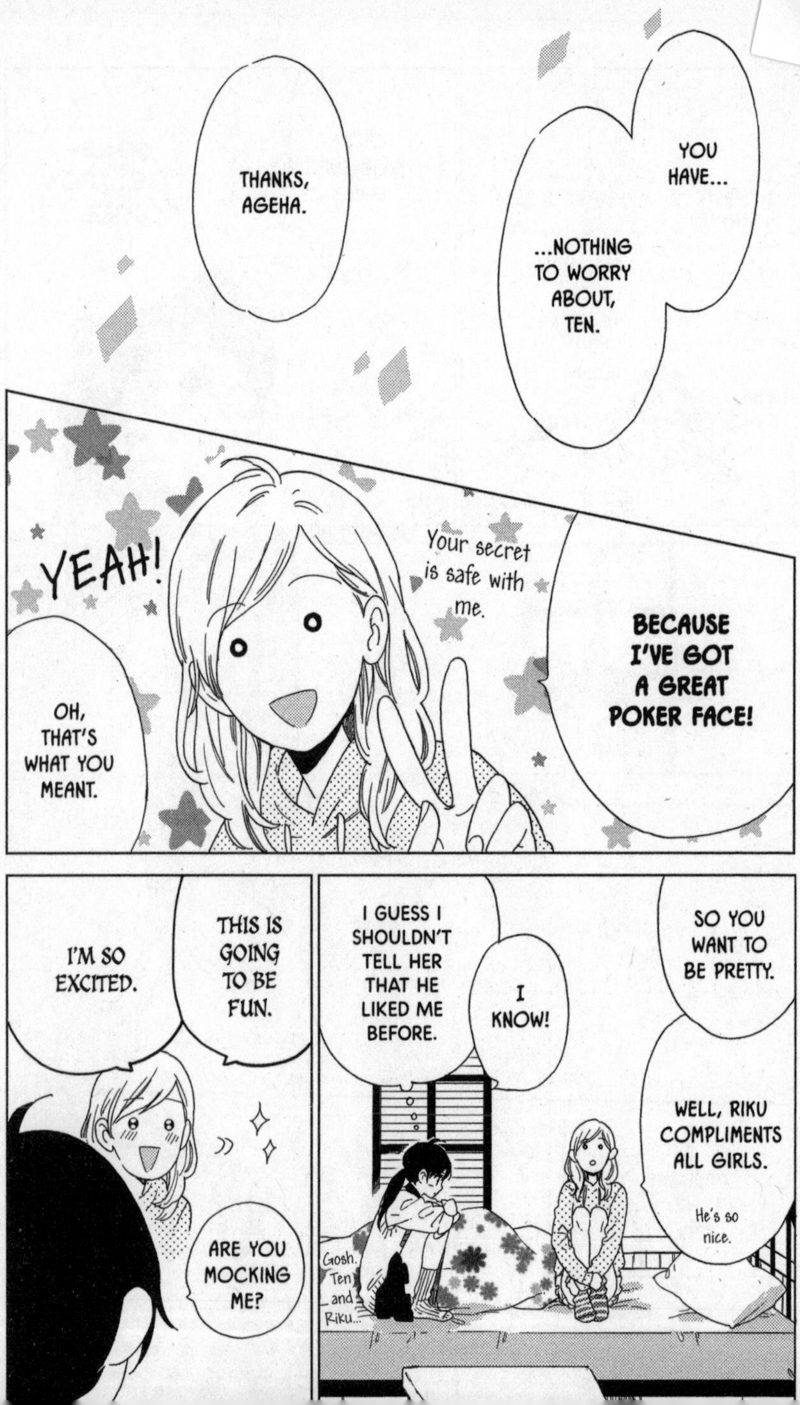
YOU HAVE...
...NOTHING TO WORRY ABOUT, TEN.
THANKS, AGEHA.
BECAUSE I'VE GOT A GREAT POKER FACE!
Your secret is safe with me.
YEAH!
OH, THAT'S WHAT YOU MEANT.
SO YOU WANT TO BE PRETTY.
WELL, RIKU COMPLIMENTS ALL GIRLS.
He's so nice.
I KNOW!
I GUESS I SHOULDN'T TELL HER THAT HE LIKED ME BEFORE.
Gosh. Ten and Riku...
THIS IS GOING TO BE FUN.
I'M SO EXCITED.
ARE YOU MOCKING ME?

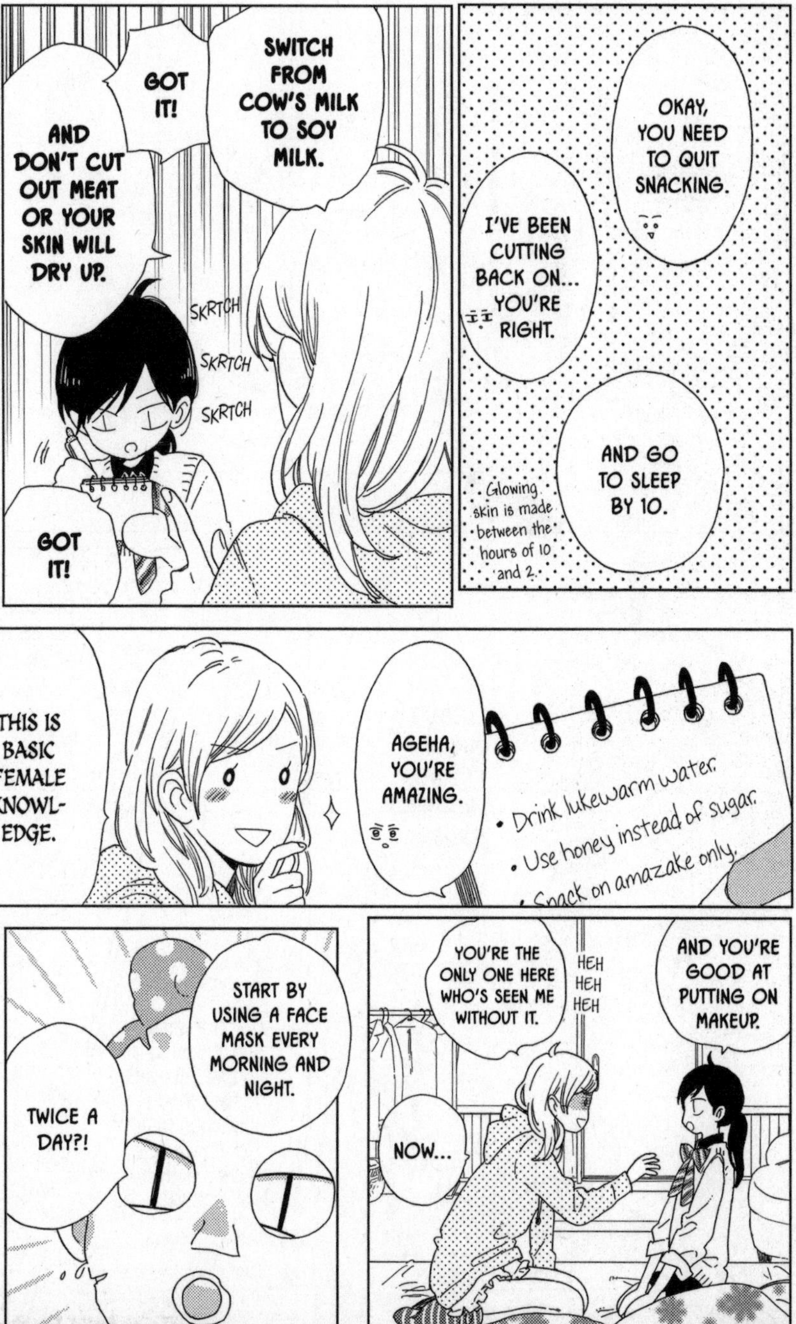
OKAY, YOU NEED TO QUIT SNACKING.
I'VE BEEN CUTTING BACK ON... YOU'RE RIGHT.
AND GO TO SLEEP BY 10.
Glowing skin is made between the hours of 10 and 2.
SWITCH FROM COW'S MILK TO SOY MILK.
GOT IT!
AND DON'T CUT OUT MEAT OR YOUR SKIN WILL DRY UP.
SKRTCH
SKRTCH
SKRTCH
GOT IT!
• Drink lukewarm water.
• Use honey instead of sugar.
• Snack on amazake only.
AGEHA, YOU'RE AMAZING.
THIS IS BASIC FEMALE KNOWL-EDGE.
AND YOU'RE GOOD AT PUTTING ON MAKEUP.
HEH HEH HEH
YOU'RE THE ONLY ONE HERE WHO'S SEEN ME WITHOUT IT.
NOW...
START BY USING A FACE MASK EVERY MORNING AND NIGHT.
TWICE A DAY?!

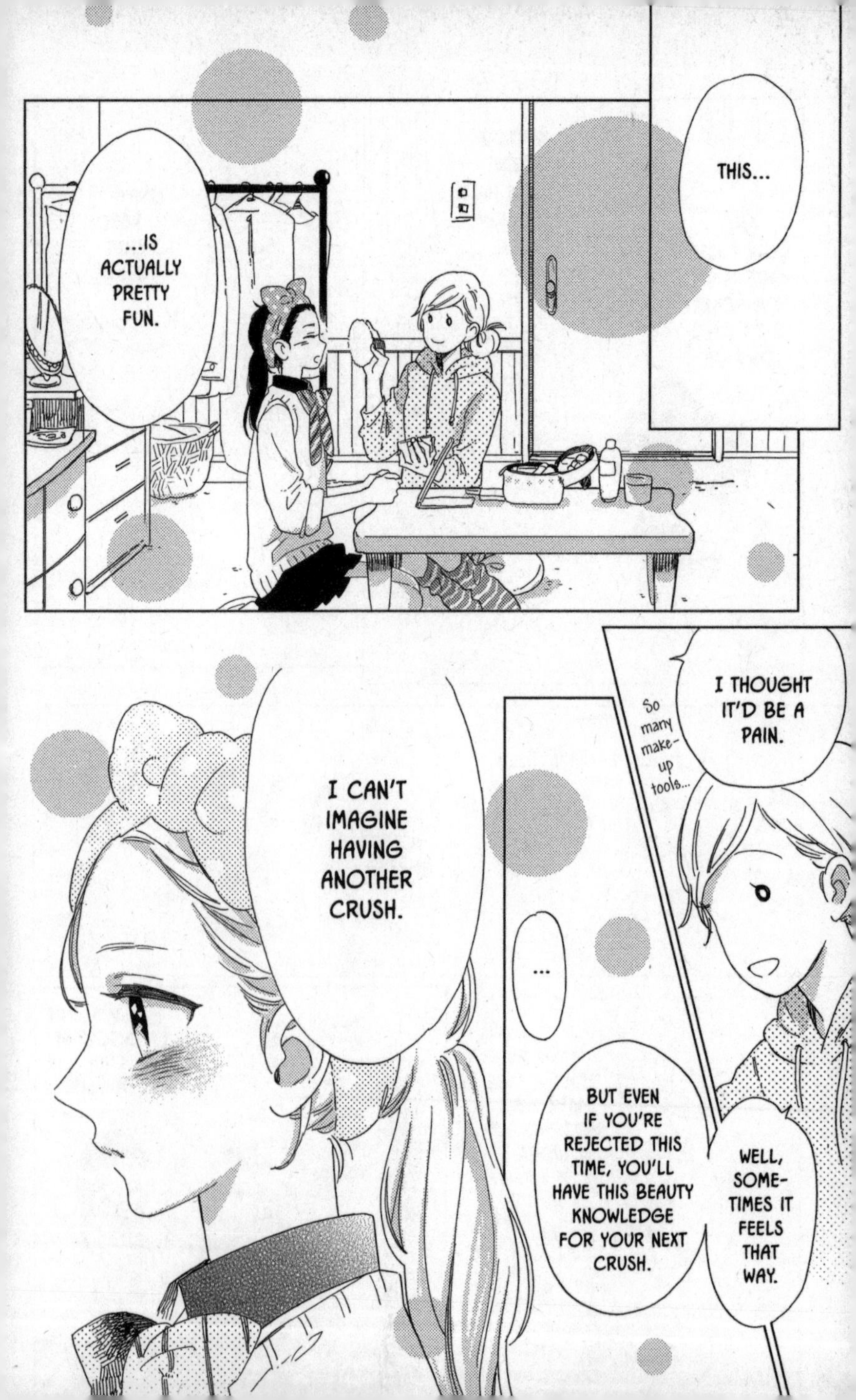
THIS...
...IS ACTUALLY PRETTY FUN.
I THOUGHT IT'D BE A PAIN.
So many make-up tools...
WELL, SOME-TIMES IT FEELS THAT WAY.
...
BUT EVEN IF YOU'RE REJECTED THIS TIME, YOU'LL HAVE THIS BEAUTY KNOWLEDGE FOR YOUR NEXT CRUSH.
I CAN'T IMAGINE HAVING ANOTHER CRUSH.

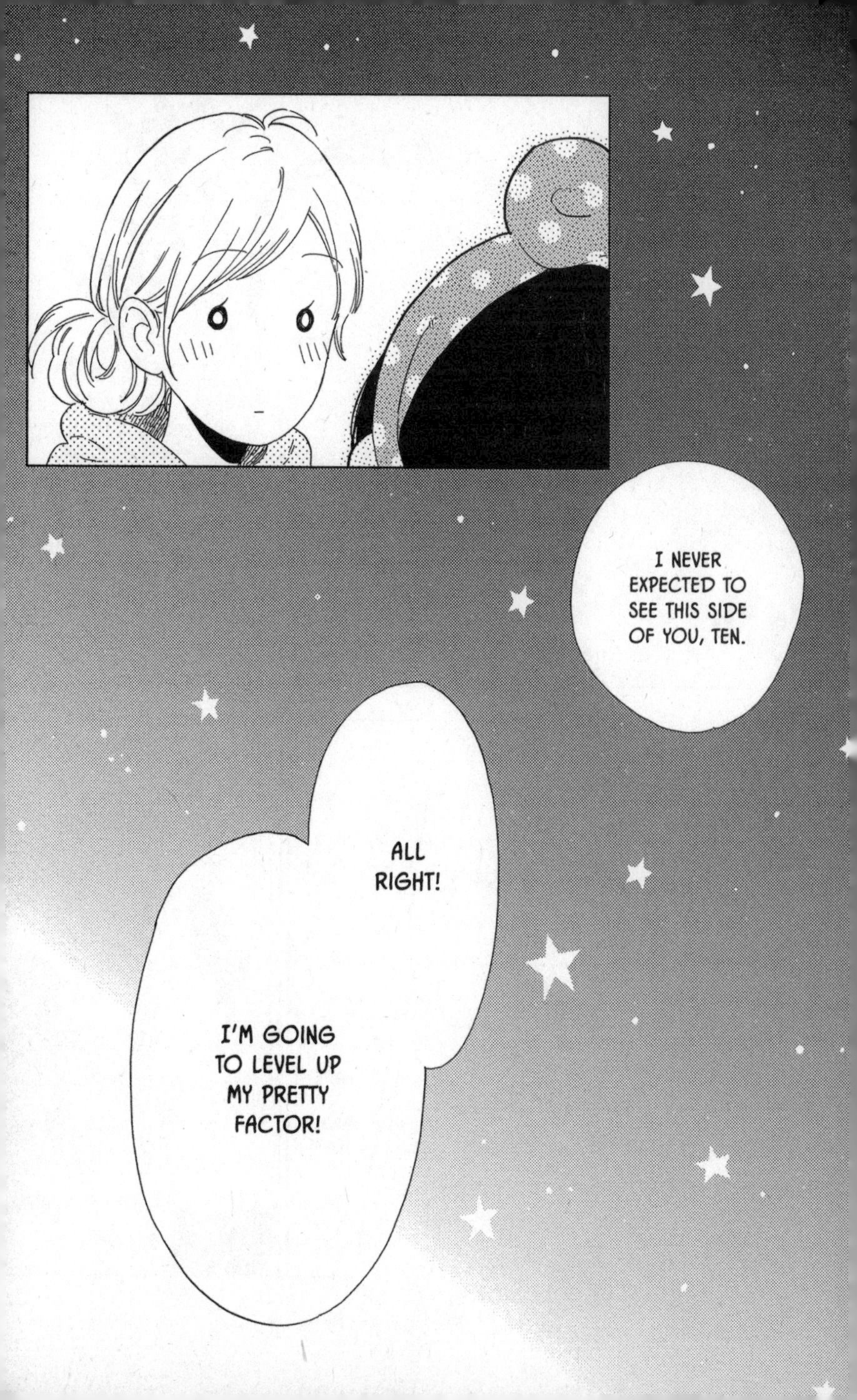
I NEVER EXPECTED TO SEE THIS SIDE OF YOU, TEN.
ALL RIGHT!
I'M GOING TO LEVEL UP MY PRETTY FACTOR!

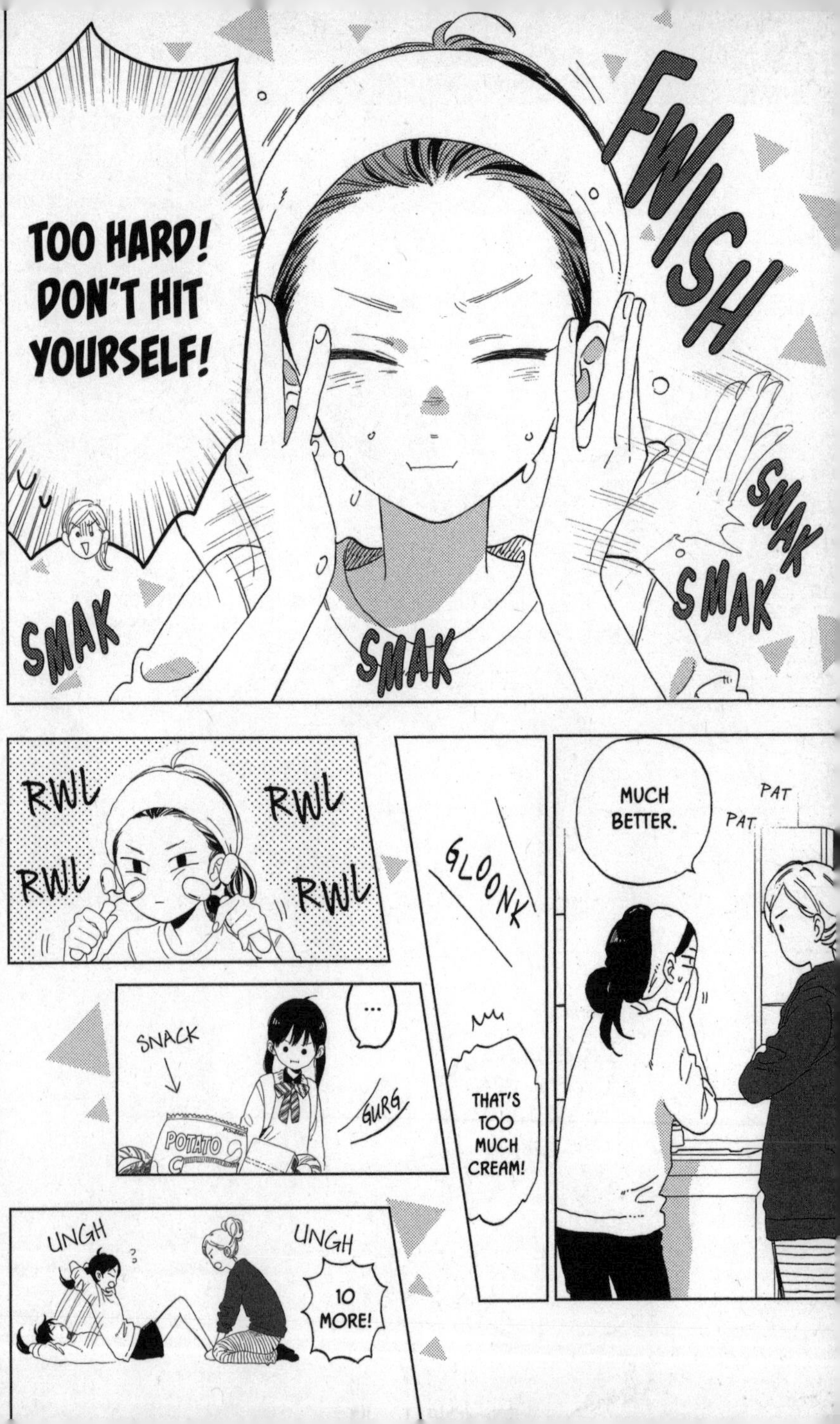
FWISH
SMAK
SMAK
TOO HARD! DON'T HIT YOURSELF!
SMAK
SMAK
PAT
PAT
MUCH BETTER.
GLOONK
THAT'S TOO MUCH CREAM!
RWL
RWL
RWL
RWL
...
GURG
SNACK
POTATO
10 MORE!
UNGH
UNGH

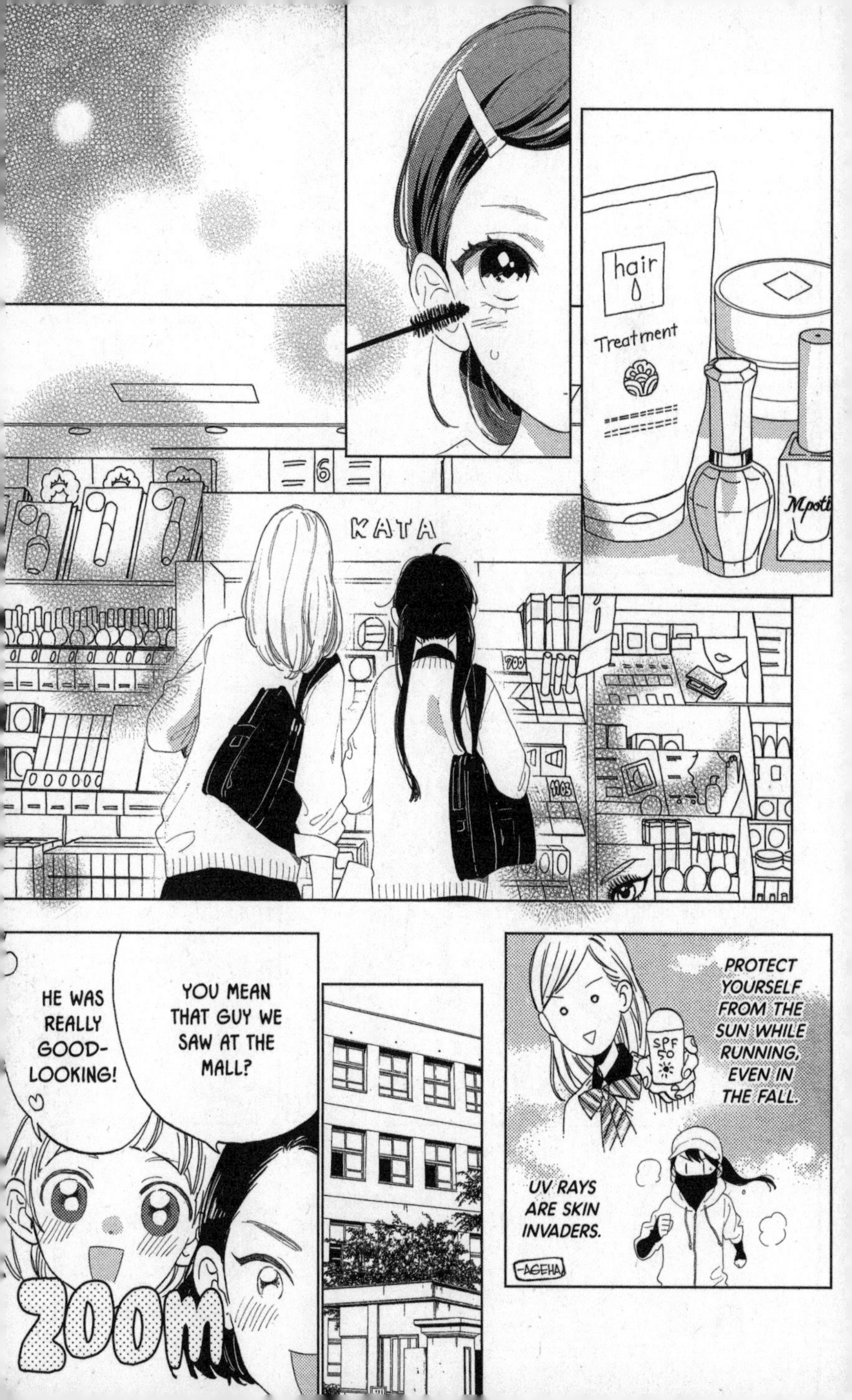
hair
Treatment
KATA
PROTECT YOURSELF FROM THE SUN WHILE RUNNING, EVEN IN THE FALL.
SPF 50
UV RAYS ARE SKIN INVADERS.
-AGEHA
YOU MEAN THAT GUY WE SAW AT THE MALL?
HE WAS REALLY GOOD-LOOKING!
ZOOM

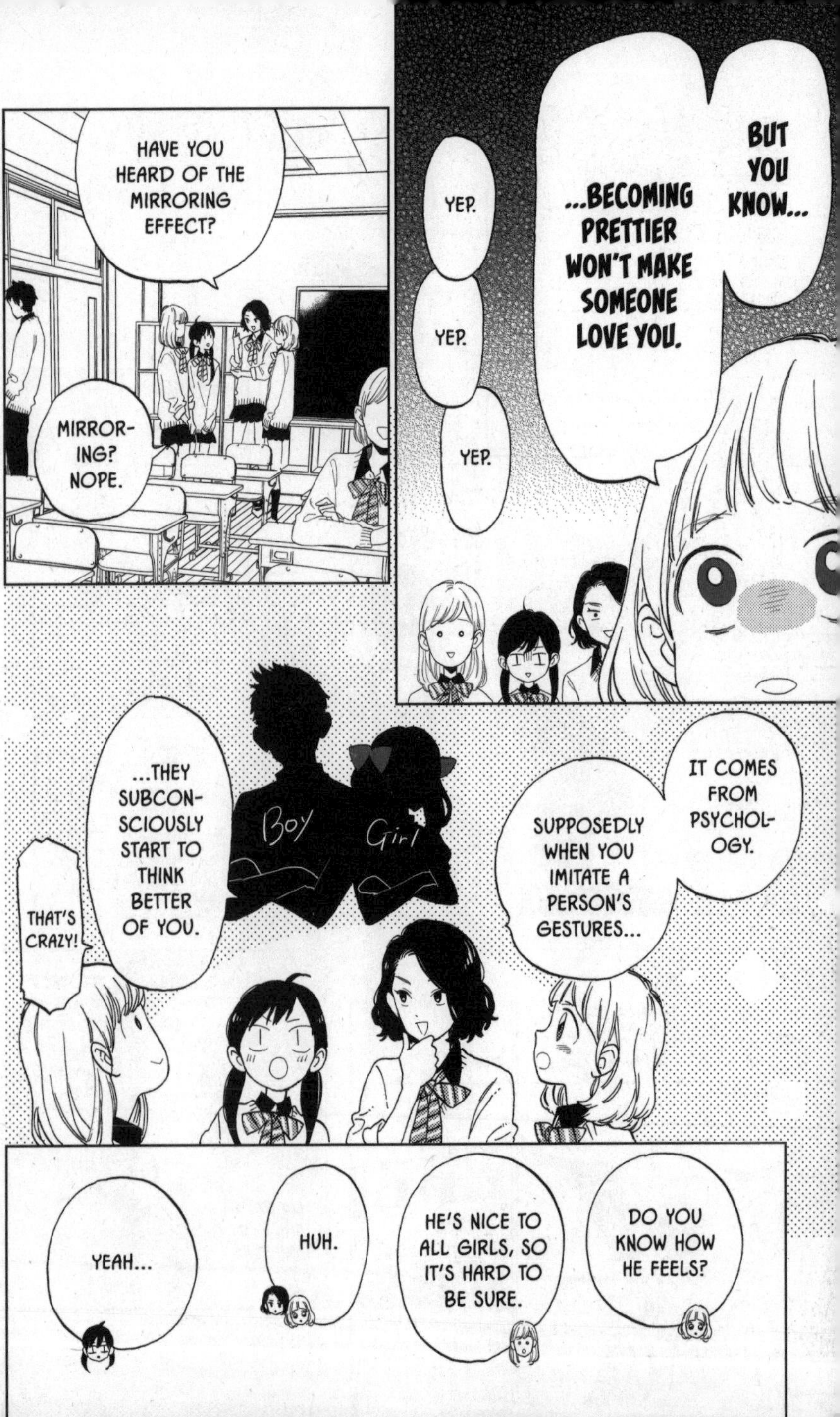
BUT YOU KNOW...
...BECOMING PRETTIER WON'T MAKE SOMEONE LOVE YOU.
YEP.
YEP.
YEP.
HAVE YOU HEARD OF THE MIRRORING EFFECT?
MIRROR-ING? NOPE.
IT COMES FROM PSYCHOL-OGY.
SUPPOSEDLY WHEN YOU IMITATE A PERSON'S GESTURES...
...THEY SUBCON-SCIOUSLY START TO THINK BETTER OF YOU.
Girl
Boy
THAT'S CRAZY!
DO YOU KNOW HOW HE FEELS?
HE'S NICE TO ALL GIRLS, SO IT'S HARD TO BE SURE.
HUH.
YEAH...

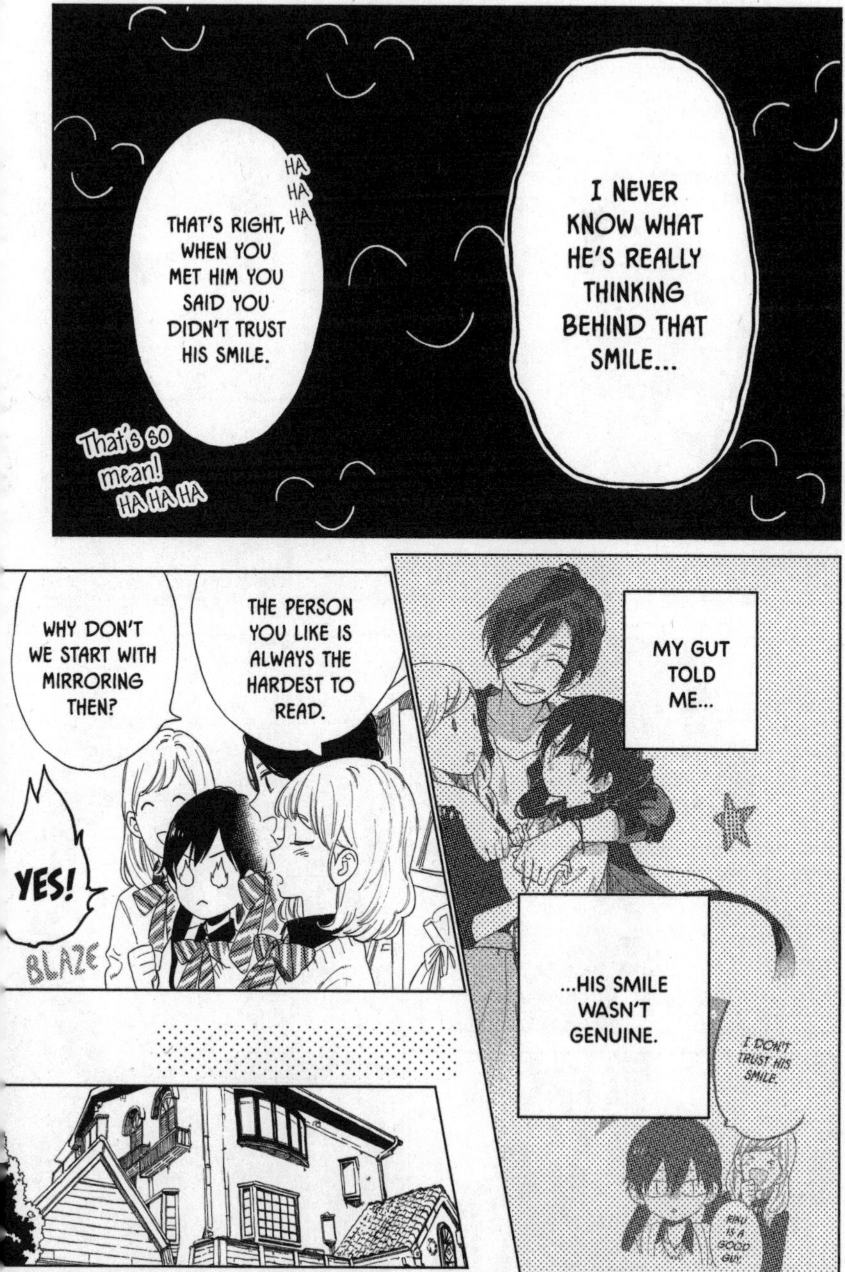
I NEVER KNOW WHAT HE'S REALLY THINKING BEHIND THAT SMILE...
HA HA HA
THAT'S RIGHT, WHEN YOU MET HIM YOU SAID YOU DIDN'T TRUST HIS SMILE.
That's so mean! HA HA HA
MY GUT TOLD ME...
...HIS SMILE WASN'T GENUINE.
I DON'T TRUST HIS SMILE.
RIKU IS A GOOD GUY
THE PERSON YOU LIKE IS ALWAYS THE HARDEST TO READ.
WHY DON'T WE START WITH MIRRORING THEN?
YES!
BLAZE

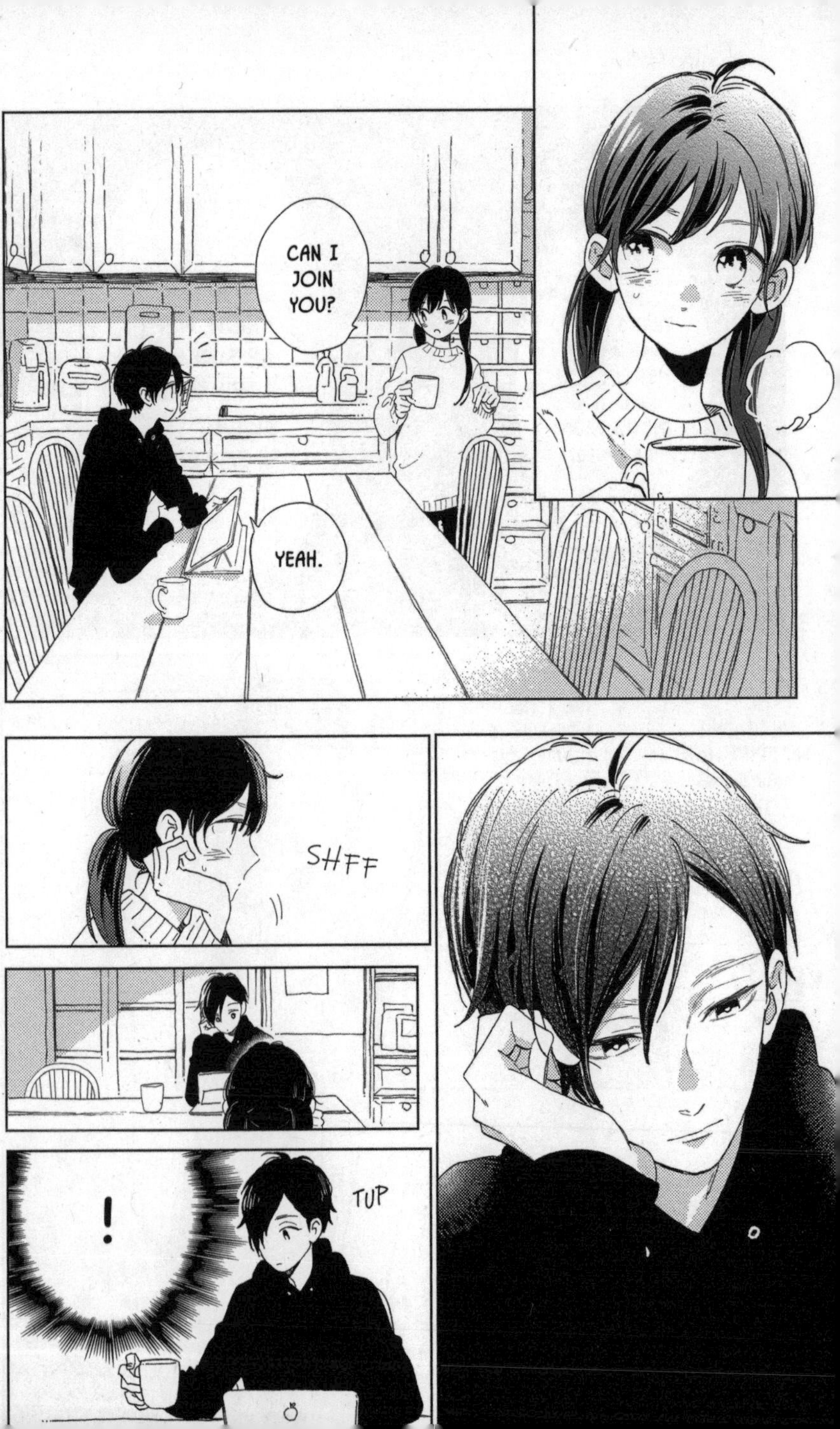
CAN I JOIN YOU?
YEAH.
SHFF
TUP
!

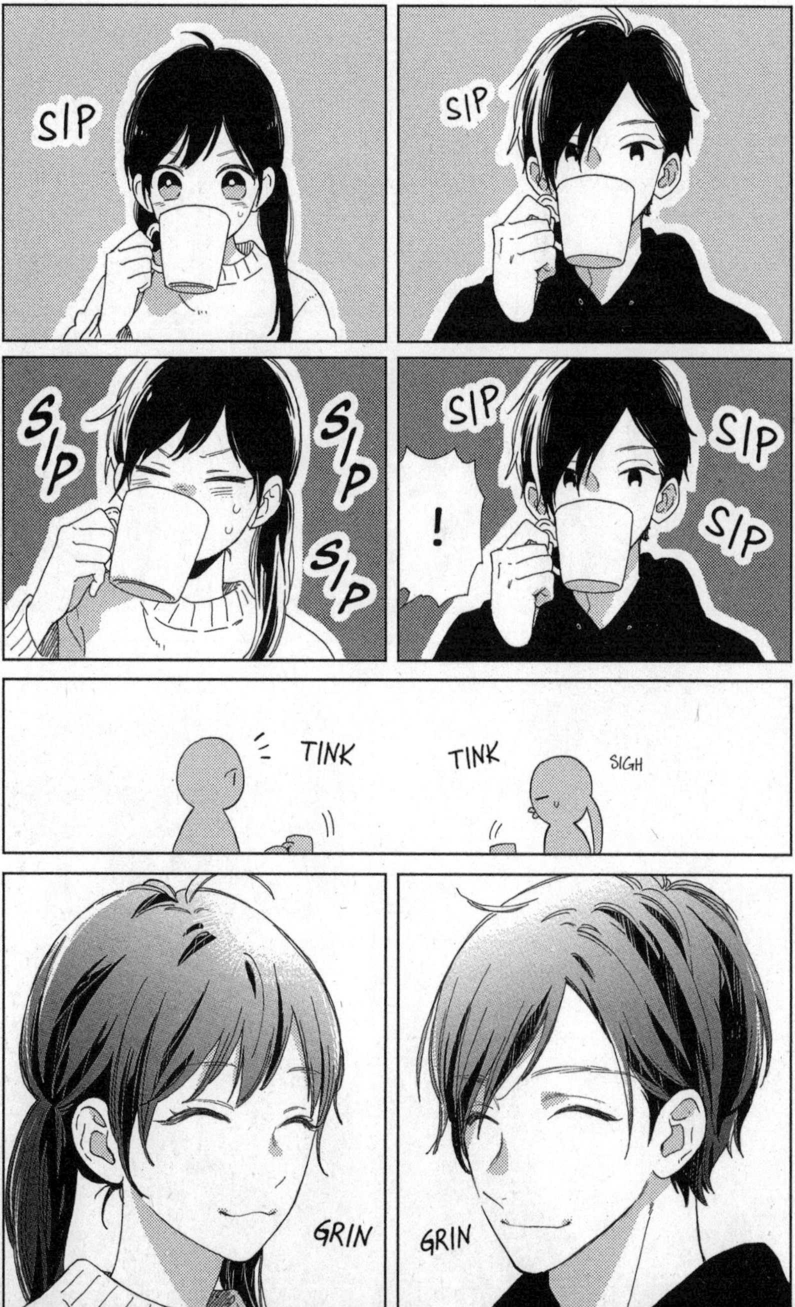
SIP
SIP
SIP
SIP
SIP
!
SIP
SIP
SIP
SIGH
TINK
TINK
GRIN
GRIN

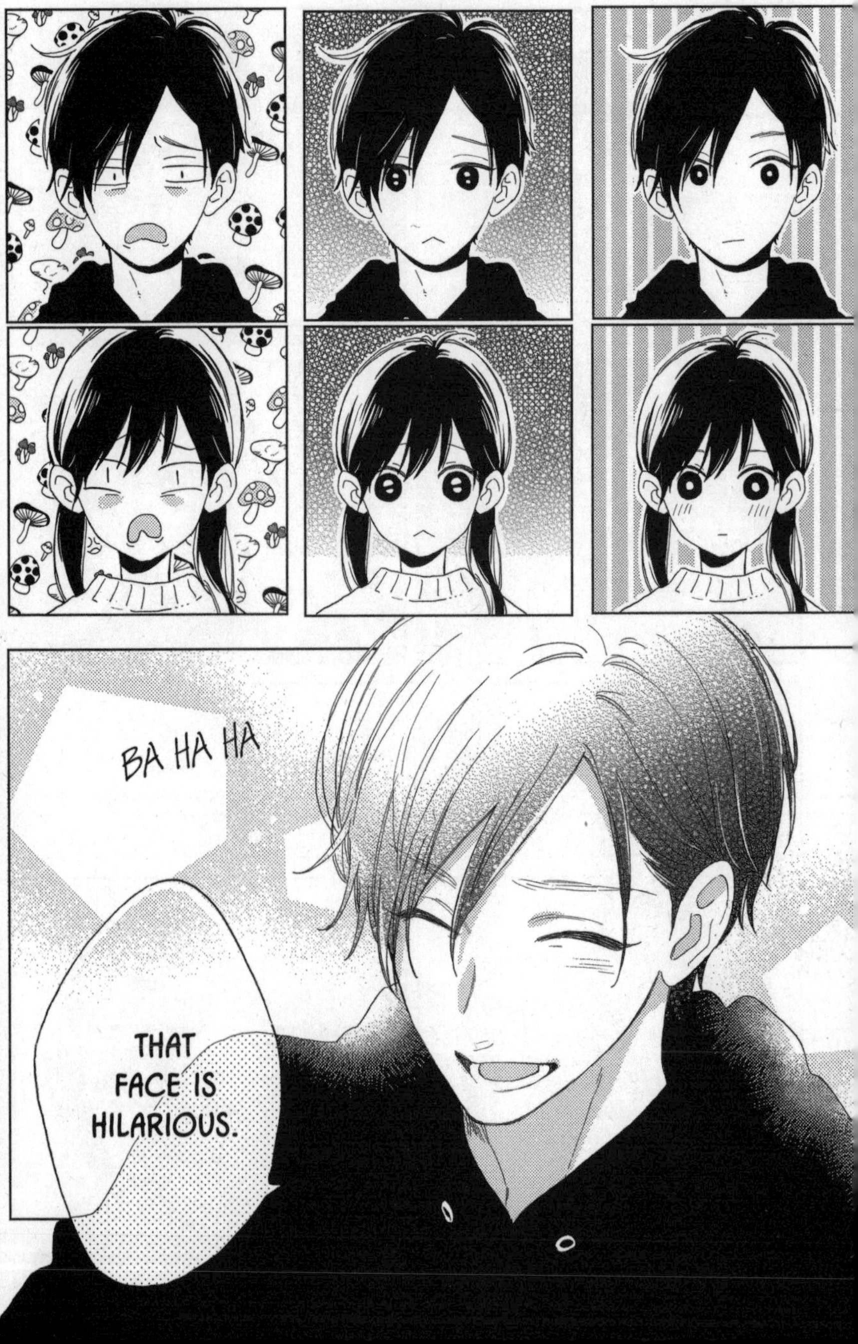
BA HA HA
THAT FACE IS HILARIOUS.

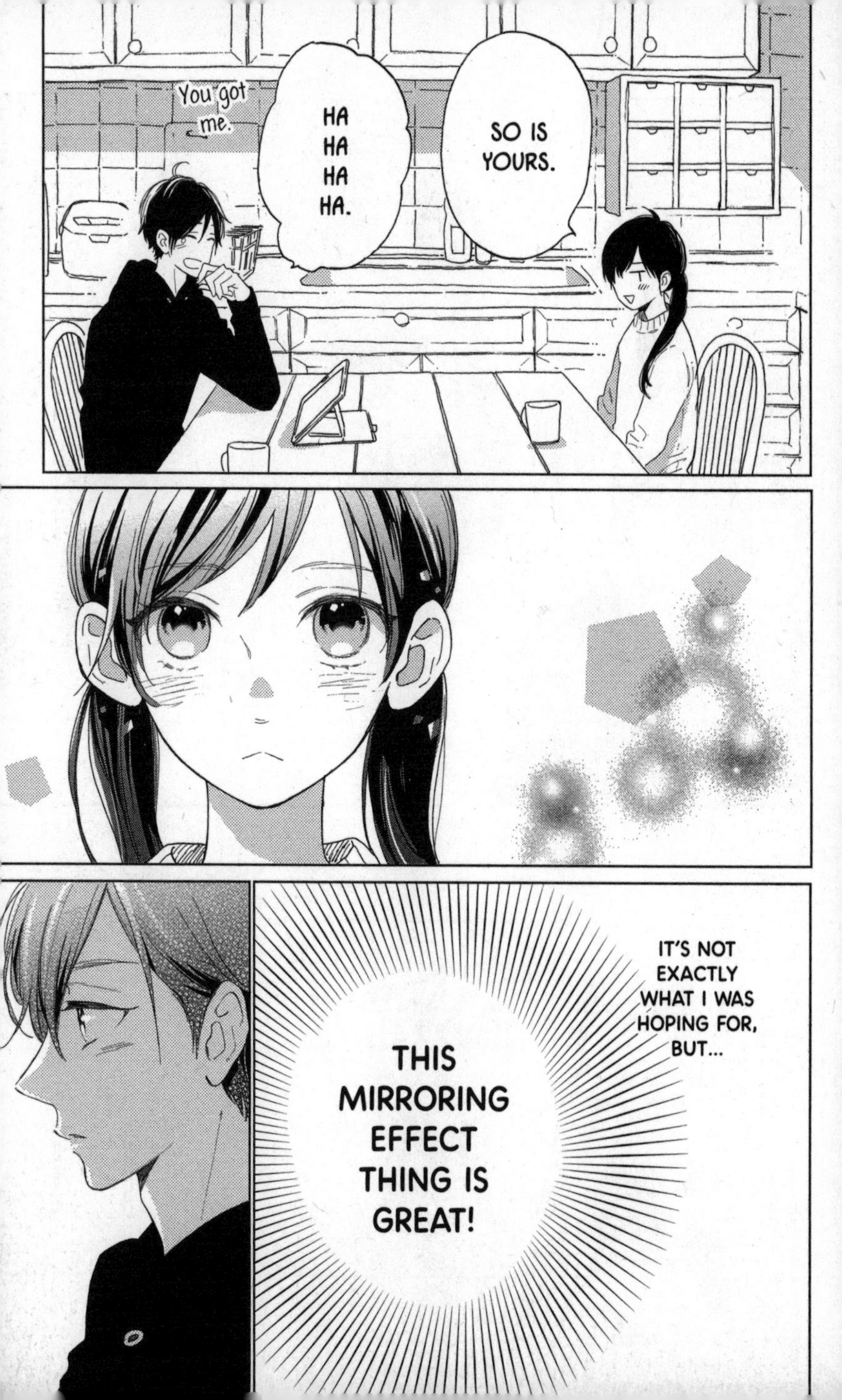
SO IS YOURS.
HA HA HA HA.
You got me.
IT'S NOT EXACTLY WHAT I WAS HOPING FOR, BUT...
THIS MIRRORING EFFECT THING IS GREAT!

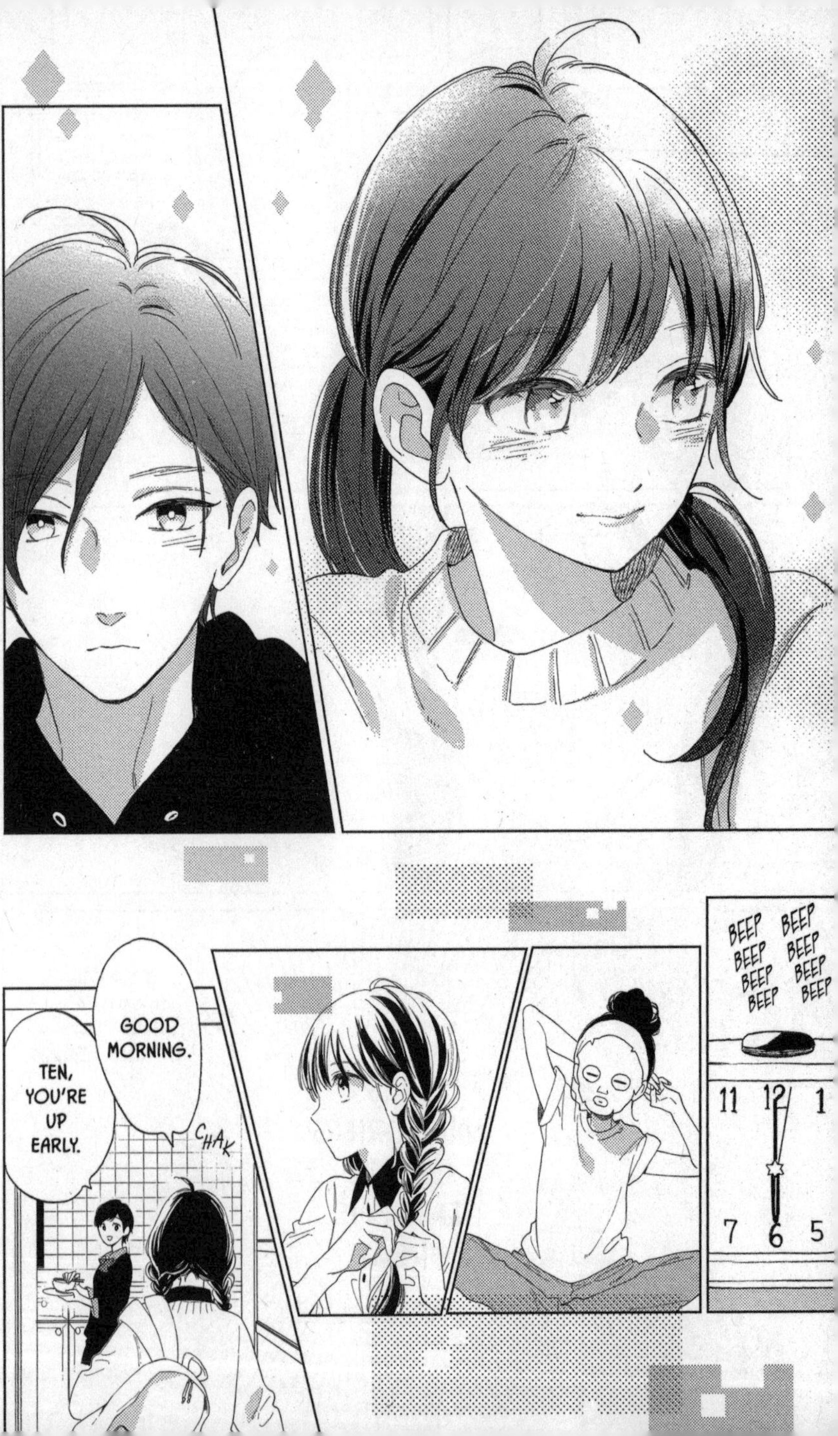
BEEP BEEP BEEP BEEP
BEEP BEEP BEEP BEEP
GOOD MORNING.
CHAK
TEN, YOU'RE UP EARLY.

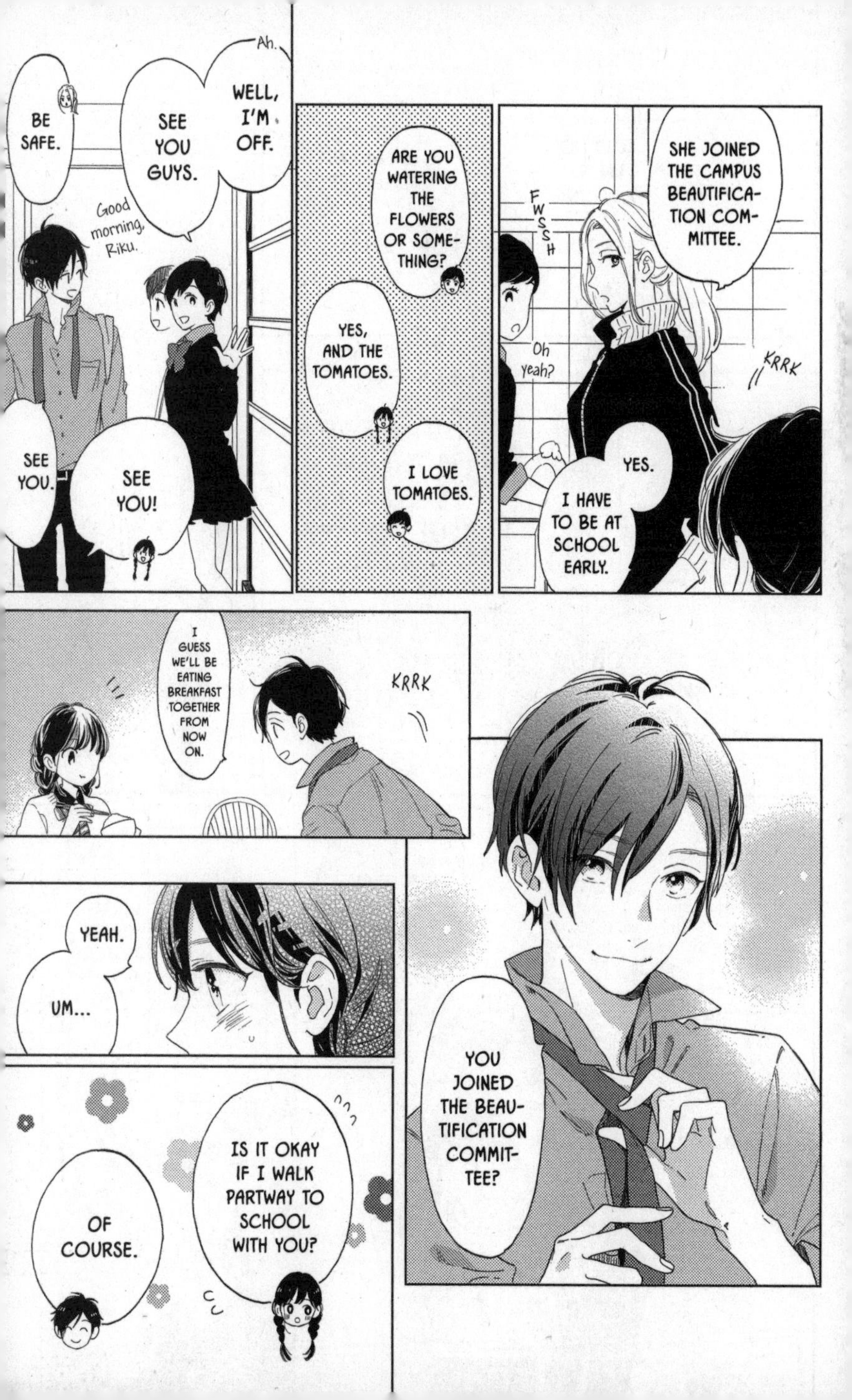

SHE JOINED THE CAMPUS BEAUTIFICATION COMMITTEE.
FWSSH
KRRK
Oh yeah?
YES. I HAVE TO BE AT SCHOOL EARLY.
ARE YOU WATERING THE FLOWERS OR SOMETHING?
YES, AND THE TOMATOES.
I LOVE TOMATOES.
Ah.
WELL, I'M OFF.
SEE YOU GUYS.
BE SAFE.
Good morning, Riku.
SEE YOU!
SEE YOU.
I GUESS WE'LL BE EATING BREAKFAST TOGETHER FROM NOW ON.
KRRK
YOU JOINED THE BEAUTIFICATION COMMITTEE?
YEAH.
UM...
IS IT OKAY IF I WALK PARTWAY TO SCHOOL WITH YOU?
OF COURSE.

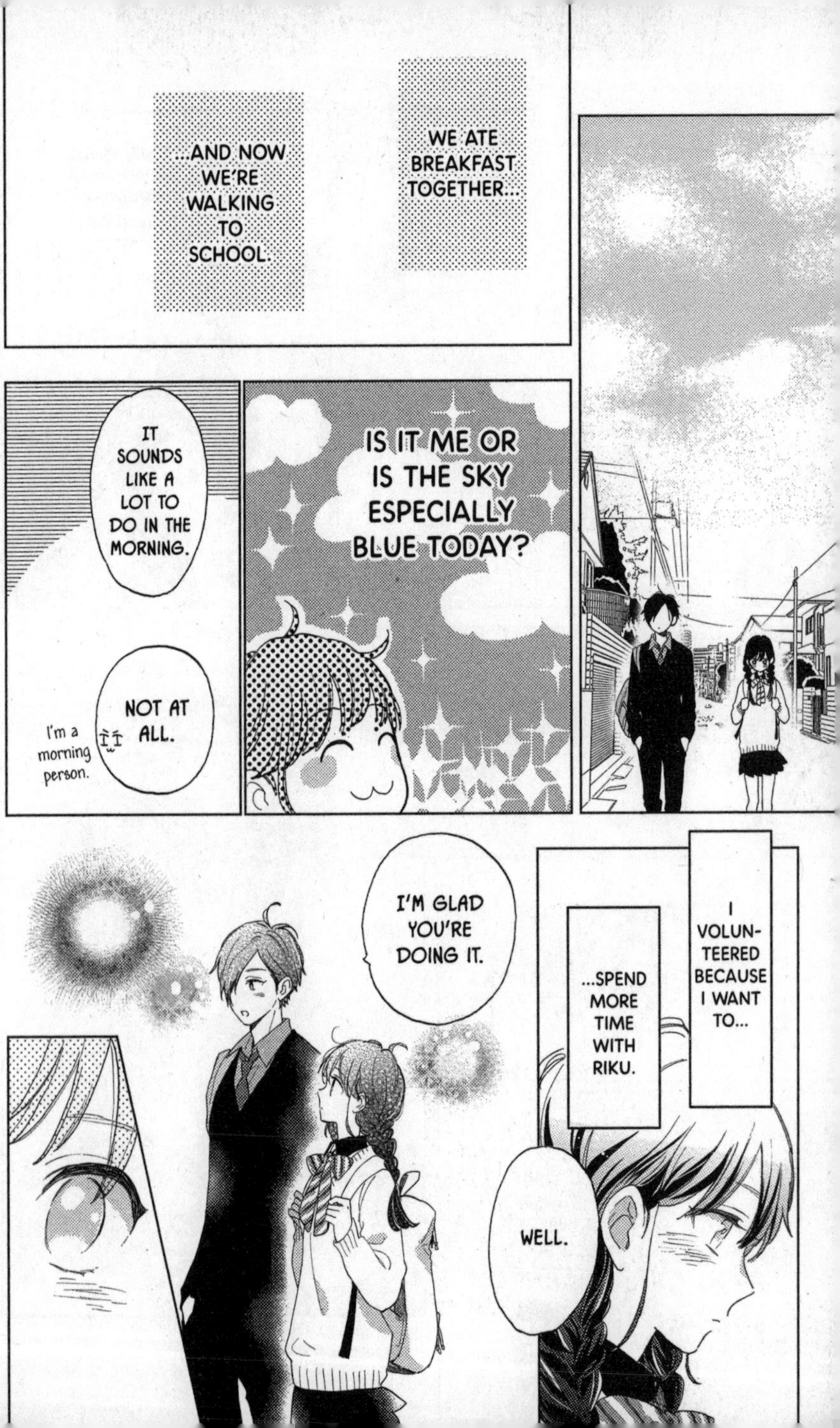
WE ATE BREAKFAST TOGETHER...
...AND NOW WE'RE WALKING TO SCHOOL.
IS IT ME OR IS THE SKY ESPECIALLY BLUE TODAY?
IT SOUNDS LIKE A LOT TO DO IN THE MORNING.
NOT AT ALL.
I'm a morning person.
I VOLUNTEERED BECAUSE I WANT TO...
...SPEND MORE TIME WITH RIKU.
WELL.
I'M GLAD YOU'RE DOING IT.

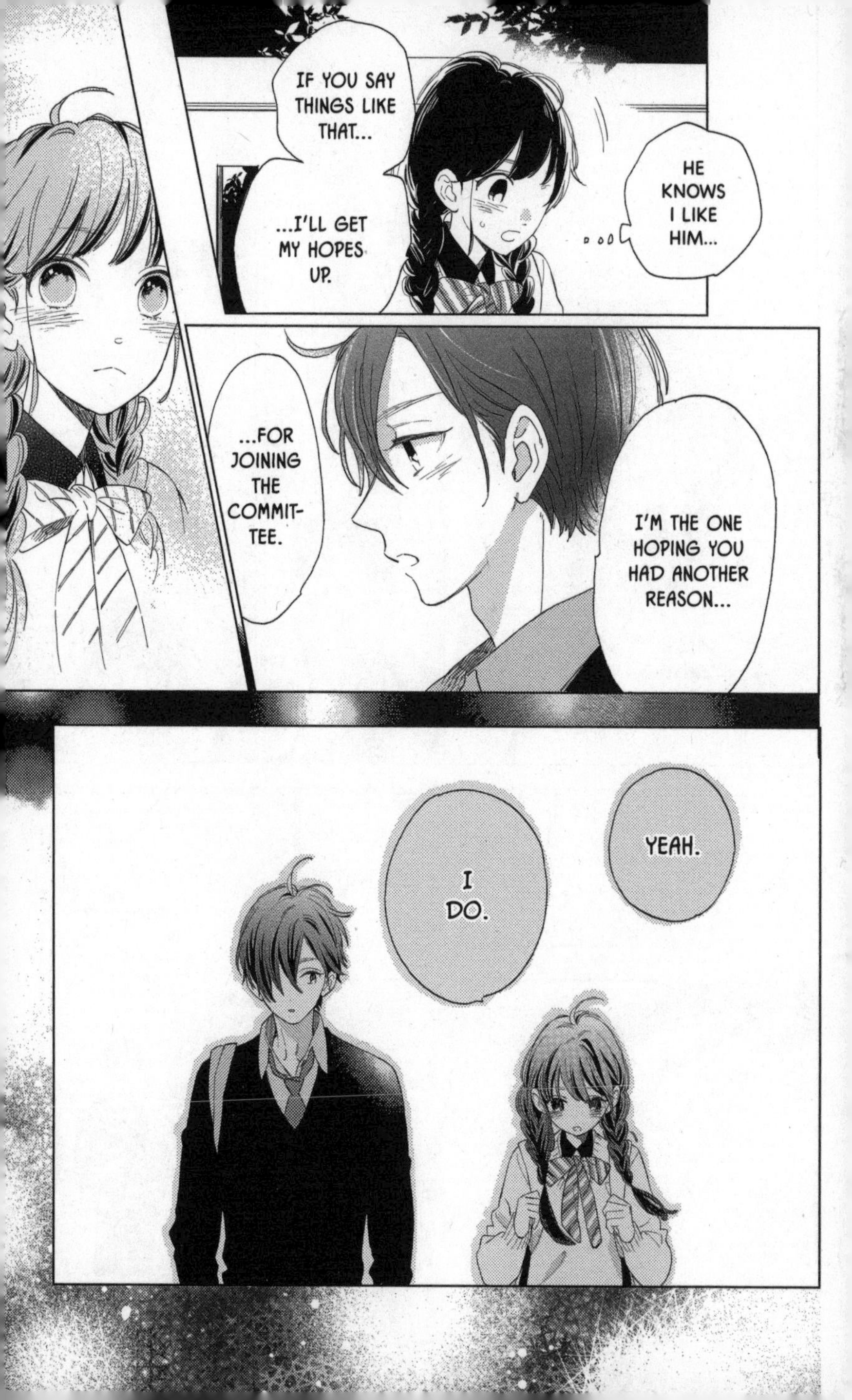
HE KNOWS I LIKE HIM...
IF YOU SAY THINGS LIKE THAT...
...I'LL GET MY HOPES UP.
I'M THE ONE HOPING YOU HAD ANOTHER REASON...
...FOR JOINING THE COMMIT-TEE.
YEAH.
I DO.

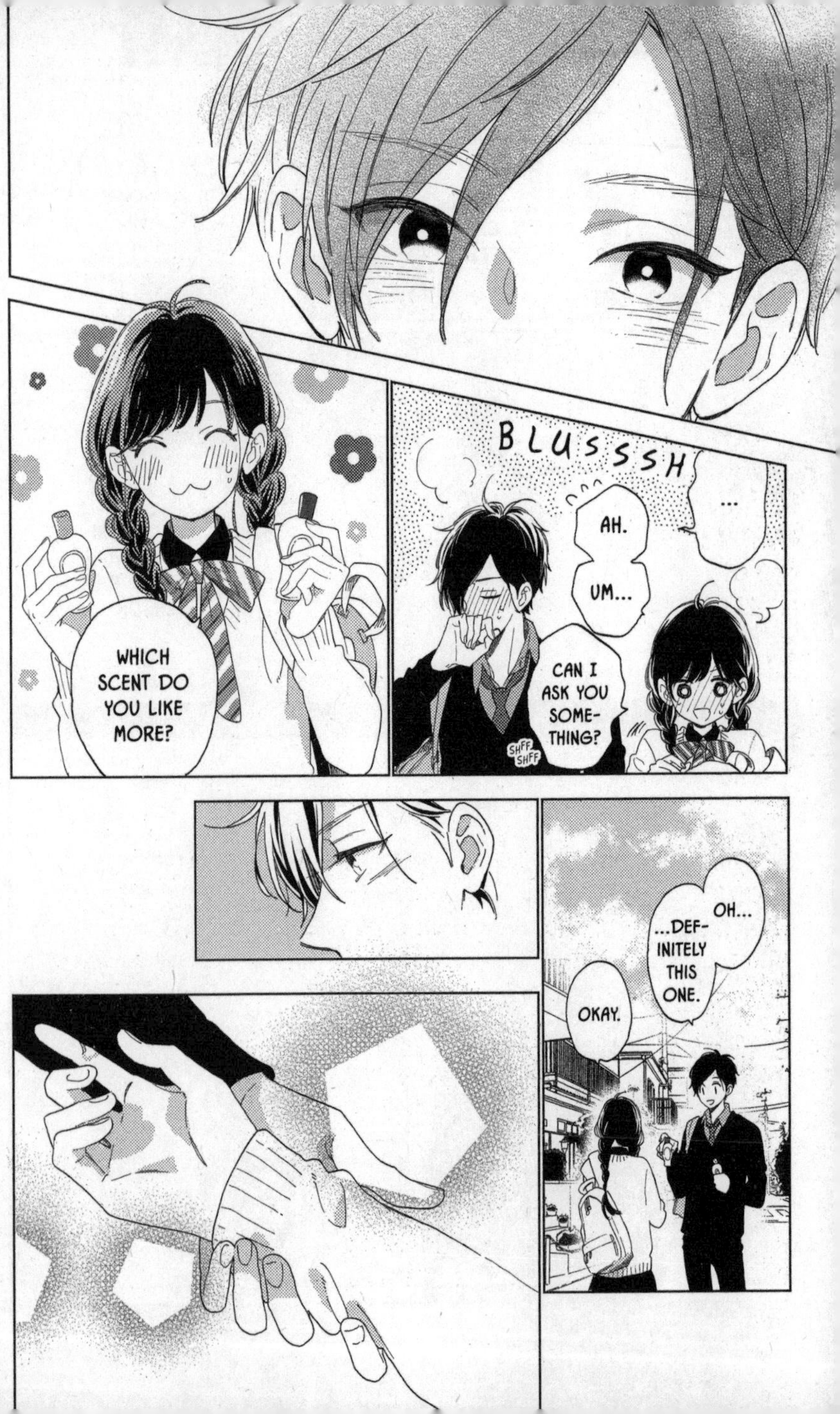
BLUSSSH
...
AH.
UM...
CAN I ASK YOU SOMETHING?
SHFF SHFF
WHICH SCENT DO YOU LIKE MORE?
OH...
...DEF-INITELY THIS ONE.
OKAY.

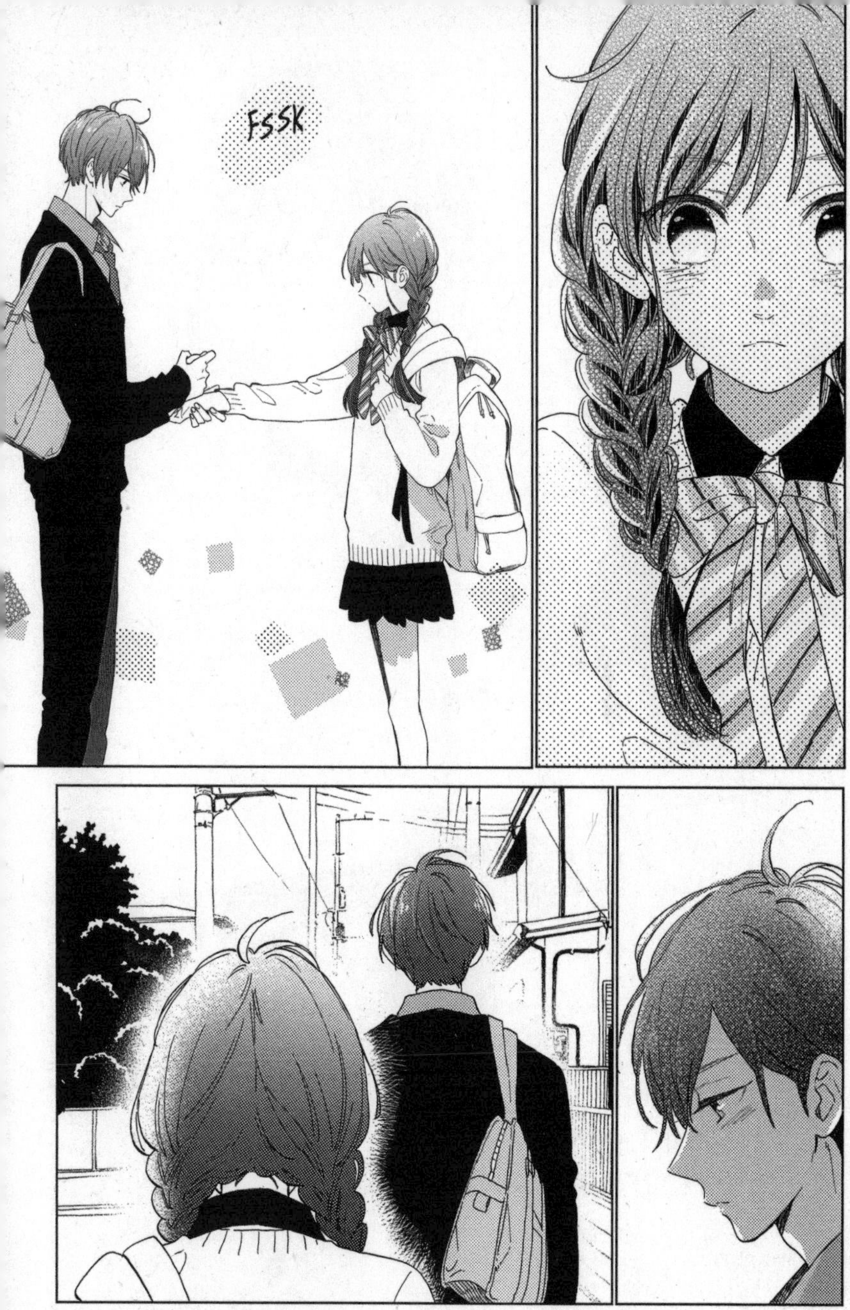
FSSK

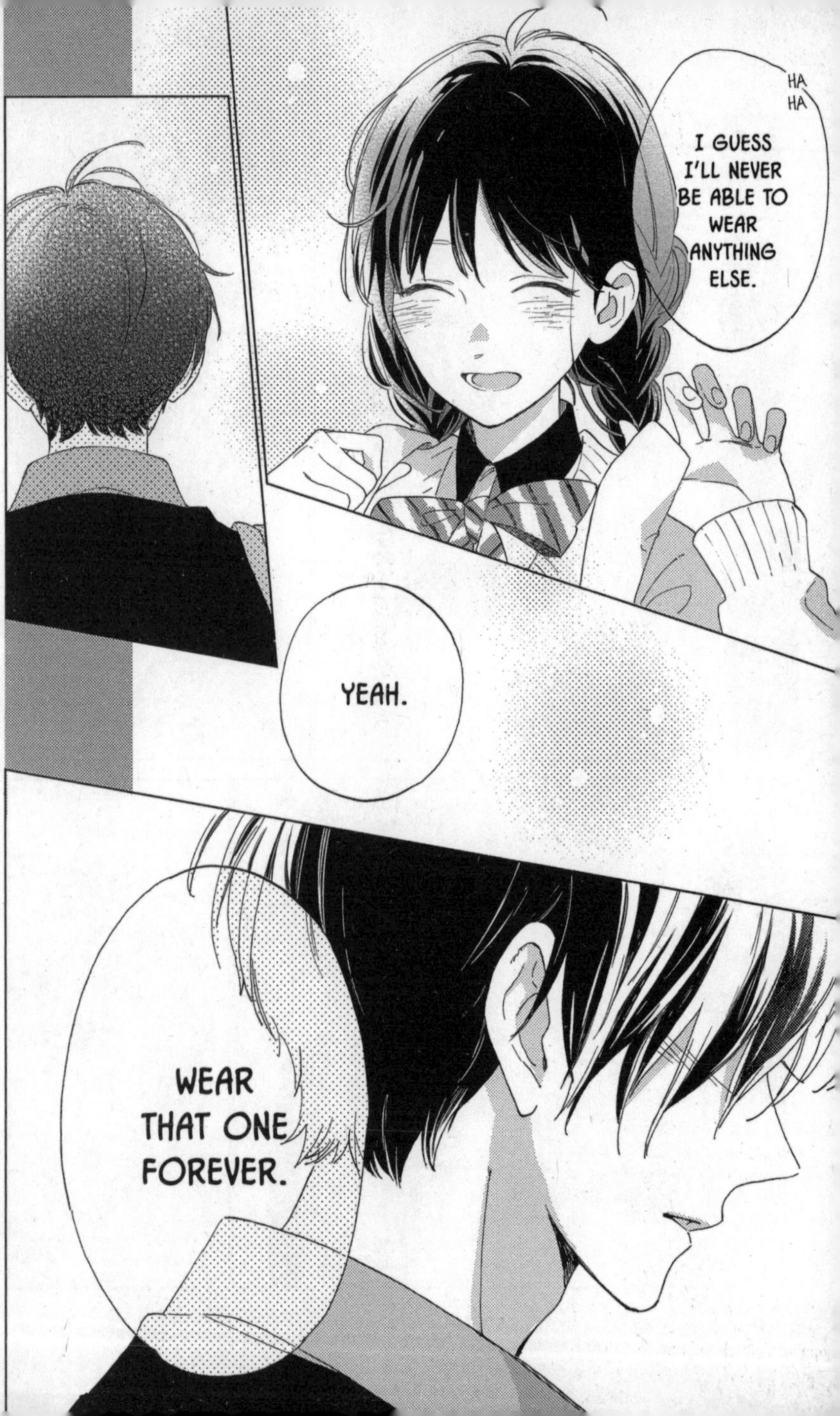
HA HA
I GUESS I'LL NEVER BE ABLE TO WEAR ANYTHING ELSE.
YEAH.
WEAR THAT ONE FOREVER.

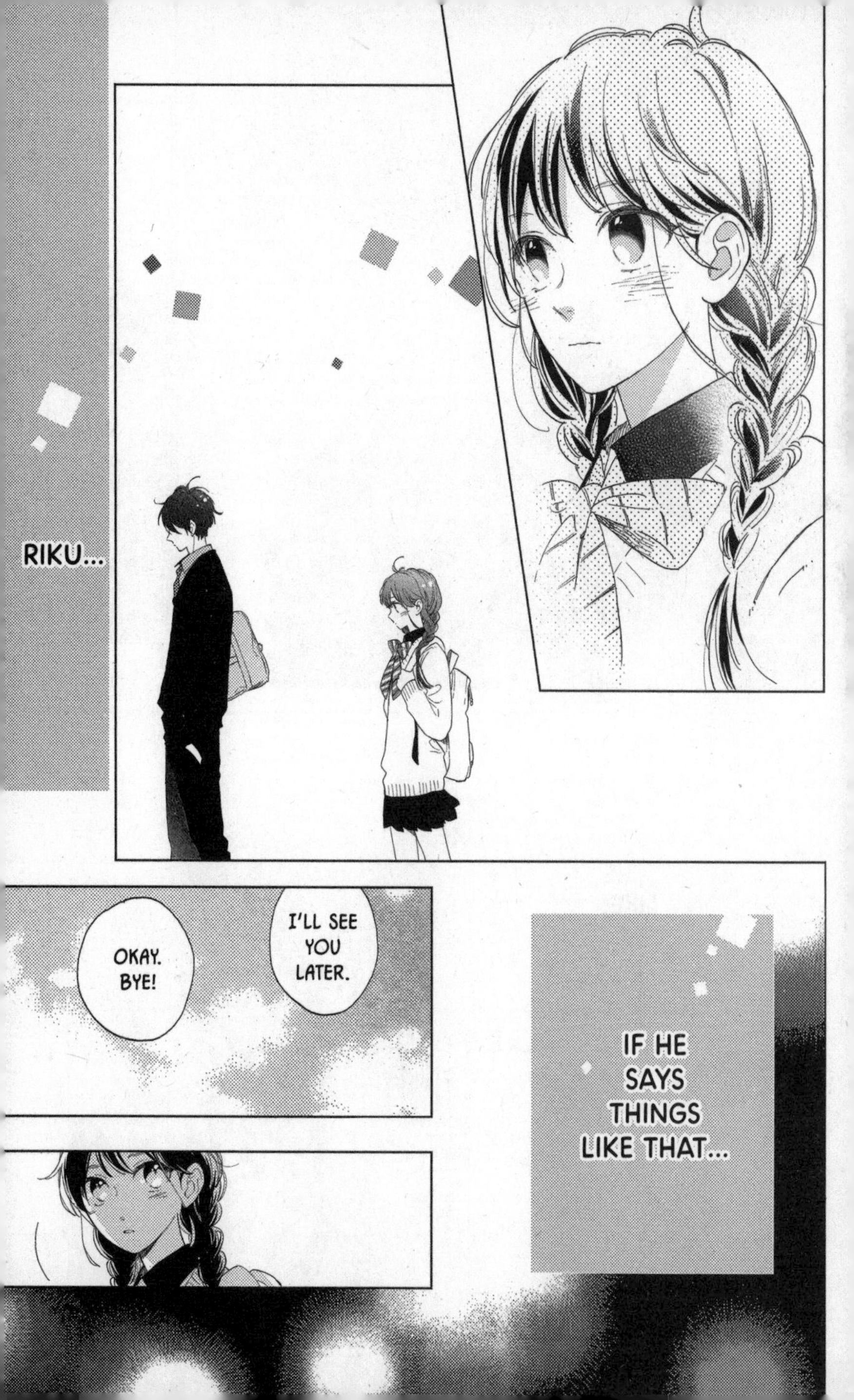
RIKU...
IF HE SAYS THINGS LIKE THAT...
I'LL SEE YOU LATER.
OKAY. BYE!

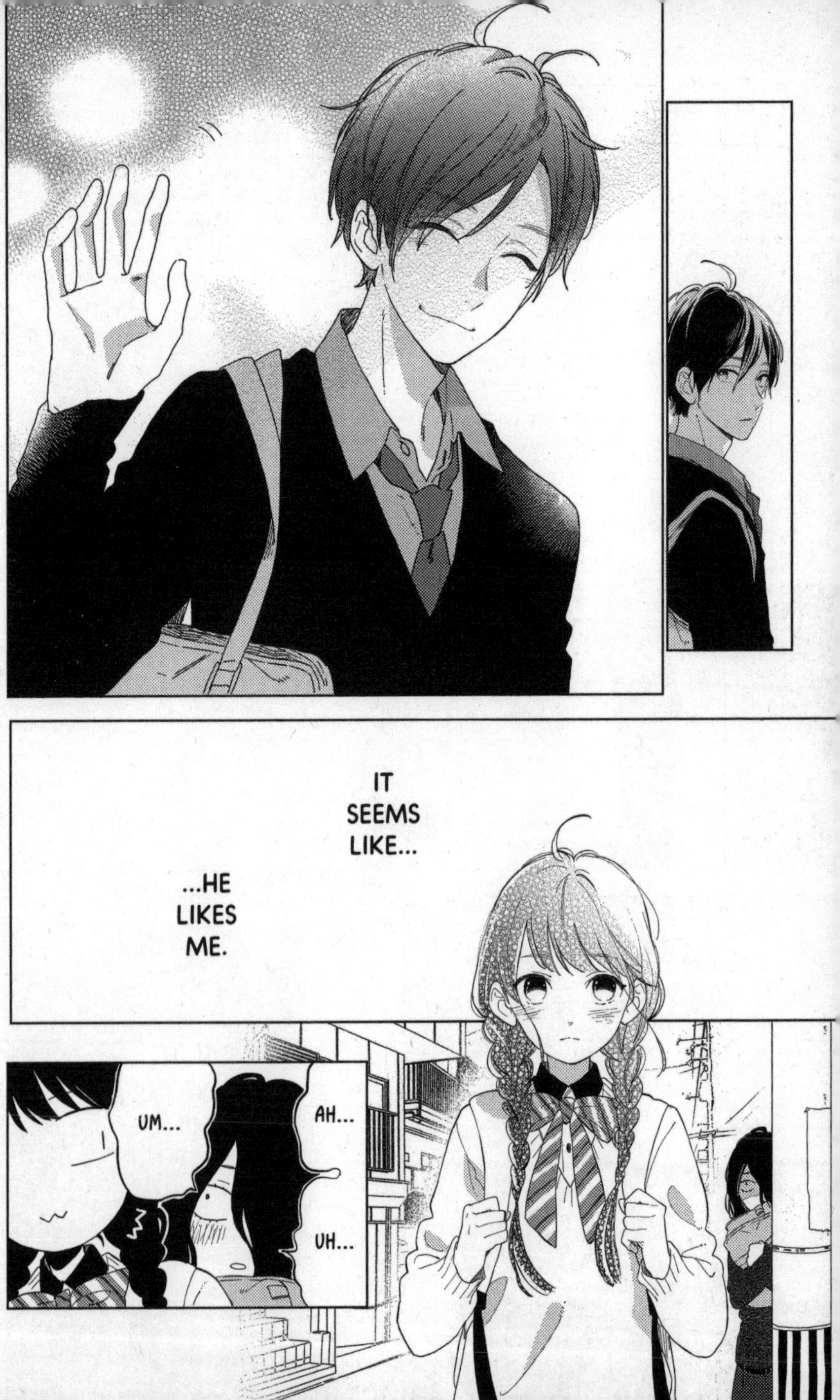
IT SEEMS LIKE...
...HE LIKES ME.
AH...
UM...
UH...

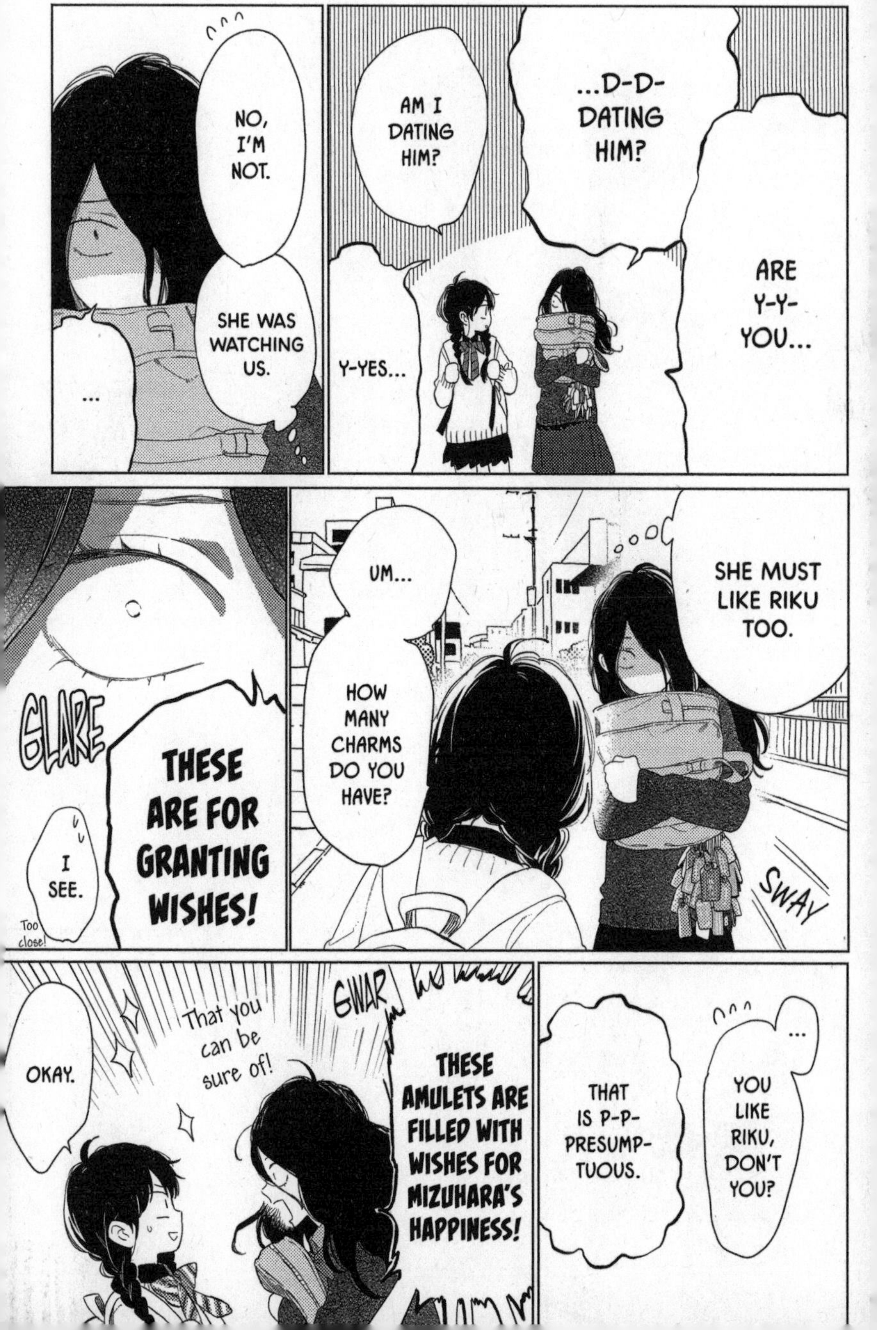
ARE Y-Y-YOU...
...D-D-DATING HIM?
AM I DATING HIM?
Y-YES...
NO, I'M NOT.
SHE WAS WATCHING US.
...
SHE MUST LIKE RIKU TOO.
UM...
HOW MANY CHARMS DO YOU HAVE?
SWAY
GLARE
THESE ARE FOR GRANTING WISHES!
I SEE.
Too close!
...
YOU LIKE RIKU, DON'T YOU?
THAT IS P-P-PRESUMPTUOUS.
GWAR
THESE AMULETS ARE FILLED WITH WISHES FOR MIZUHARA'S HAPPINESS!
That you can be sure of!
OKAY.

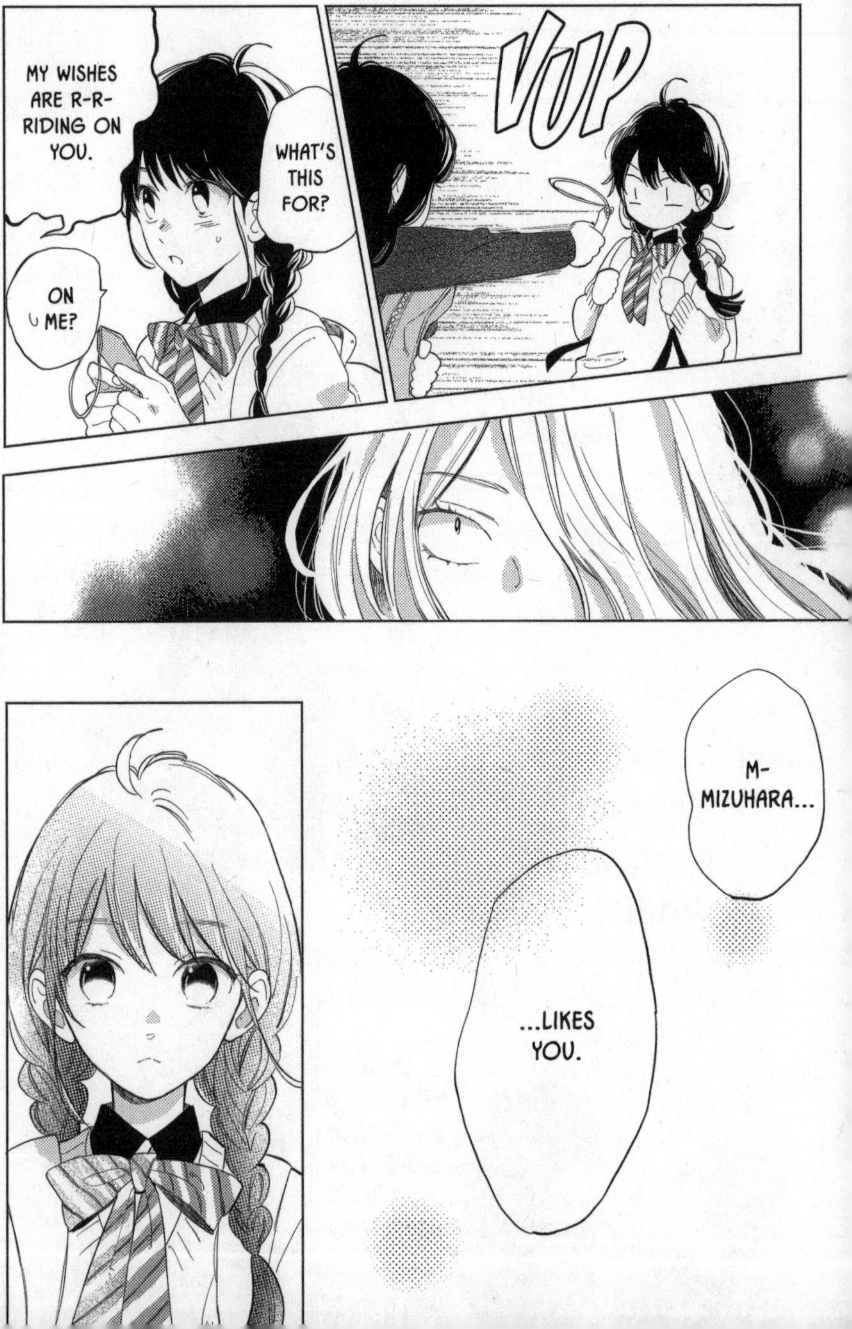
VUIP
WHAT'S THIS FOR?
MY WISHES ARE R-R-RIDING ON YOU.
ON ME?
M-MIZUHARA...
...LIKES YOU.

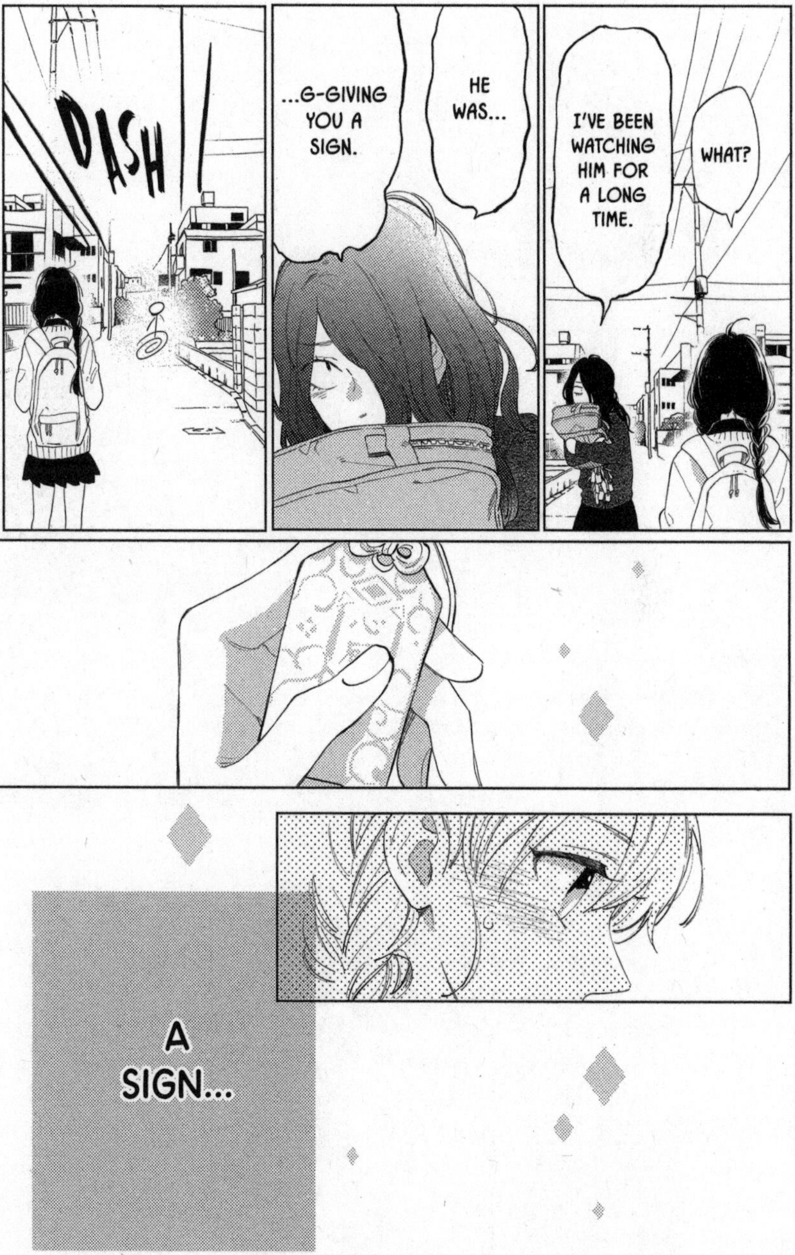
WHAT?
I'VE BEEN WATCHING HIM FOR A LONG TIME.
HE WAS...
...G-GIVING YOU A SIGN.
DASH
A SIGN...

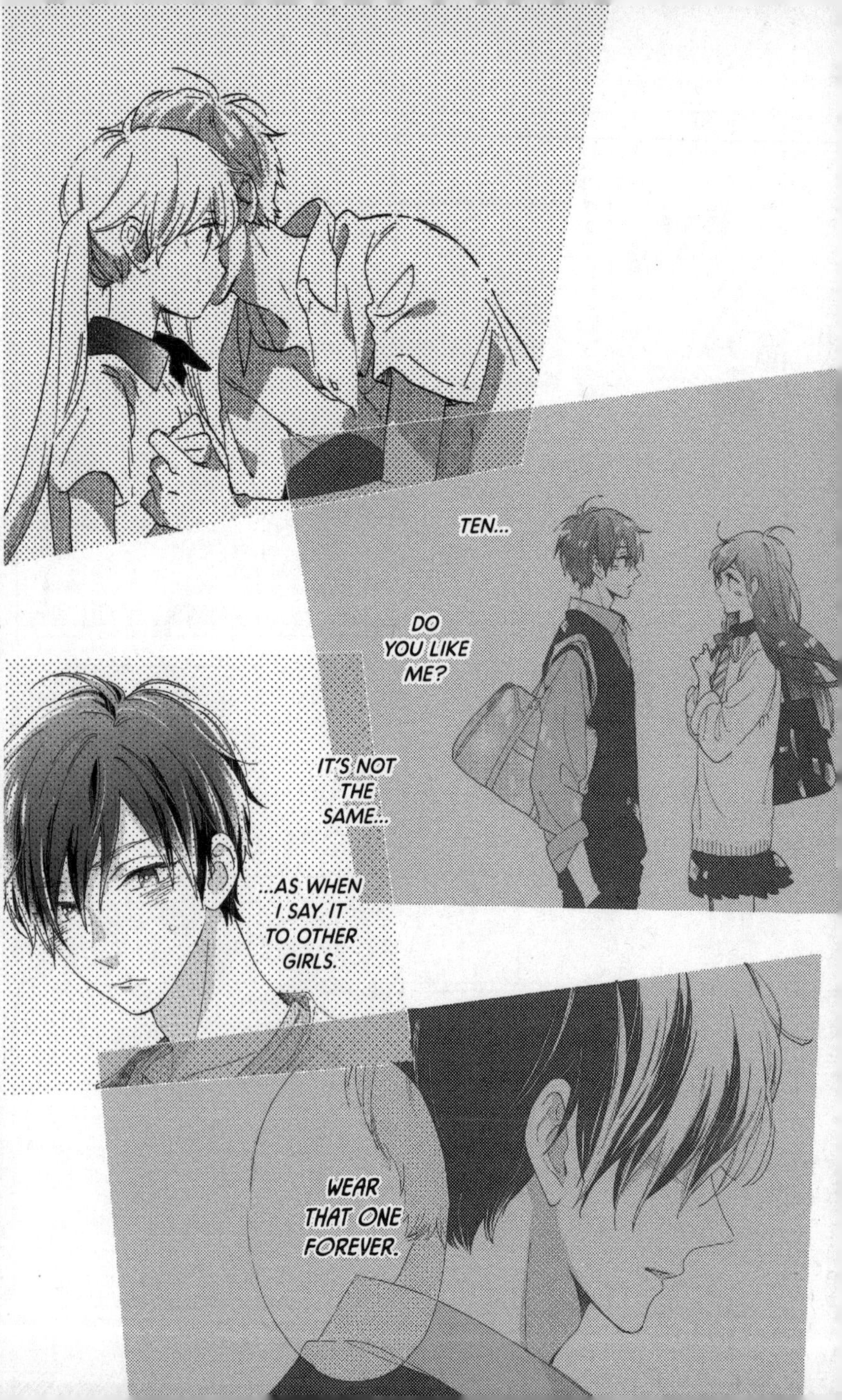
TEN...
DO YOU LIKE ME?
IT'S NOT THE SAME...
...AS WHEN I SAY IT TO OTHER GIRLS.
WEAR THAT ONE FOREVER.

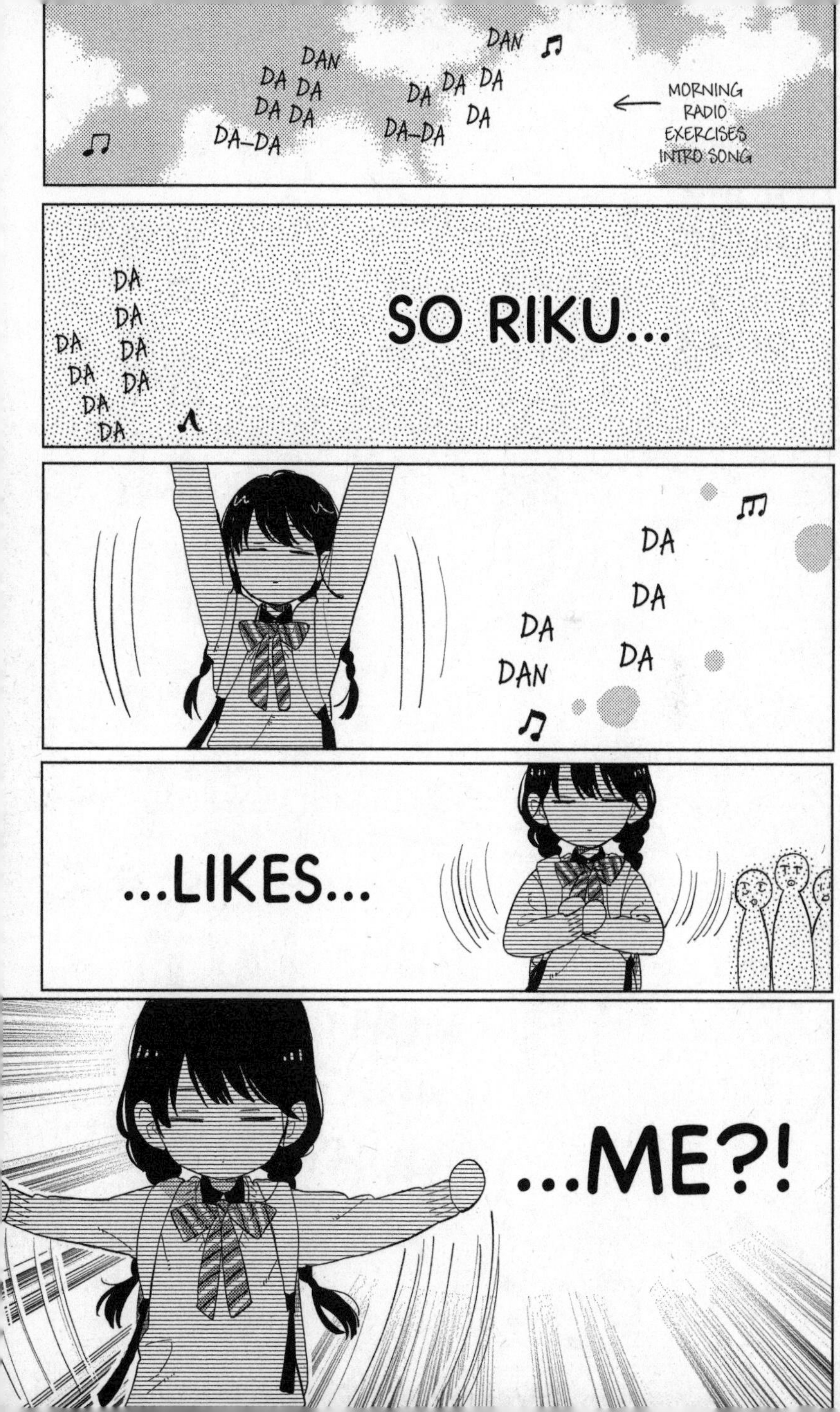

DAN
DA DA DA
DA
DA-DA
MORNING RADIO EXERCISES INTRO SONG
DAN
DA DA
DA DA
DA-DA
SO RIKU...
DA DA DA DA
DA DA DA DA
DA DA DA DA
DAN
...LIKES...
...ME?!

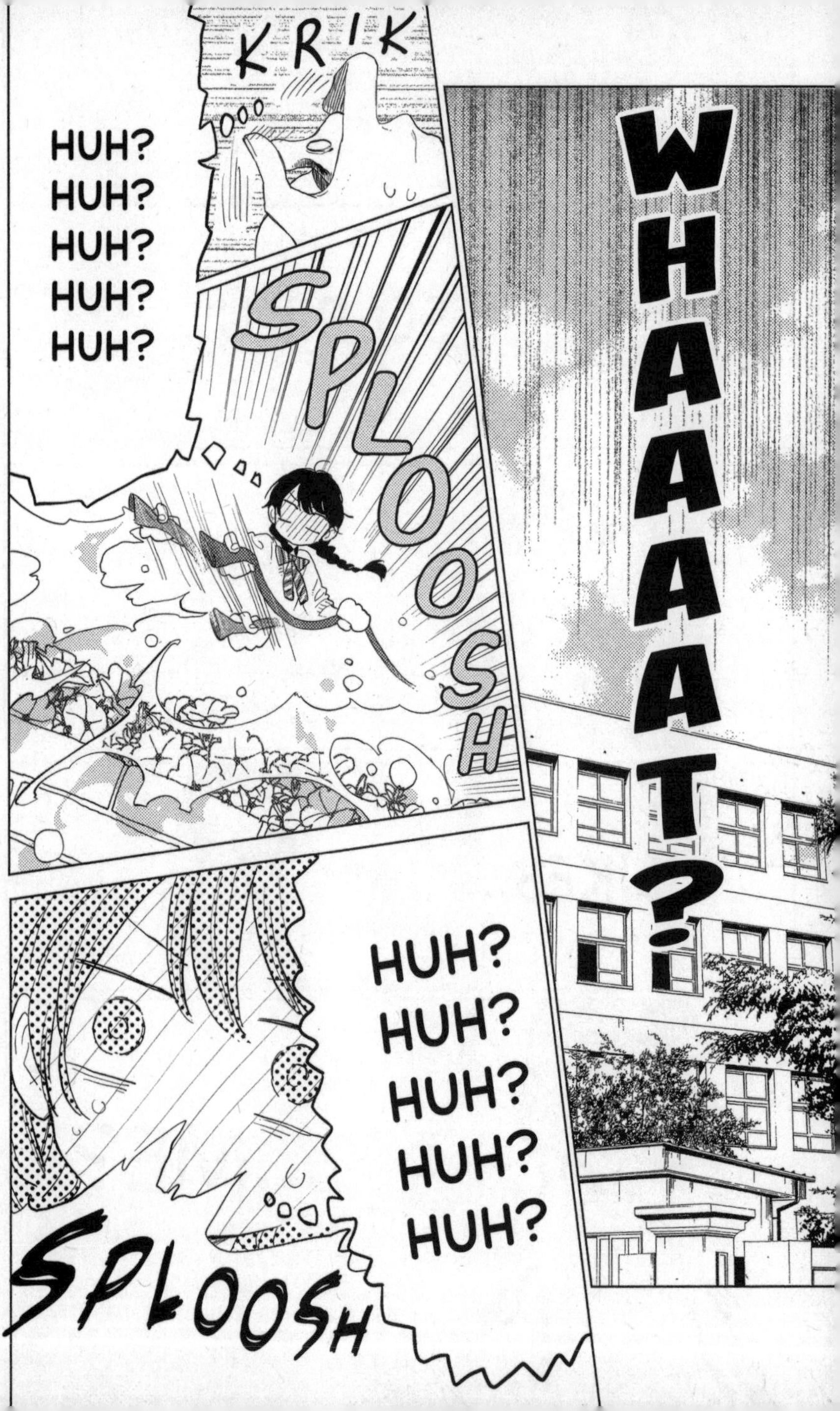
WHAAAAT?!
KRIK
HUH? HUH? HUH? HUH? HUH?
SPLOOSH
HUH? HUH? HUH? HUH? HUH?
SPLOOSH

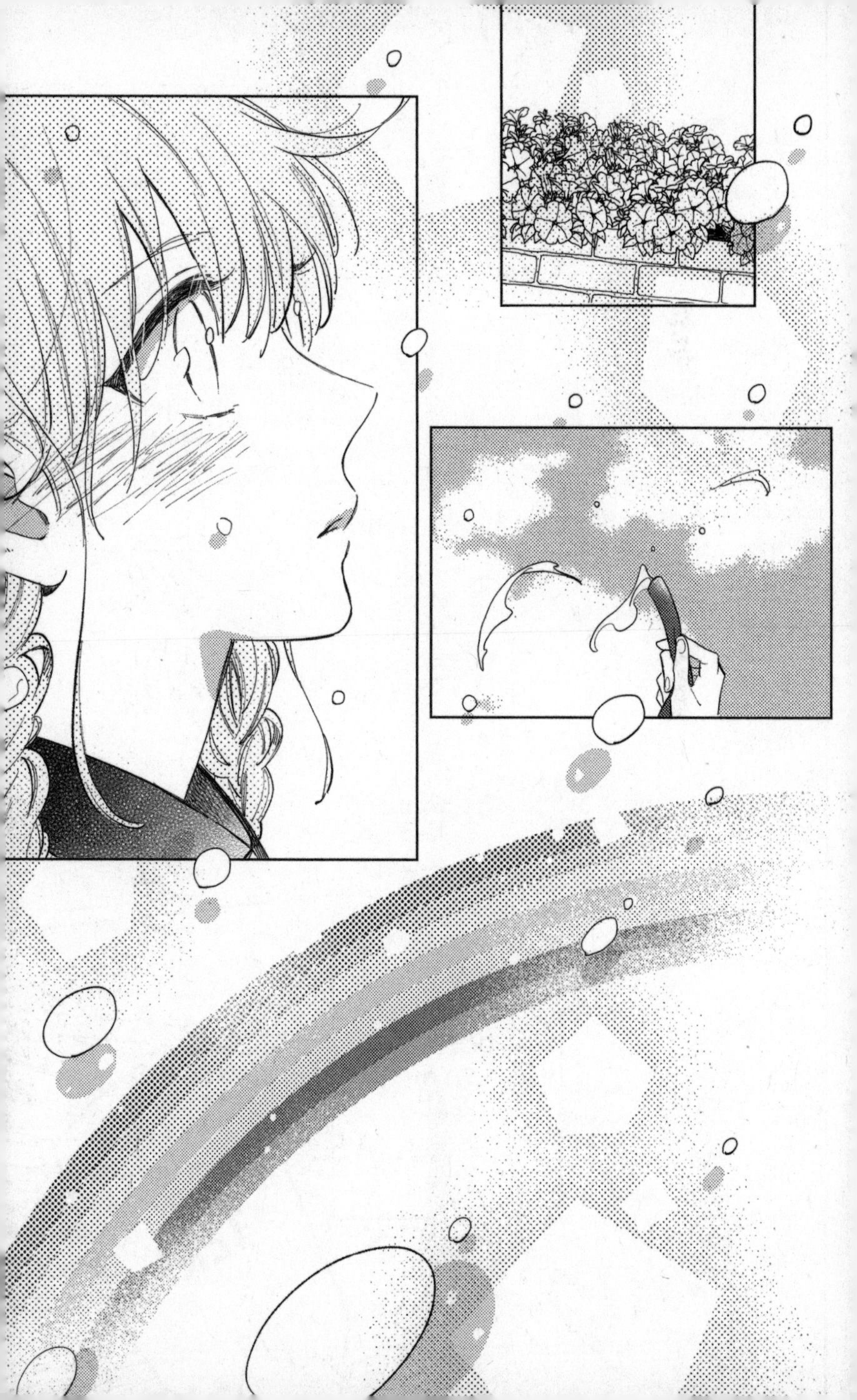

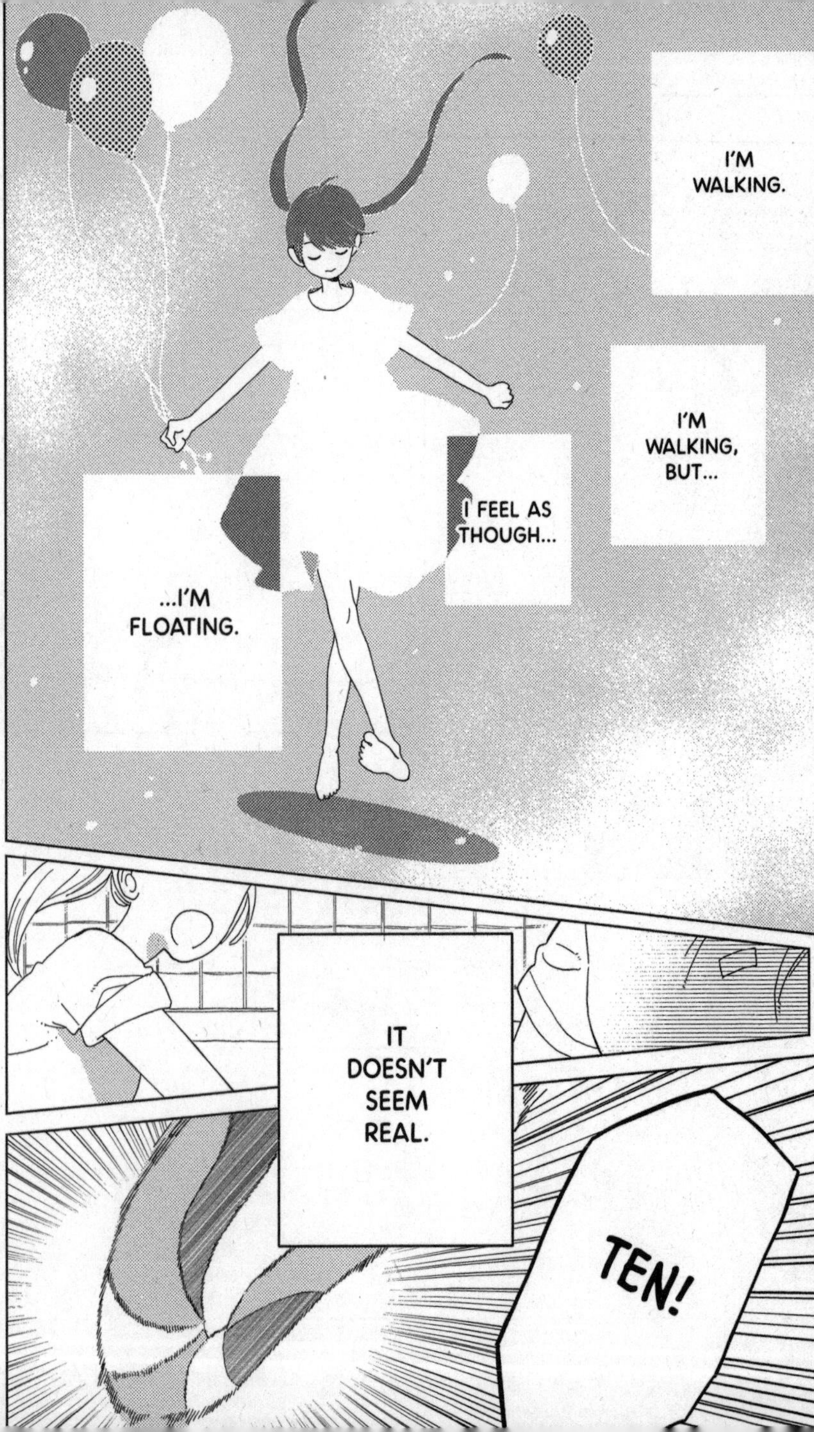
I'M WALKING.
I'M WALKING, BUT...
I FEEL AS THOUGH...
...I'M FLOATING.
IT DOESN'T SEEM REAL.
TEN!

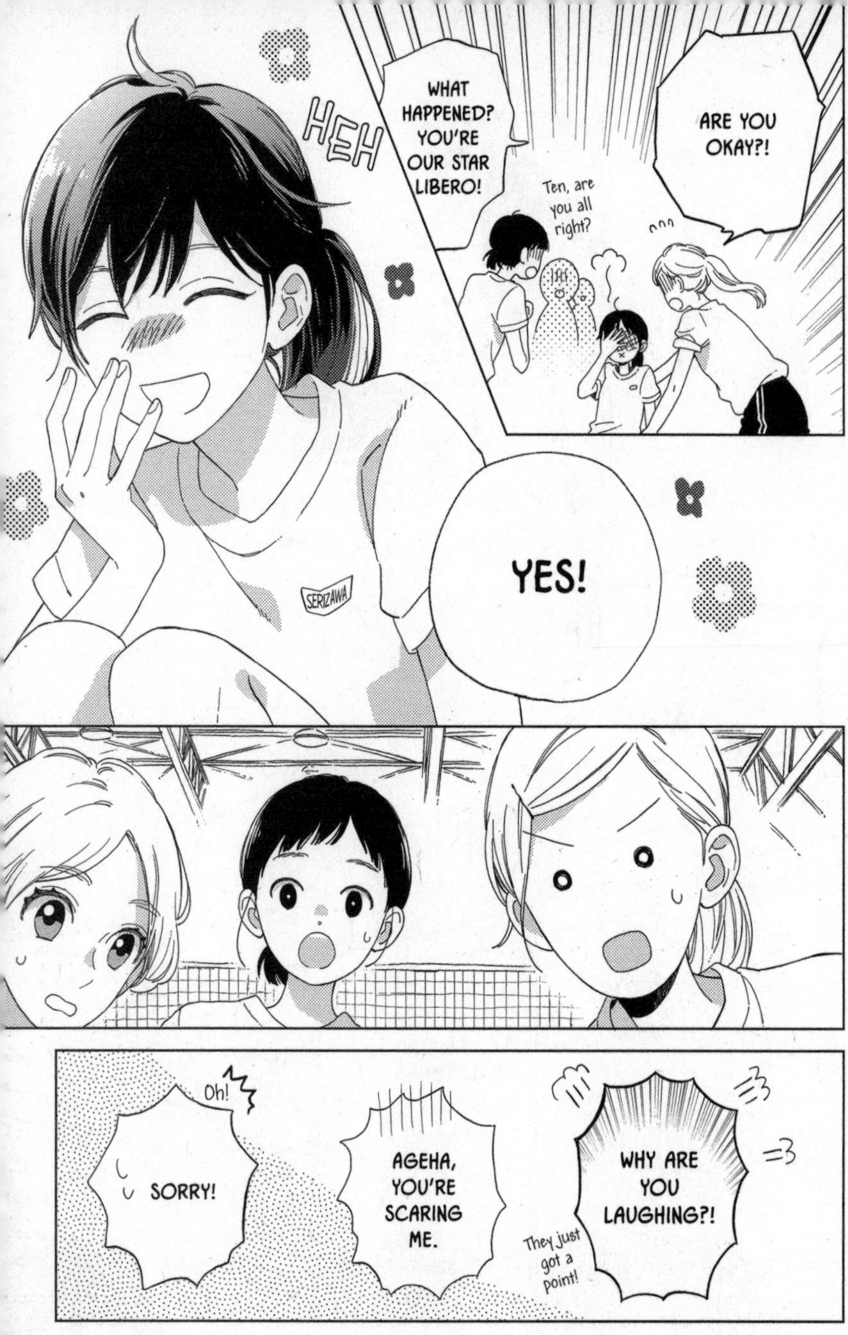
ARE YOU OKAY?!
WHAT HAPPENED? YOU'RE OUR STAR LIBERO!
Ten, are you all right?
HEH
YES!
SERIZAWA
WHY ARE YOU LAUGHING?!
They just got a point!
AGEHA, YOU'RE SCARING ME.
Oh!
SORRY!

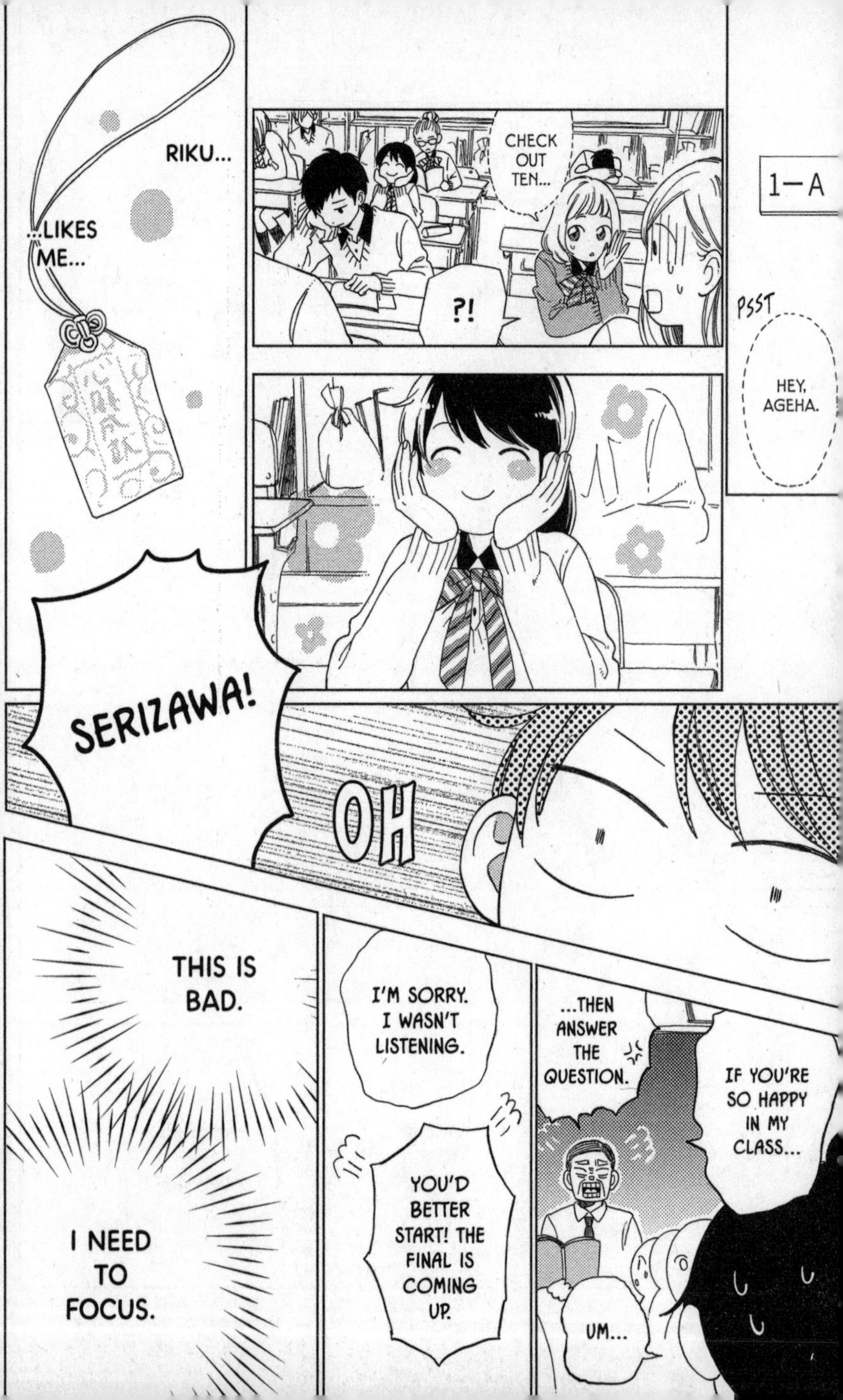
1-A
PSST
HEY, AGEHA.
CHECK OUT TEN...
?!
RIKU...
...LIKES ME...
SERIZAWA!
OH
IF YOU'RE SO HAPPY IN MY CLASS...
...THEN ANSWER THE QUESTION.
UM...
I'M SORRY. I WASN'T LISTENING.
YOU'D BETTER START! THE FINAL IS COMING UP.
THIS IS BAD.
I NEED TO FOCUS.

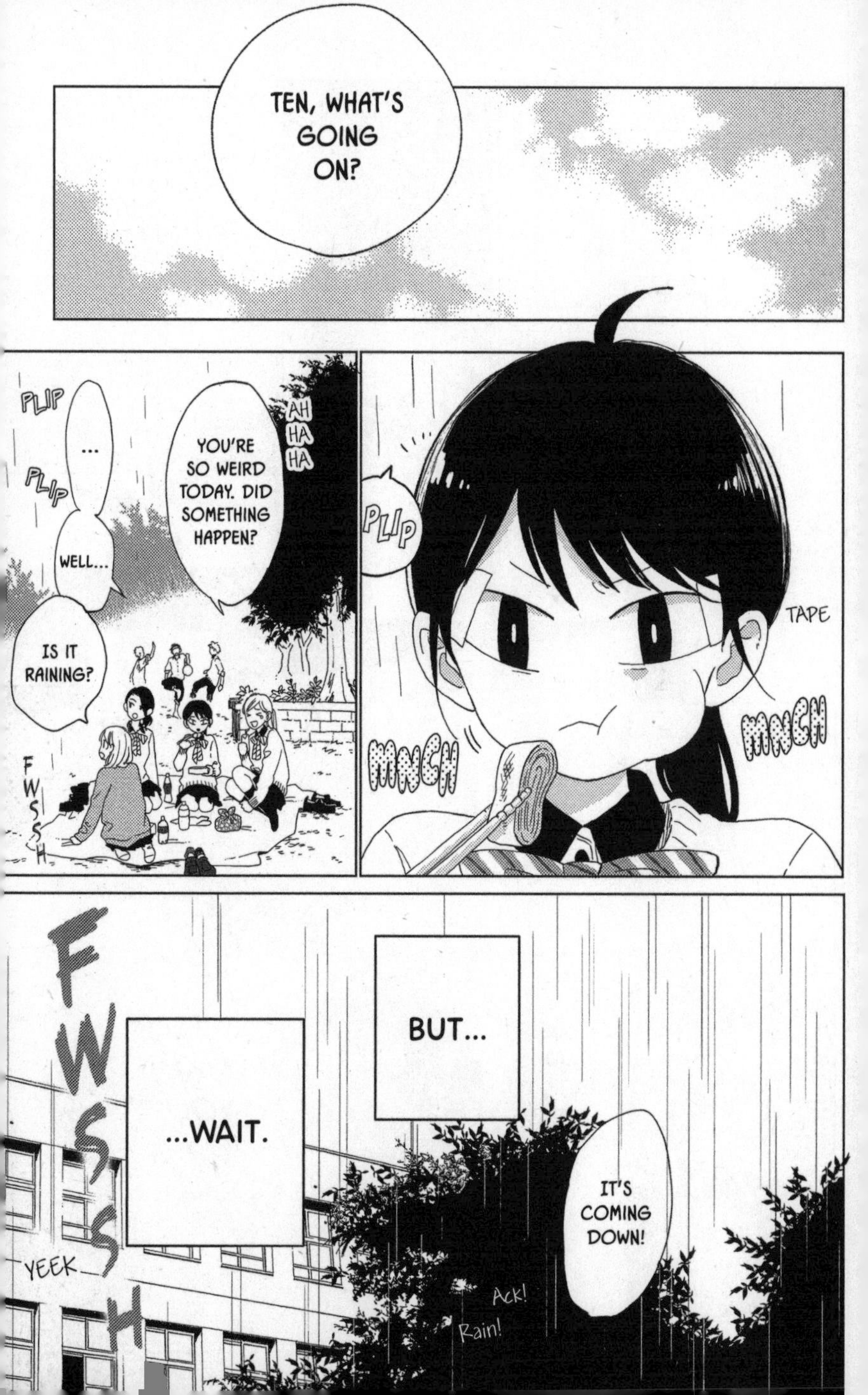
TEN, WHAT'S GOING ON?
PLIP
TAPE
MNCH
MNCH
AH HA HA
YOU'RE SO WEIRD TODAY. DID SOMETHING HAPPEN?
PLIP
...
PLIP
WELL...
IS IT RAINING?
FWSSH
BUT...
...WAIT.
IT'S COMING DOWN!
Ack!
Rain!
FWSSH
YEEK

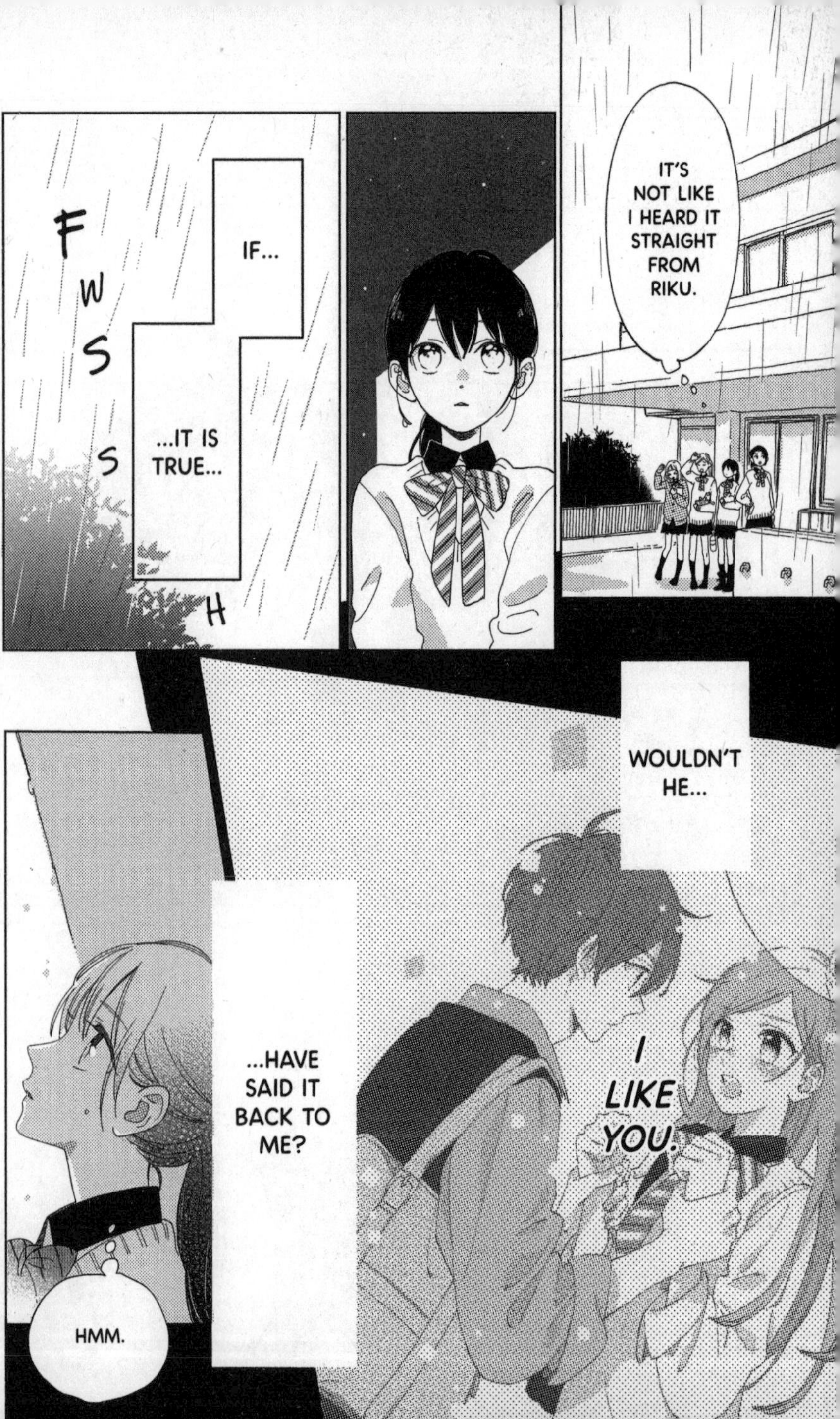
IT'S NOT LIKE I HEARD IT STRAIGHT FROM RIKU.
IF...
...IT IS TRUE...
FWSSH
WOULDN'T HE...
I LIKE YOU.
...HAVE SAID IT BACK TO ME?
HMM.

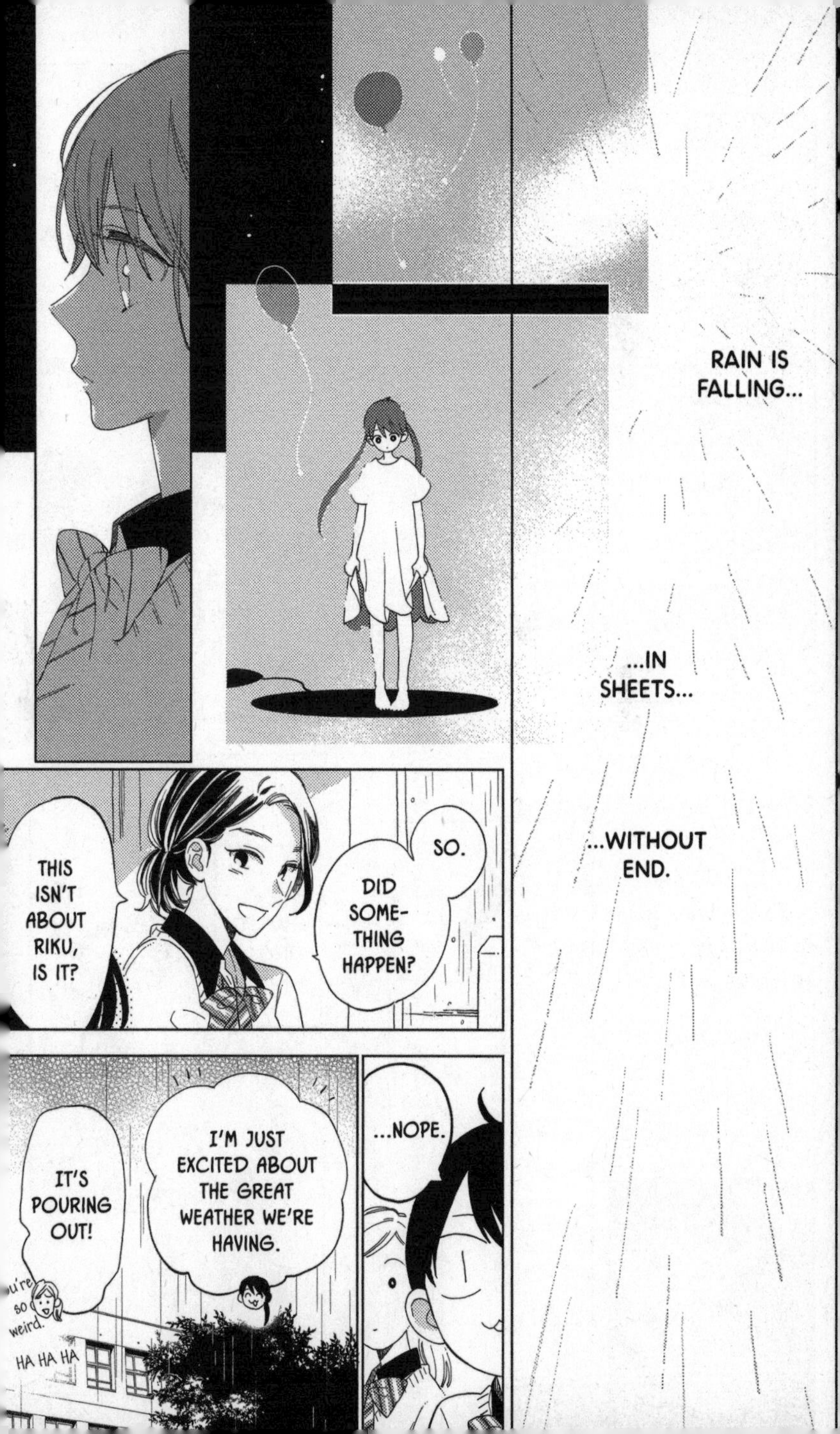
RAIN IS FALLING...
...IN SHEETS...
...WITHOUT END.
SO.
DID SOMETHING HAPPEN?
THIS ISN'T ABOUT RIKU, IS IT?
...NOPE.
I'M JUST EXCITED ABOUT THE GREAT WEATHER WE'RE HAVING.
IT'S POURING OUT!
u're so weird.
HA HA HA

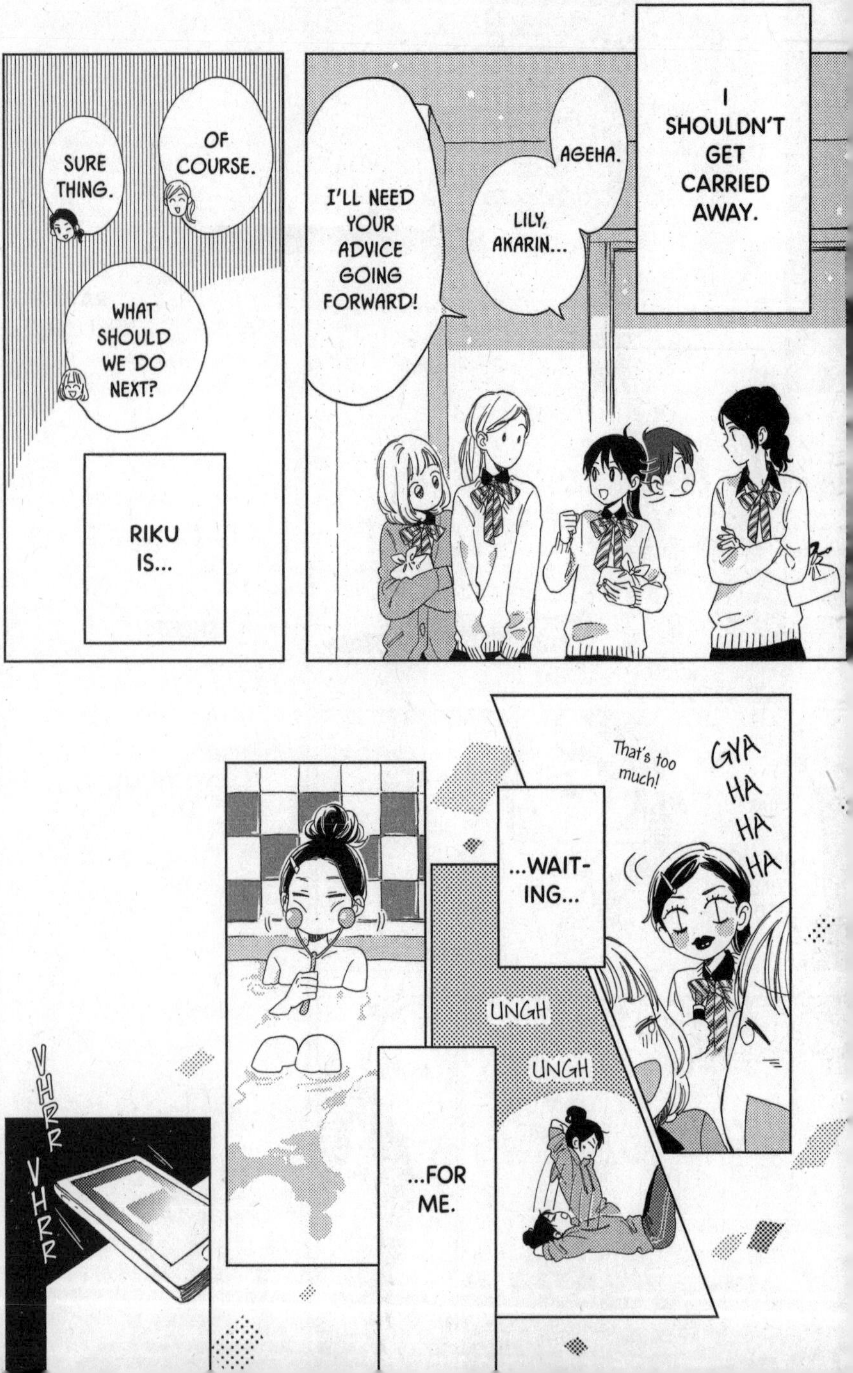
I SHOULDN'T GET CARRIED AWAY.
AGEHA.
LILY, AKARIN...
I'LL NEED YOUR ADVICE GOING FORWARD!
OF COURSE.
SURE THING.
WHAT SHOULD WE DO NEXT?
RIKU IS...
GYA HA HA HA
That's too much!
...WAIT-ING...
UNGH
UNGH
...FOR ME.
VHRR
VHRR

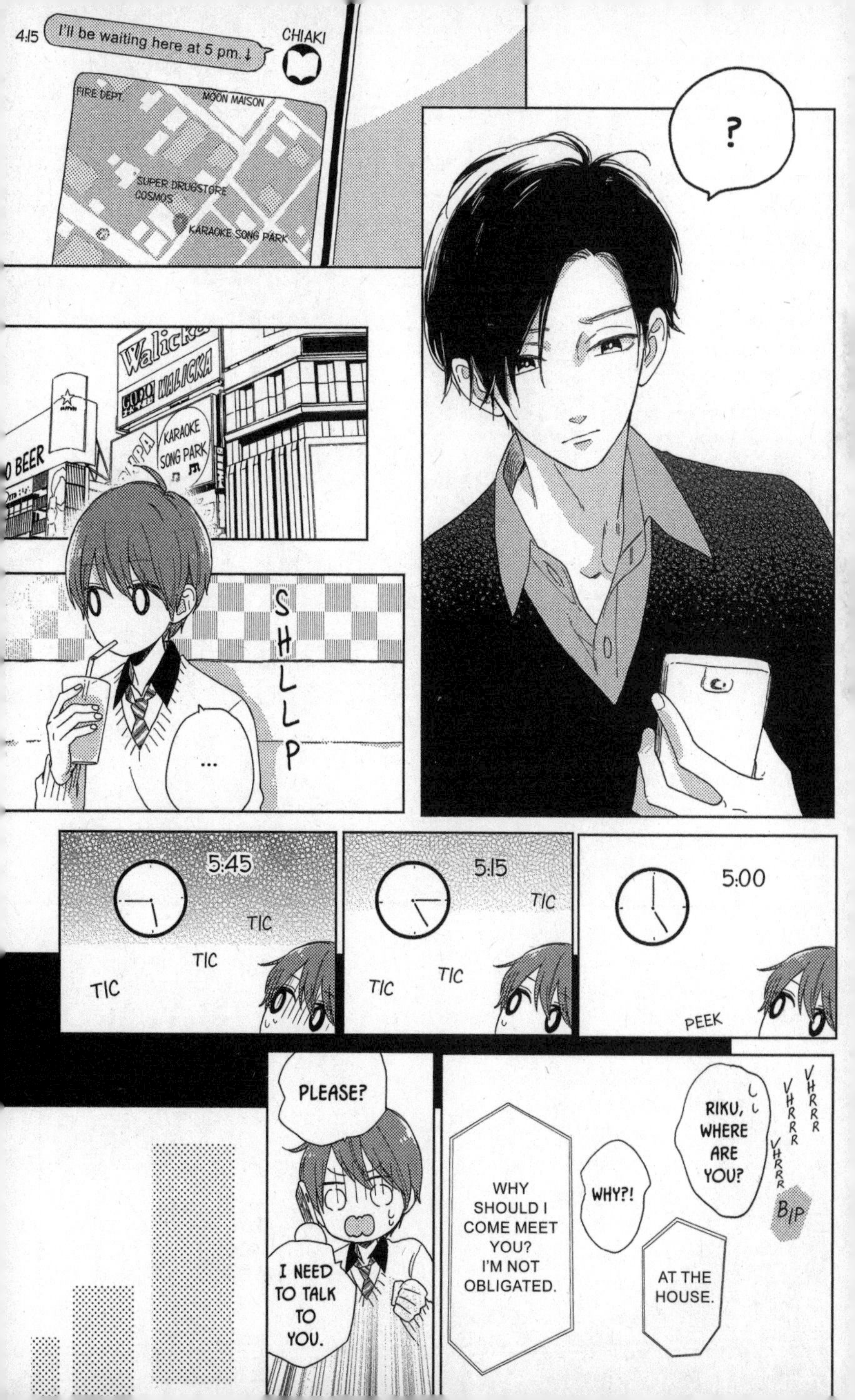

4:15
I'll be waiting here at 5 pm.↓
CHIAKI
FIRE DEPT.
MOON MAISON
SUPER DRUGSTORE COSMOS
KARAOKE SONG PARK
?
Walicka
WALICKA
KARAOKE SONG PARK
BEER
SHLLP
...
5:00
PEEK
5:15
TIC
TIC
TIC
5:45
TIC
TIC
TIC
VHRRR
VHRRR
VHRRR
BIP
RIKU, WHERE ARE YOU?
AT THE HOUSE.
WHY?!
WHY SHOULD I COME MEET YOU? I'M NOT OBLIGATED.
PLEASE?
I NEED TO TALK TO YOU.

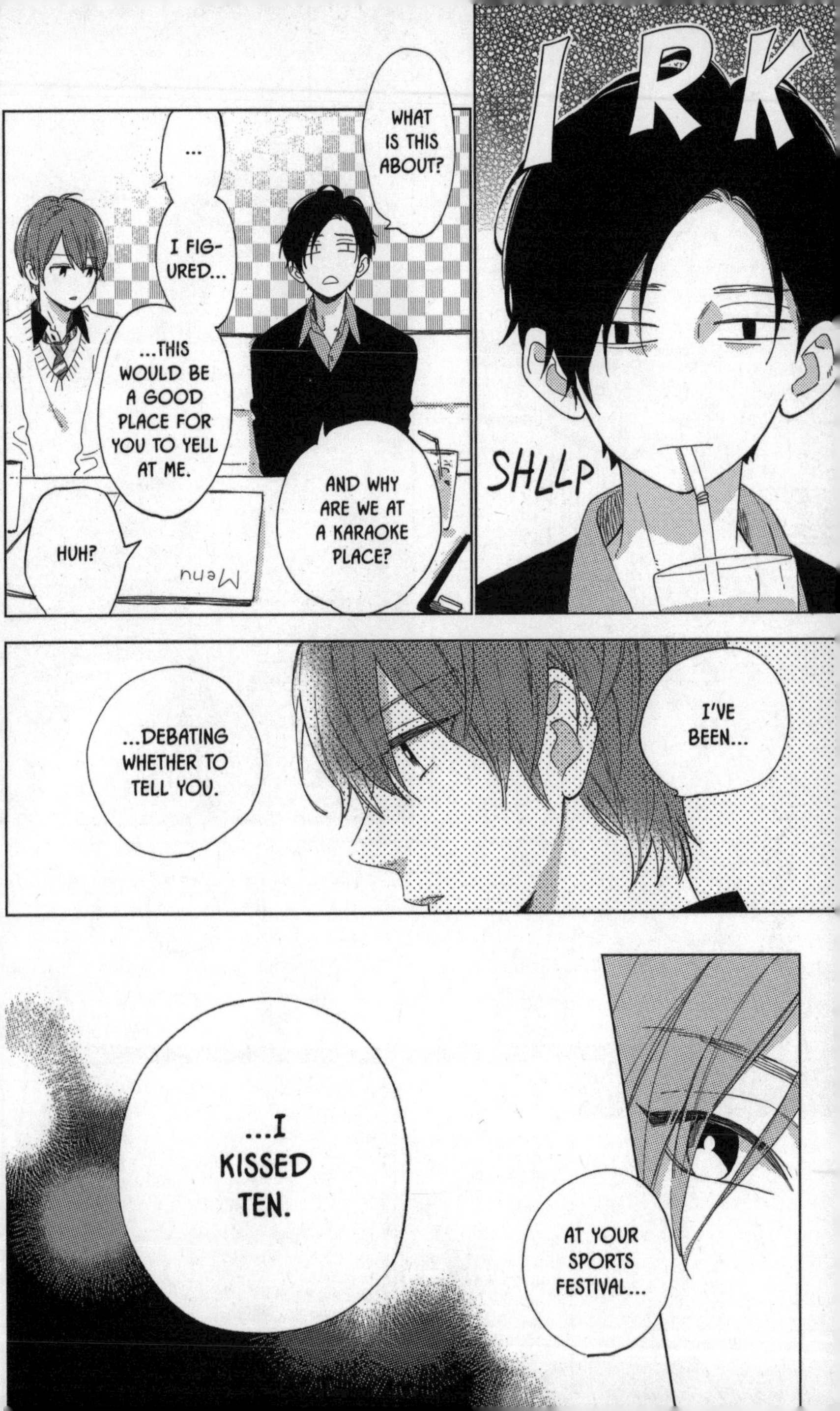
IRK
SHLLP
WHAT IS THIS ABOUT?
AND WHY ARE WE AT A KARAOKE PLACE?
HUH?
...
I FIG-URED...
...THIS WOULD BE A GOOD PLACE FOR YOU TO YELL AT ME.
Menu
I'VE BEEN...
...DEBATING WHETHER TO TELL YOU.
AT YOUR SPORTS FESTIVAL...
...I KISSED TEN.

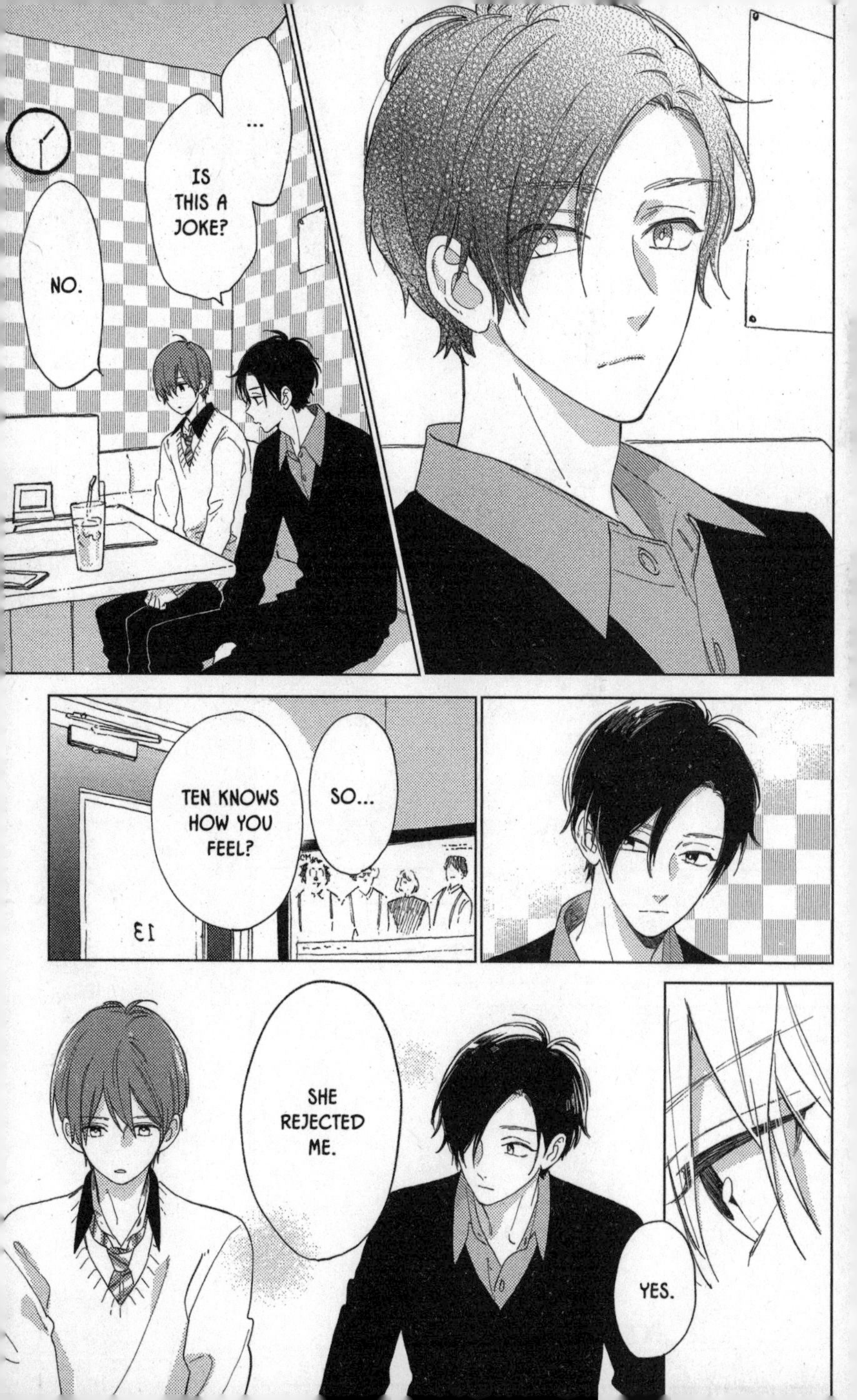
...
IS THIS A JOKE?
NO.
SO...
TEN KNOWS HOW YOU FEEL?
YES.
SHE REJECTED ME.

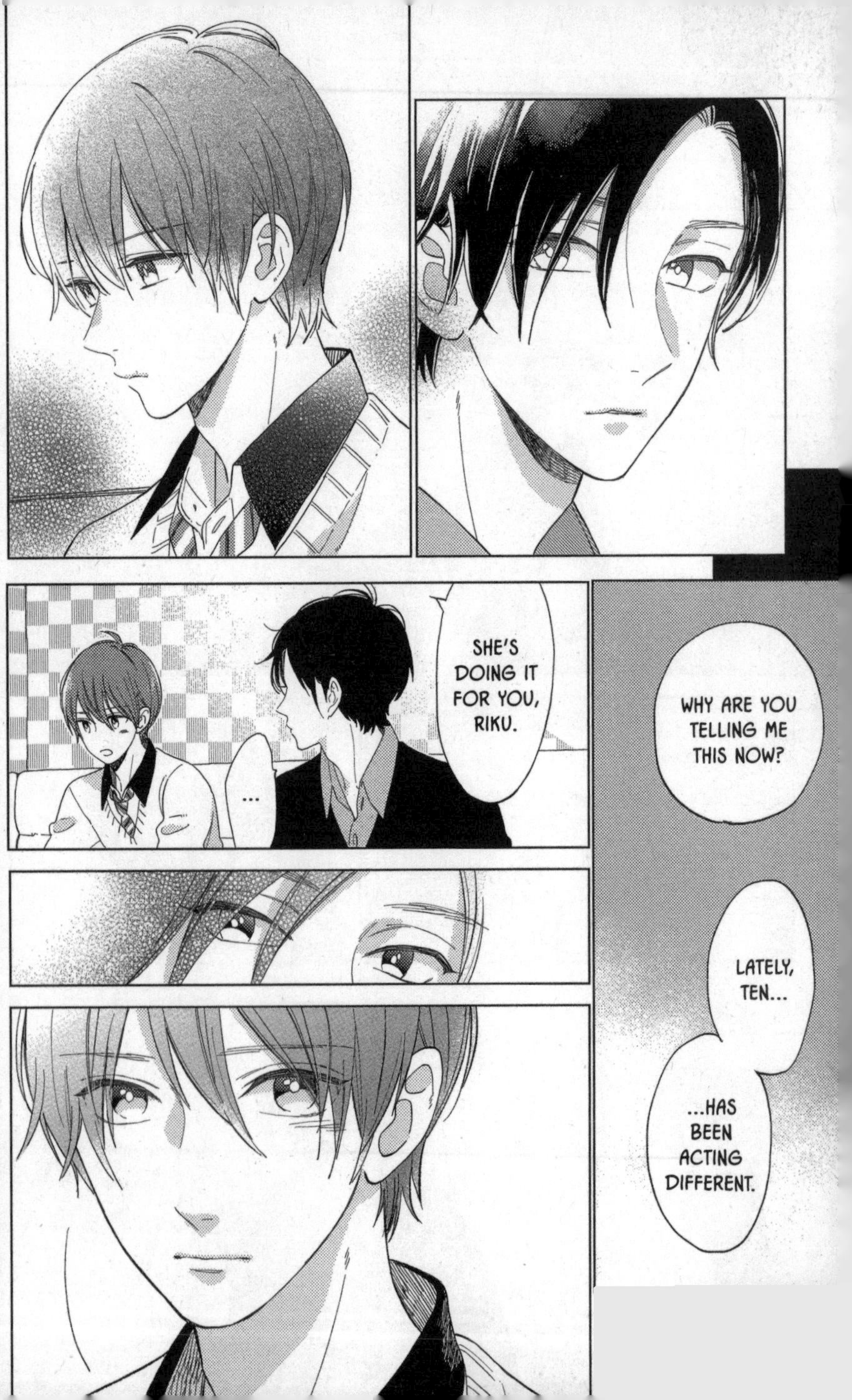
SHE'S DOING IT FOR YOU, RIKU.
...
WHY ARE YOU TELLING ME THIS NOW?
LATELY, TEN...
...HAS BEEN ACTING DIFFERENT.

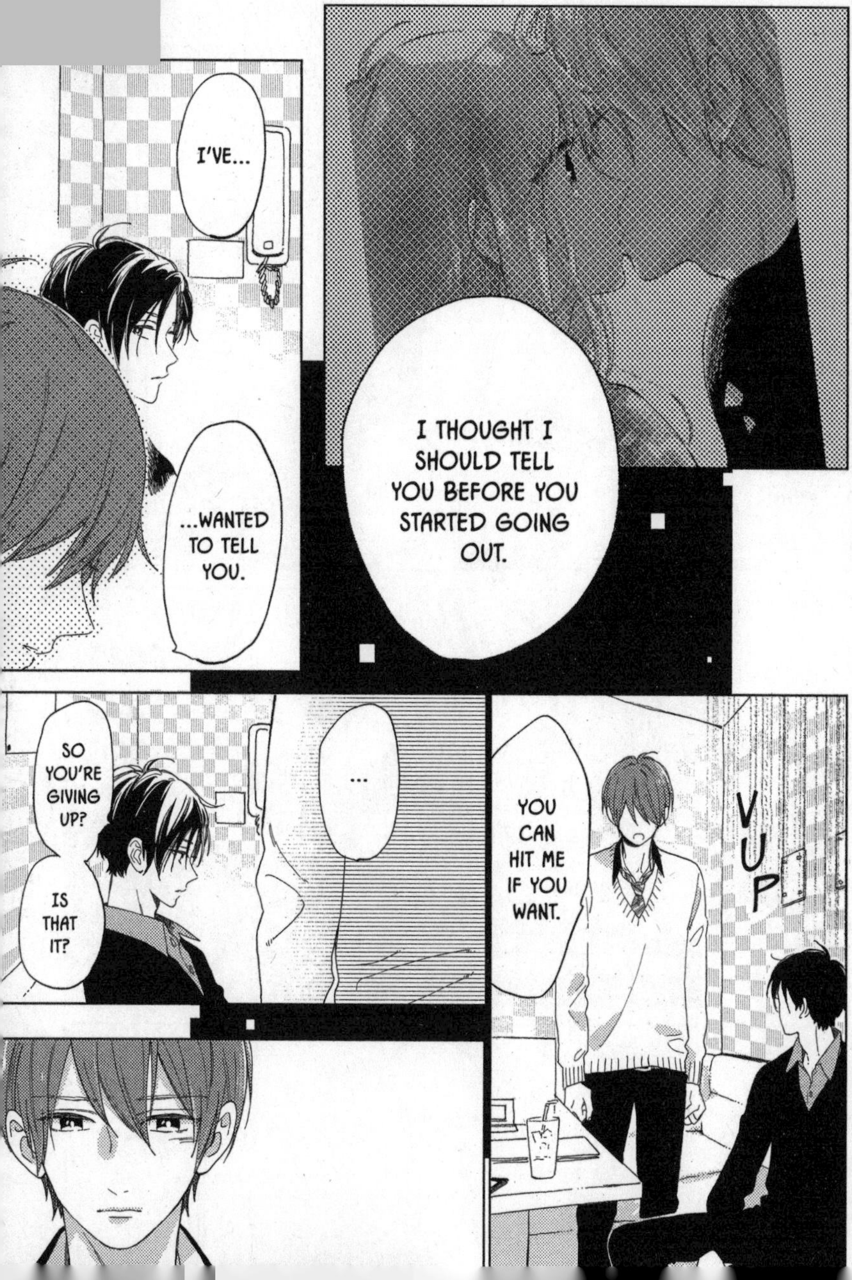
I THOUGHT I SHOULD TELL YOU BEFORE YOU STARTED GOING OUT.
I'VE...
...WANTED TO TELL YOU.
YOU CAN HIT ME IF YOU WANT.
VUP
...
SO YOU'RE GIVING UP?
IS THAT IT?

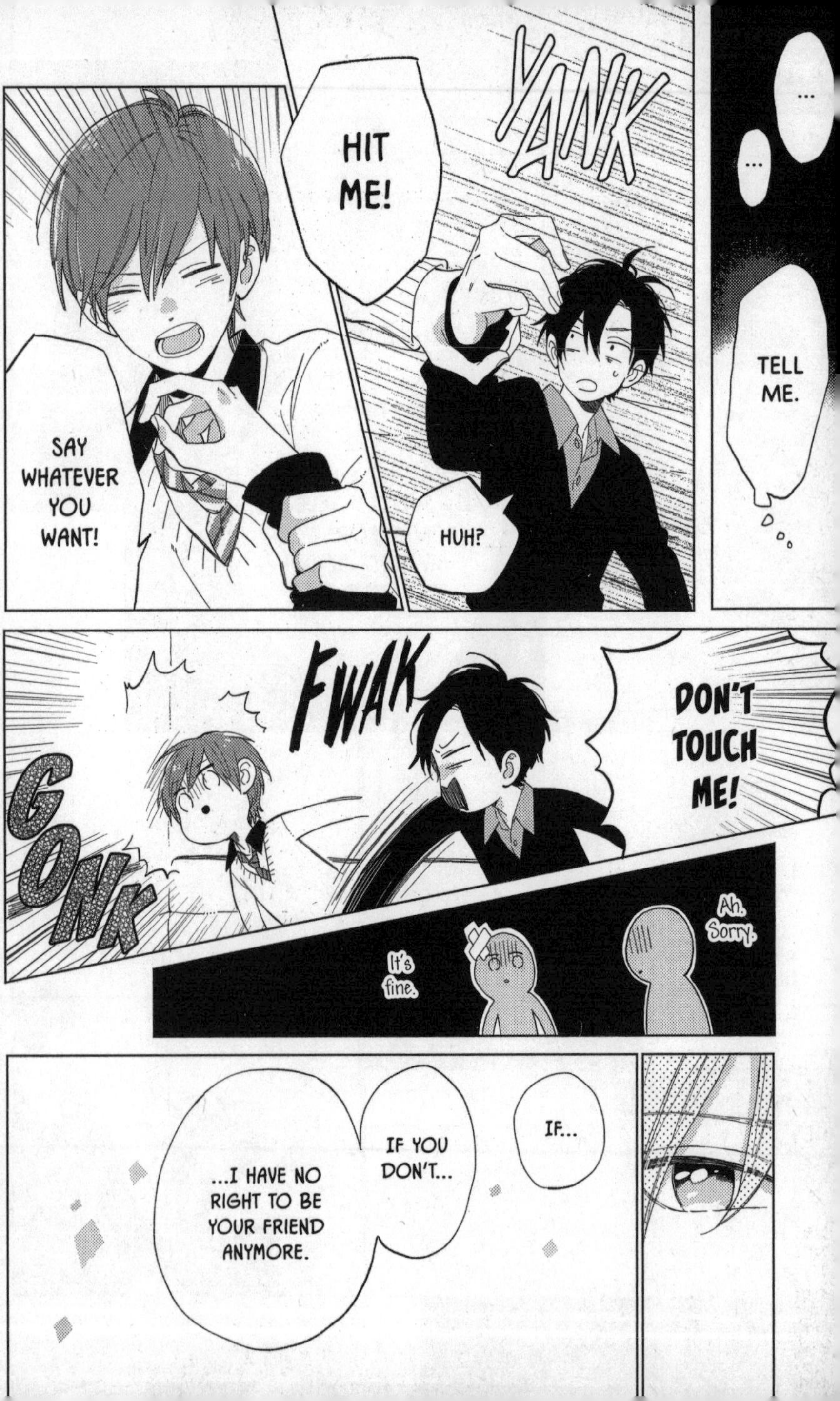
...
...
TELL ME.
YANK
HIT ME!
HUH?
SAY WHATEVER YOU WANT!
DON'T TOUCH ME!
FWAK
GONK
Ah. Sorry.
It's fine.
IF...
IF YOU DON'T...
...I HAVE NO RIGHT TO BE YOUR FRIEND ANYMORE.

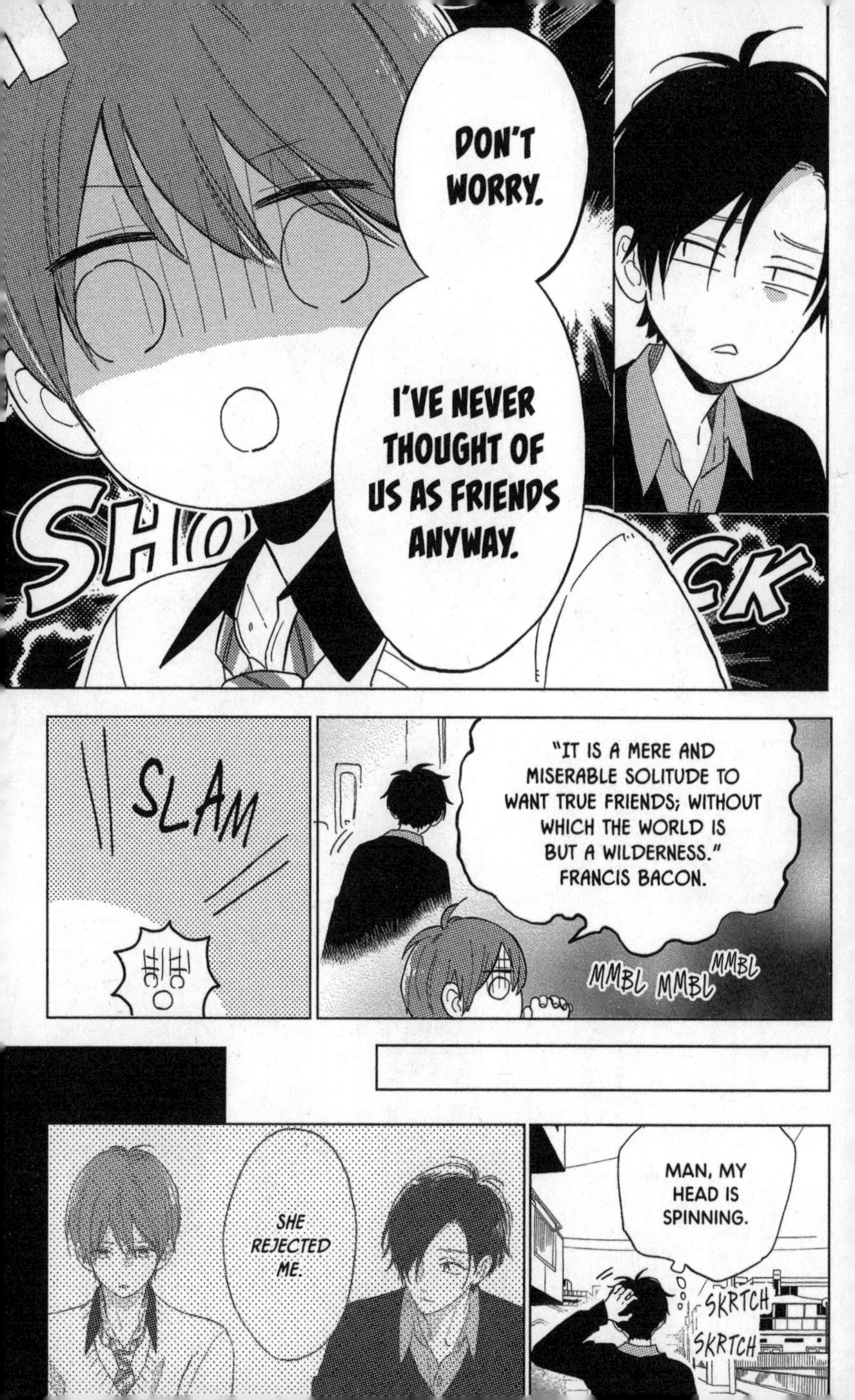
DON'T WORRY.
I'VE NEVER THOUGHT OF US AS FRIENDS ANYWAY.
SHO
CK
"IT IS A MERE AND MISERABLE SOLITUDE TO WANT TRUE FRIENDS; WITHOUT WHICH THE WORLD IS BUT A WILDERNESS." FRANCIS BACON.
MMBL MMBL MMBL
SLAM
MAN, MY HEAD IS SPINNING.
SKRTCH
SKRTCH
SHE REJECTED ME.

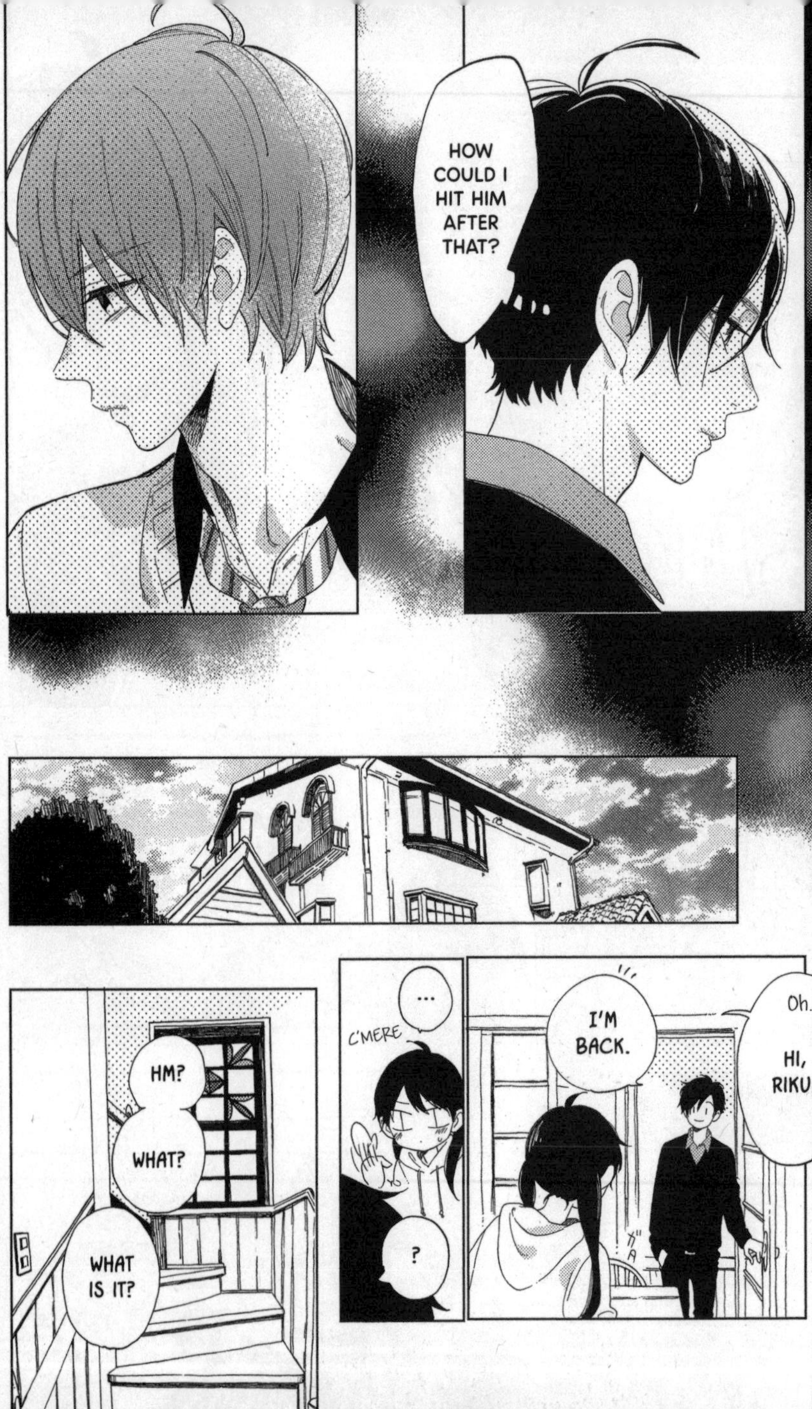
HOW COULD I HIT HIM AFTER THAT?
I'M BACK.
Oh.
HI, RIKU.
...
C'MERE
?
HM?
WHAT?
WHAT IS IT?

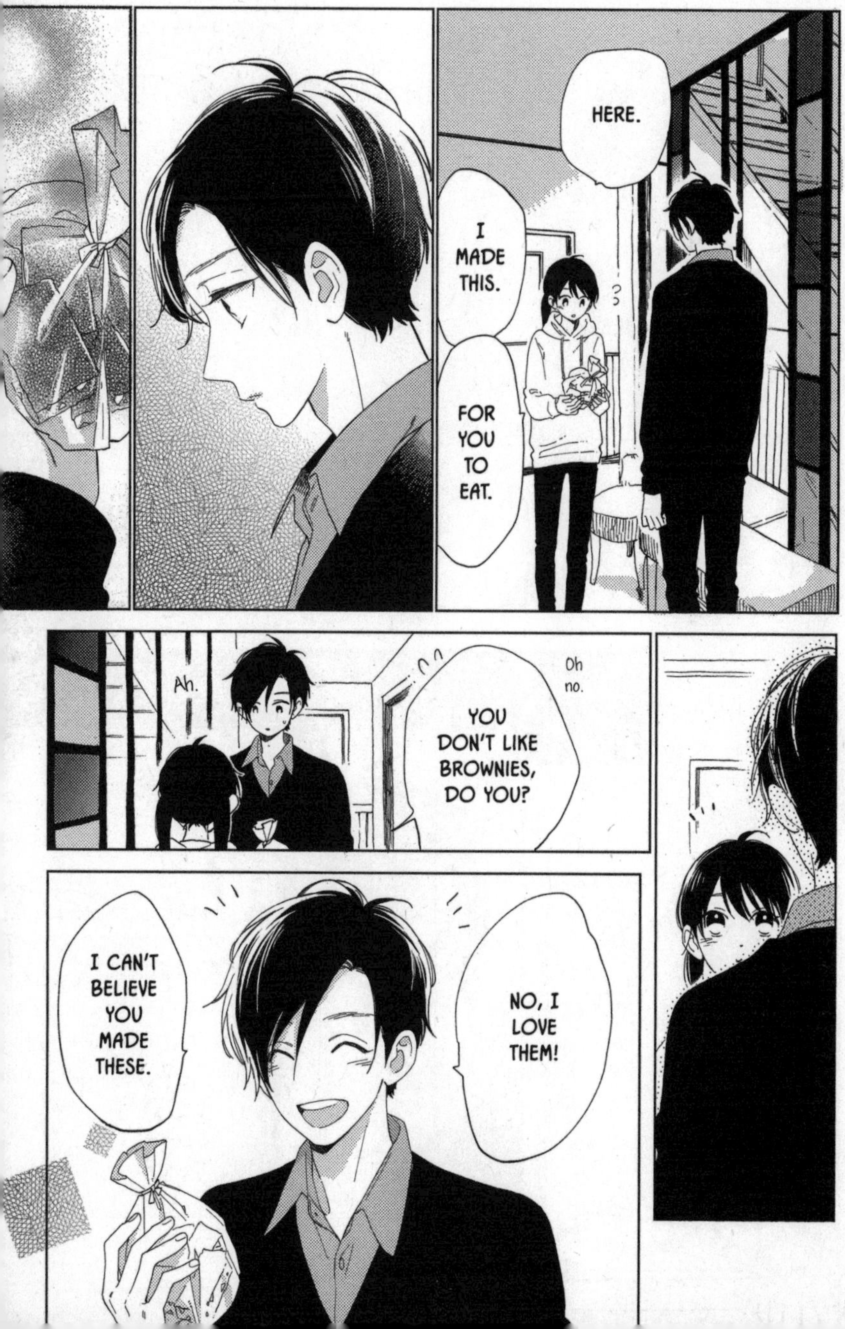
HERE.
I MADE THIS.
FOR YOU TO EAT.
?
Oh no.
YOU DON'T LIKE BROWNIES, DO YOU?
Ah.
NO, I LOVE THEM!
I CAN'T BELIEVE YOU MADE THESE.

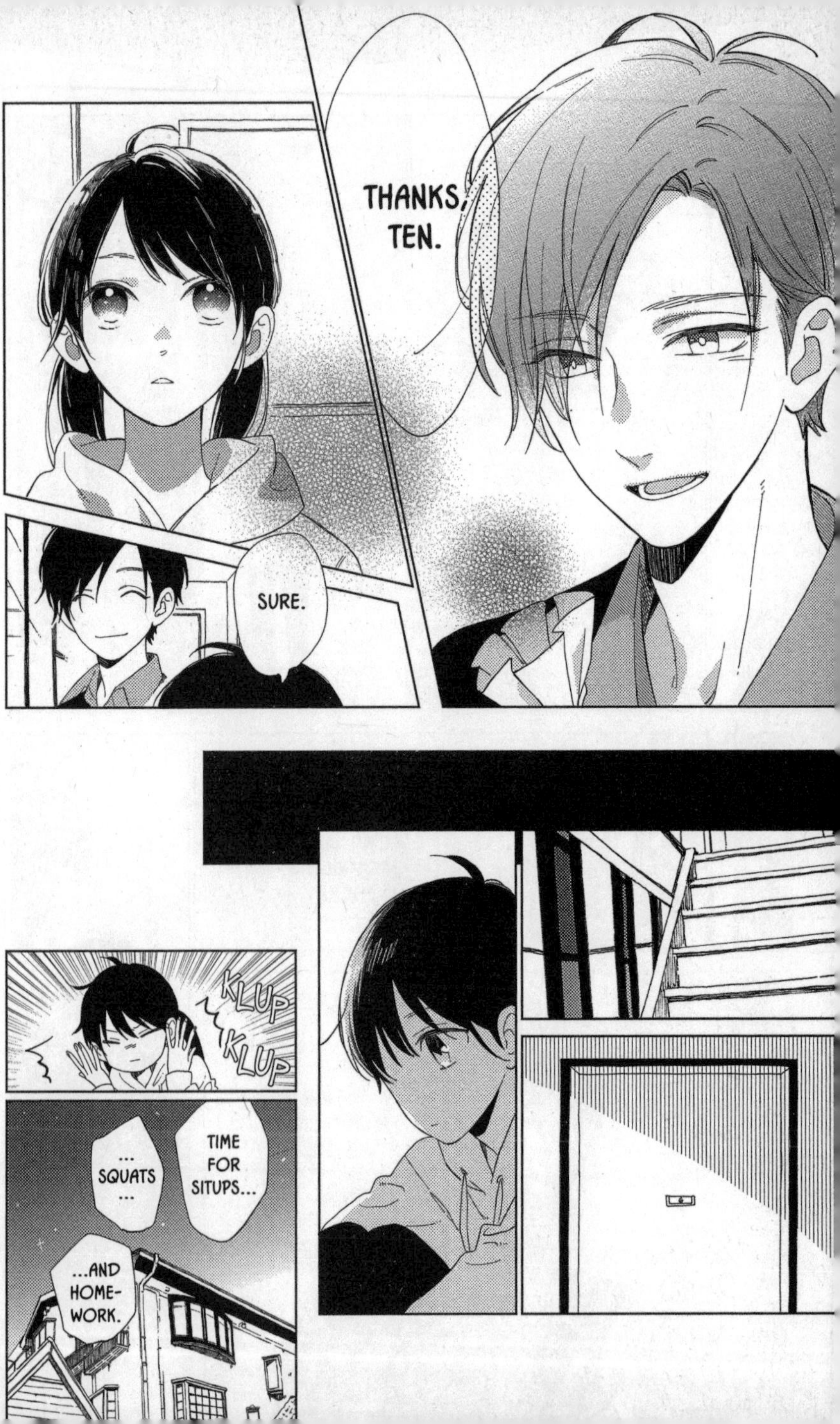
THANKS, TEN.
SURE.
KLUP KLUP
TIME FOR SITUPS...
... SQUATS ...
...AND HOMEWORK.

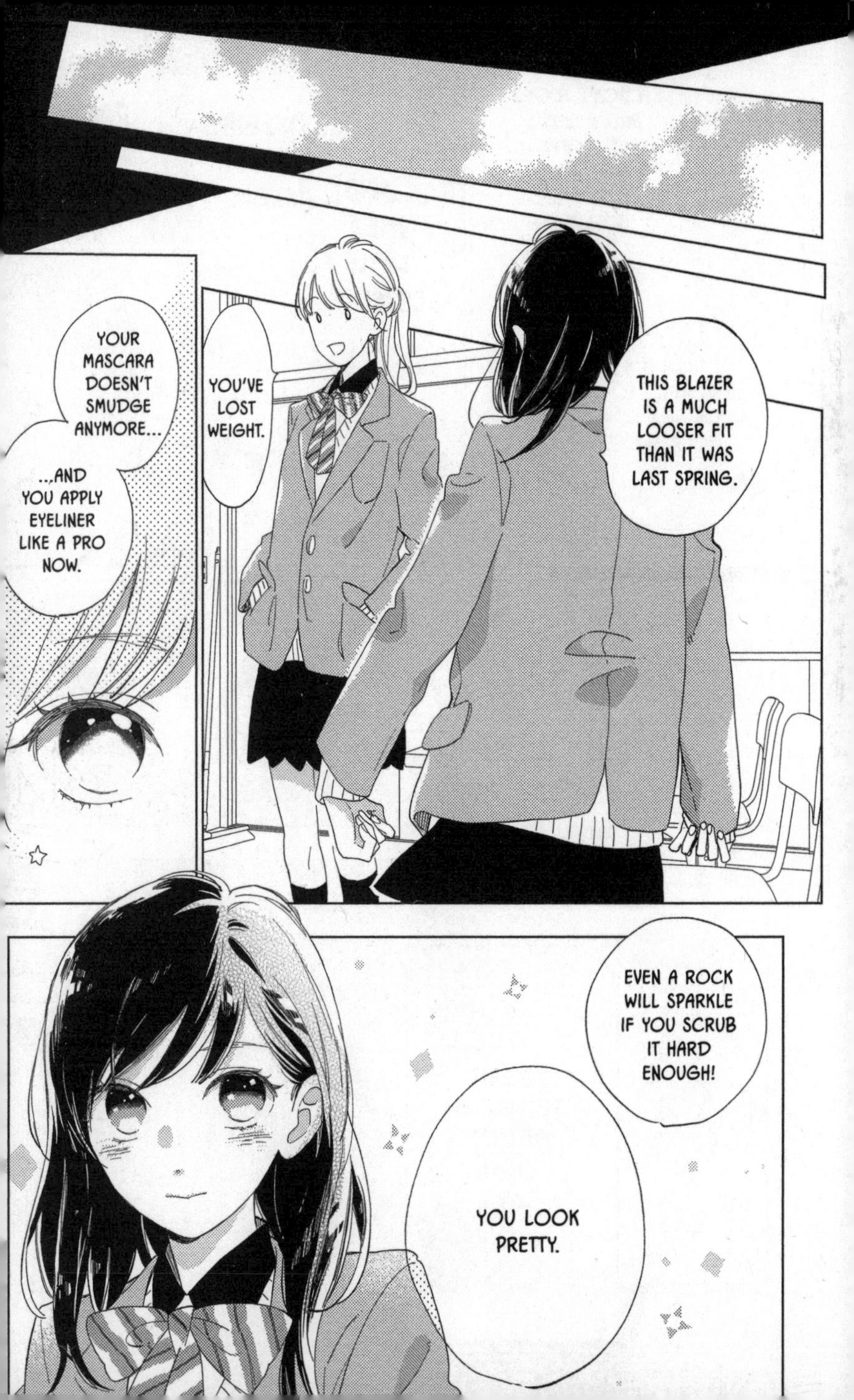
THIS BLAZER IS A MUCH LOOSER FIT THAN IT WAS LAST SPRING.
YOU'VE LOST WEIGHT.
YOUR MASCARA DOESN'T SMUDGE ANYMORE...
...AND YOU APPLY EYELINER LIKE A PRO NOW.
EVEN A ROCK WILL SPARKLE IF YOU SCRUB IT HARD ENOUGH!
YOU LOOK PRETTY.

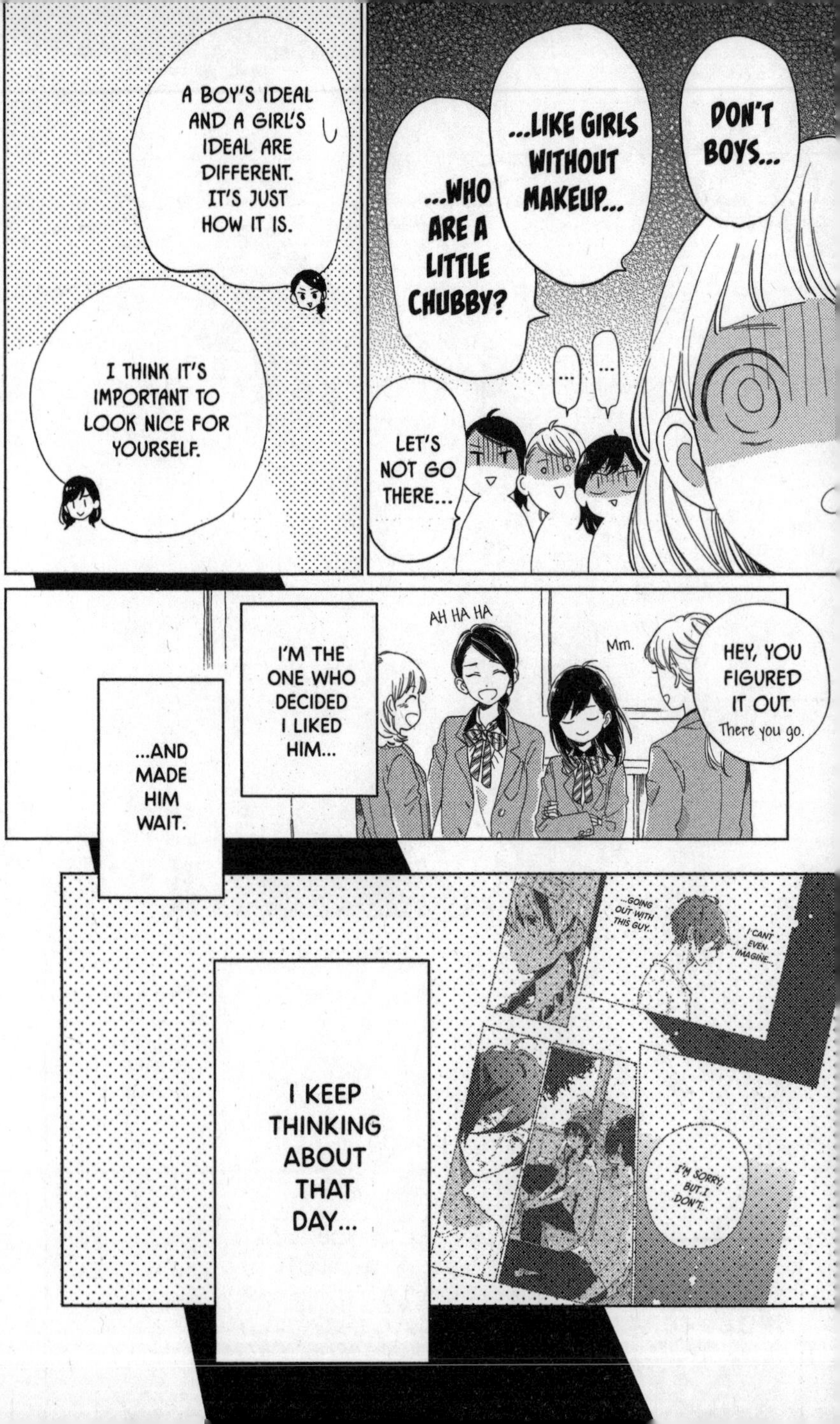
DON'T BOYS...
...LIKE GIRLS WITHOUT MAKEUP...
...WHO ARE A LITTLE CHUBBY?
...
...
LET'S NOT GO THERE...
A BOY'S IDEAL AND A GIRL'S IDEAL ARE DIFFERENT. IT'S JUST HOW IT IS.
I THINK IT'S IMPORTANT TO LOOK NICE FOR YOURSELF.
HEY, YOU FIGURED IT OUT. There you go.
Mm.
AH HA HA
I'M THE ONE WHO DECIDED I LIKED HIM...
...AND MADE HIM WAIT.
...GOING OUT WITH THIS GUY...
I CANT EVEN IMAGINE...
I'M SORRY, BUT I DON'T...
I KEEP THINKING ABOUT THAT DAY...

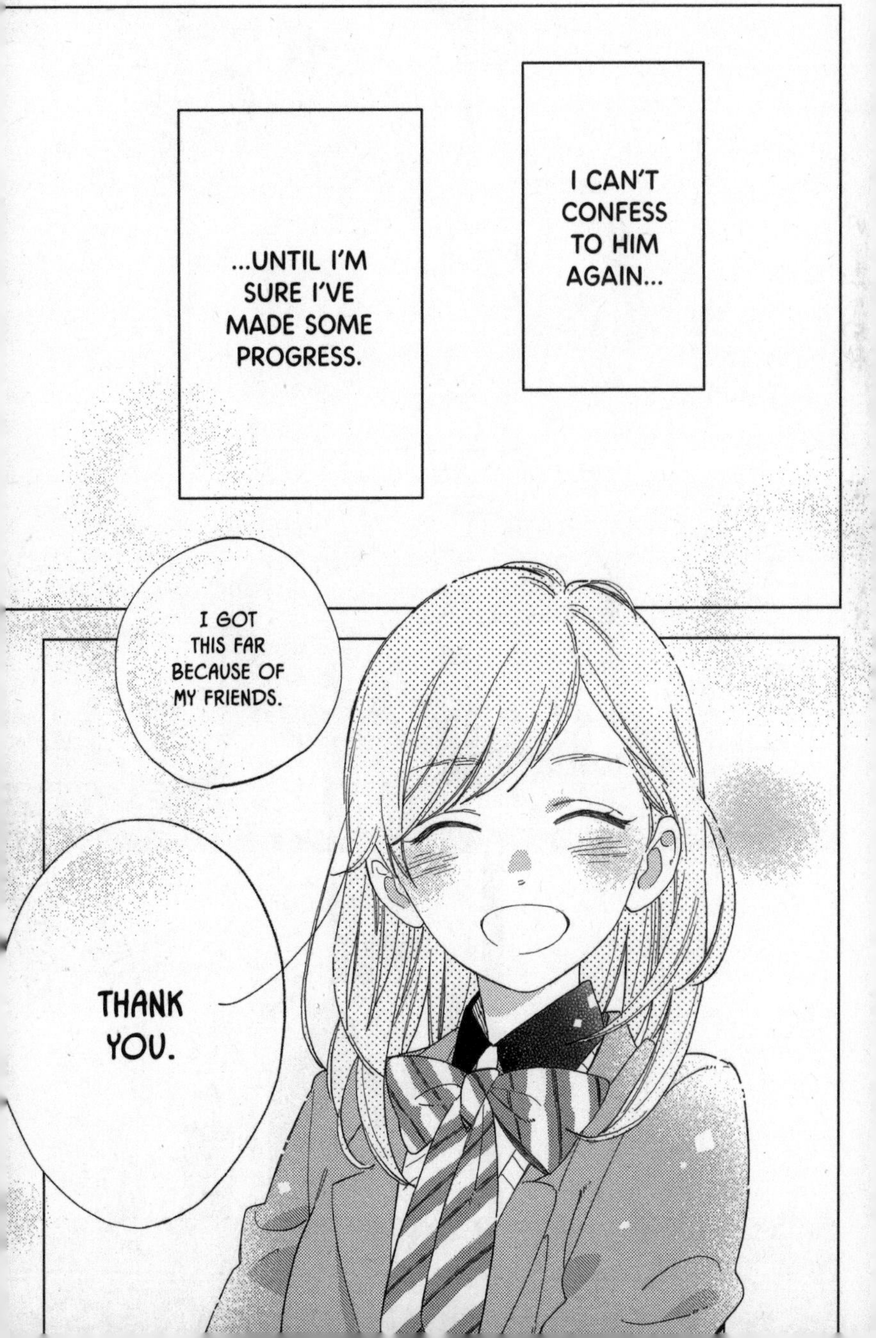
I CAN'T CONFESS TO HIM AGAIN...
...UNTIL I'M SURE I'VE MADE SOME PROGRESS.
I GOT THIS FAR BECAUSE OF MY FRIENDS.
THANK YOU.

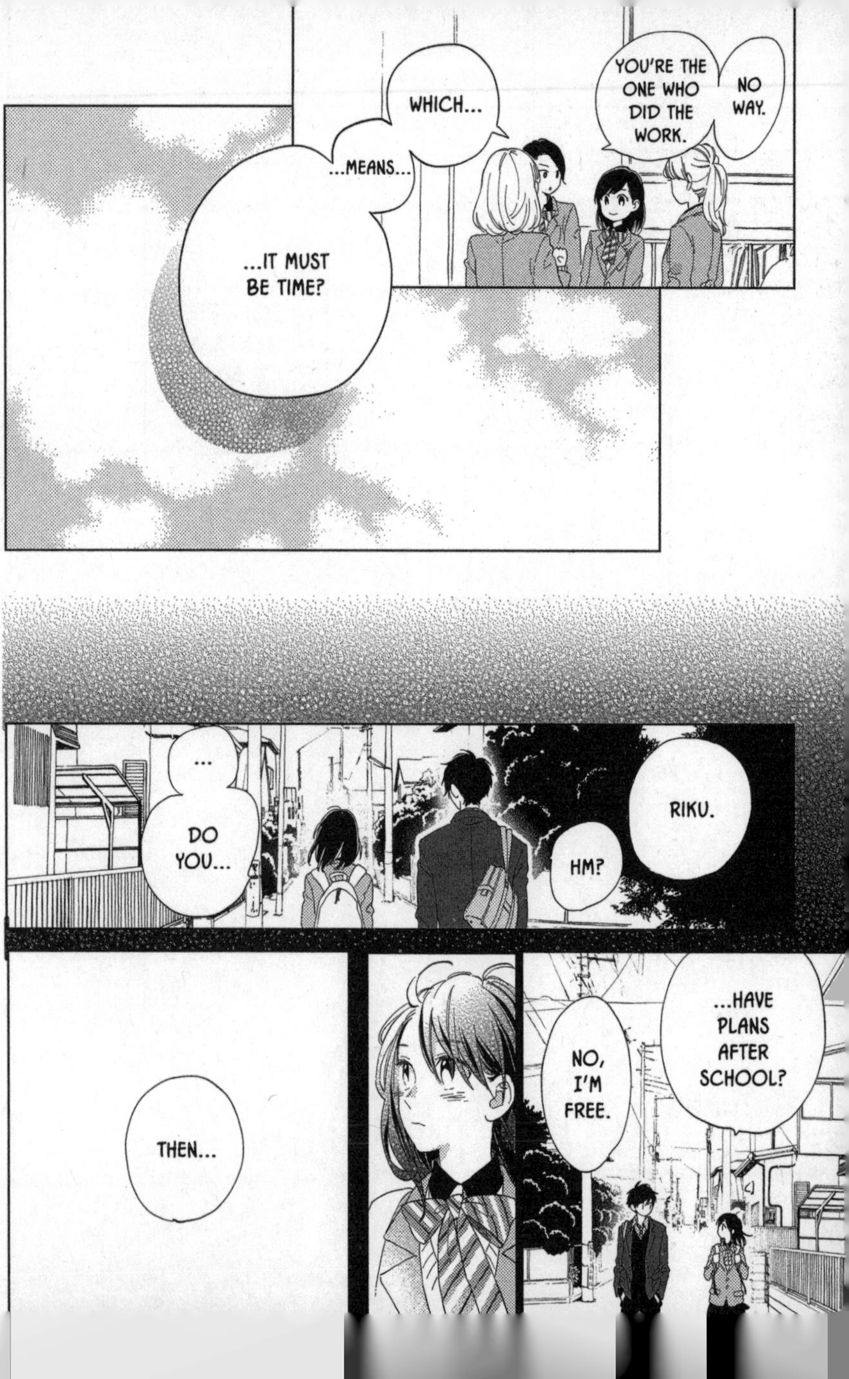
NO WAY.
YOU'RE THE ONE WHO DID THE WORK.
WHICH...
...MEANS...
...IT MUST BE TIME?
RIKU.
HM?
...
DO YOU...
...HAVE PLANS AFTER SCHOOL?
NO, I'M FREE.
THEN...

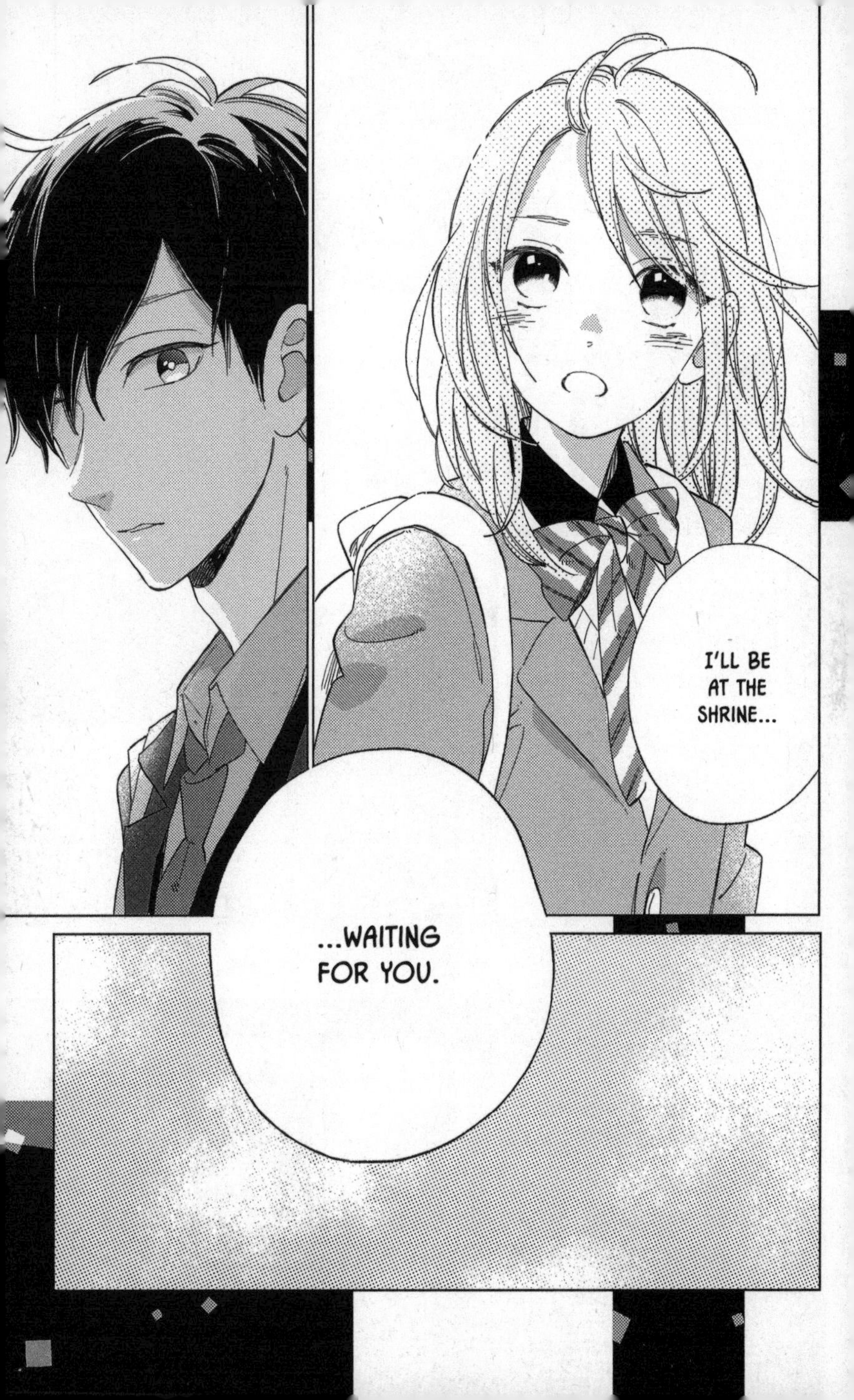
I'LL BE AT THE SHRINE...
...WAITING FOR YOU.

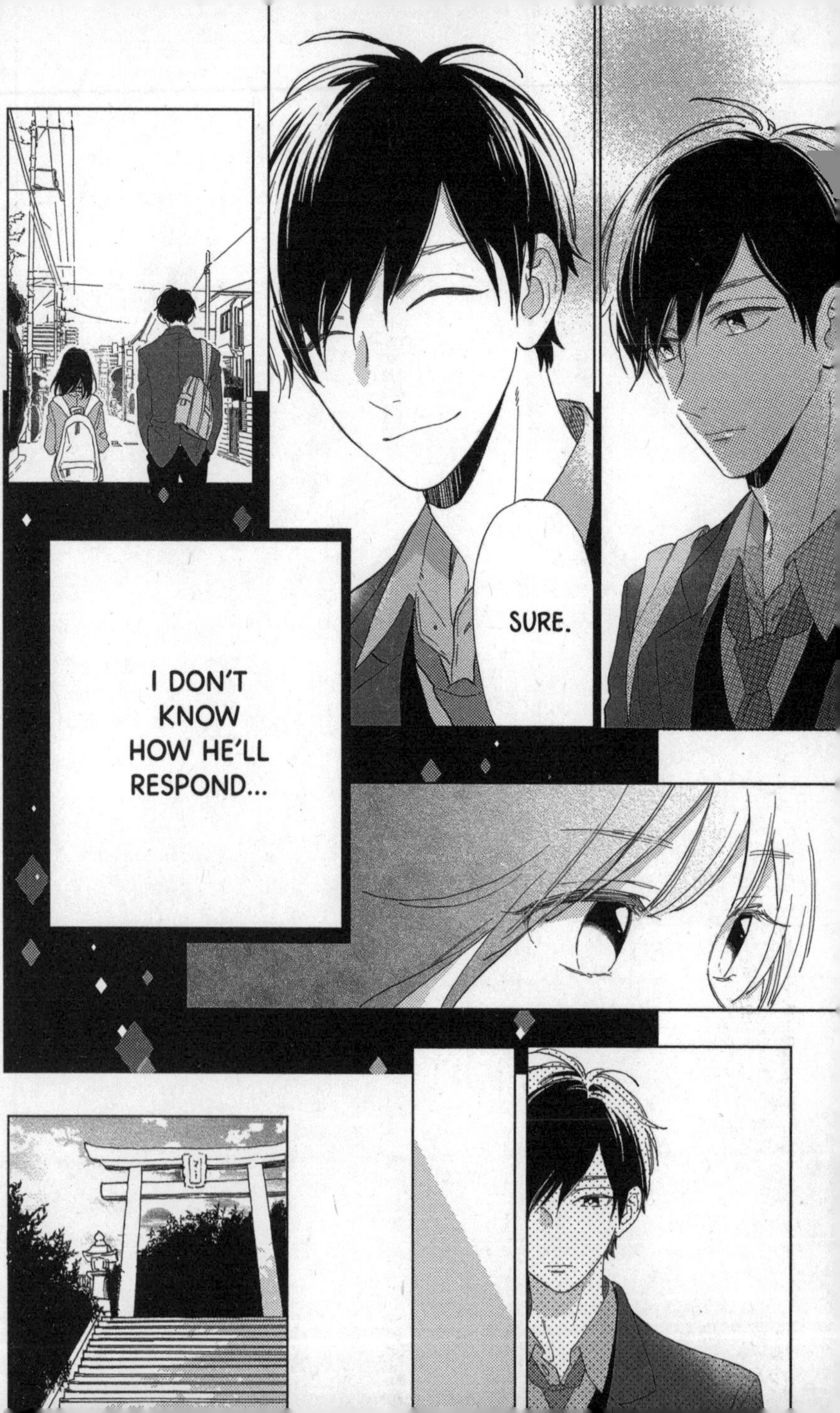
SURE.
I DON'T KNOW HOW HE'LL RESPOND...

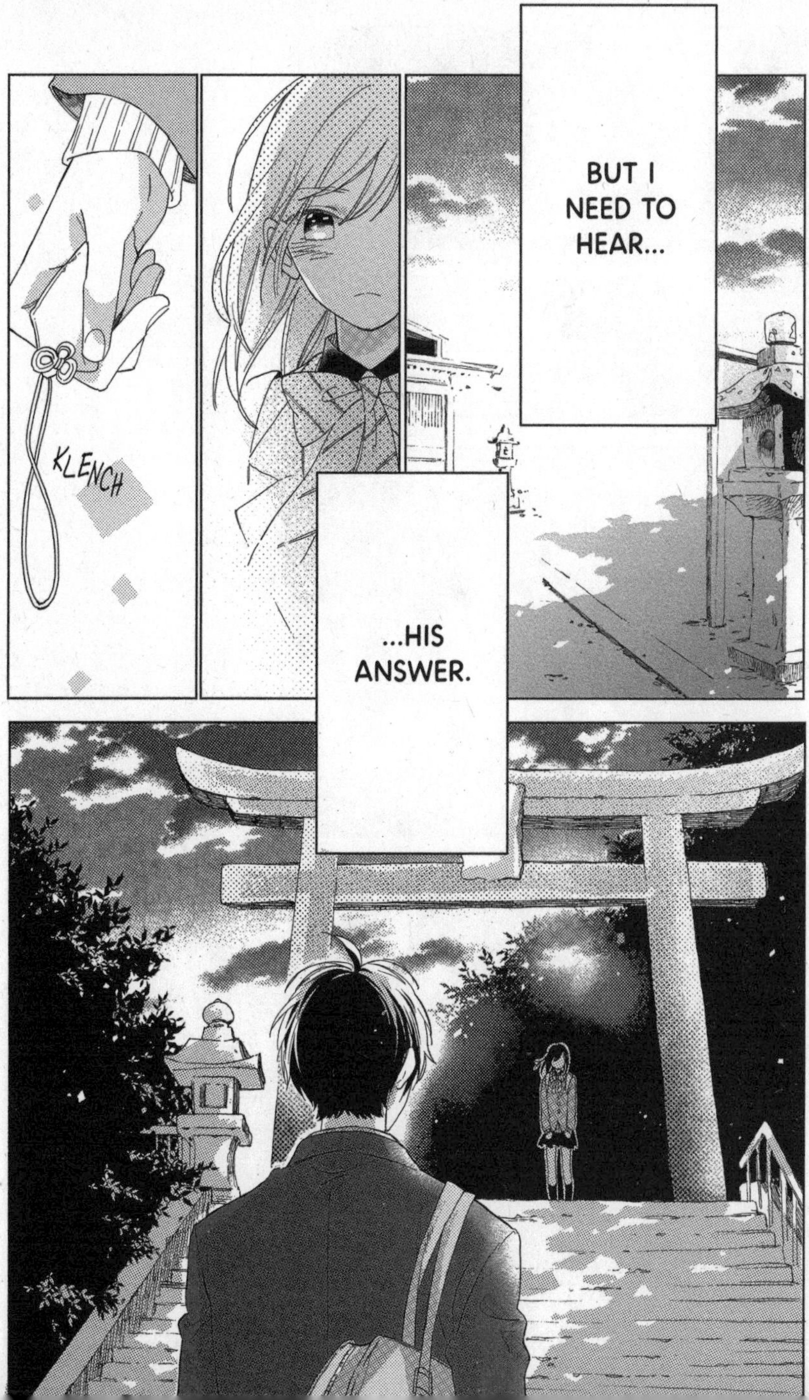
BUT I NEED TO HEAR...
KLENCH
...HIS ANSWER.

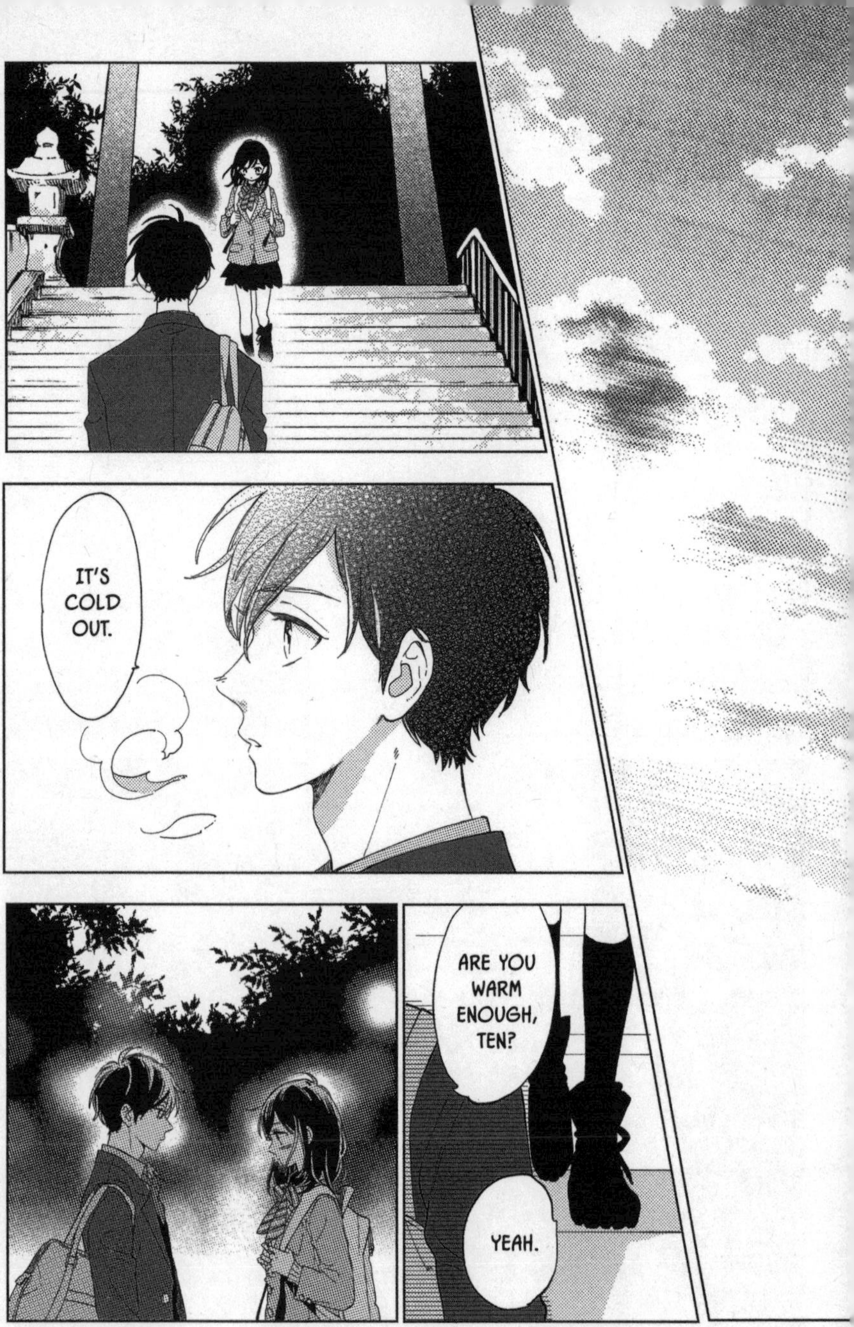
IT'S COLD OUT.
ARE YOU WARM ENOUGH, TEN?
YEAH.

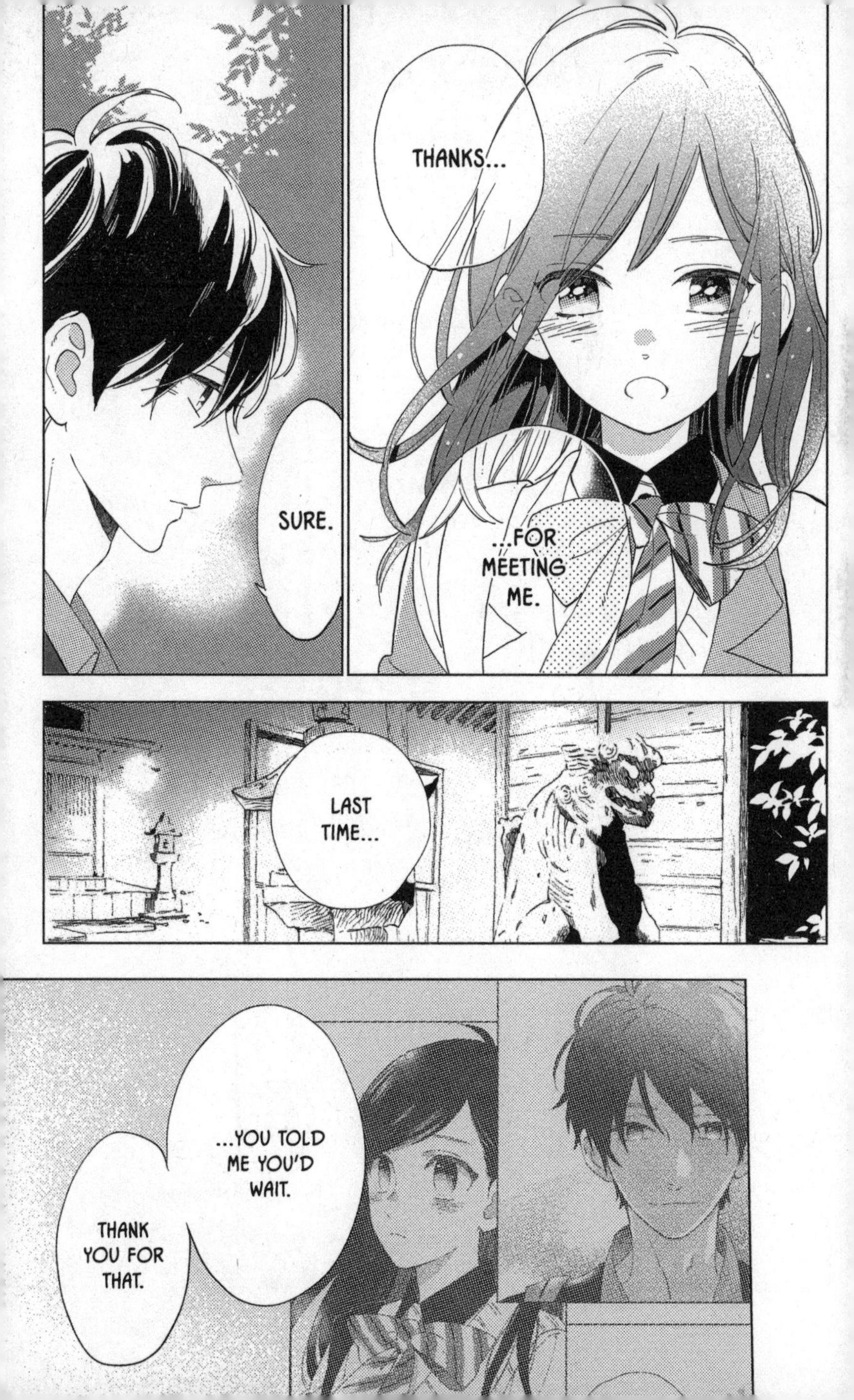
THANKS...
...FOR MEETING ME.
SURE.
LAST TIME...
...YOU TOLD ME YOU'D WAIT.
THANK YOU FOR THAT.

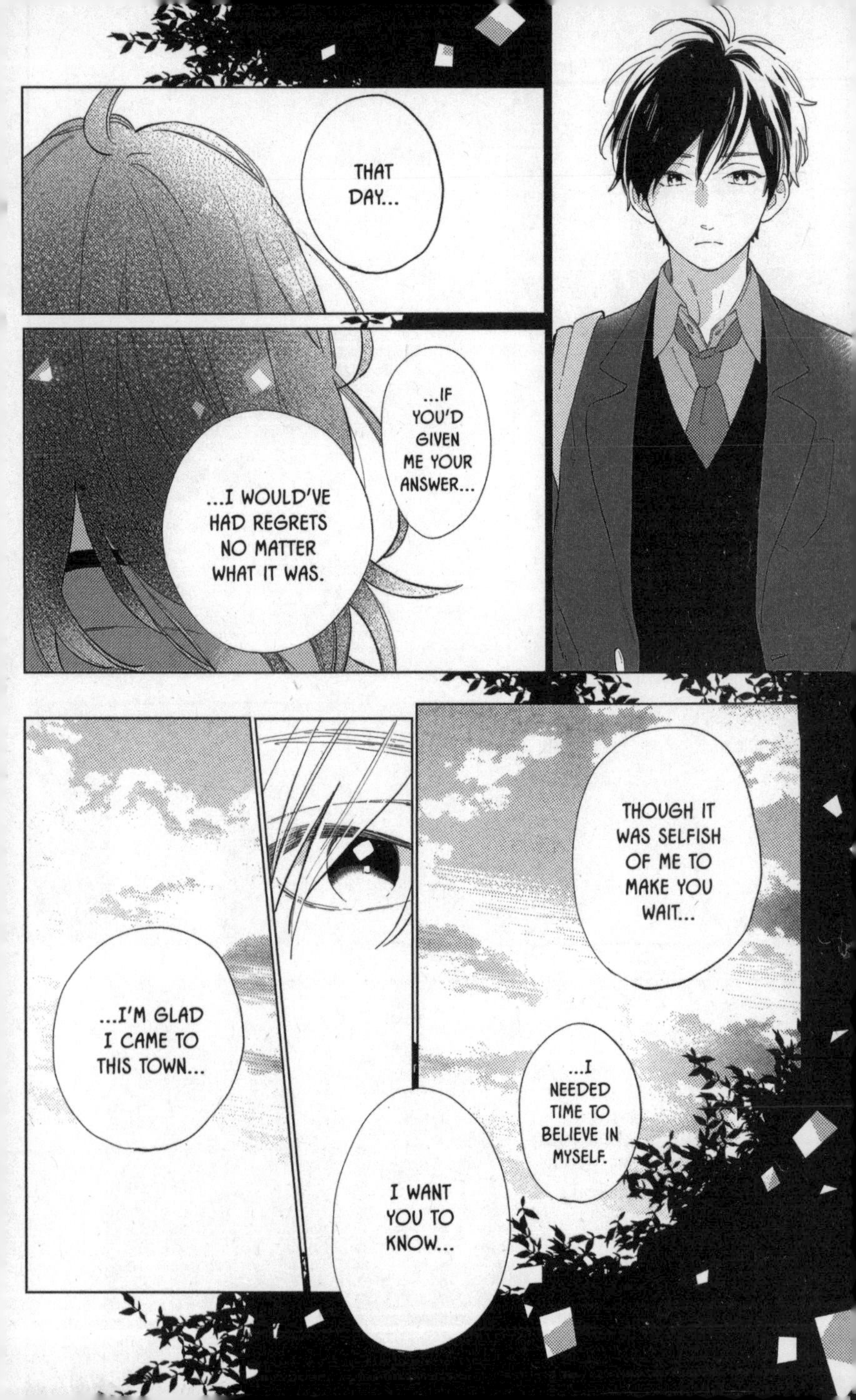
THAT DAY...
...IF YOU'D GIVEN ME YOUR ANSWER...
...I WOULD'VE HAD REGRETS NO MATTER WHAT IT WAS.
THOUGH IT WAS SELFISH OF ME TO MAKE YOU WAIT...
...I NEEDED TIME TO BELIEVE IN MYSELF.
I WANT YOU TO KNOW...
...I'M GLAD I CAME TO THIS TOWN...

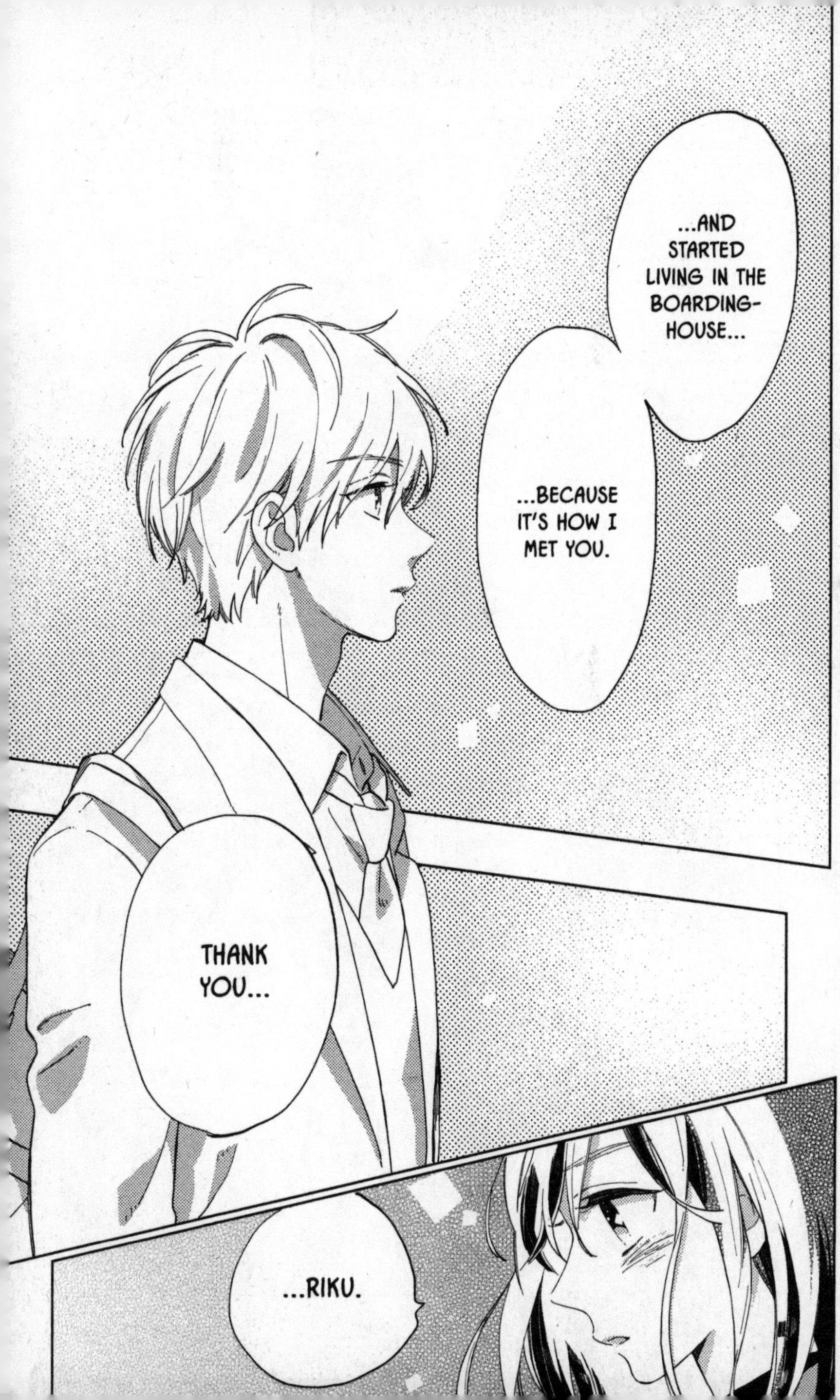
...AND STARTED LIVING IN THE BOARDING-HOUSE...
...BECAUSE IT'S HOW I MET YOU.
THANK YOU...
...RIKU.

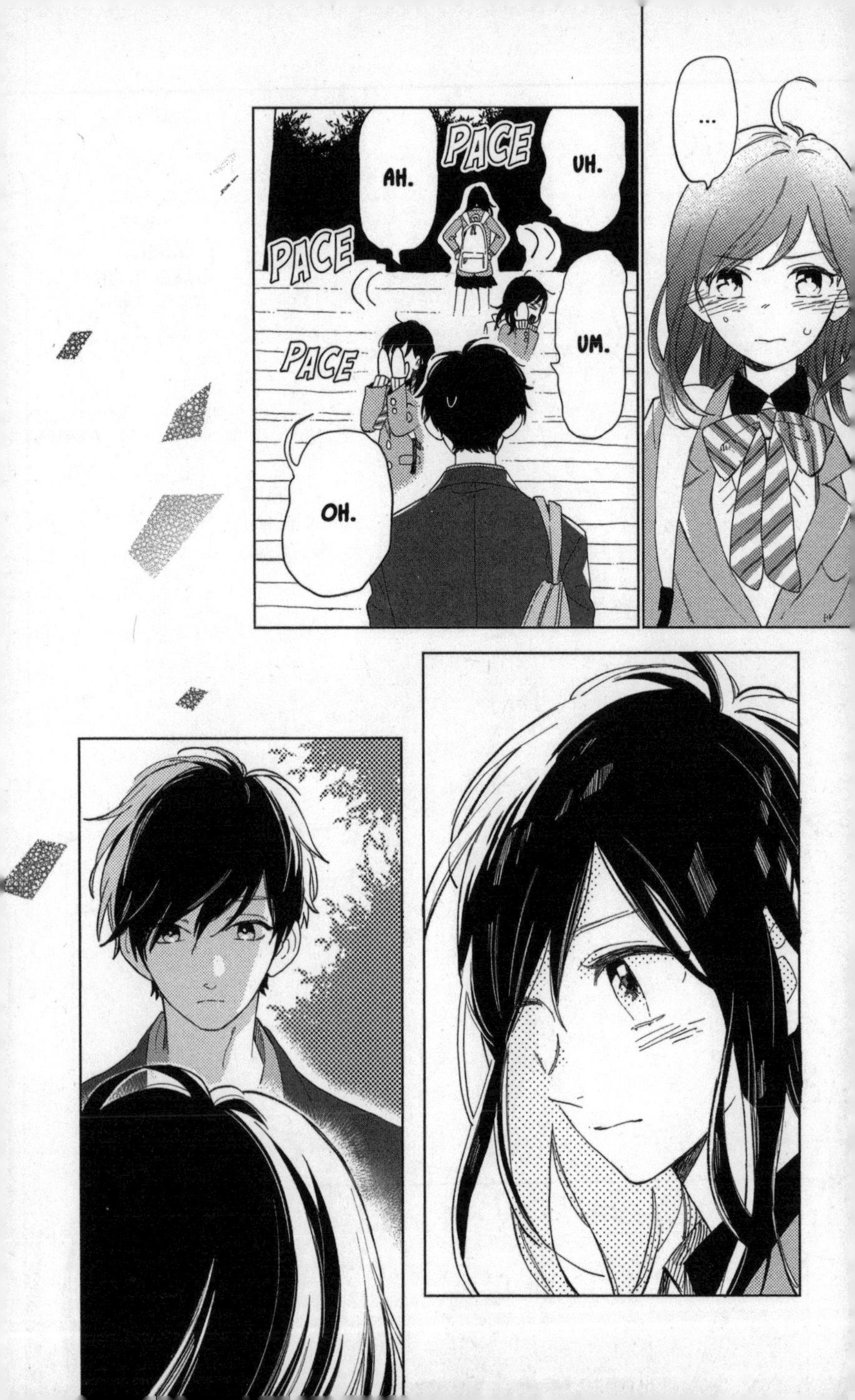
...
UH.
PACE
AH.
PACE
UM.
PACE
OH.

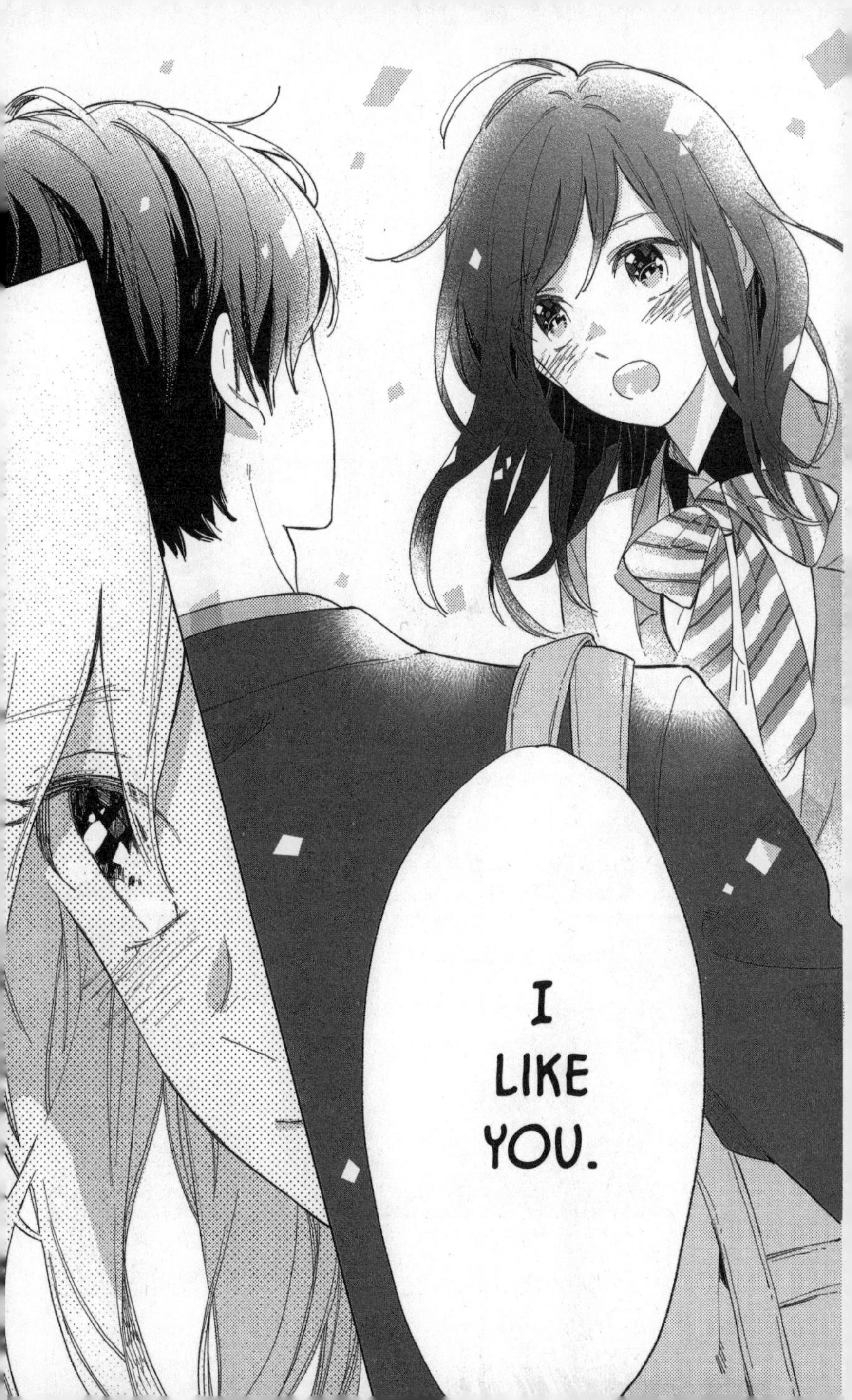
I LIKE YOU.

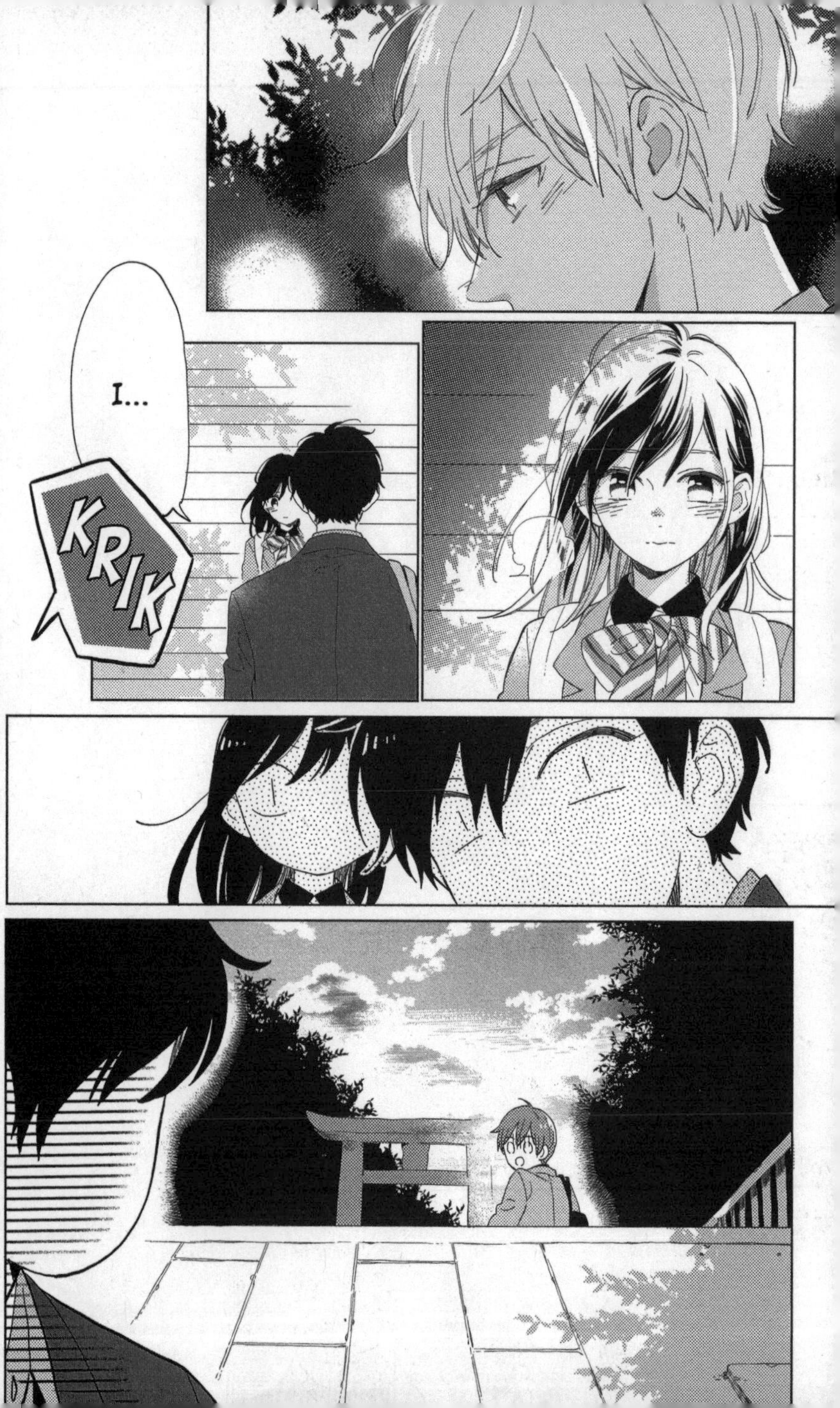
I...
KRIK

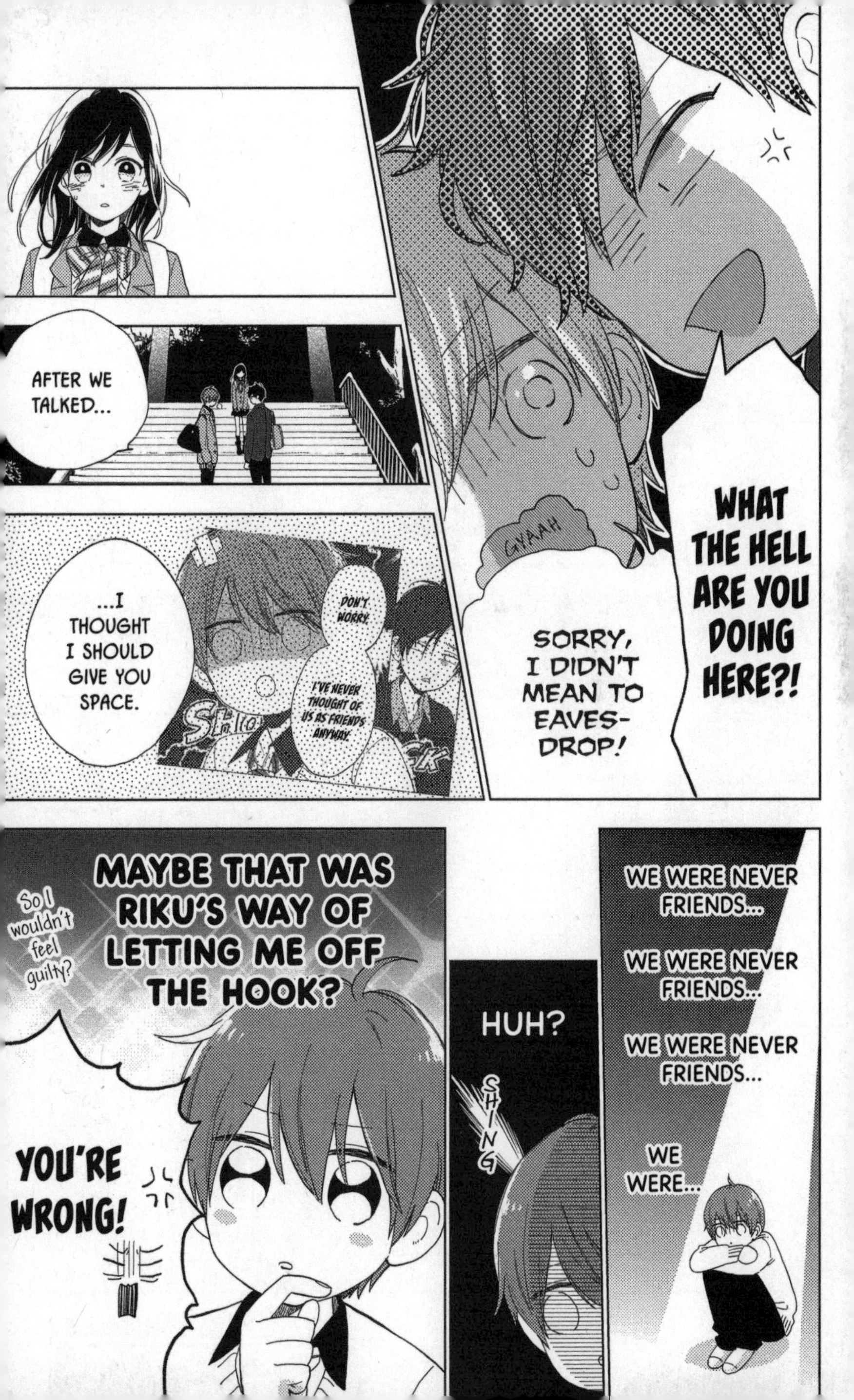
WHAT THE HELL ARE YOU DOING HERE?!
GYAAH
SORRY, I DIDN'T MEAN TO EAVES-DROP!
AFTER WE TALKED...
...I THOUGHT I SHOULD GIVE YOU SPACE.
DON'T WORRY.
I'VE NEVER THOUGHT OF US AS FRIENDS ANYWAY.
WE WERE NEVER FRIENDS...
WE WERE NEVER FRIENDS...
WE WERE NEVER FRIENDS...
WE WERE...
HUH?
SHING
MAYBE THAT WAS RIKU'S WAY OF LETTING ME OFF THE HOOK?
So I wouldn't feel guilty?
YOU'RE WRONG!

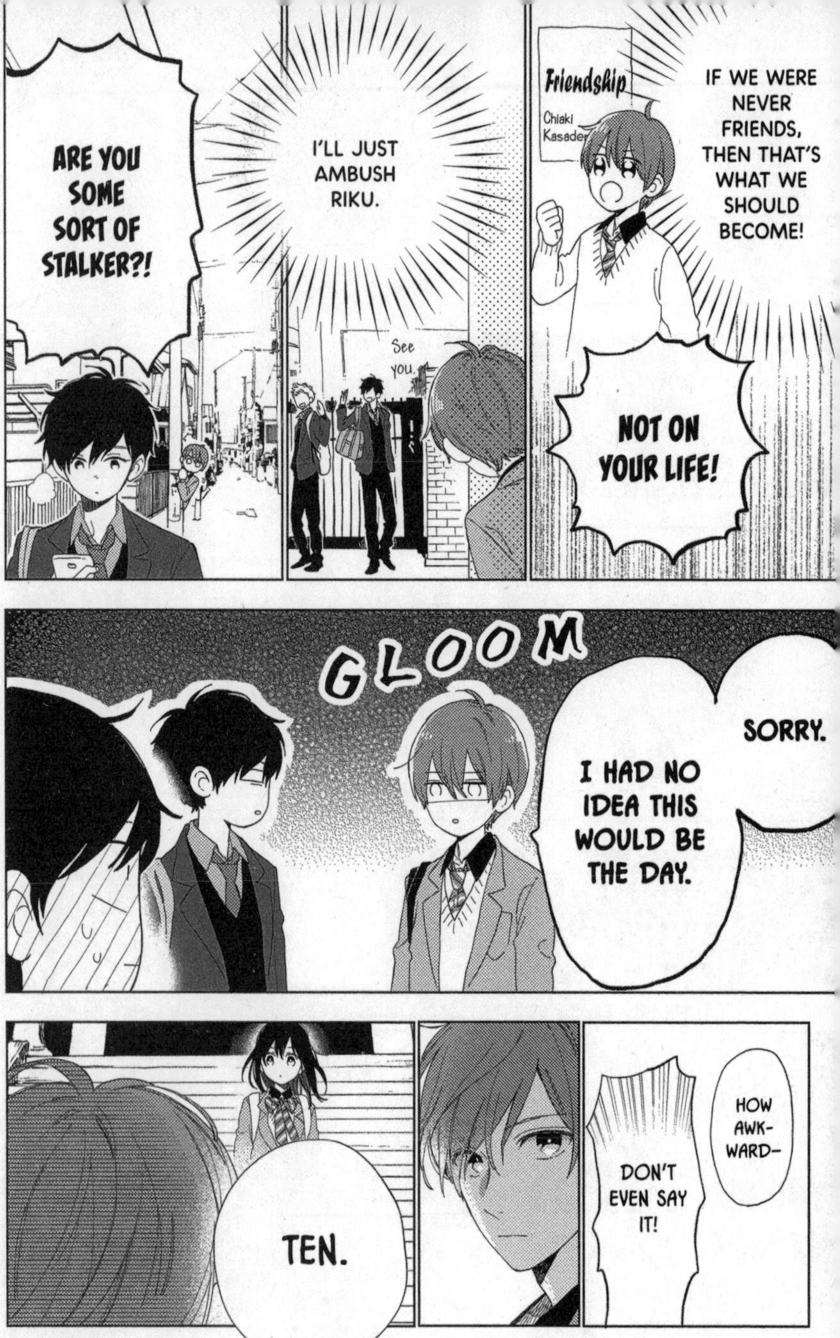
Friendship
Chiaki Kasade
IF WE WERE NEVER FRIENDS, THEN THAT'S WHAT WE SHOULD BECOME!
NOT ON YOUR LIFE!
I'LL JUST AMBUSH RIKU.
See you.
ARE YOU SOME SORT OF STALKER?!
GLOOM
SORRY.
I HAD NO IDEA THIS WOULD BE THE DAY.
HOW AWK-WARD—
DON'T EVEN SAY IT!
TEN.

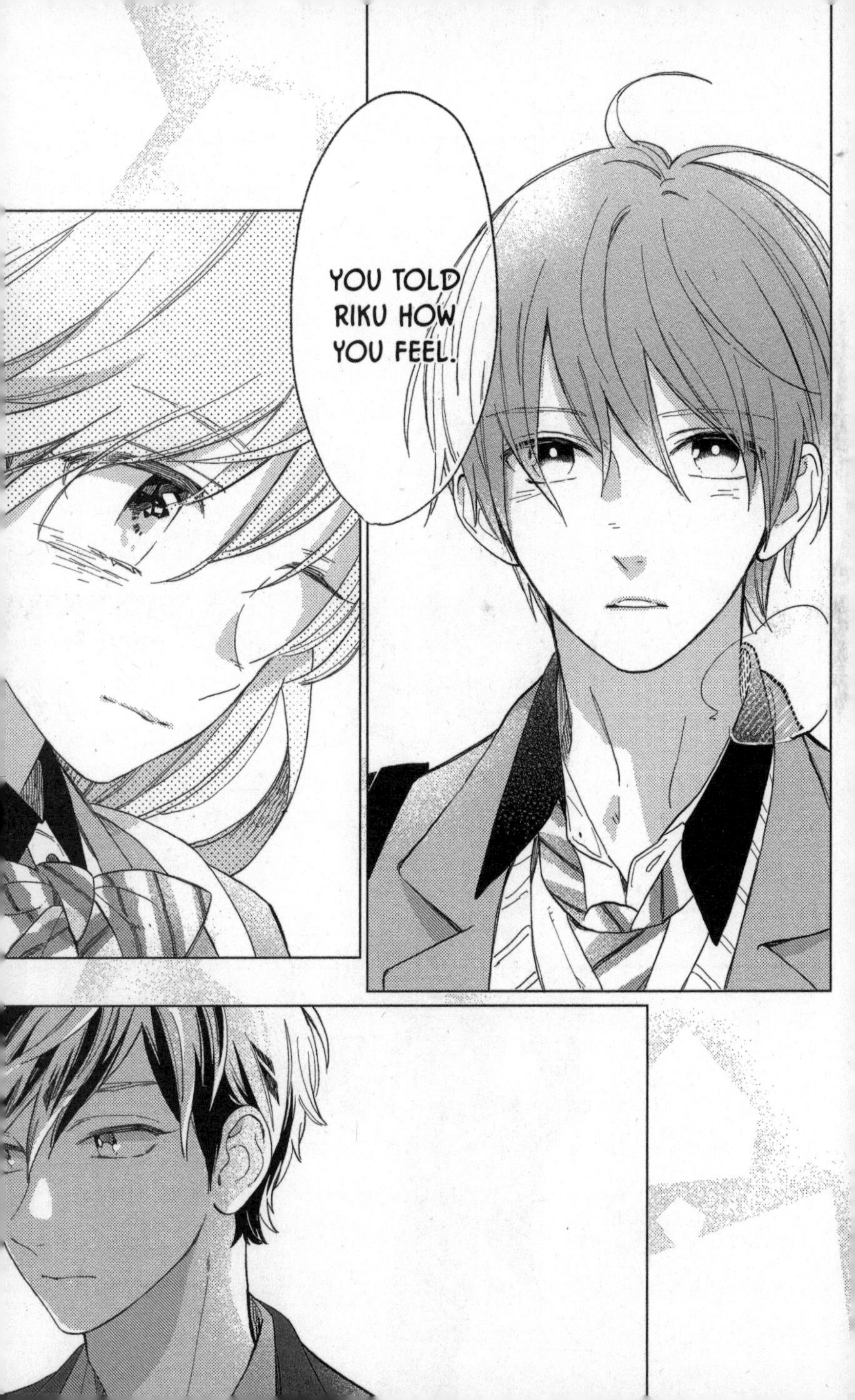
YOU TOLD RIKU HOW YOU FEEL.

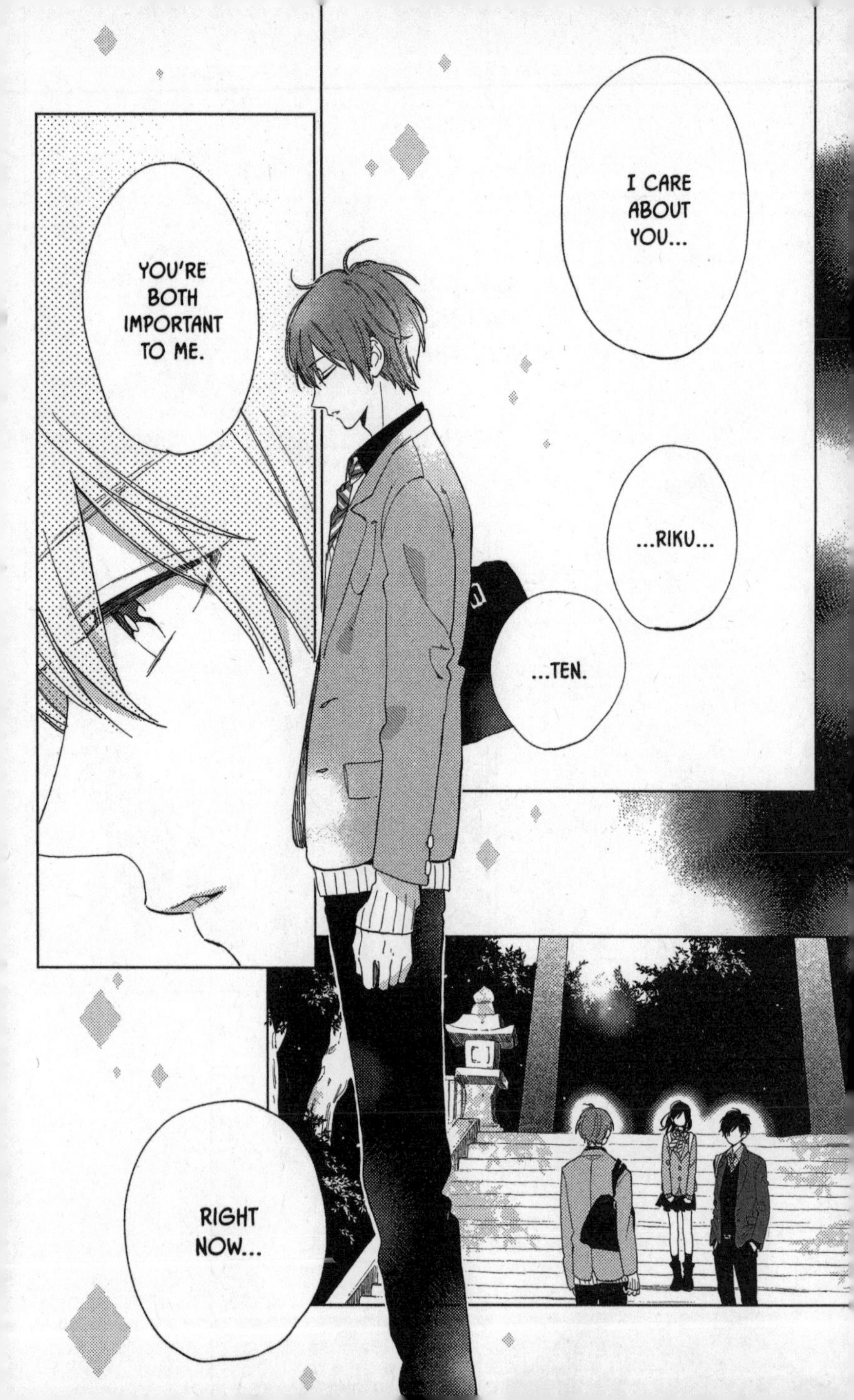
I CARE ABOUT YOU...
...RIKU...
...TEN.
YOU'RE BOTH IMPORTANT TO ME.
RIGHT NOW...

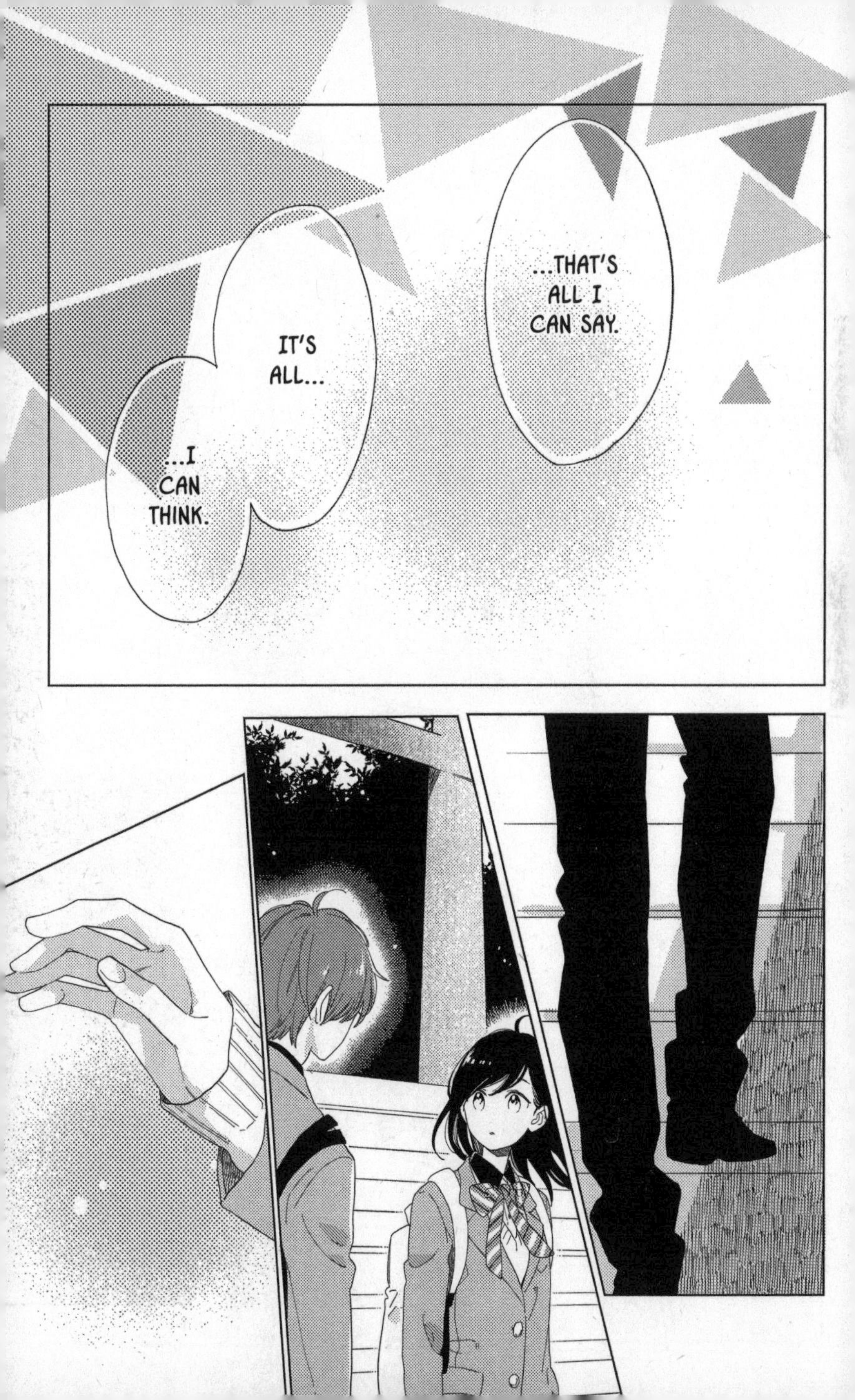
...THAT'S ALL I CAN SAY.
IT'S ALL...
...I CAN THINK.

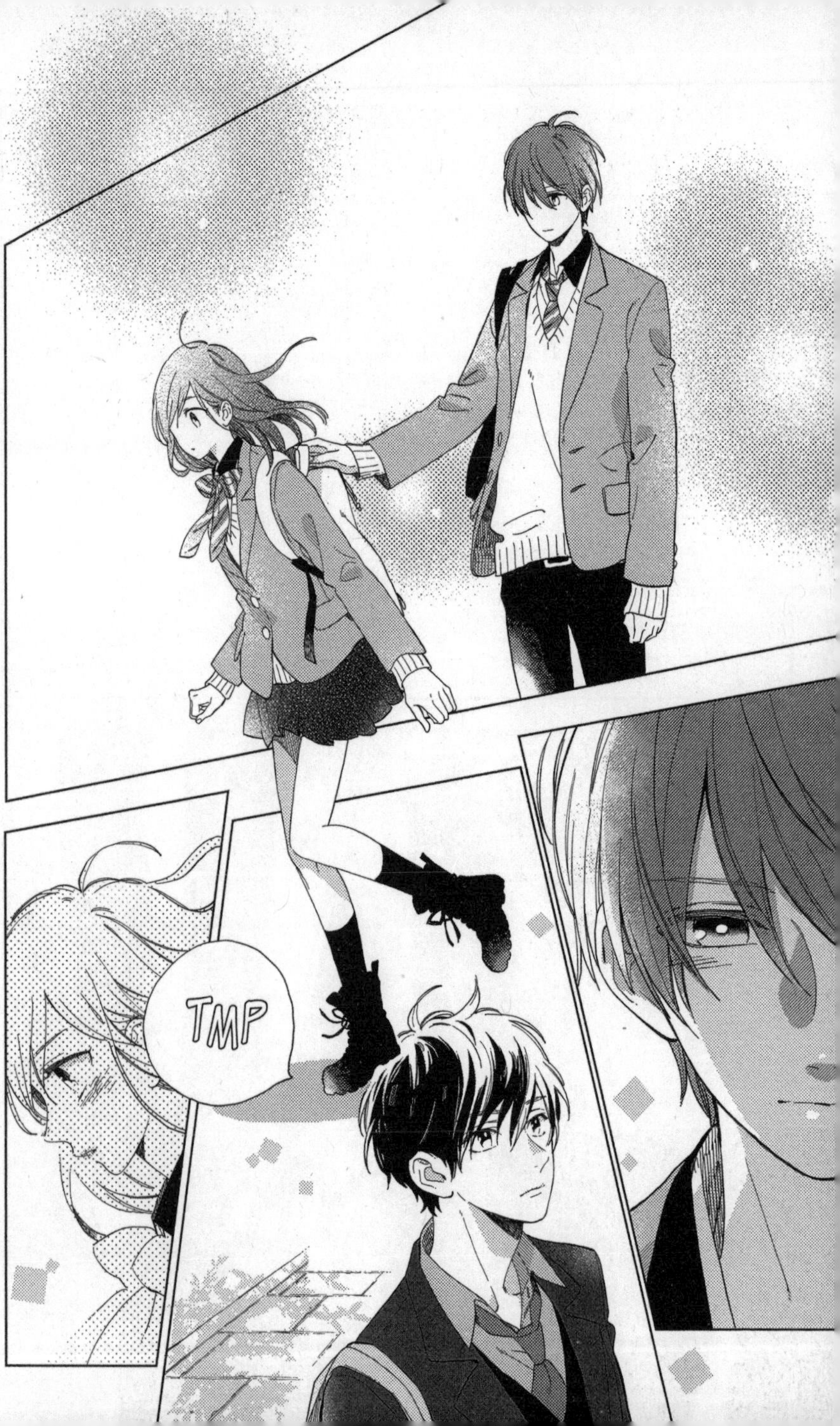
TMP

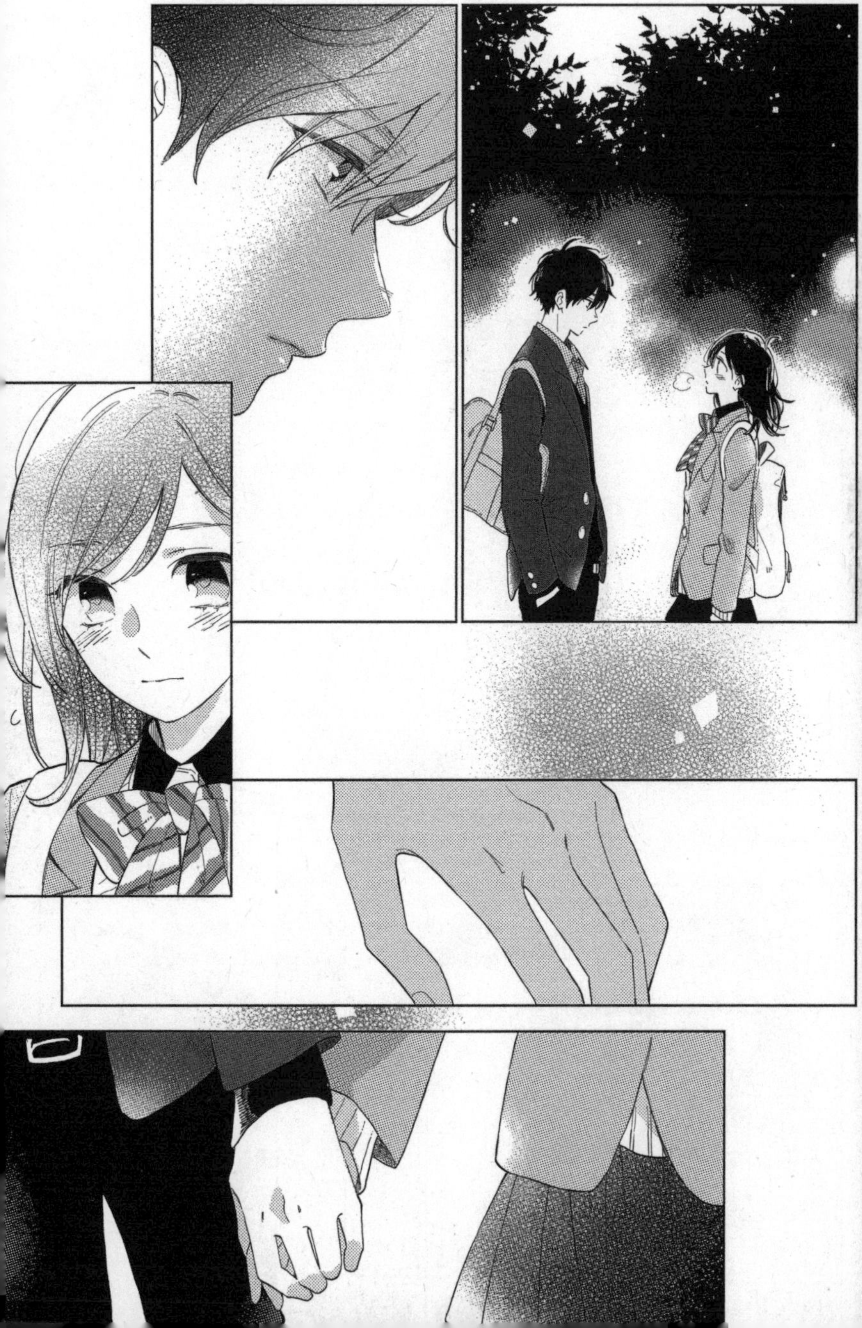

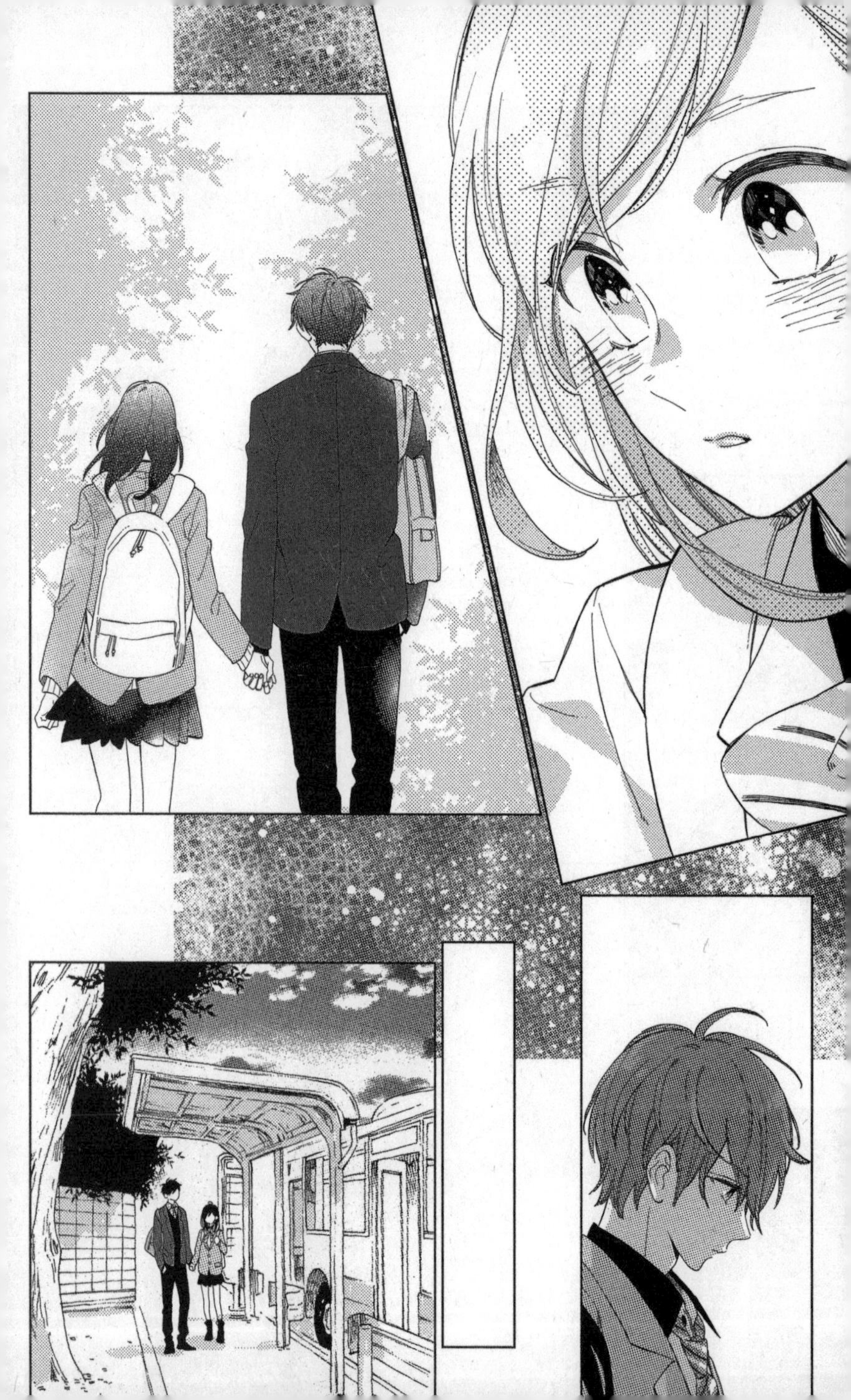

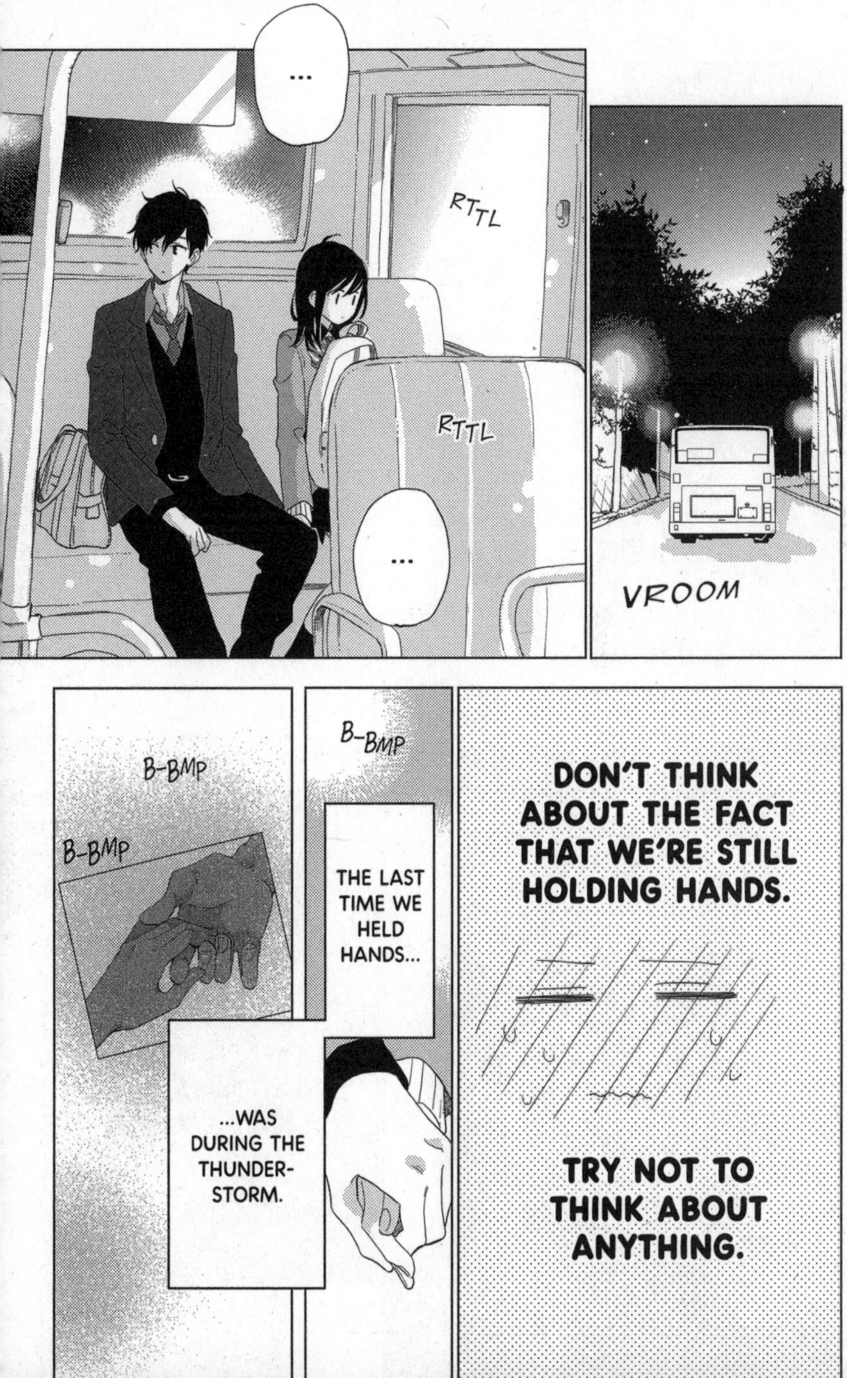
VROOM
...
RTTL
RTTL
...
DON'T THINK ABOUT THE FACT THAT WE'RE STILL HOLDING HANDS.
TRY NOT TO THINK ABOUT ANYTHING.
B-BMP
THE LAST TIME WE HELD HANDS...
B-BMP
B-BMP
...WAS DURING THE THUNDER-STORM.

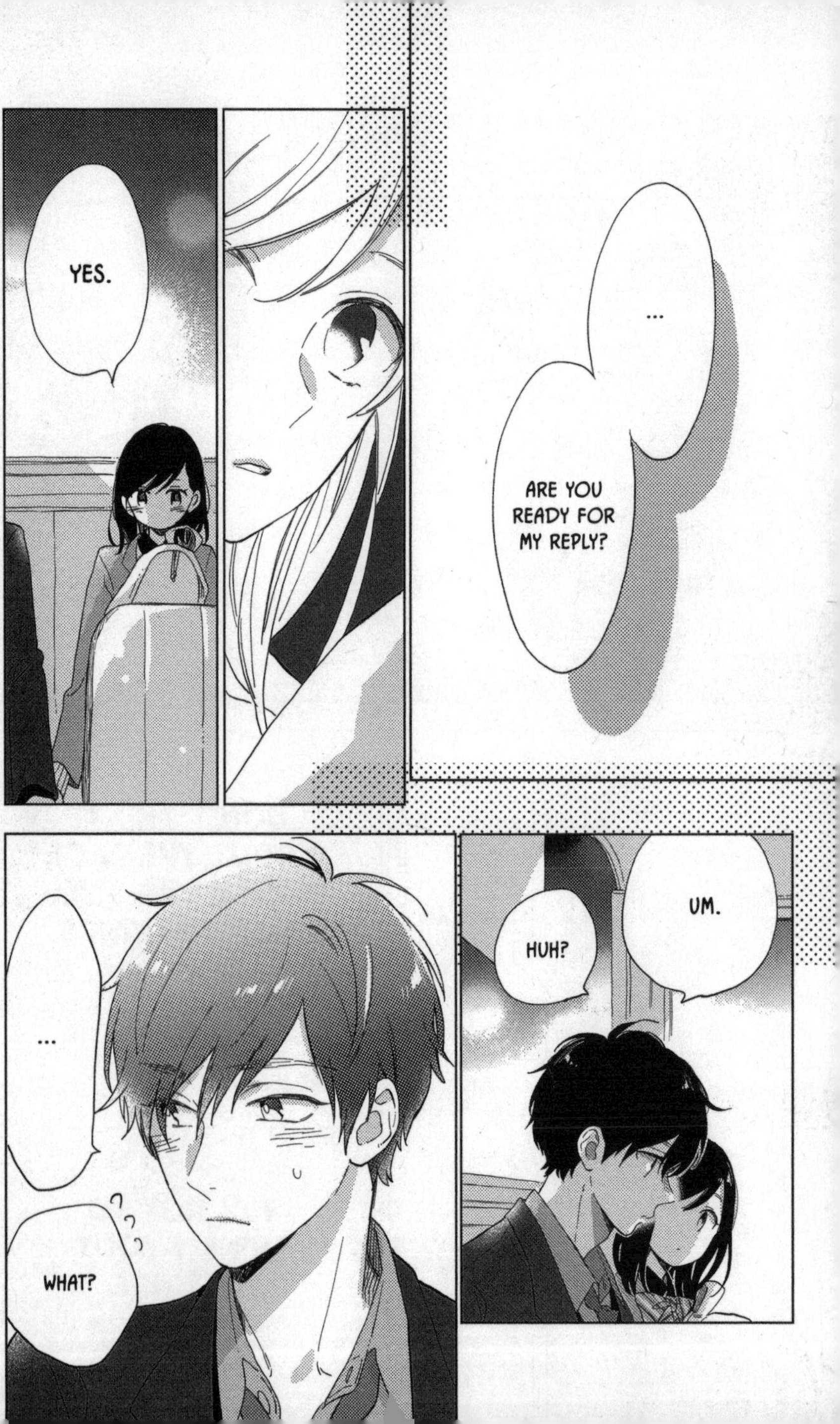
...
ARE YOU READY FOR MY REPLY?
YES.
UM.
HUH?
...
WHAT?

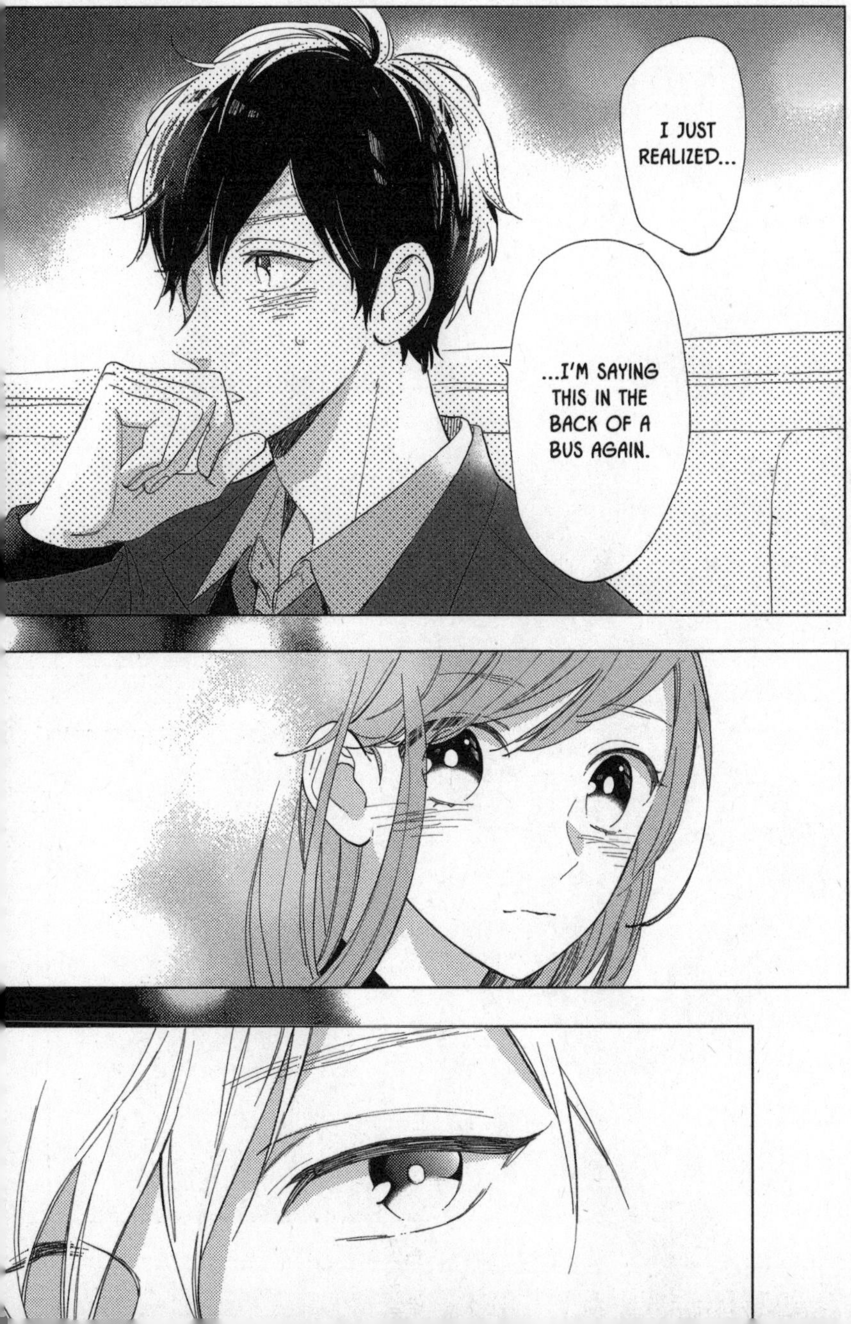
I JUST REALIZED...
...I'M SAYING THIS IN THE BACK OF A BUS AGAIN.

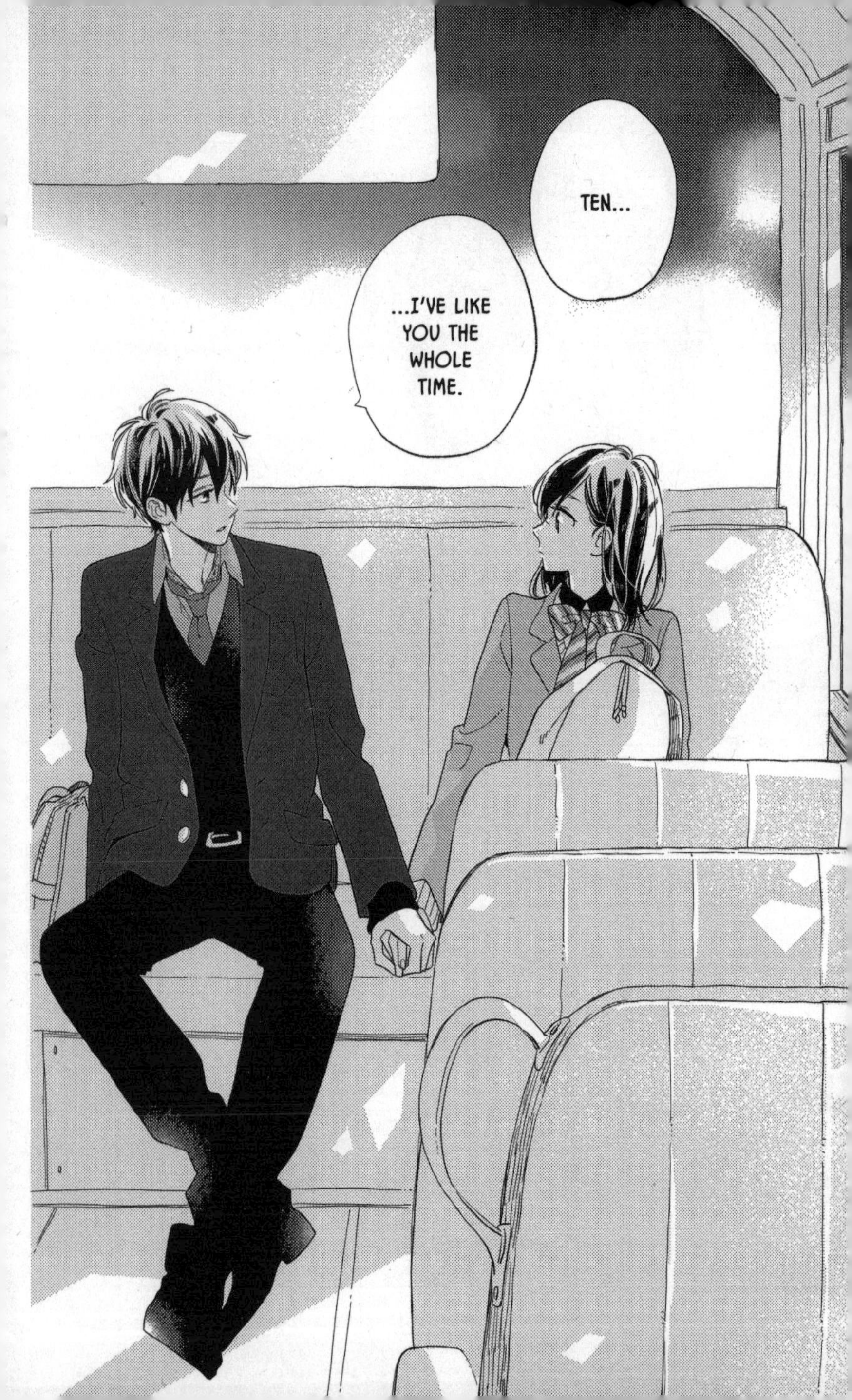
TEN...
...I'VE LIKE YOU THE WHOLE TIME.

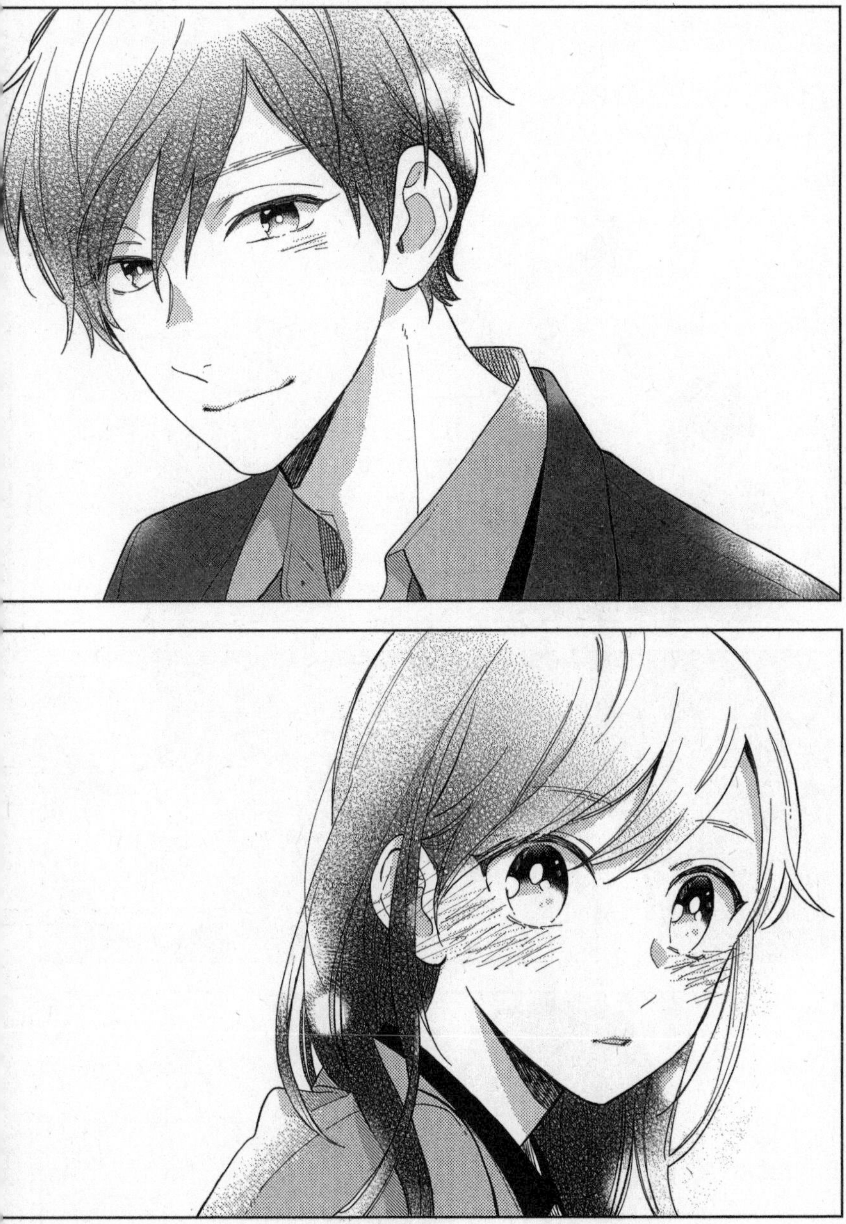

WAIT.

B-BMP

WHAT?

B-BMP

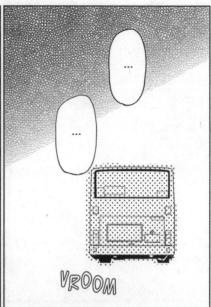

...

...

VROOM

FRET
FRET

ARE...

...YOU JOKING?

I'M SERIOUS.

SKWEEZ

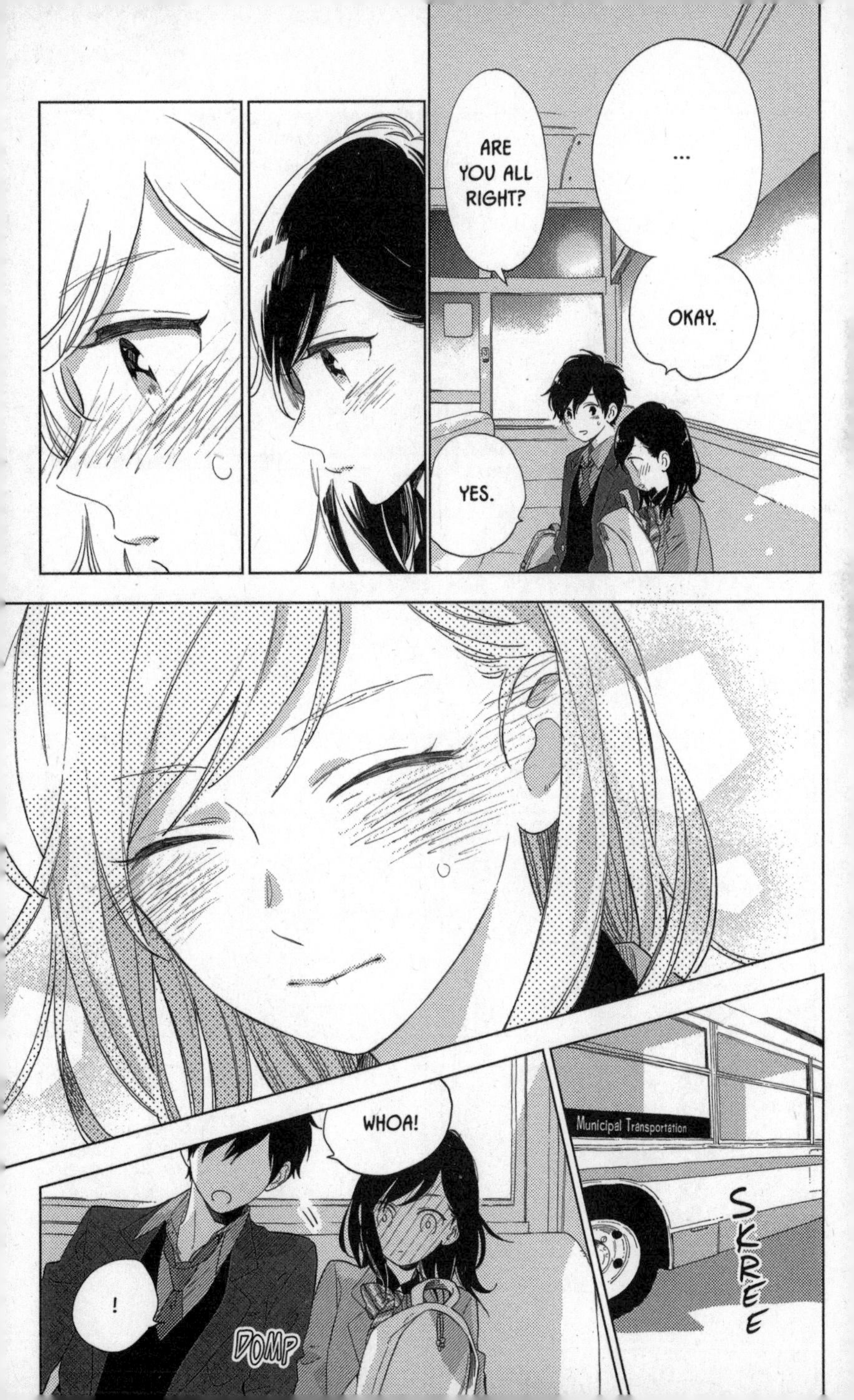
...
OKAY.
ARE YOU ALL RIGHT?
YES.
Municipal Transportation
SKREE
WHOA!
!
DOMP

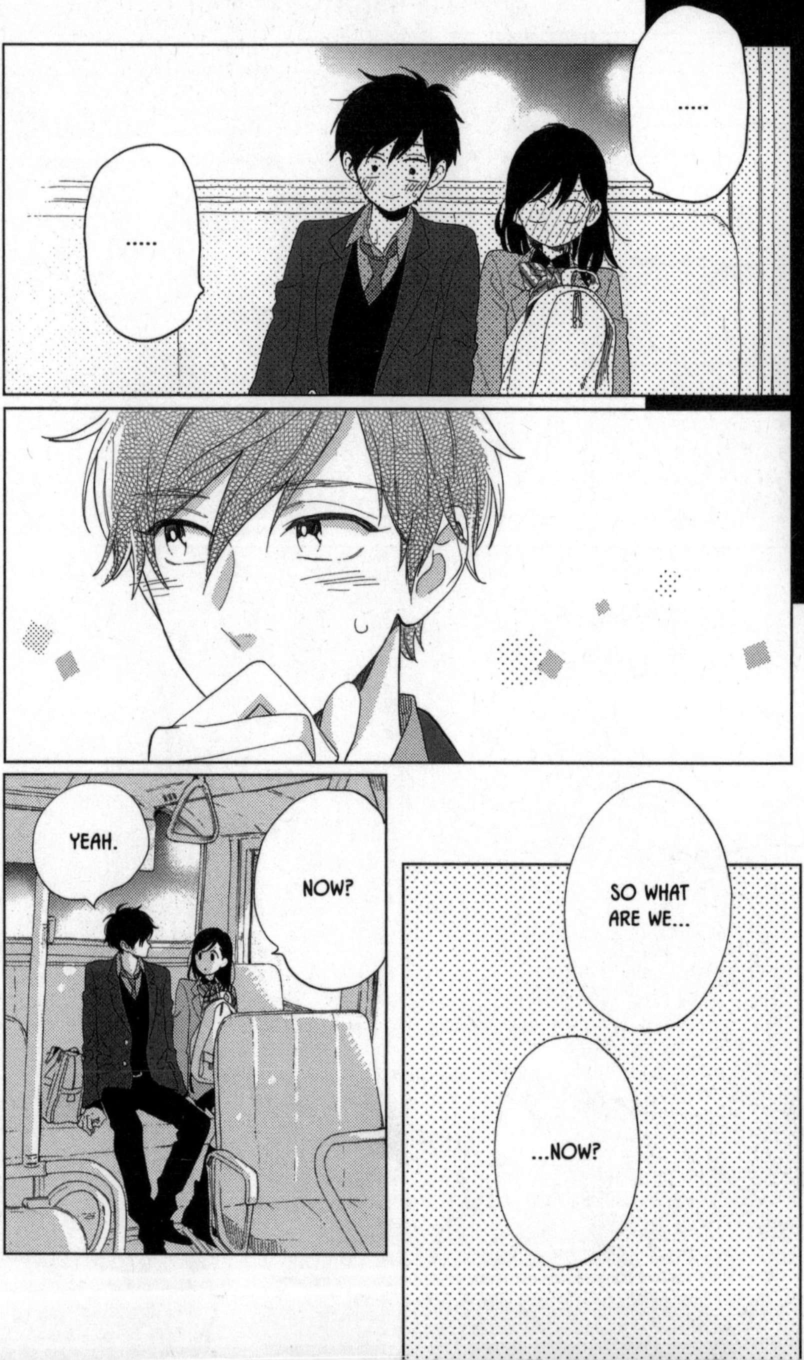
.....
.....
SO WHAT ARE WE...
...NOW?
NOW?
YEAH.

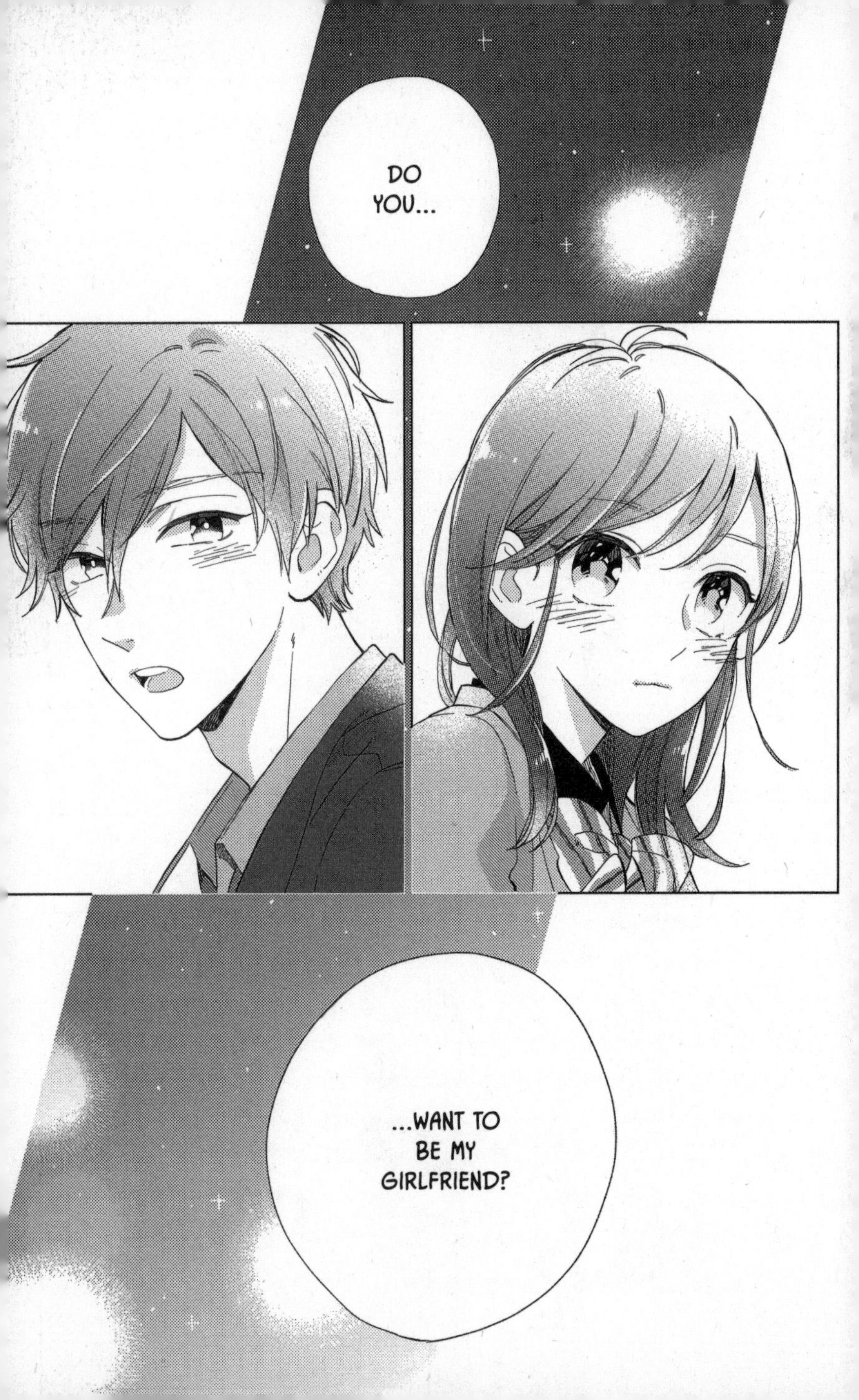
DO YOU...
...WANT TO BE MY GIRLFRIEND?

SHORTCAKE
CAKE

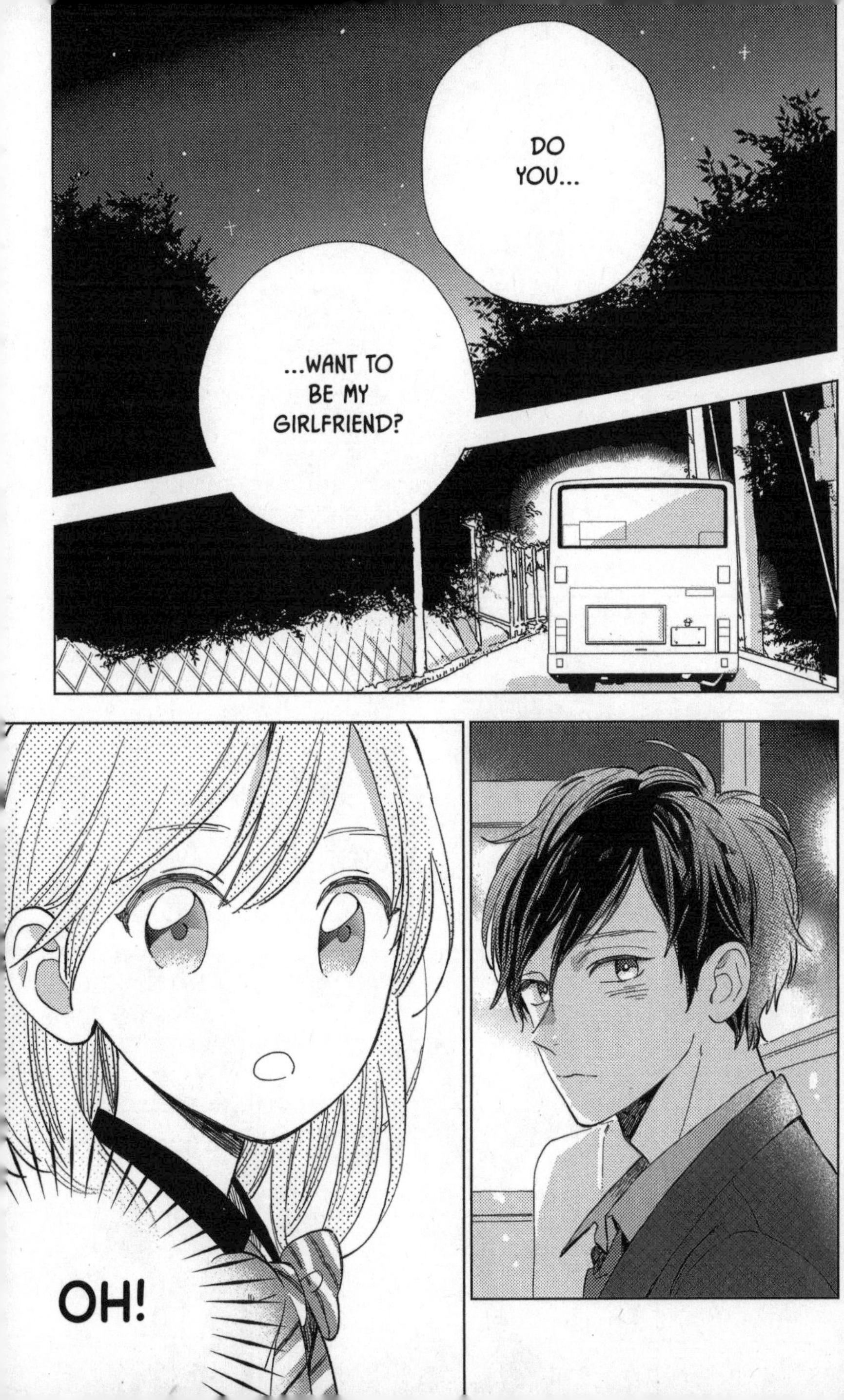
DO YOU...
...WANT TO BE MY GIRLFRIEND?
OH!

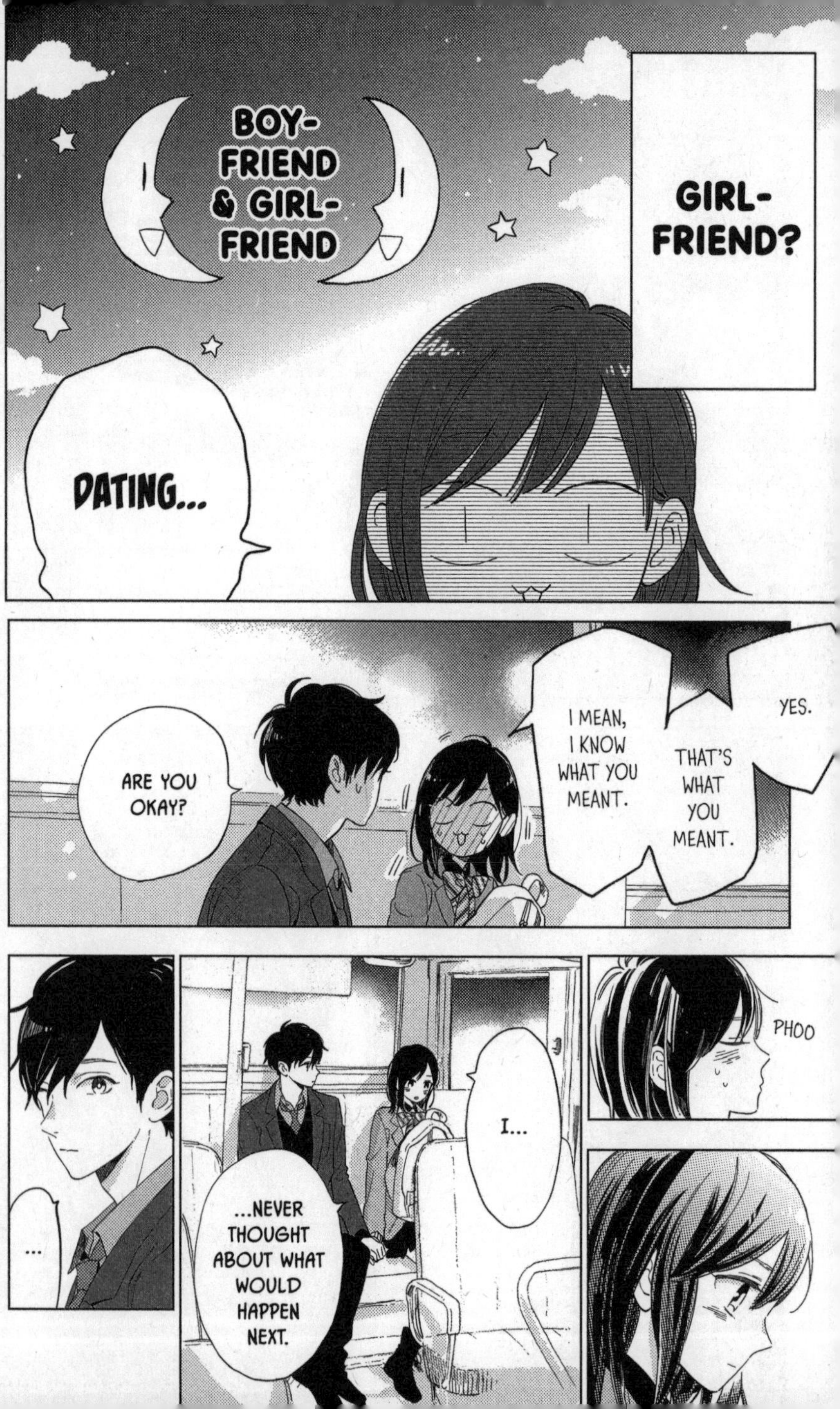
GIRL-FRIEND?
BOY-FRIEND & GIRL-FRIEND
DATING...
YES. THAT'S WHAT YOU MEANT.
I MEAN, I KNOW WHAT YOU MEANT.
ARE YOU OKAY?
PHOO
I...
...NEVER THOUGHT ABOUT WHAT WOULD HAPPEN NEXT.
...

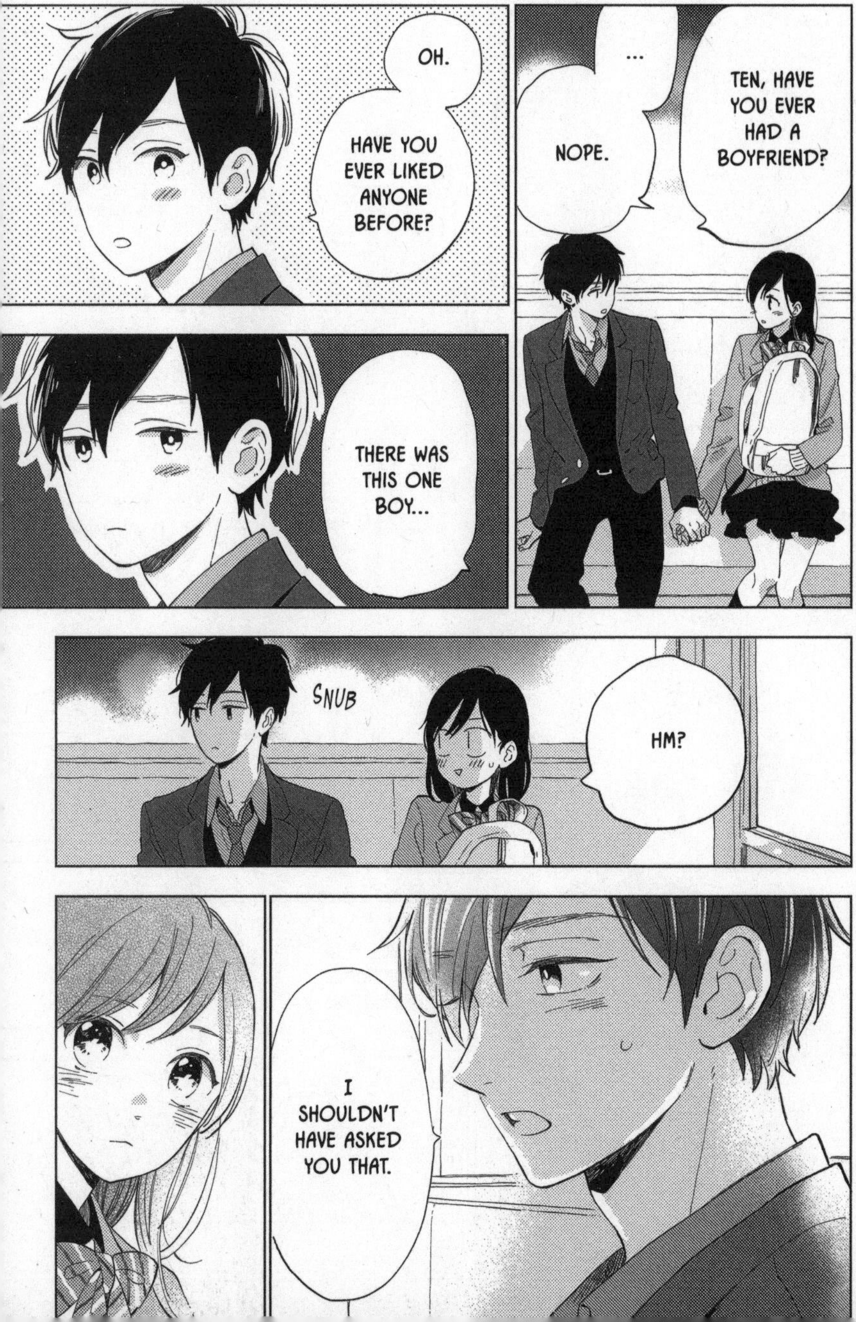
TEN, HAVE YOU EVER HAD A BOYFRIEND?
...
NOPE.
OH.
HAVE YOU EVER LIKED ANYONE BEFORE?
THERE WAS THIS ONE BOY...
HM?
SNUB
I SHOULDN'T HAVE ASKED YOU THAT.

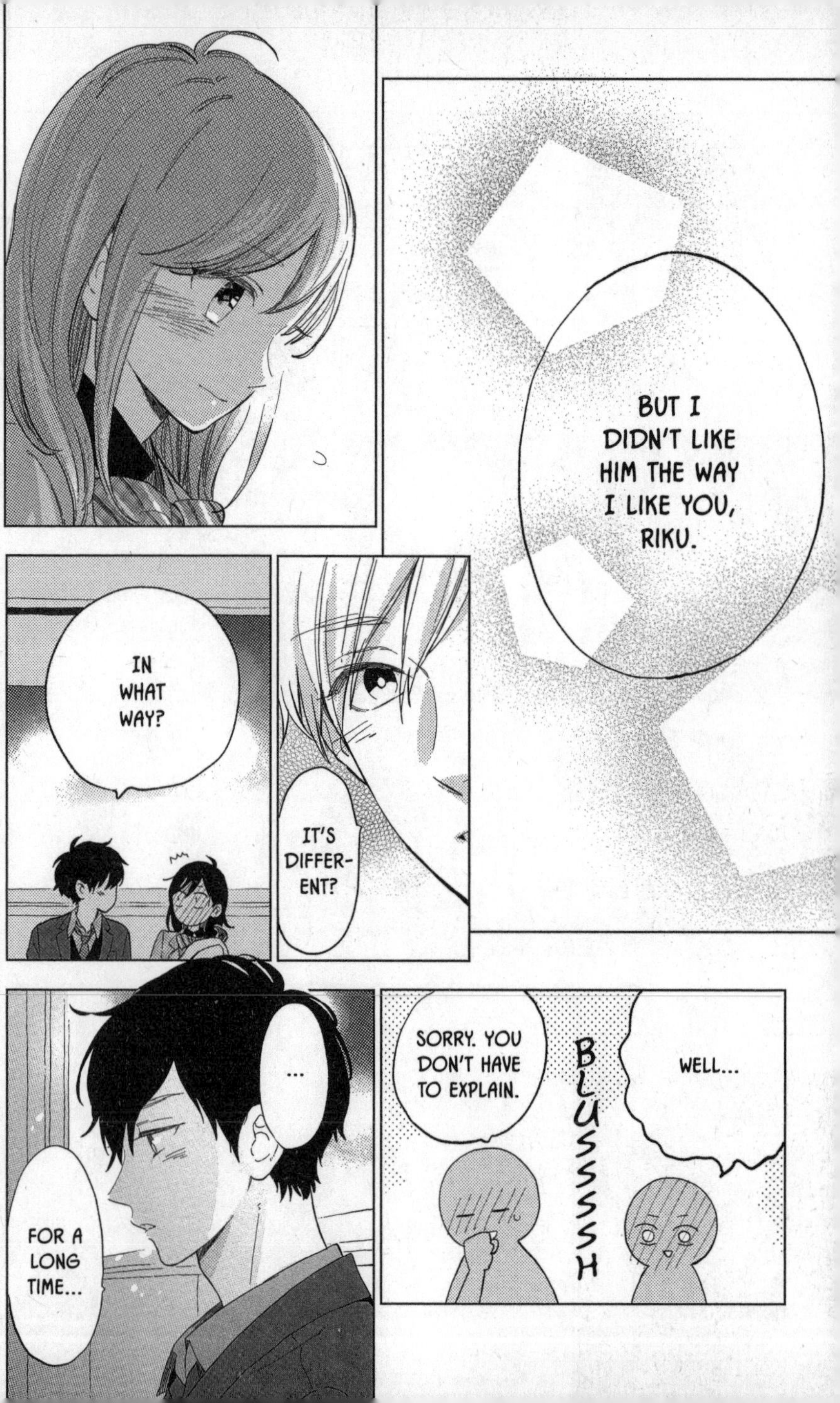
BUT I DIDN'T LIKE HIM THE WAY I LIKE YOU, RIKU.
IT'S DIFFER-ENT?
IN WHAT WAY?
WELL...
BLUSSSSH
SORRY. YOU DON'T HAVE TO EXPLAIN.
...
FOR A LONG TIME...

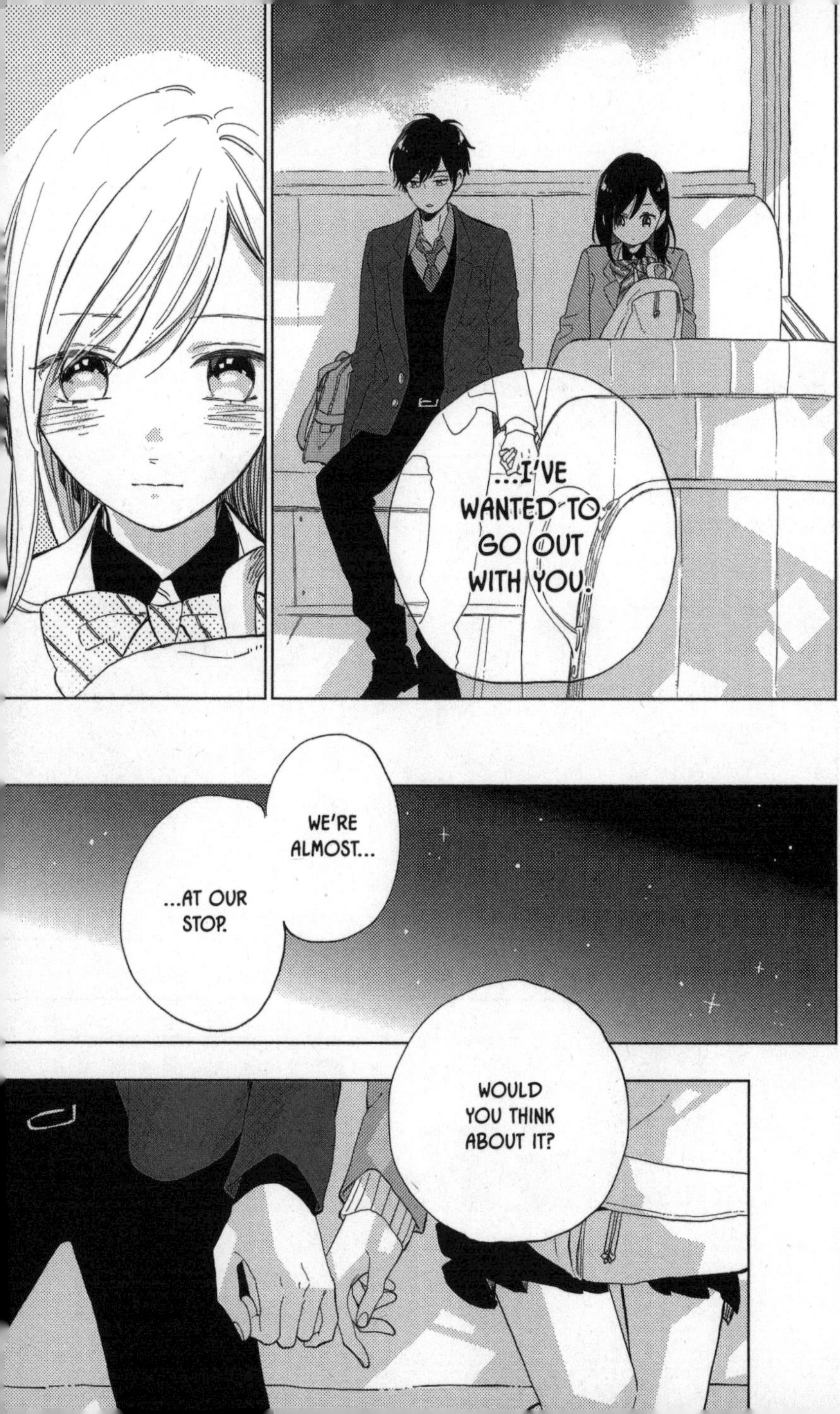
...I'VE WANTED TO GO OUT WITH YOU.
WE'RE ALMOST...
...AT OUR STOP.
WOULD YOU THINK ABOUT IT?

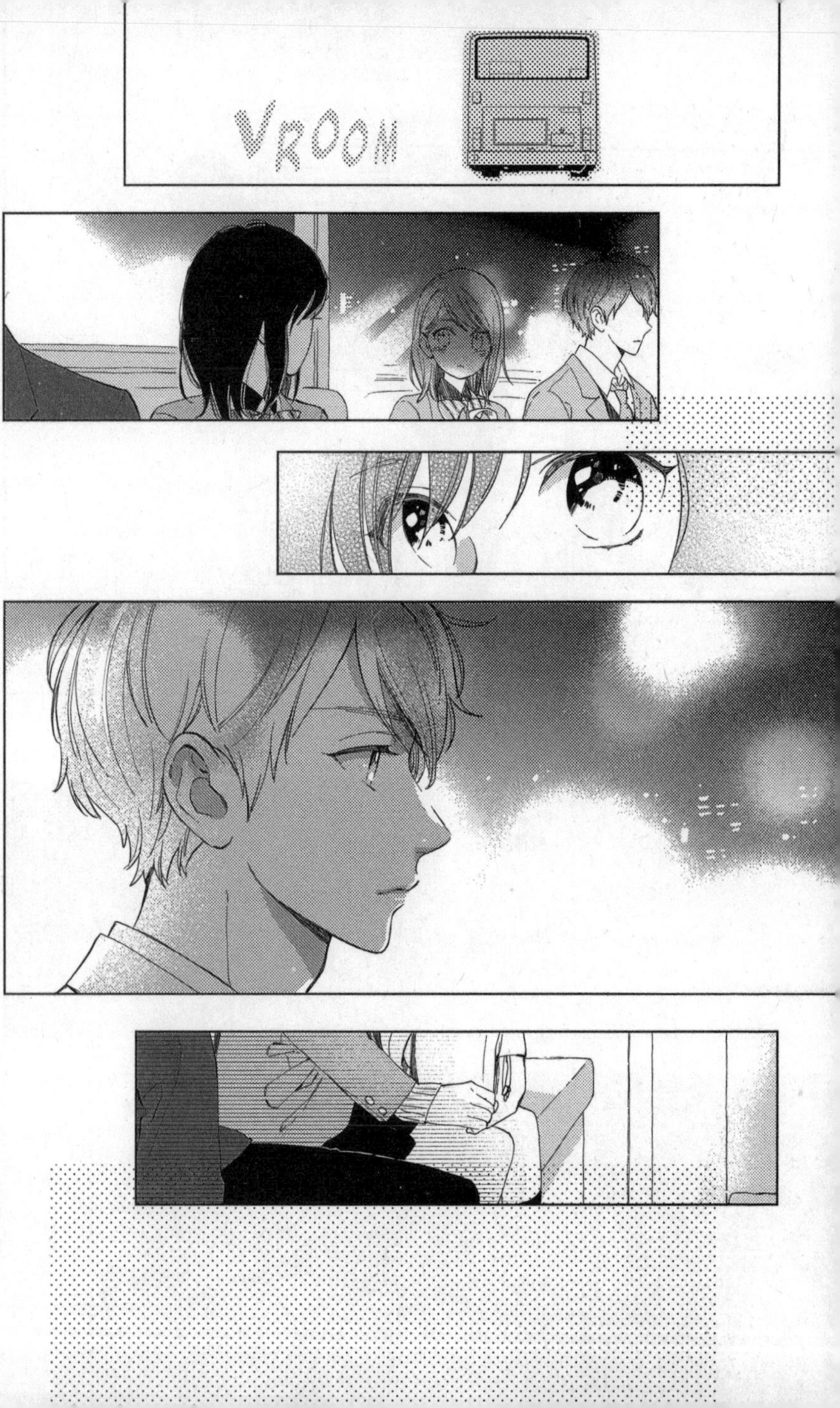
VROOM

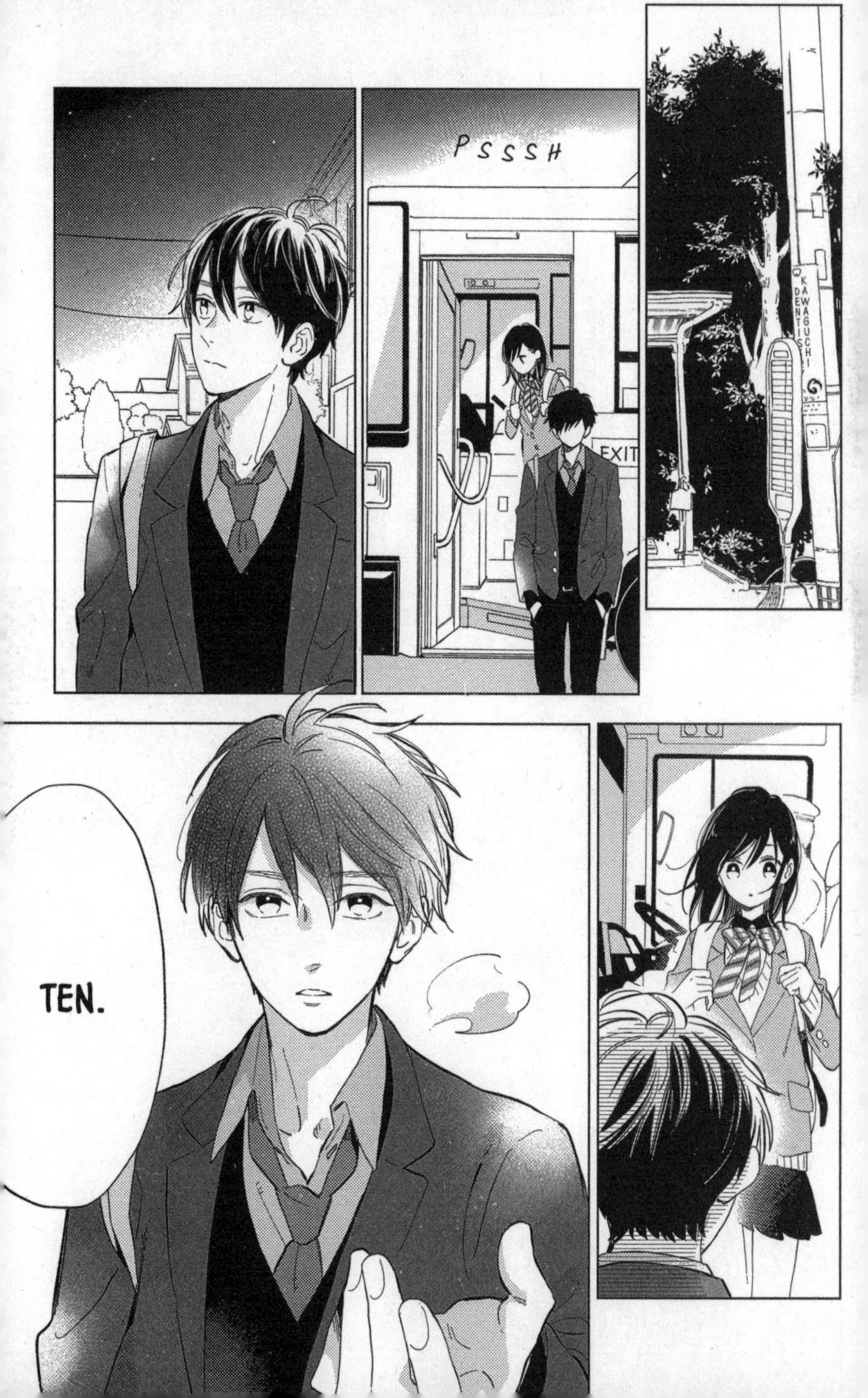
KAWAGUCHI
DENTIS
PSSSH
EXIT
TEN.

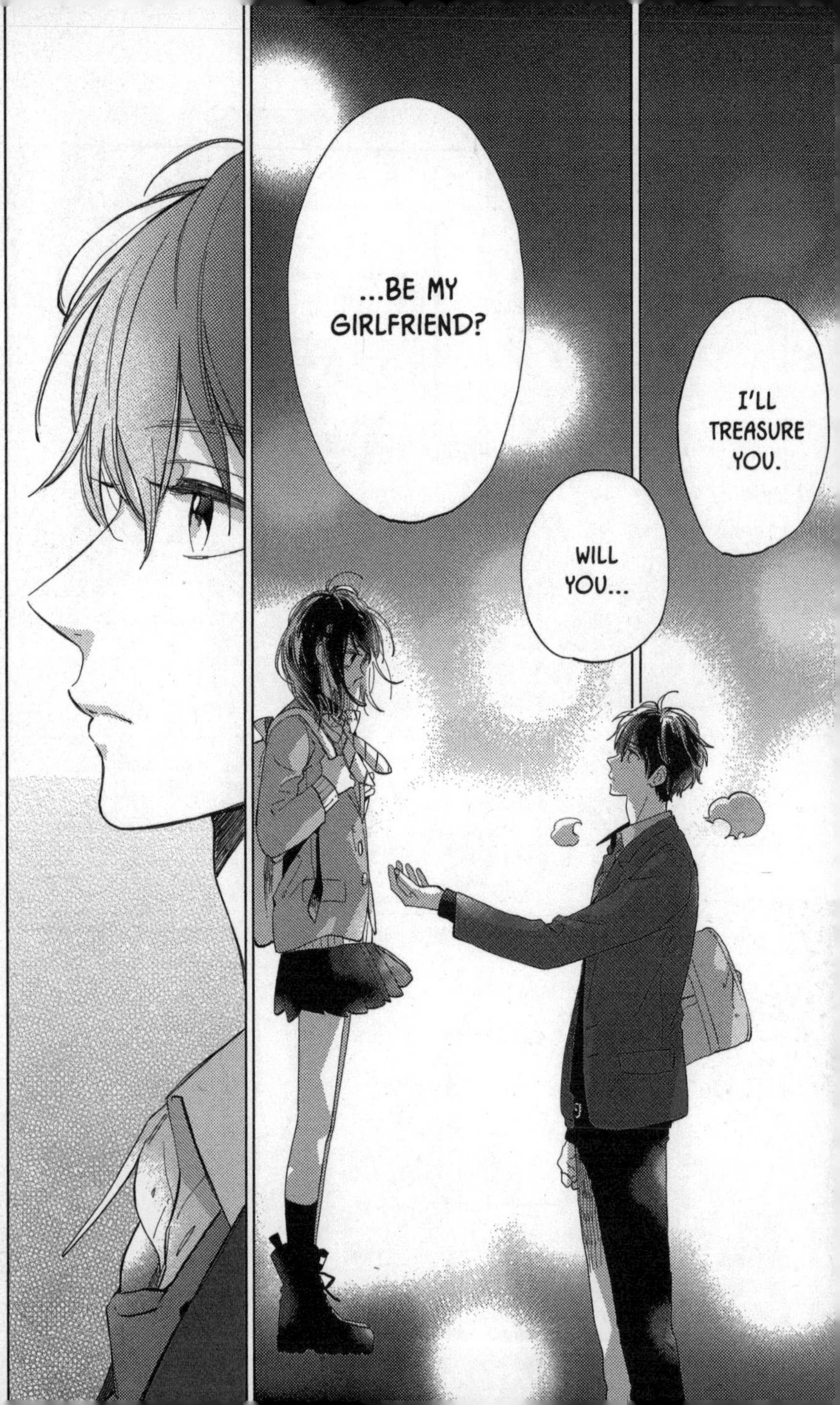
I'LL TREASURE YOU.
WILL YOU...
...BE MY GIRLFRIEND?

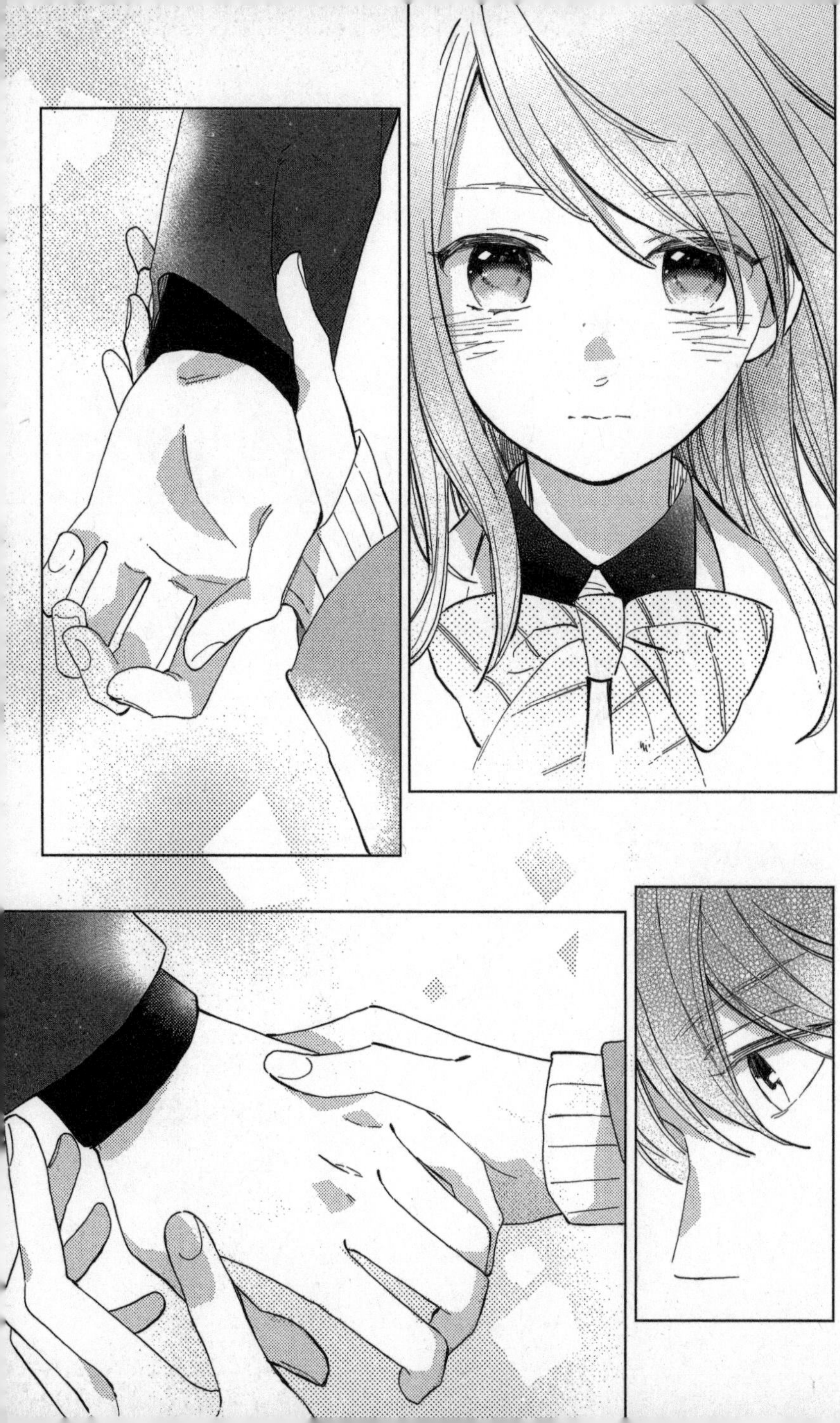

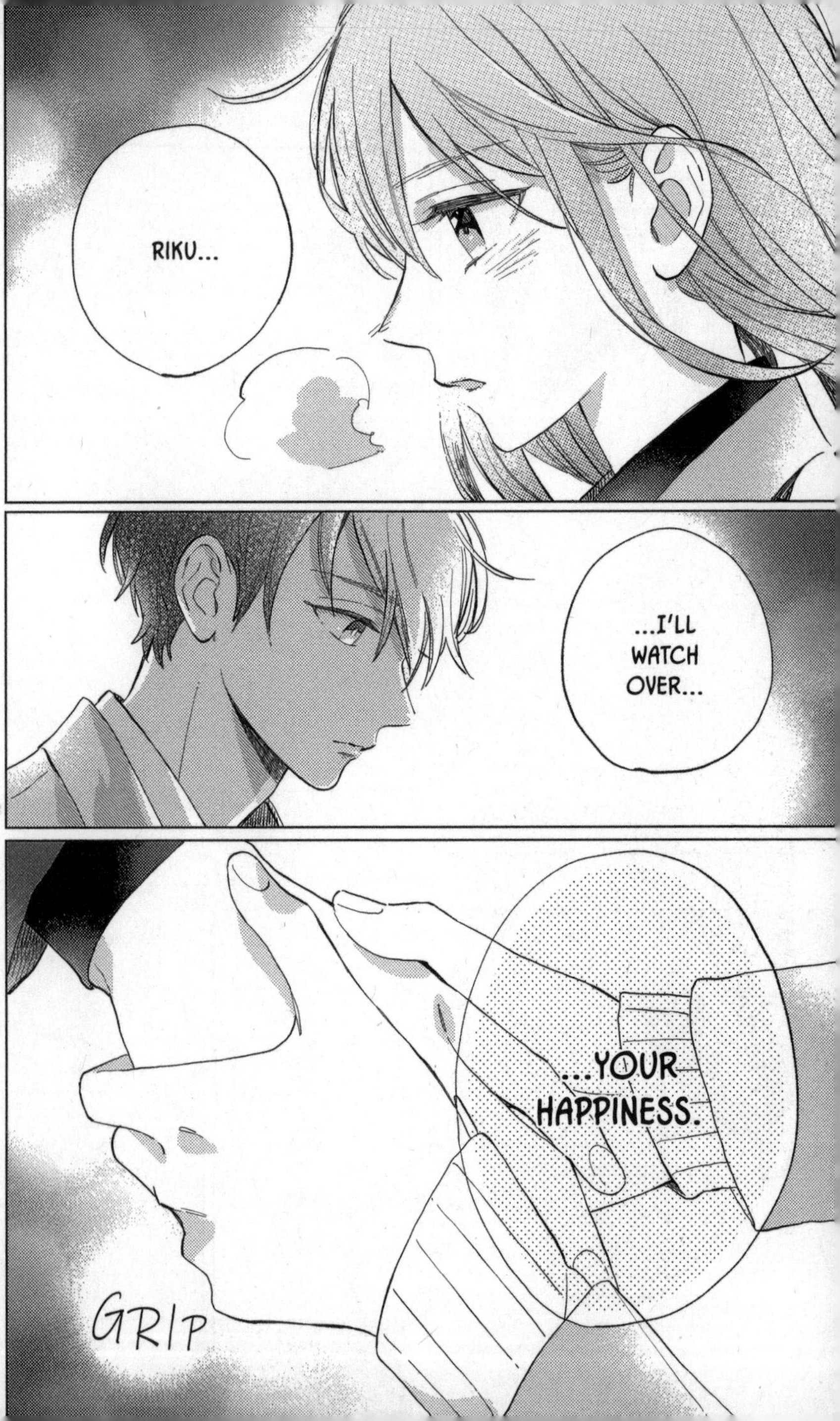
RIKU...
...I'LL WATCH OVER...
...YOUR HAPPINESS.
GRIP

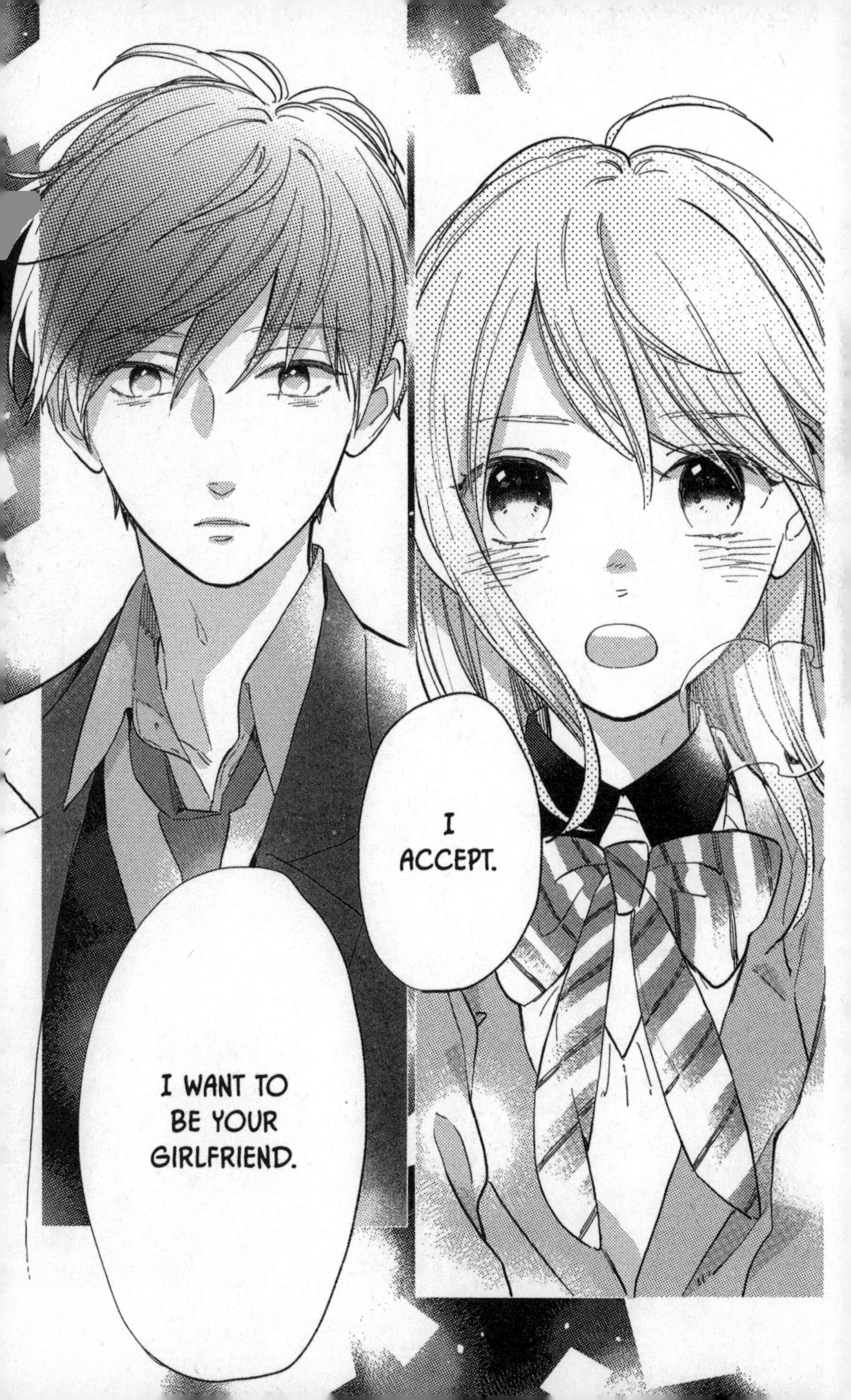
I ACCEPT.
I WANT TO BE YOUR GIRLFRIEND.

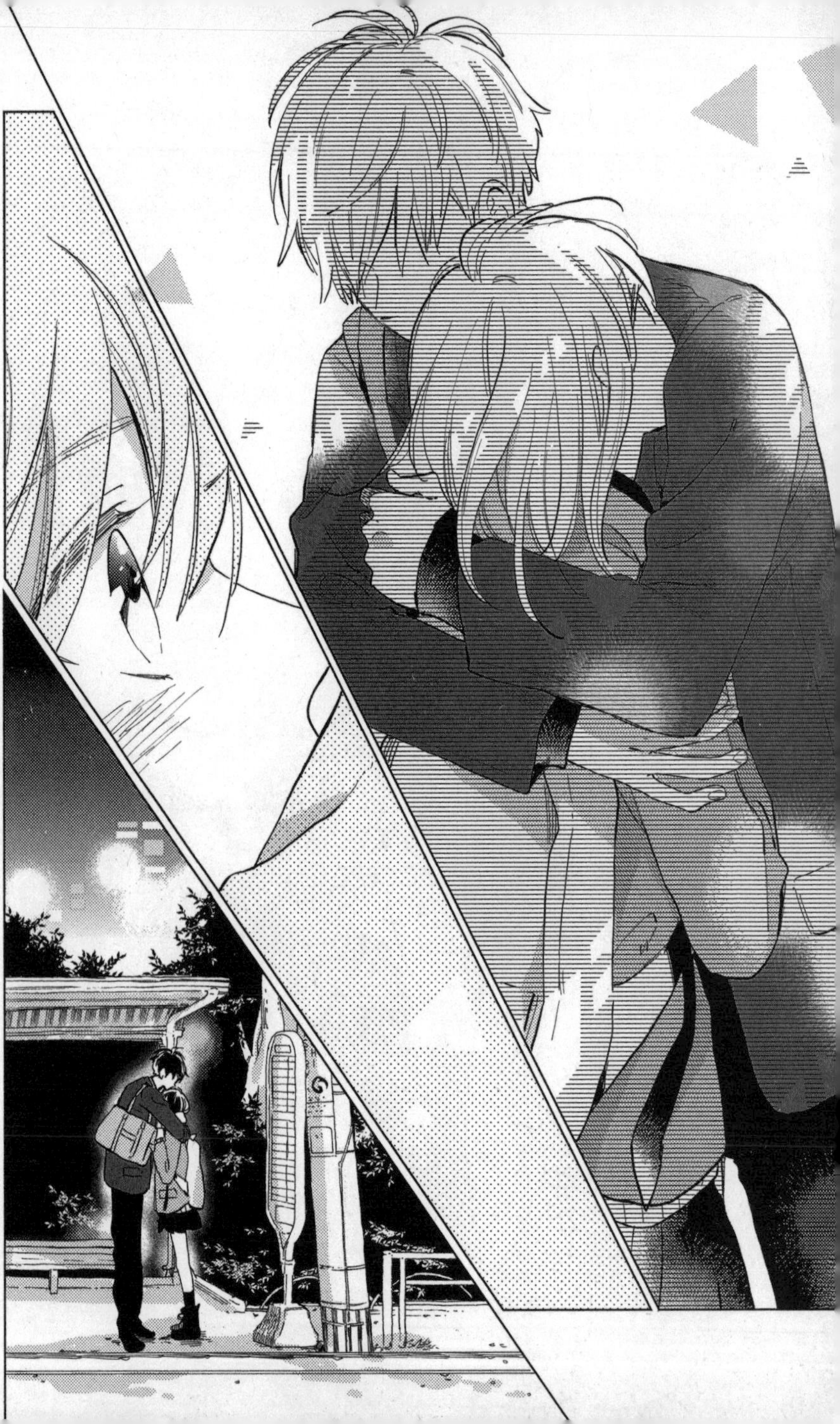

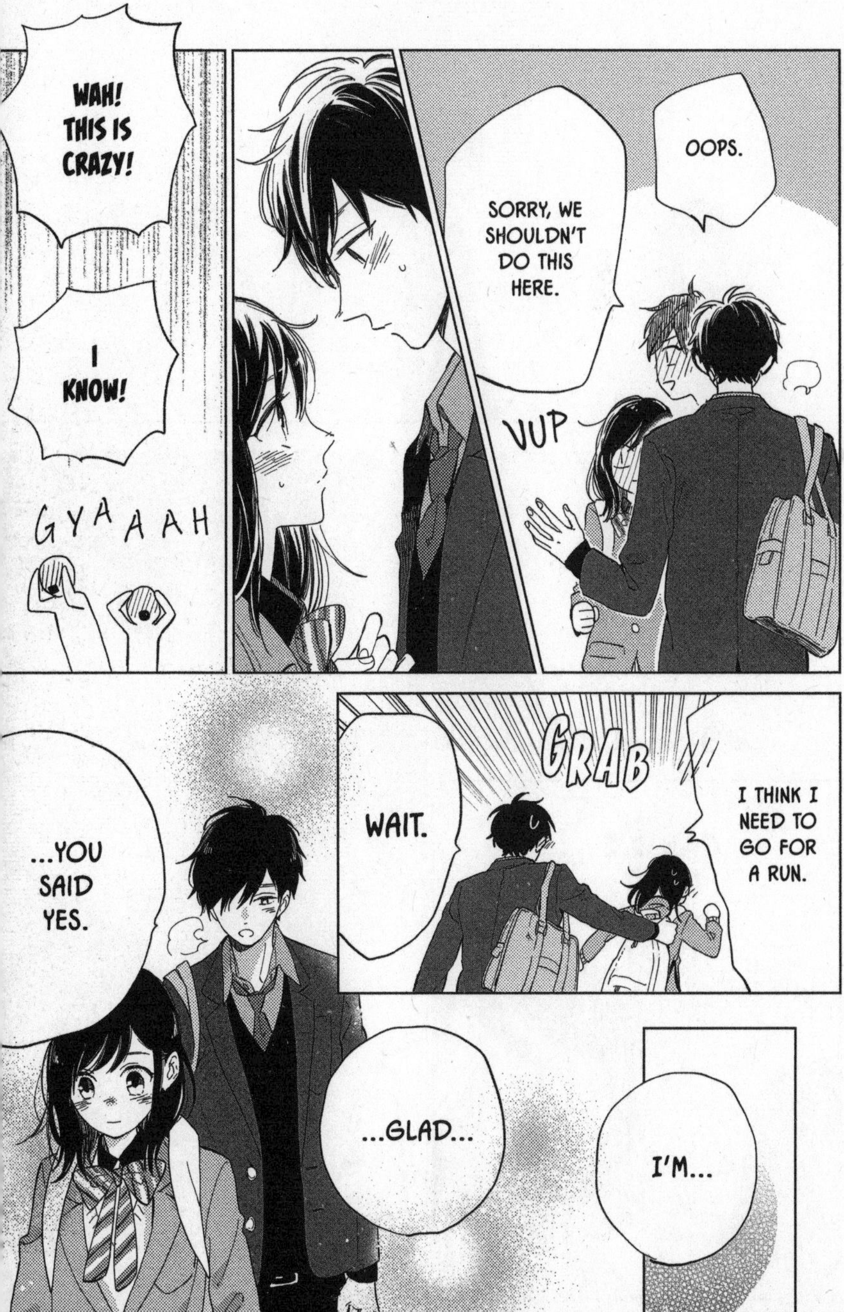
OOPS.
SORRY, WE SHOULDN'T DO THIS HERE.
VUP
WAH! THIS IS CRAZY!
I KNOW!
GYAAAAH
I THINK I NEED TO GO FOR A RUN.
GRAB
WAIT.
I'M...
...GLAD...
...YOU SAID YES.

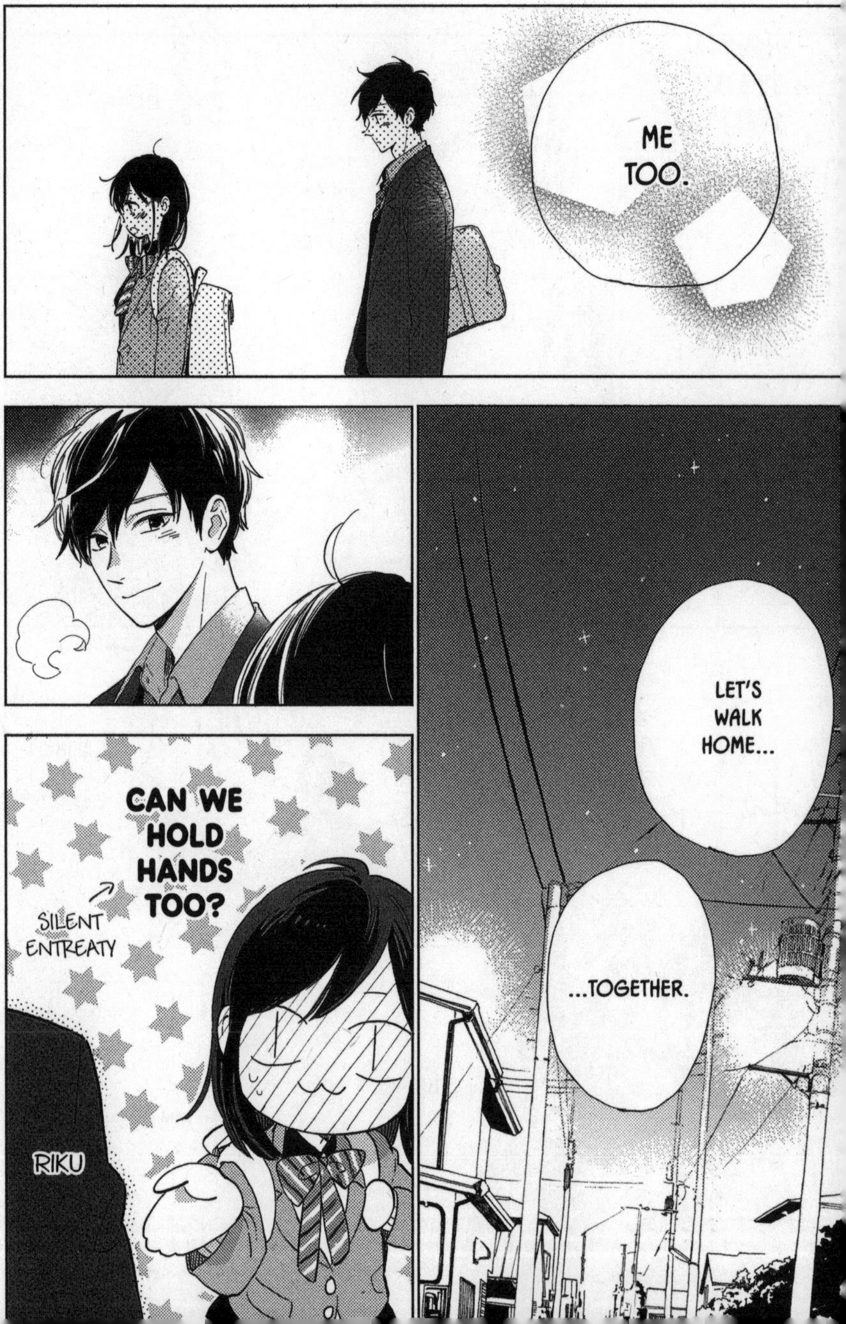
ME TOO.
LET'S WALK HOME...
...TOGETHER.
CAN WE HOLD HANDS TOO?
SILENT ENTREATY
RIKU

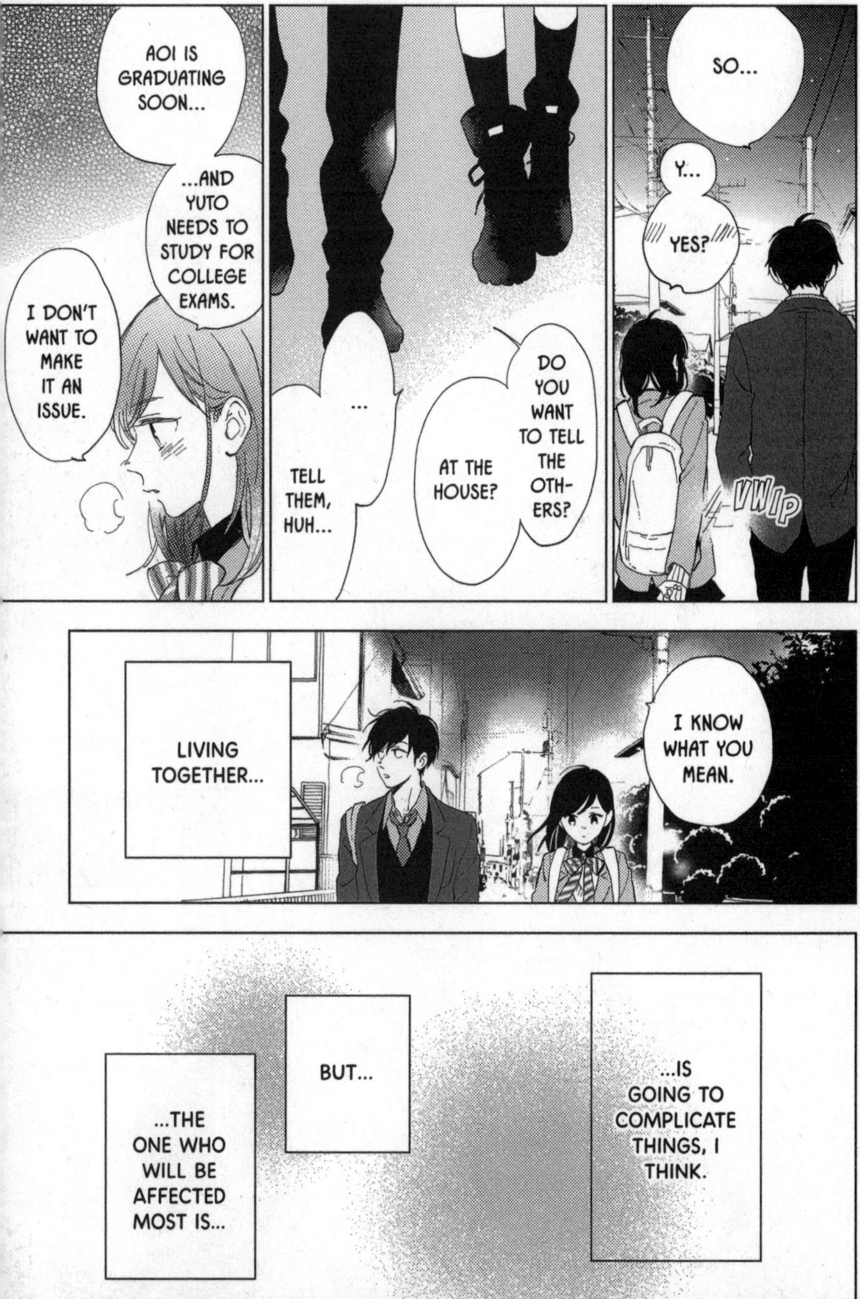
SO...
Y...
YES?
VWIP
DO YOU WANT TO TELL THE OTHERS?
AT THE HOUSE?
...
TELL THEM, HUH...
AOI IS GRADUATING SOON...
...AND YUTO NEEDS TO STUDY FOR COLLEGE EXAMS.
I DON'T WANT TO MAKE IT AN ISSUE.
I KNOW WHAT YOU MEAN.
LIVING TOGETHER...
...IS GOING TO COMPLICATE THINGS, I THINK.
BUT...
...THE ONE WHO WILL BE AFFECTED MOST IS...

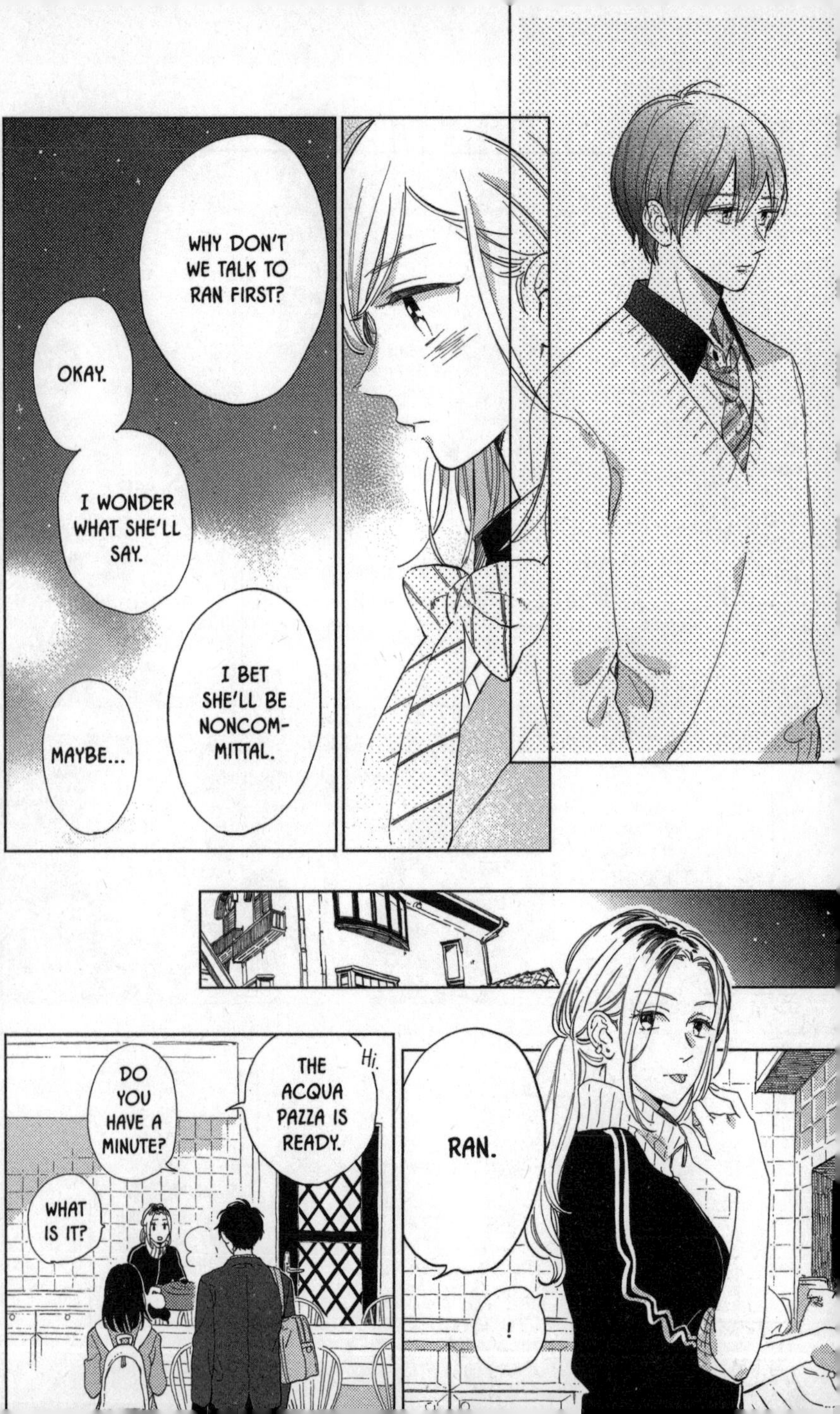
WHY DON'T WE TALK TO RAN FIRST?
OKAY.
I WONDER WHAT SHE'LL SAY.
I BET SHE'LL BE NONCOM-MITTAL.
MAYBE...
RAN.
!
Hi.
THE ACQUA PAZZA IS READY.
DO YOU HAVE A MINUTE?
WHAT IS IT?

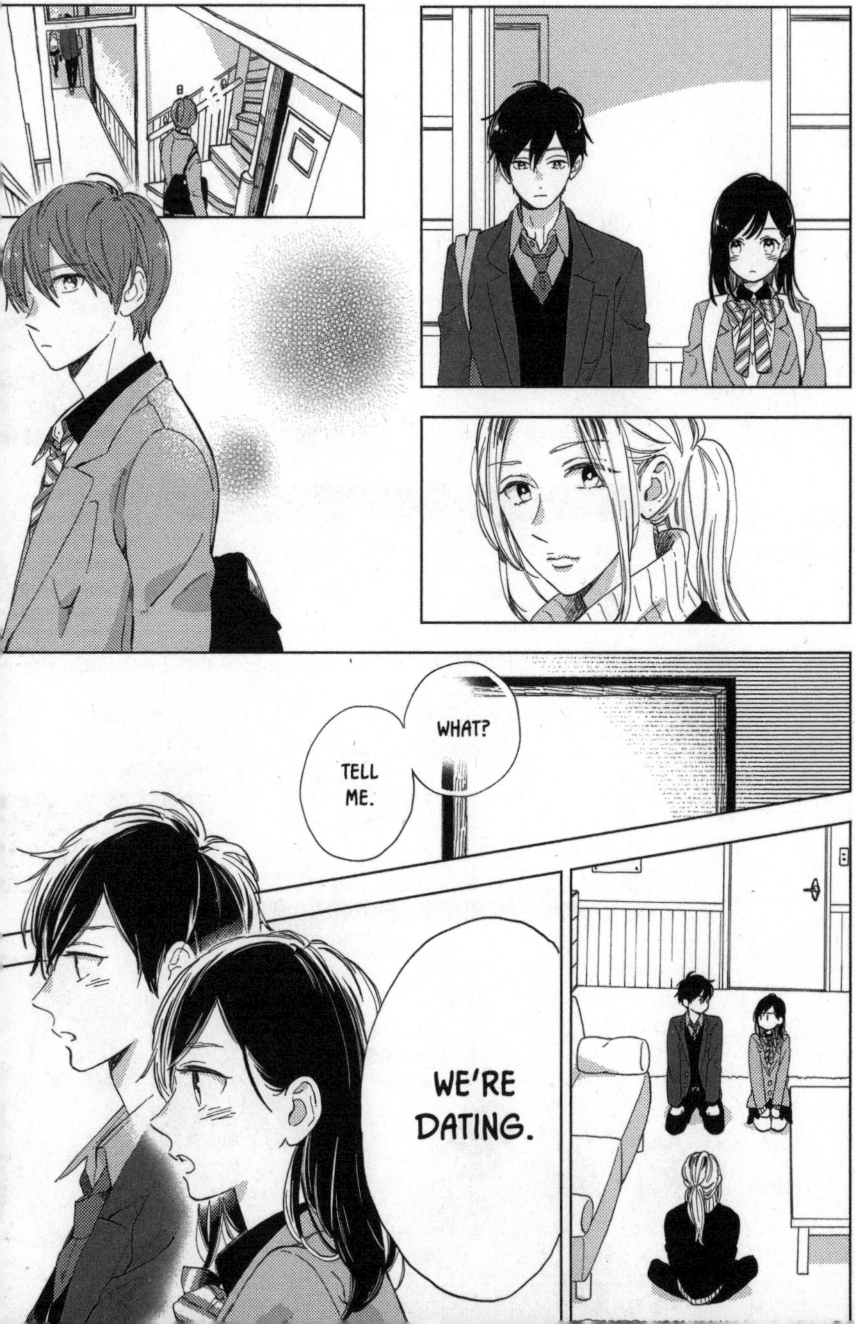
WHAT?
TELL ME.
WE'RE DATING.

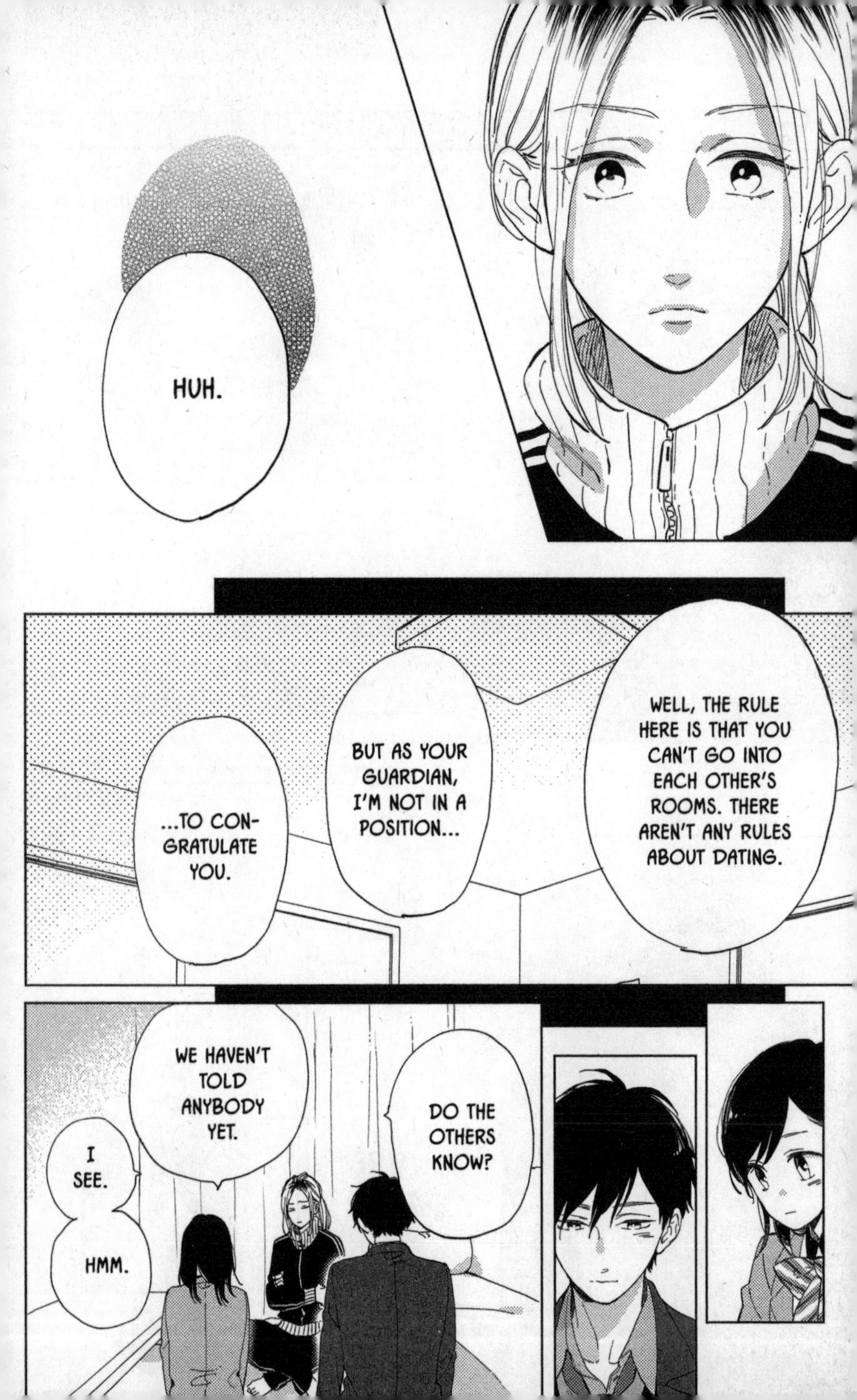
HUH.
WELL, THE RULE HERE IS THAT YOU CAN'T GO INTO EACH OTHER'S ROOMS. THERE AREN'T ANY RULES ABOUT DATING.
BUT AS YOUR GUARDIAN, I'M NOT IN A POSITION...
...TO CON-GRATULATE YOU.
DO THE OTHERS KNOW?
WE HAVEN'T TOLD ANYBODY YET.
I SEE.
HMM.

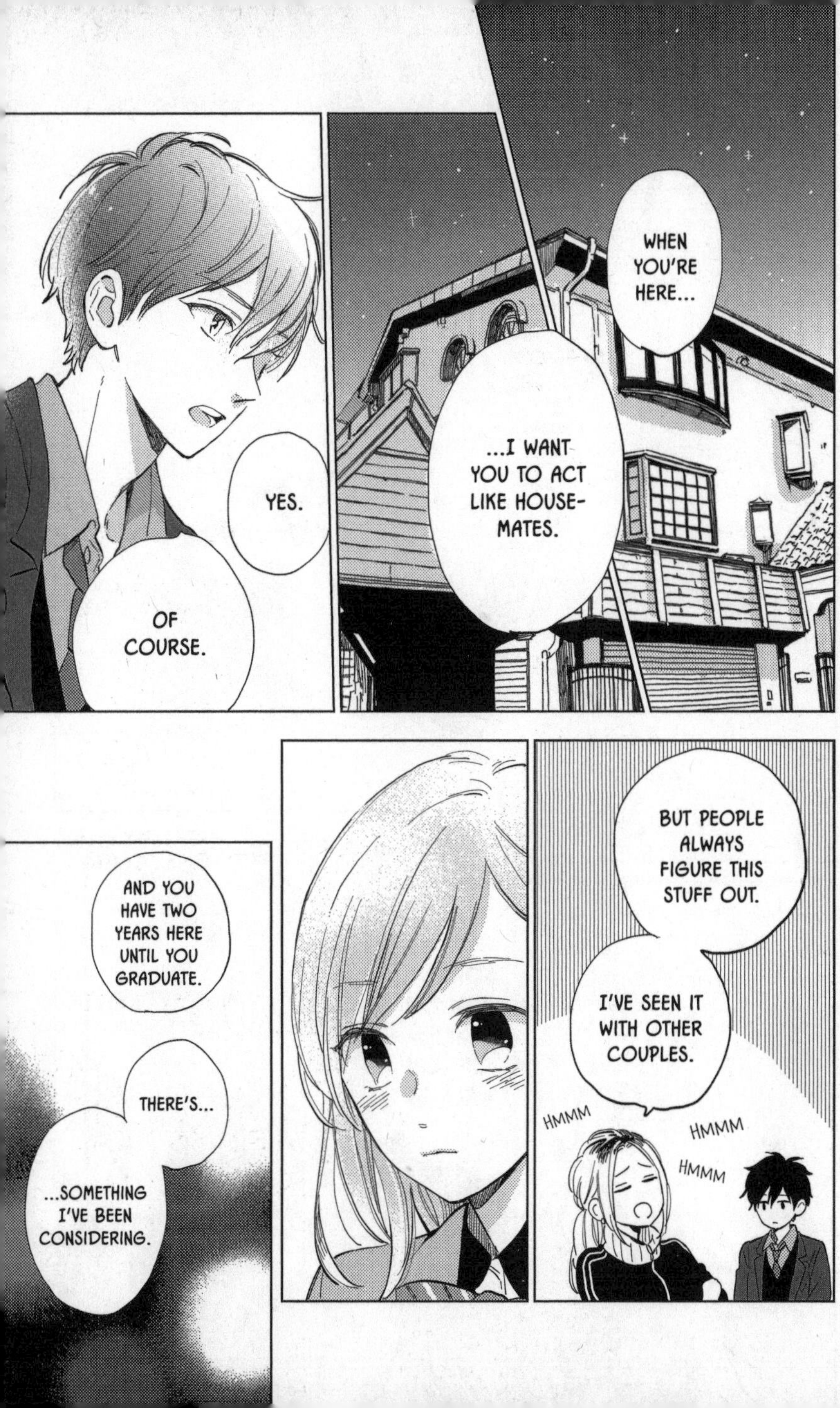
WHEN YOU'RE HERE...
...I WANT YOU TO ACT LIKE HOUSE-MATES.
YES.
OF COURSE.
BUT PEOPLE ALWAYS FIGURE THIS STUFF OUT.
I'VE SEEN IT WITH OTHER COUPLES.
HMMM
HMMM
HMMM
AND YOU HAVE TWO YEARS HERE UNTIL YOU GRADUATE.
THERE'S...
...SOMETHING I'VE BEEN CONSIDERING.

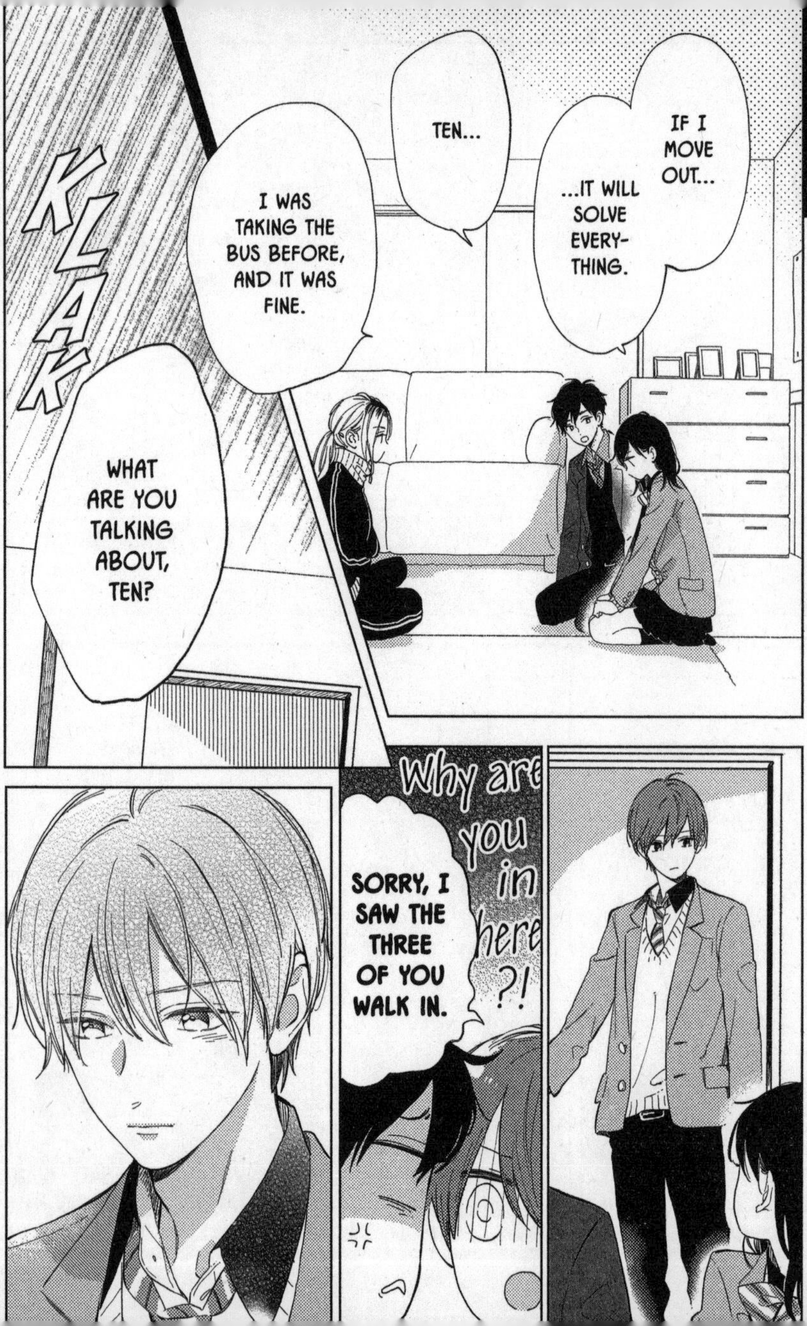
IF I MOVE OUT...
...IT WILL SOLVE EVERYTHING.
TEN...
I WAS TAKING THE BUS BEFORE, AND IT WAS FINE.
KLAK
WHAT ARE YOU TALKING ABOUT, TEN?
Why are you in here?!
SORRY, I SAW THE THREE OF YOU WALK IN.

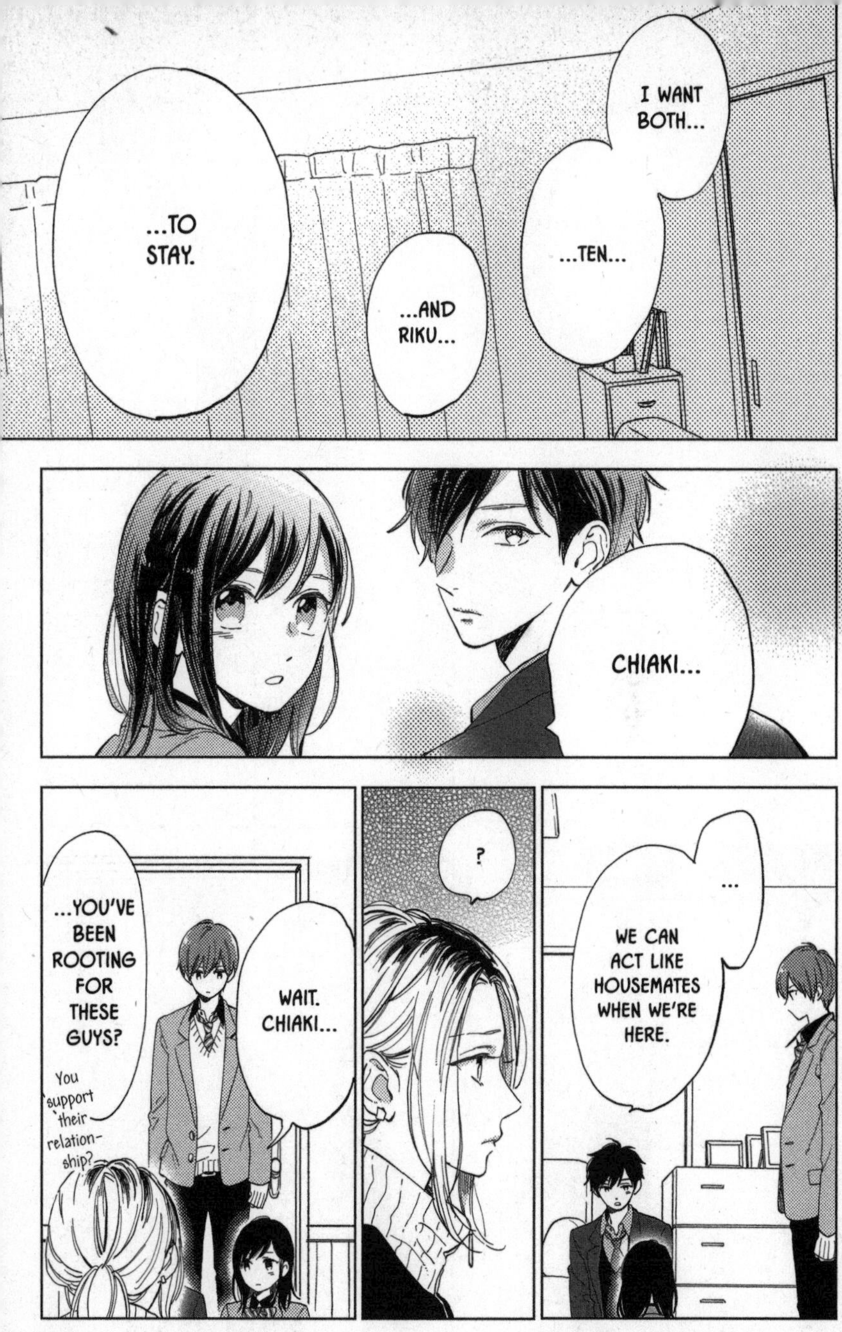
I WANT BOTH...
...TEN...
...AND RIKU...
...TO STAY.
CHIAKI...
...
WE CAN ACT LIKE HOUSEMATES WHEN WE'RE HERE.
?
WAIT. CHIAKI...
...YOU'VE BEEN ROOTING FOR THESE GUYS?
You support their relationship?

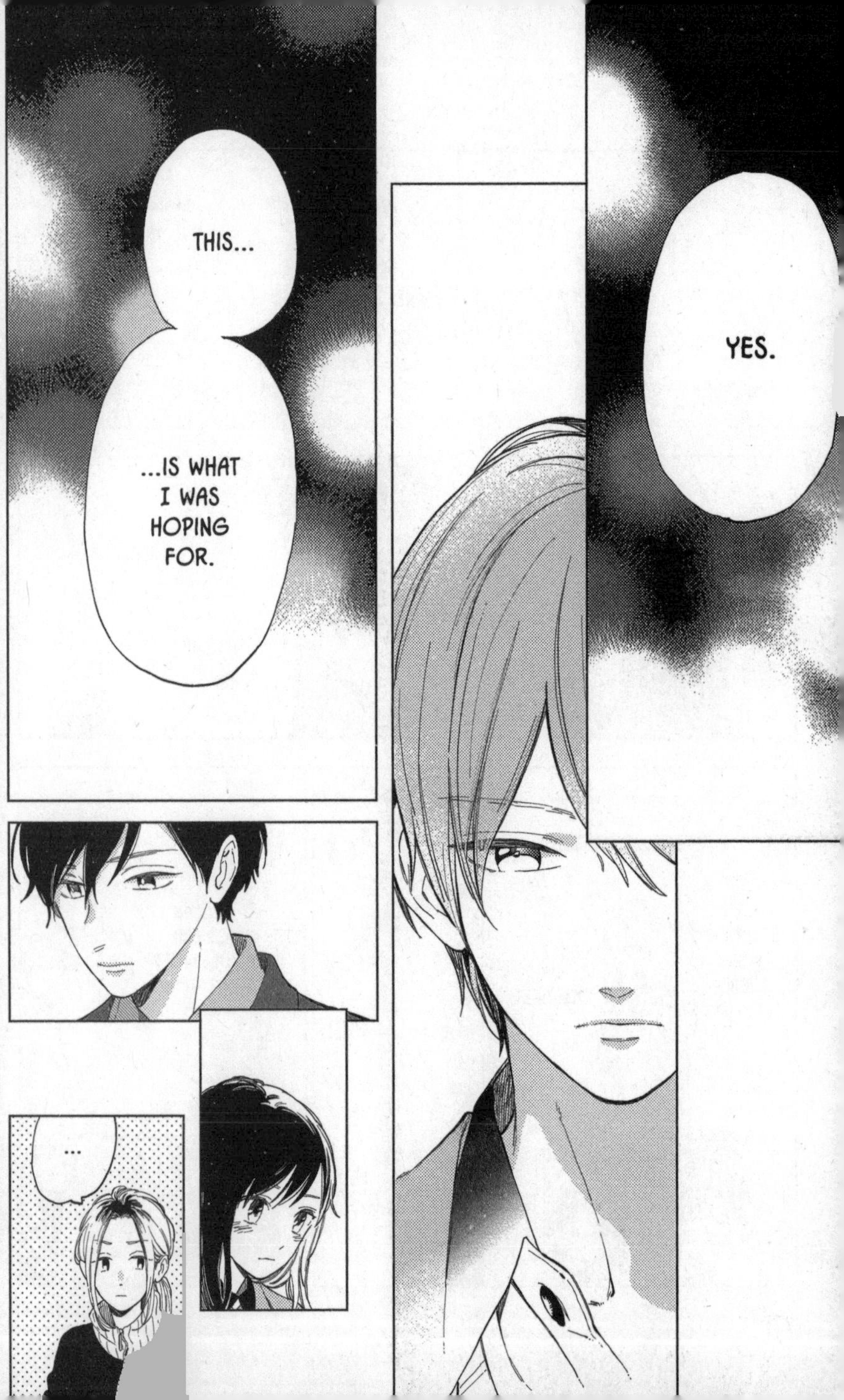
YES.
THIS...
...IS WHAT I WAS HOPING FOR.
...

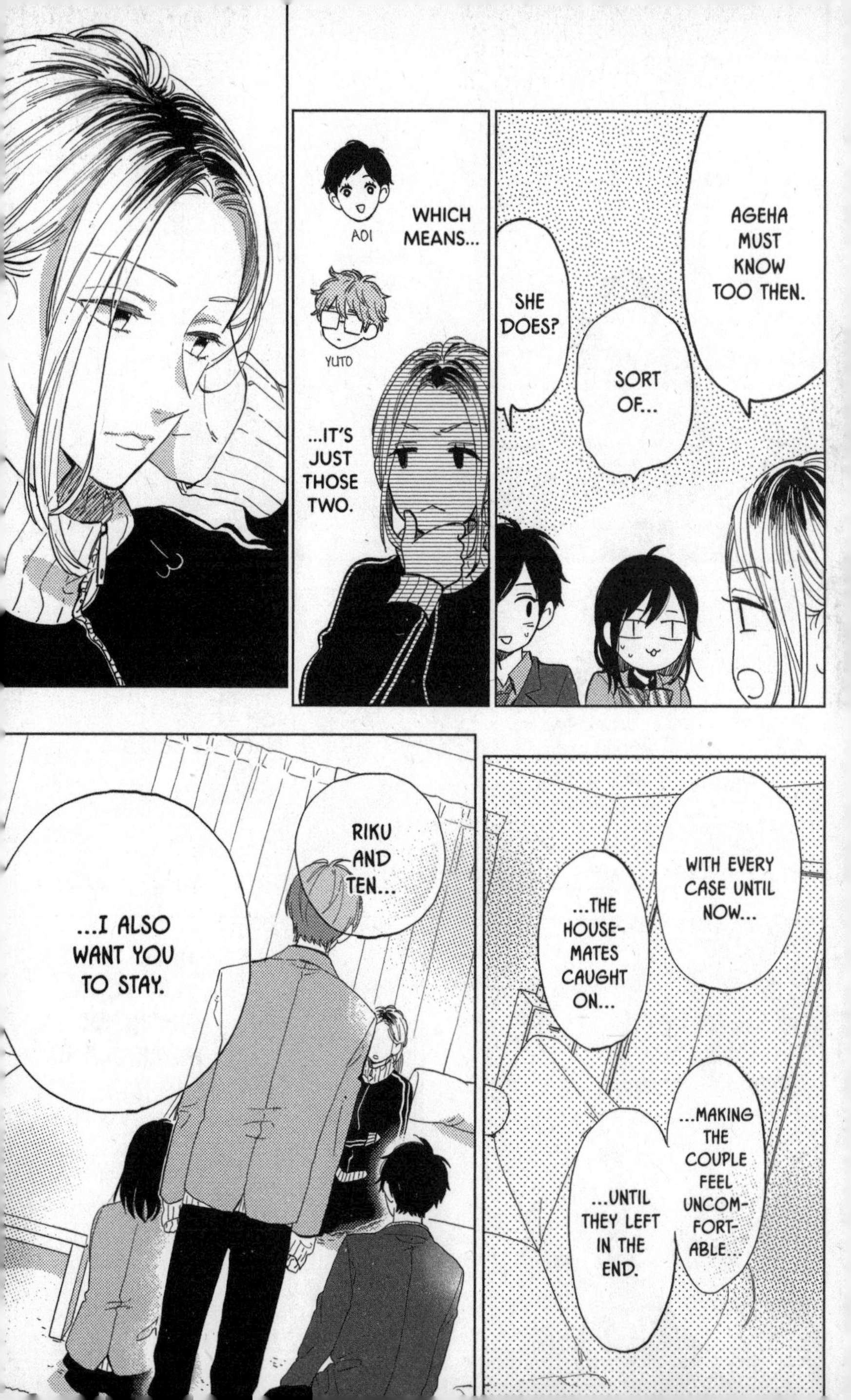
AGEHA MUST KNOW TOO THEN.
SHE DOES?
SORT OF...
WHICH MEANS...
AOI
YUTO
...IT'S JUST THOSE TWO.
WITH EVERY CASE UNTIL NOW...
...THE HOUSE-MATES CAUGHT ON...
...MAKING THE COUPLE FEEL UNCOM-FORT-ABLE...
...UNTIL THEY LEFT IN THE END.
RIKU AND TEN...
...I ALSO WANT YOU TO STAY.

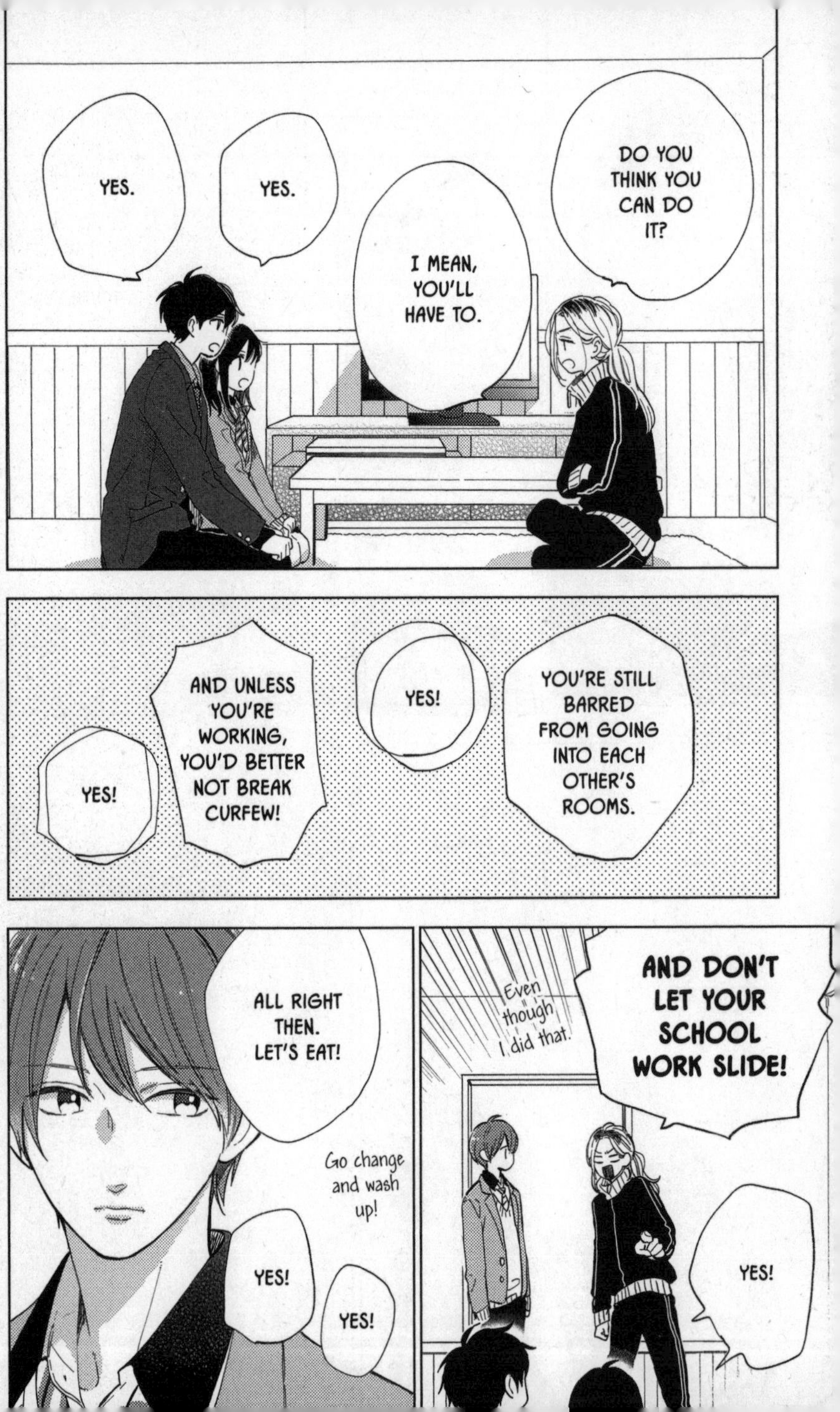
DO YOU THINK YOU CAN DO IT?
I MEAN, YOU'LL HAVE TO.
YES.
YES.
YOU'RE STILL BARRED FROM GOING INTO EACH OTHER'S ROOMS.
YES!
AND UNLESS YOU'RE WORKING, YOU'D BETTER NOT BREAK CURFEW!
YES!
AND DON'T LET YOUR SCHOOL WORK SLIDE!
Even though I did that.
YES!
ALL RIGHT THEN. LET'S EAT!
Go change and wash up!
YES!
YES!

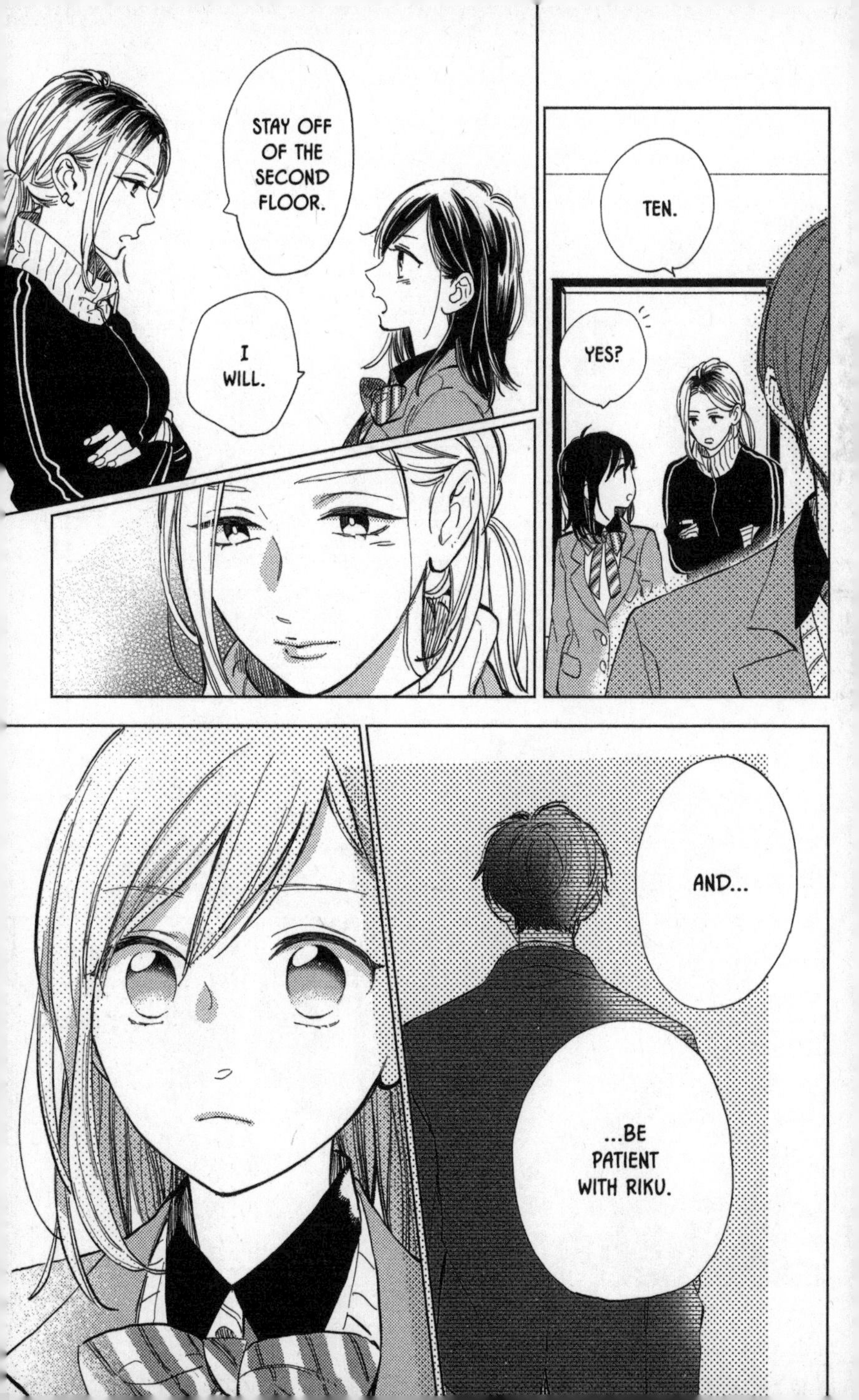
TEN.
YES?
STAY OFF OF THE SECOND FLOOR.
I WILL.
AND...
...BE PATIENT WITH RIKU.

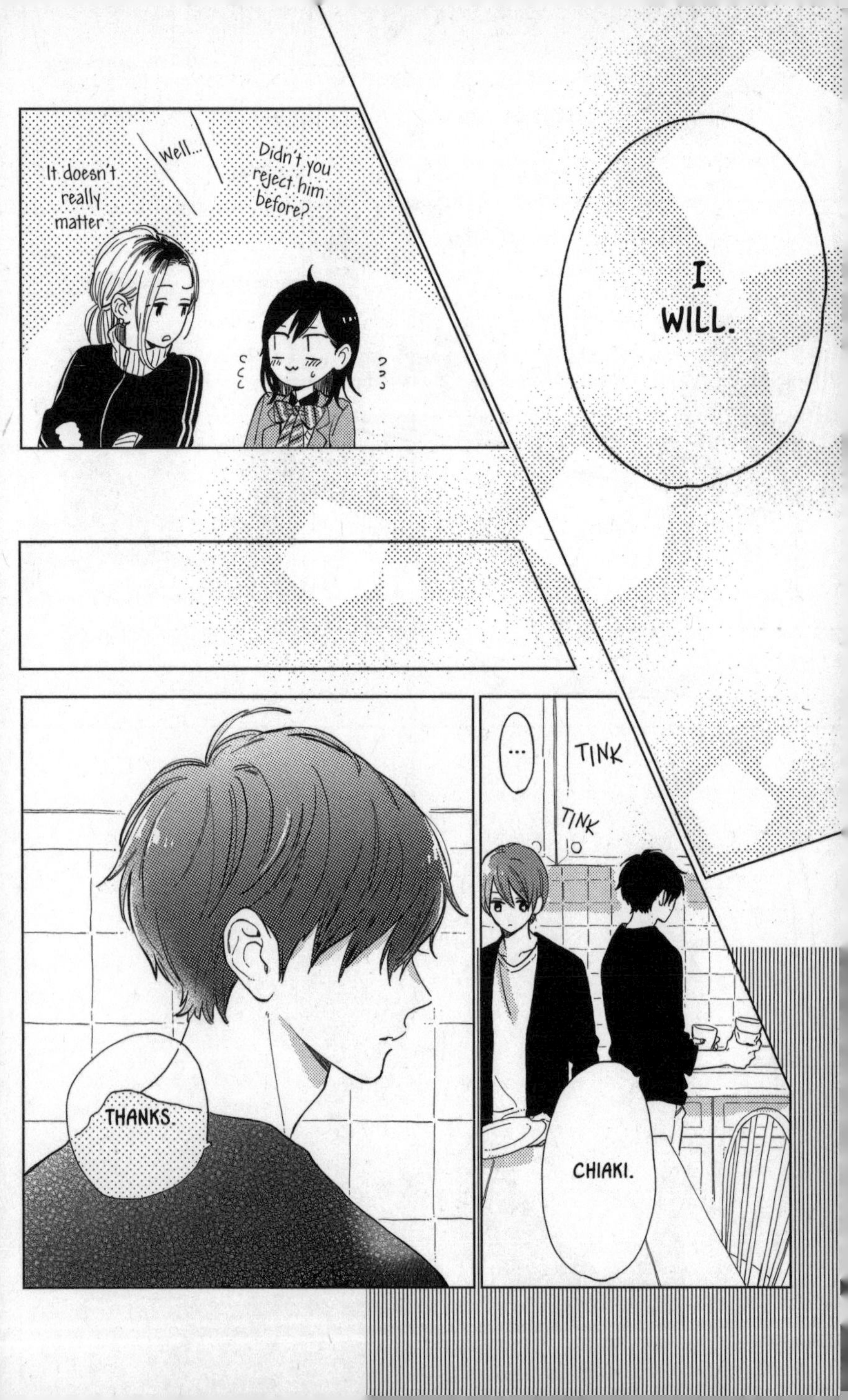
I WILL.
Didn't you reject him before?
Well...
It doesn't really matter.
...
TINK
TINK
CHIAKI.
THANKS.

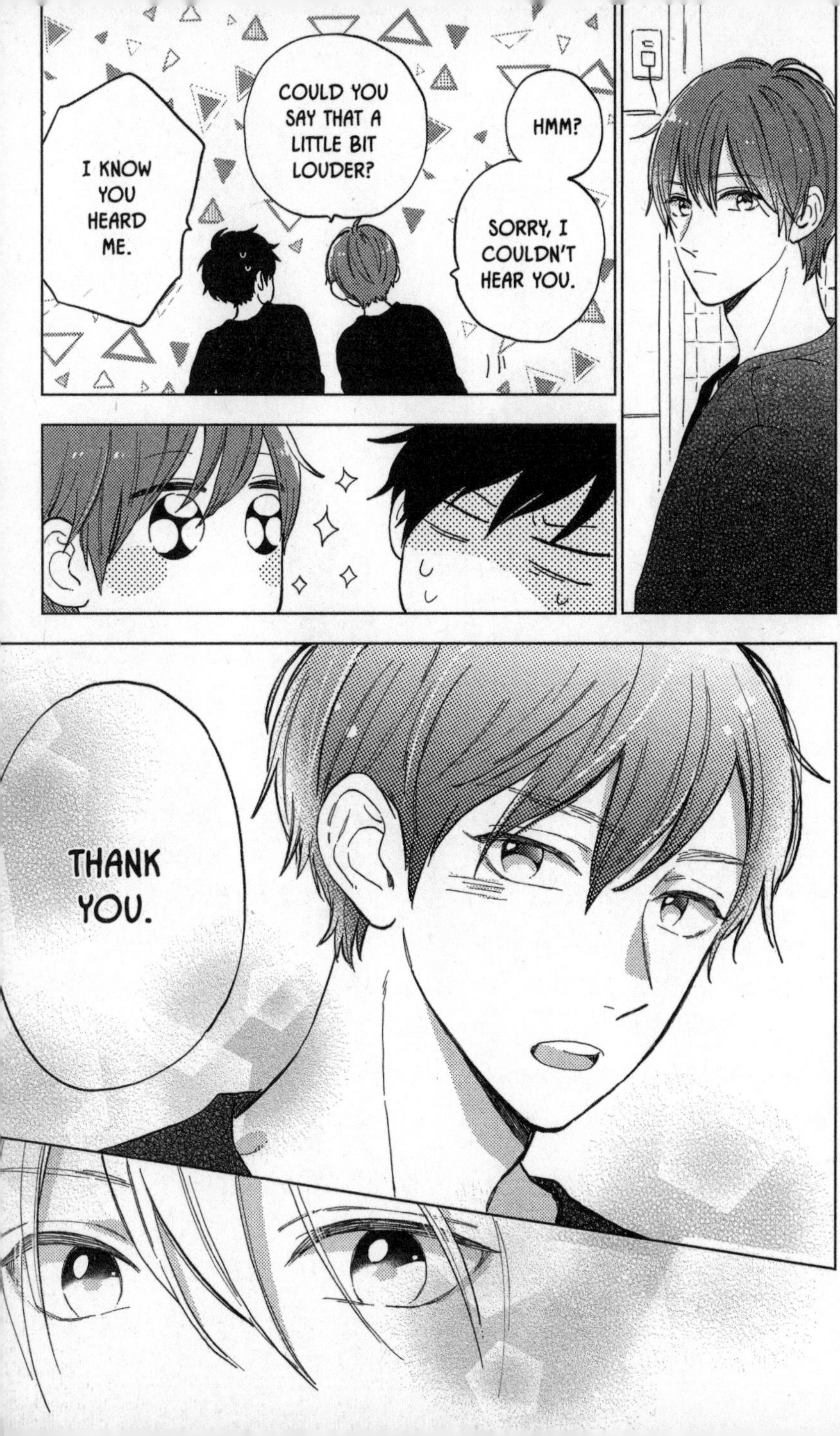
HMM?
SORRY, I COULDN'T HEAR YOU.
COULD YOU SAY THAT A LITTLE BIT LOUDER?
I KNOW YOU HEARD ME.
THANK YOU.

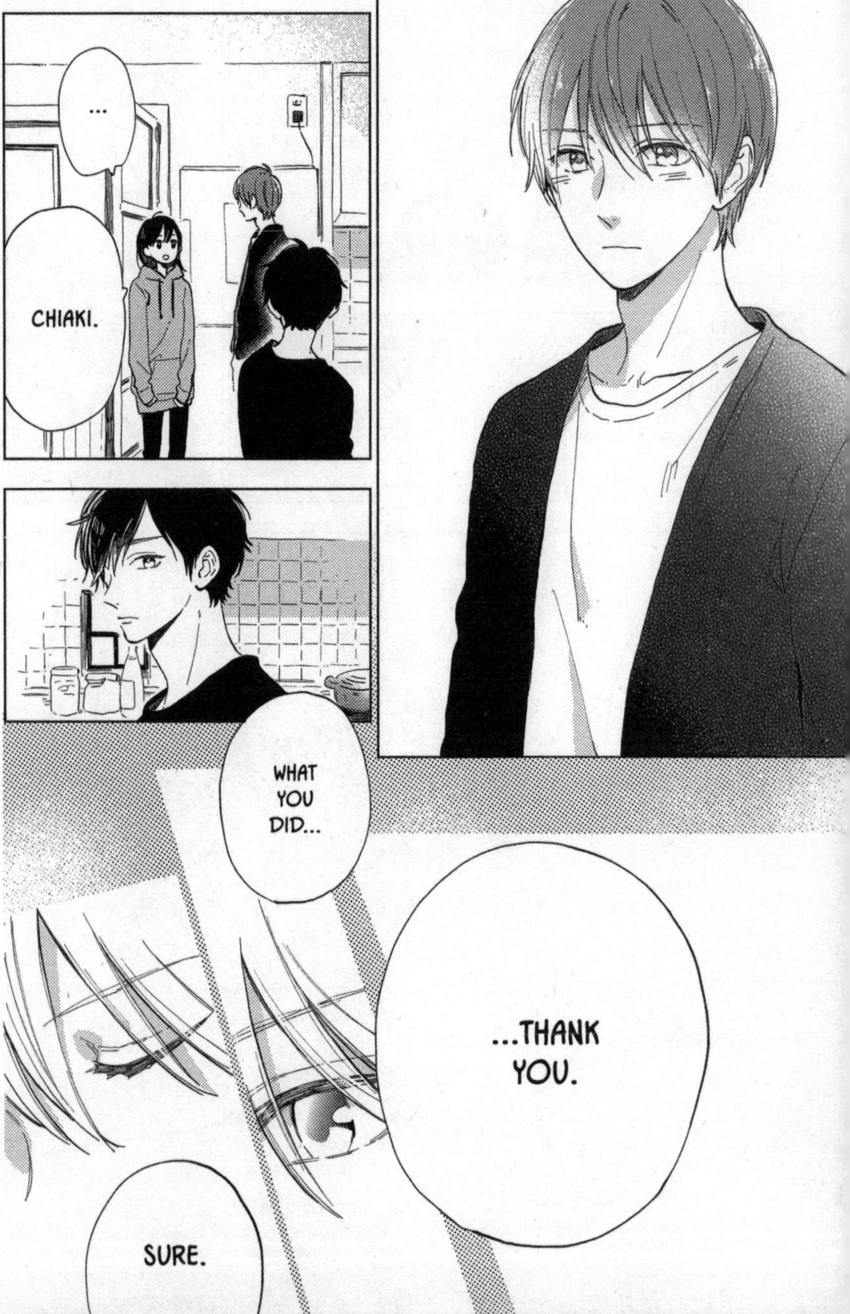
...
CHIAKI.
WHAT YOU DID...
...THANK YOU.
SURE.

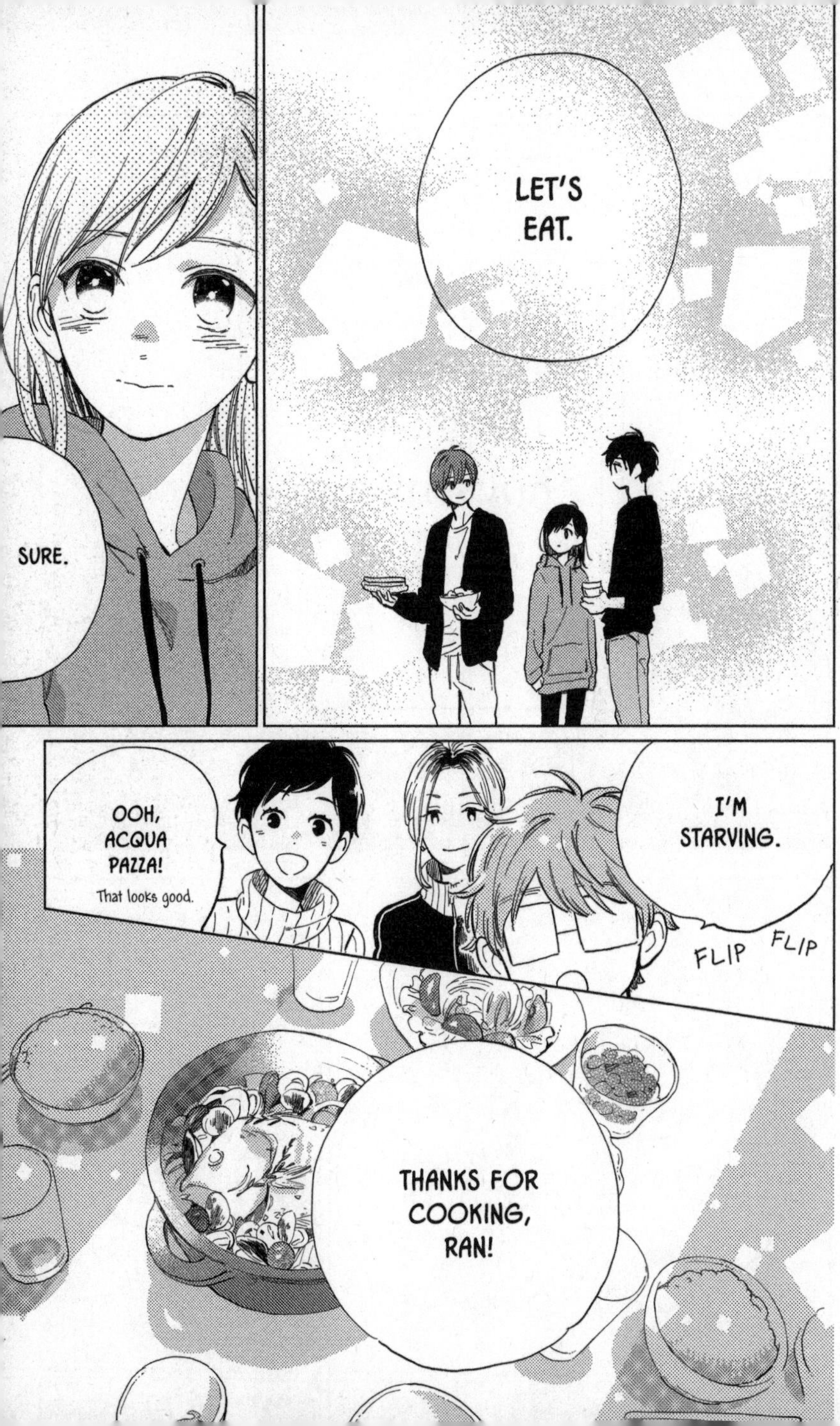
LET'S EAT.
SURE.
I'M STARVING.
FLIP FLIP
OOH, ACQUA PAZZA!
That looks good.
THANKS FOR COOKING, RAN!

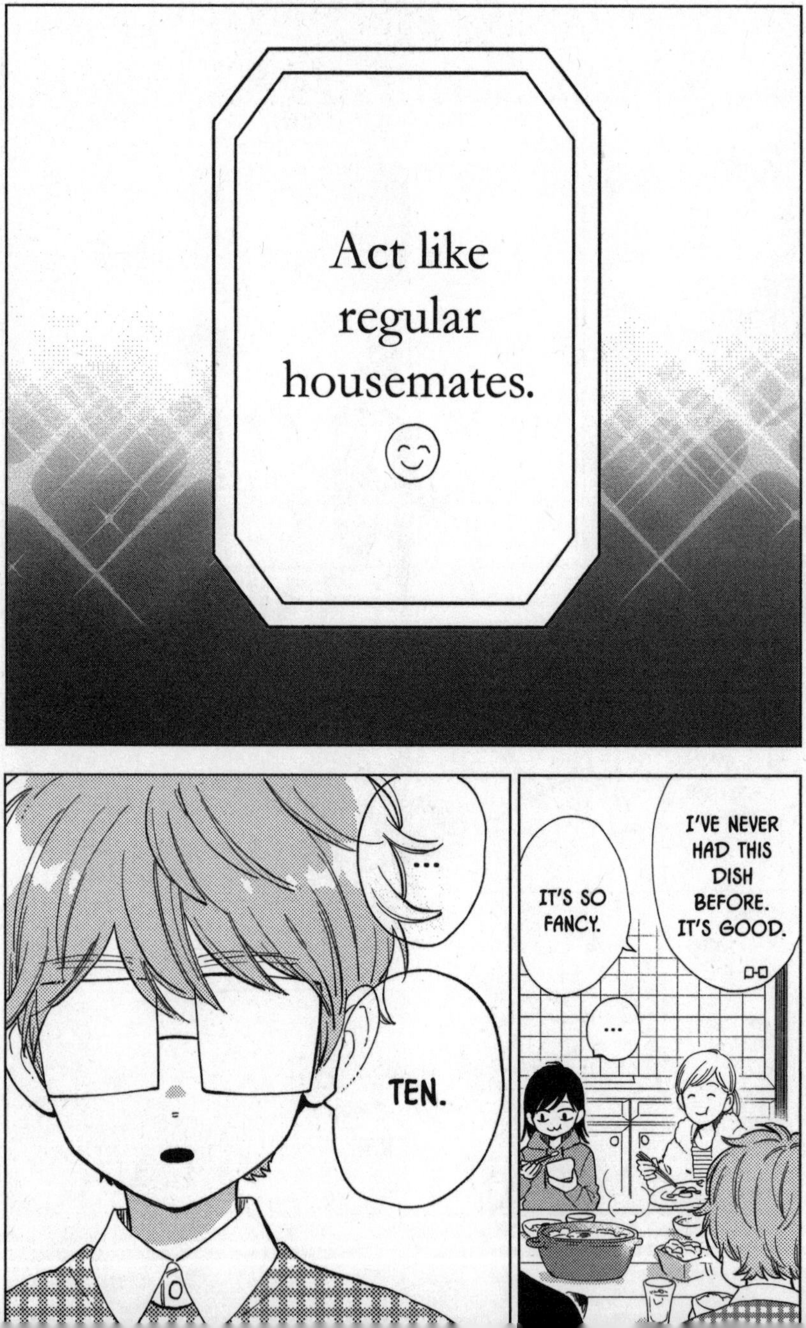
Act like regular housemates.
I'VE NEVER HAD THIS DISH BEFORE. IT'S GOOD.
IT'S SO FANCY.
...
...
TEN.

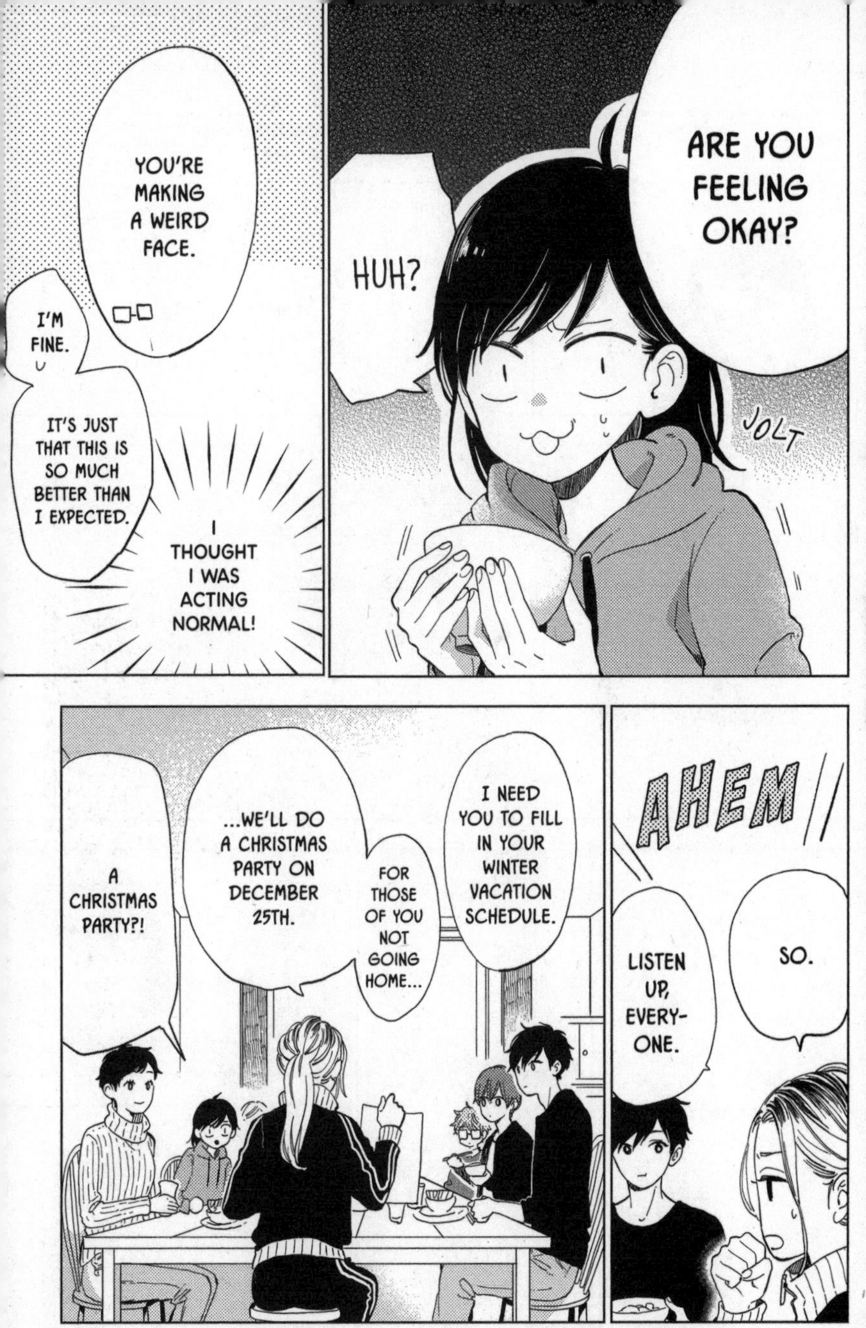
ARE YOU FEELING OKAY?
HUH?
JOLT
YOU'RE MAKING A WEIRD FACE.
I'M FINE.
IT'S JUST THAT THIS IS SO MUCH BETTER THAN I EXPECTED.
I THOUGHT I WAS ACTING NORMAL!
AHEM
SO.
LISTEN UP, EVERY-ONE.
I NEED YOU TO FILL IN YOUR WINTER VACATION SCHEDULE.
FOR THOSE OF YOU NOT GOING HOME...
...WE'LL DO A CHRISTMAS PARTY ON DECEMBER 25TH.
A CHRISTMAS PARTY?!

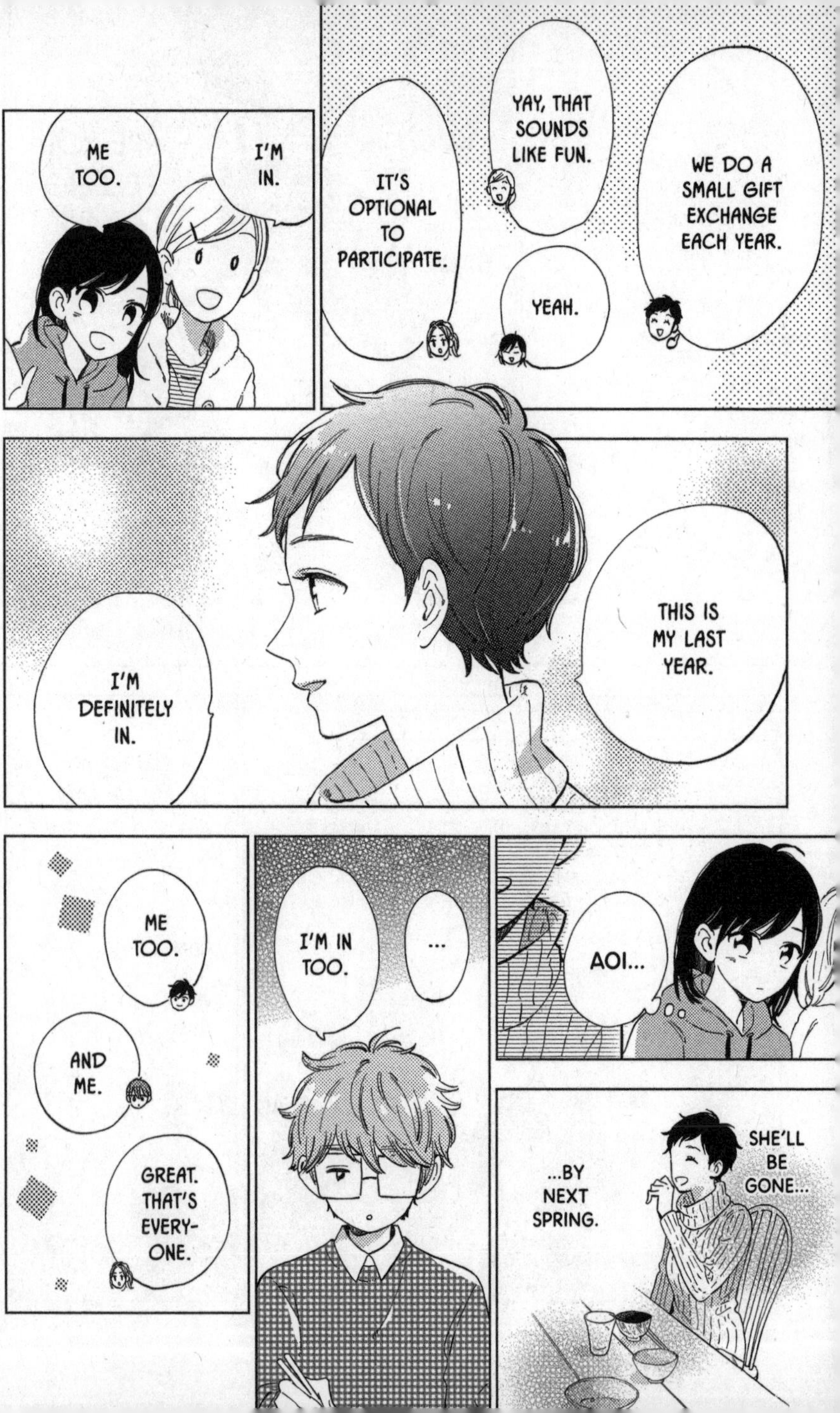
WE DO A SMALL GIFT EXCHANGE EACH YEAR.
YEAH.
YAY, THAT SOUNDS LIKE FUN.
IT'S OPTIONAL TO PARTICIPATE.
I'M IN.
ME TOO.
THIS IS MY LAST YEAR.
I'M DEFINITELY IN.
AOI...
SHE'LL BE GONE...
...BY NEXT SPRING.
...
I'M IN TOO.
ME TOO.
AND ME.
GREAT. THAT'S EVERY-ONE.

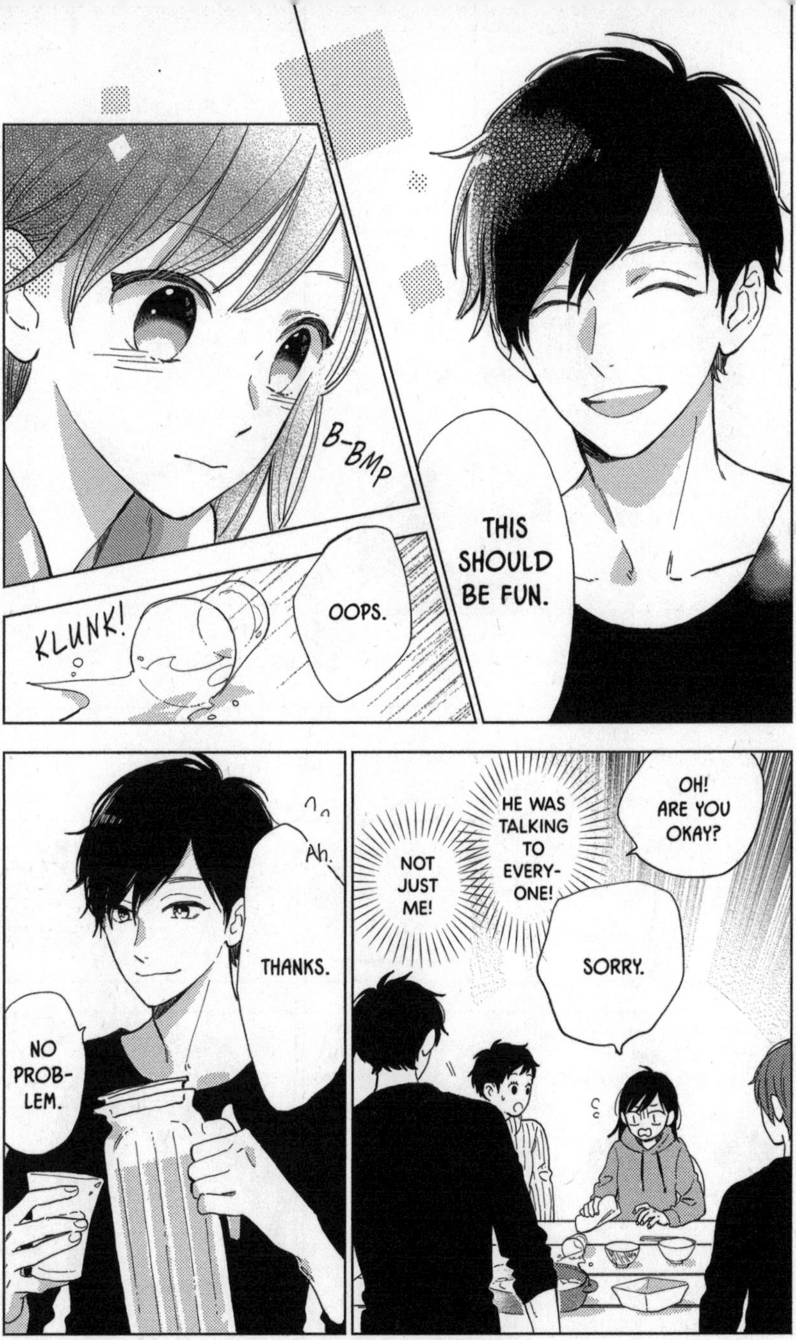
THIS SHOULD BE FUN.
B-BMP
OOPS.
KLUNK!
OH! ARE YOU OKAY?
HE WAS TALKING TO EVERY-ONE!
NOT JUST ME!
SORRY.
Ah.
THANKS.
NO PROB-LEM.

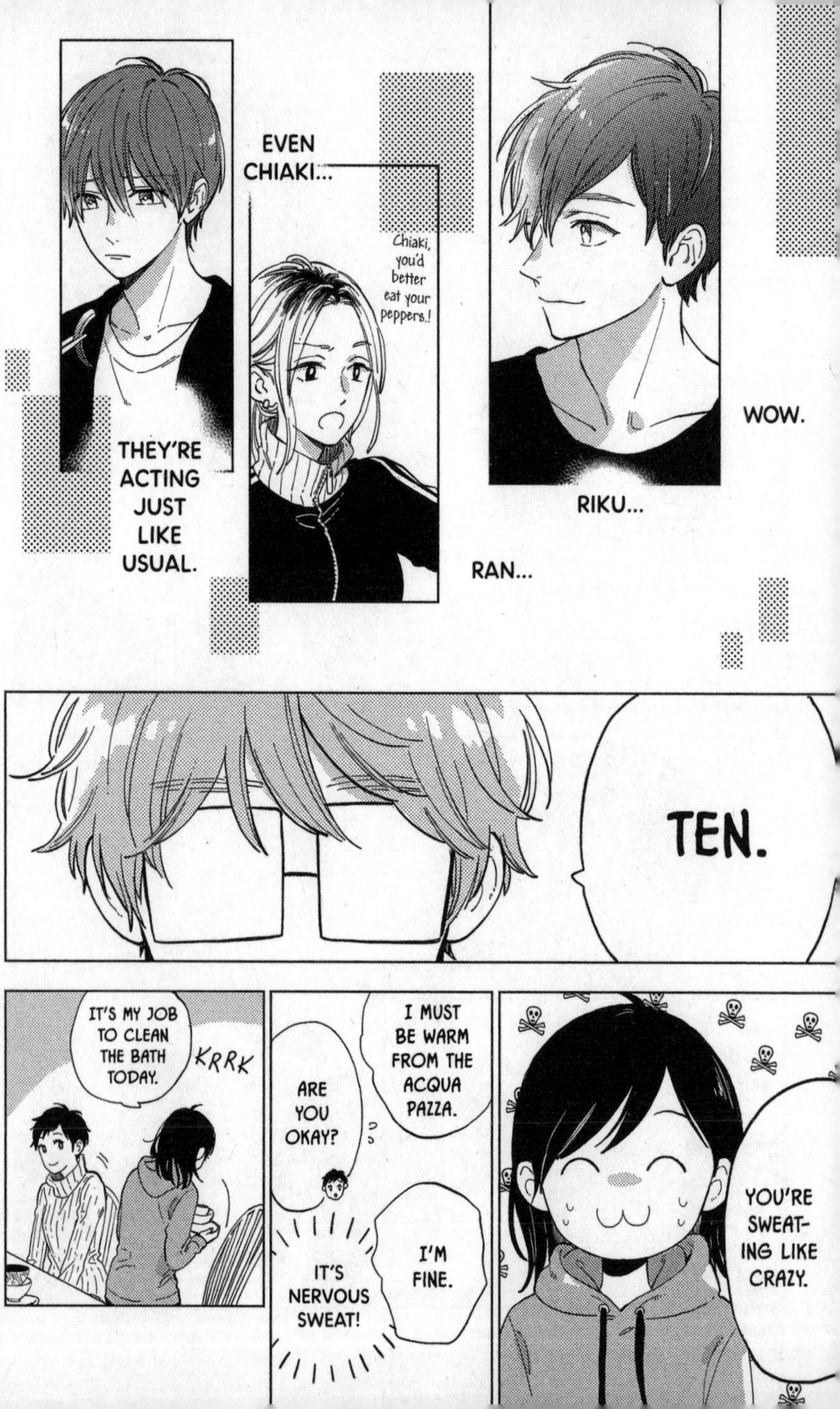
WOW.
RIKU...
RAN...
EVEN CHIAKI...
Chiaki, you'd better eat your peppers.!
THEY'RE ACTING JUST LIKE USUAL.
TEN.
YOU'RE SWEAT-ING LIKE CRAZY.
I MUST BE WARM FROM THE ACQUA PAZZA.
ARE YOU OKAY?
I'M FINE.
IT'S NERVOUS SWEAT!
IT'S MY JOB TO CLEAN THE BATH TODAY.
KRRK

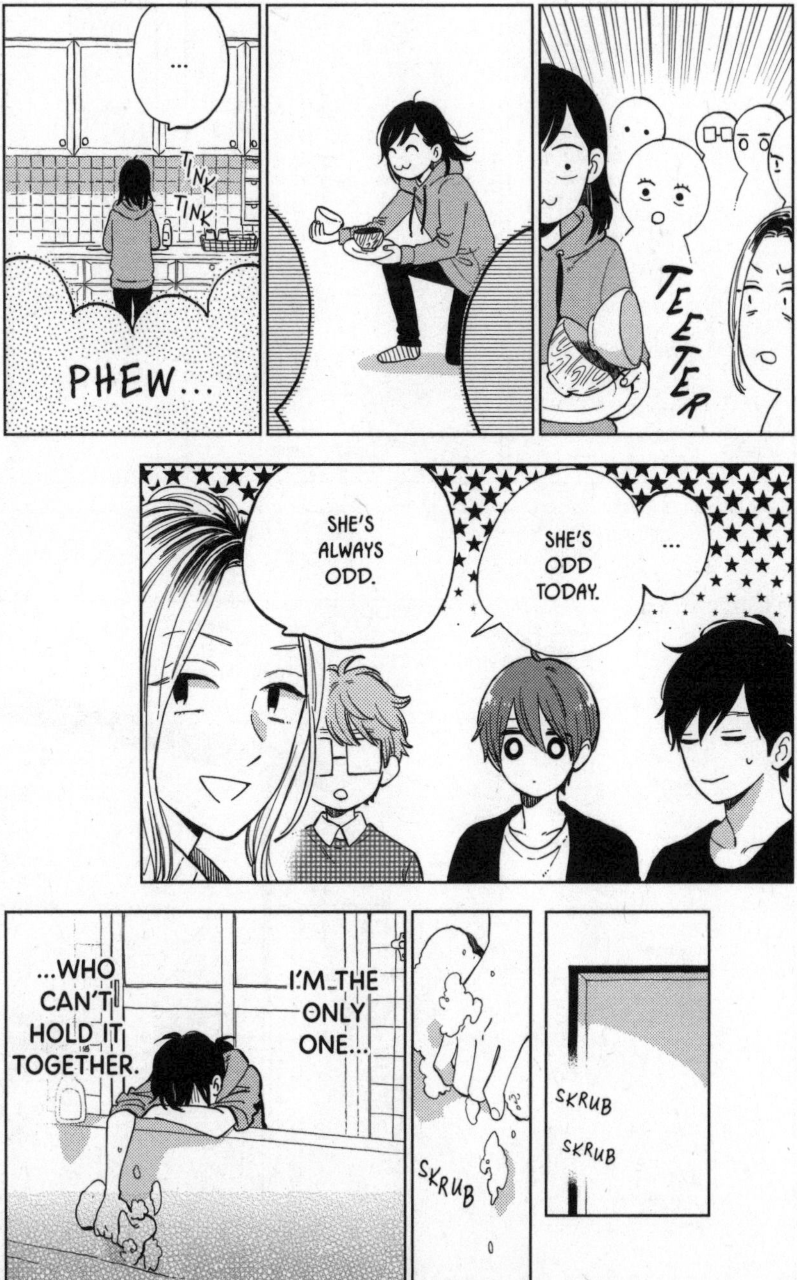
TEETER
...
TINK TINK
PHEW...
...
SHE'S ODD TODAY.
SHE'S ALWAYS ODD.
SKRUB
SKRUB
SKRUB
I'M THE ONLY ONE...
...WHO CAN'T HOLD IT TOGETHER.

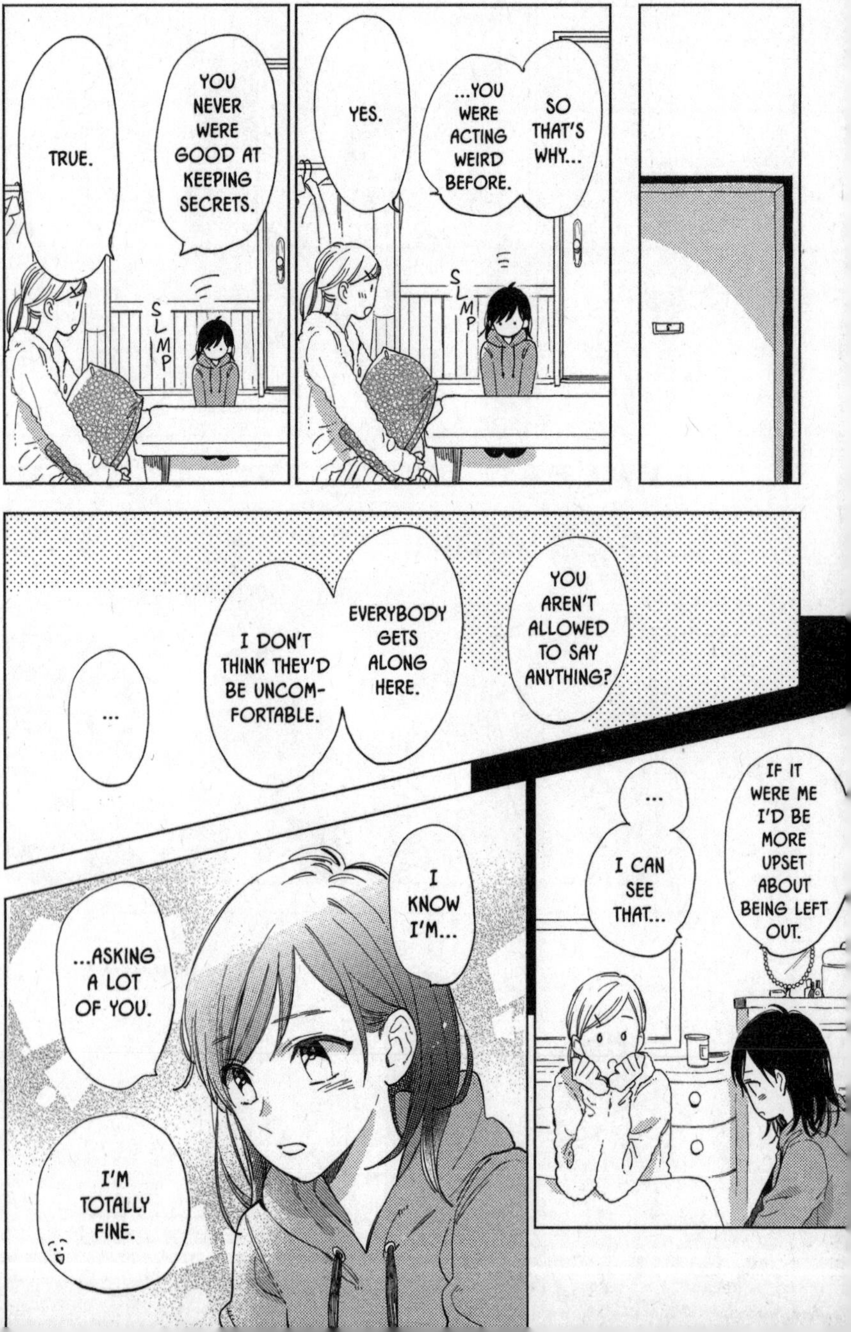
SO THAT'S WHY...
...YOU WERE ACTING WEIRD BEFORE.
YES.
S L M P
YOU NEVER WERE GOOD AT KEEPING SECRETS.
TRUE.
S L M P
YOU AREN'T ALLOWED TO SAY ANYTHING?
EVERYBODY GETS ALONG HERE.
I DON'T THINK THEY'D BE UNCOM-FORTABLE.
...
IF IT WERE ME I'D BE MORE UPSET ABOUT BEING LEFT OUT.
...
I CAN SEE THAT...
I KNOW I'M...
...ASKING A LOT OF YOU.
I'M TOTALLY FINE.

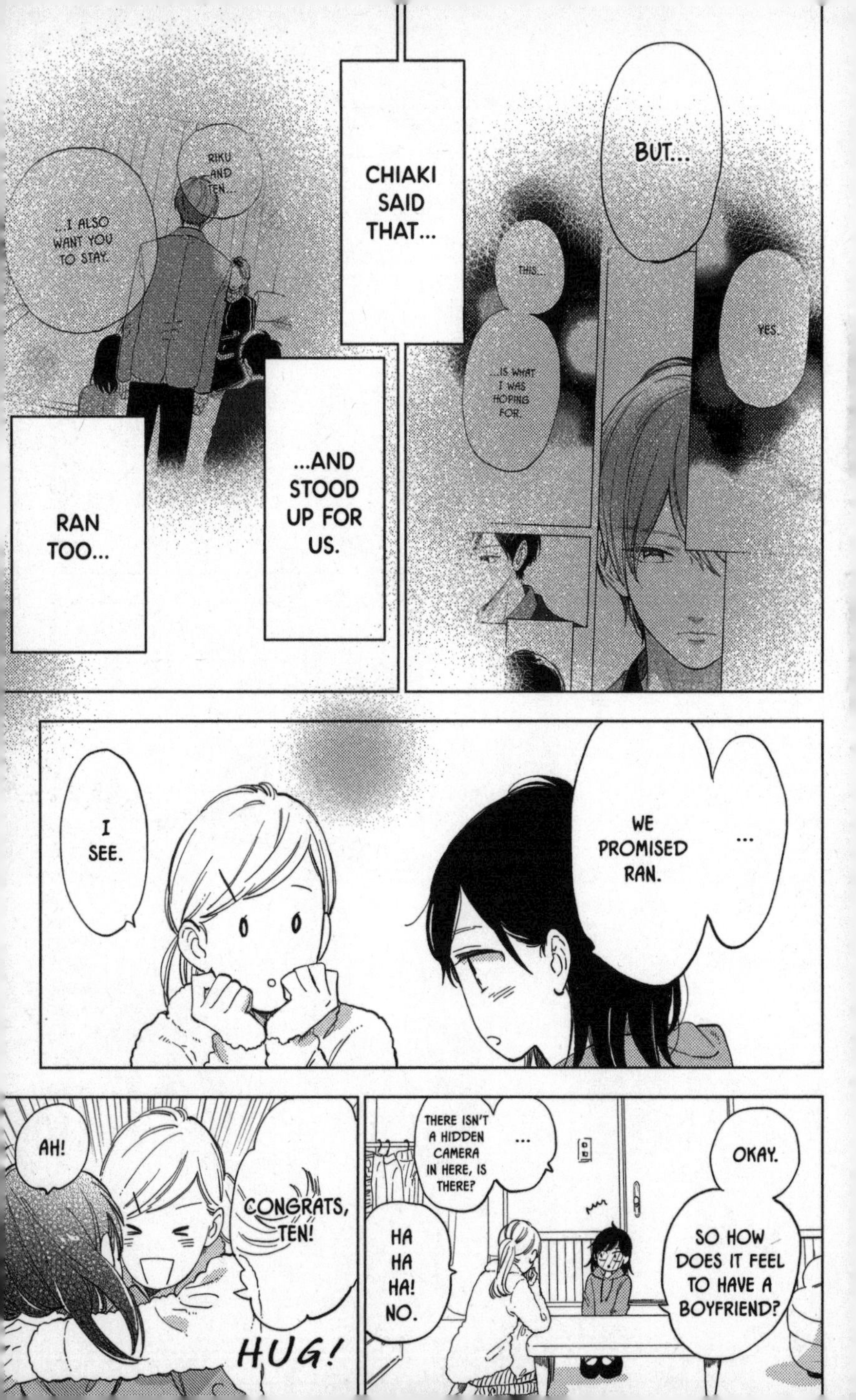
BUT...
YES.
THIS...
...IS WHAT I WAS HOPING FOR.
CHIAKI SAID THAT...
RIKU AND TEN...
...I ALSO WANT YOU TO STAY.
...AND STOOD UP FOR US.
RAN TOO...
WE PROMISED RAN.
...
I SEE.
OKAY.
SO HOW DOES IT FEEL TO HAVE A BOYFRIEND?
...
THERE ISN'T A HIDDEN CAMERA IN HERE, IS THERE?
HA HA HA! NO.
CONGRATS, TEN!
AH!
HUG!

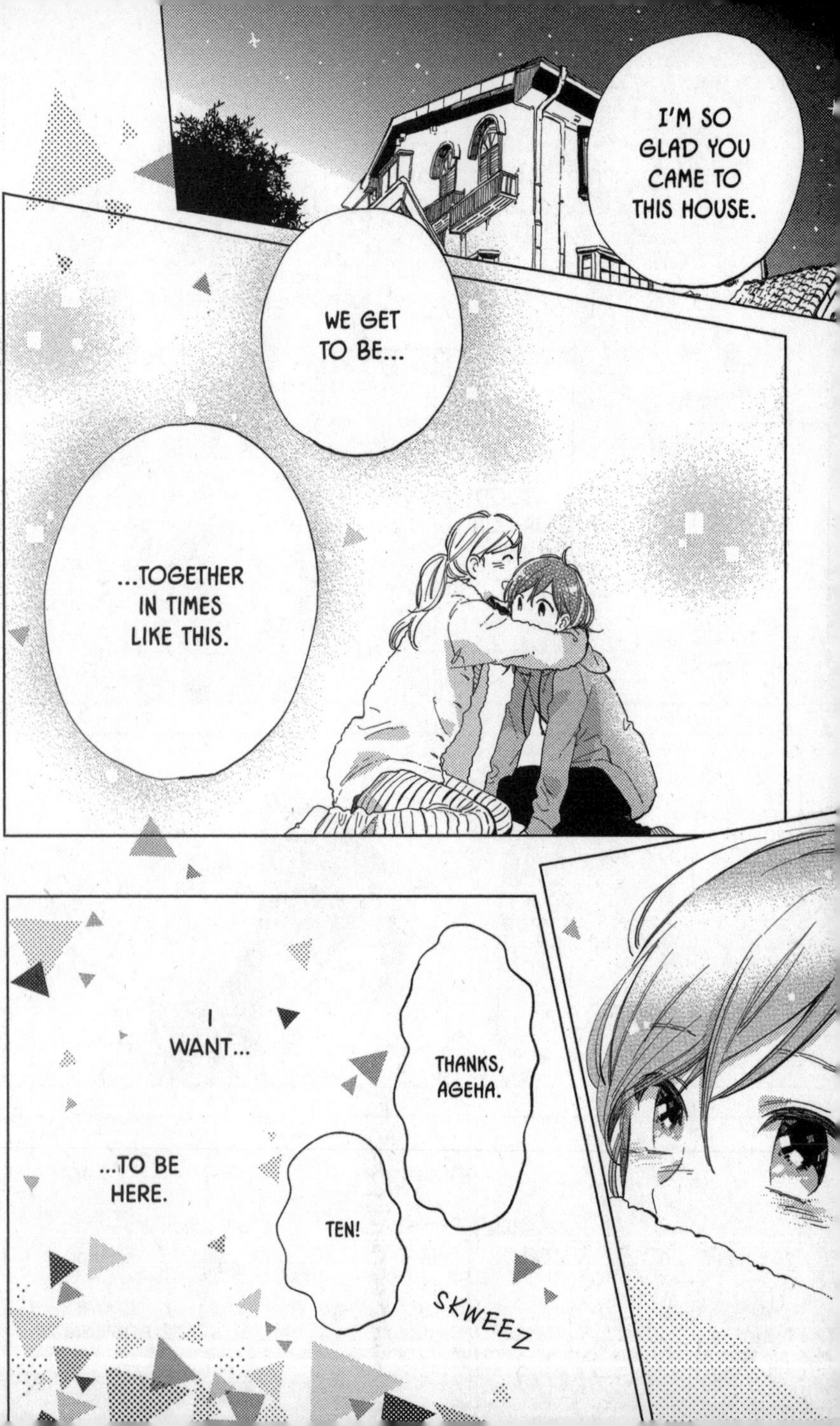
I'M SO GLAD YOU CAME TO THIS HOUSE.
WE GET TO BE...
...TOGETHER IN TIMES LIKE THIS.
THANKS, AGEHA.
TEN!
I WANT...
...TO BE HERE.
SKWEEZ

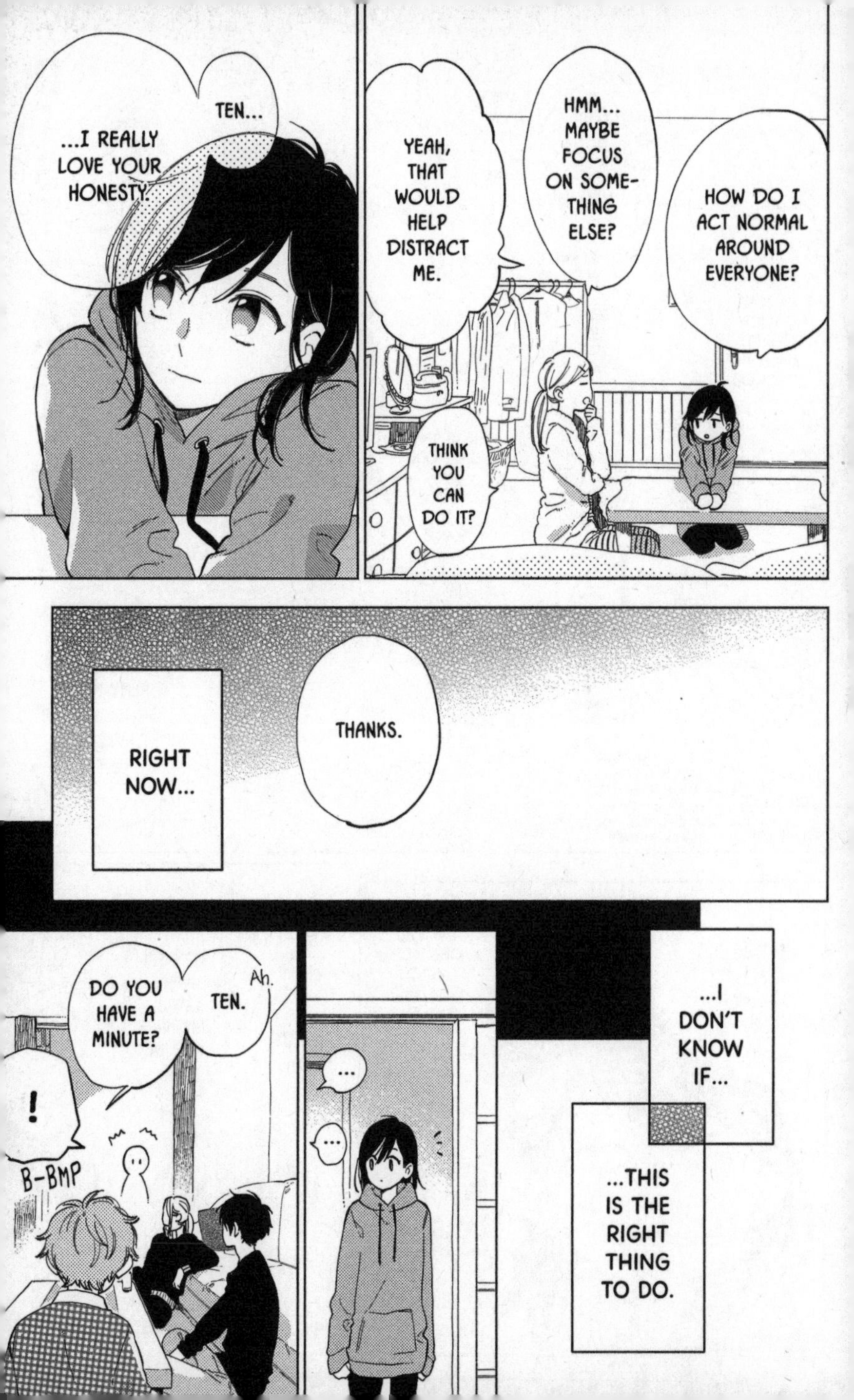
HOW DO I ACT NORMAL AROUND EVERYONE?
HMM... MAYBE FOCUS ON SOME-THING ELSE?
YEAH, THAT WOULD HELP DISTRACT ME.
THINK YOU CAN DO IT?
TEN...
...I REALLY LOVE YOUR HONESTY.
THANKS.
RIGHT NOW...
...I DON'T KNOW IF...
...THIS IS THE RIGHT THING TO DO.
...
...
Ah.
TEN.
DO YOU HAVE A MINUTE?
!
B-BMP

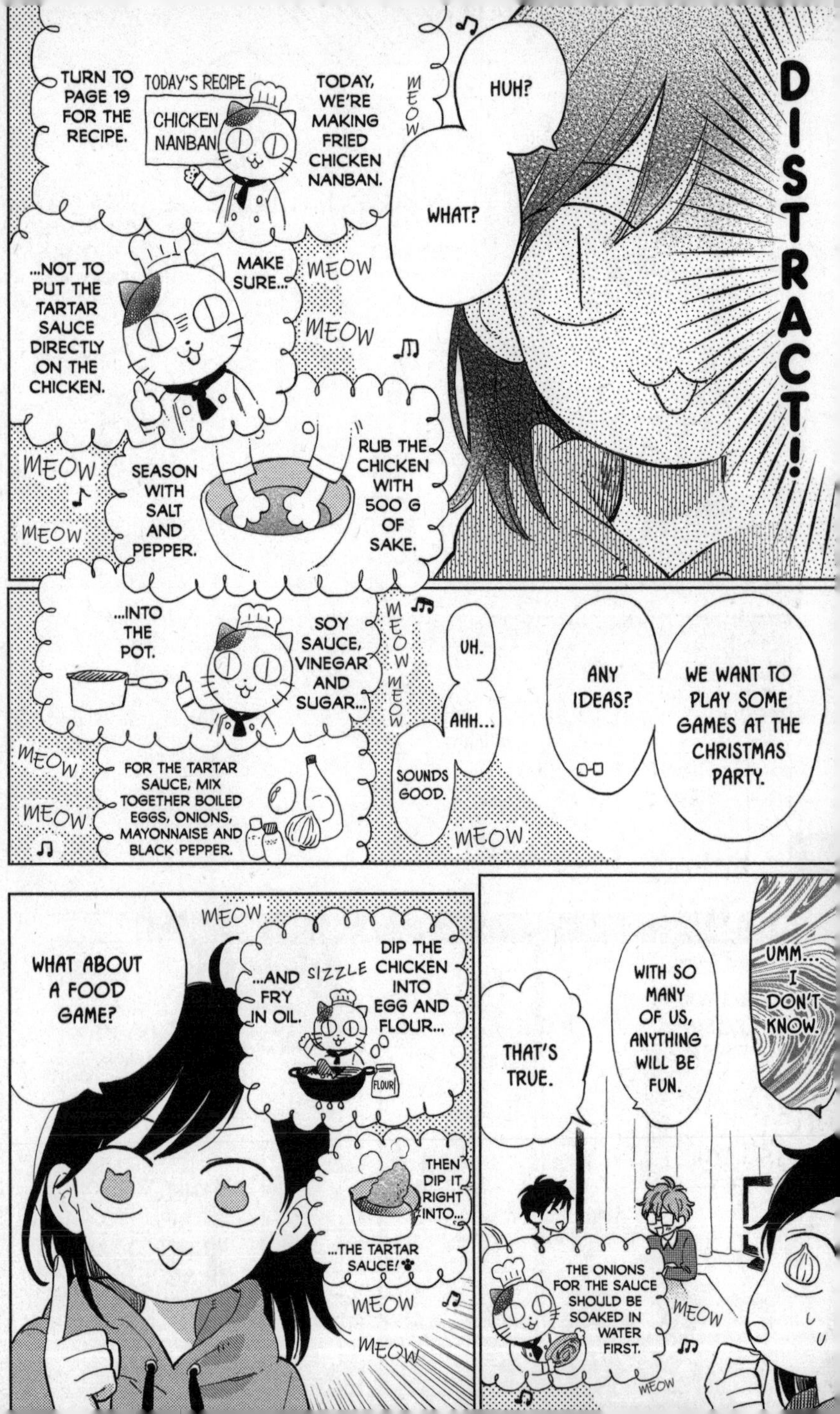
DISTRACT!
HUH?
WHAT?
TODAY, WE'RE MAKING FRIED CHICKEN NANBAN.
MEOW
TODAY'S RECIPE
CHICKEN NANBAN
TURN TO PAGE 19 FOR THE RECIPE.
MEOW
MEOW
MAKE SURE...
...NOT TO PUT THE TARTAR SAUCE DIRECTLY ON THE CHICKEN.
RUB THE CHICKEN WITH 500 G OF SAKE.
SEASON WITH SALT AND PEPPER.
MEOW
MEOW
WE WANT TO PLAY SOME GAMES AT THE CHRISTMAS PARTY.
ANY IDEAS?
UH.
AHH...
SOUNDS GOOD.
MEOW
MEOW
MEOW
SOY SAUCE, VINEGAR AND SUGAR...
...INTO THE POT.
FOR THE TARTAR SAUCE, MIX TOGETHER BOILED EGGS, ONIONS, MAYONNAISE AND BLACK PEPPER.
MEOW
MEOW
MEOW
UMM... I DON'T KNOW.
WITH SO MANY OF US, ANYTHING WILL BE FUN.
THAT'S TRUE.
THE ONIONS FOR THE SAUCE SHOULD BE SOAKED IN WATER FIRST.
MEOW
MEOW
MEOW
WHAT ABOUT A FOOD GAME?
DIP THE CHICKEN INTO EGG AND FLOUR...
...AND FRY IN OIL.
SIZZLE
FLOUR
THEN DIP IT RIGHT INTO...
...THE TARTAR SAUCE!
MEOW
MEOW

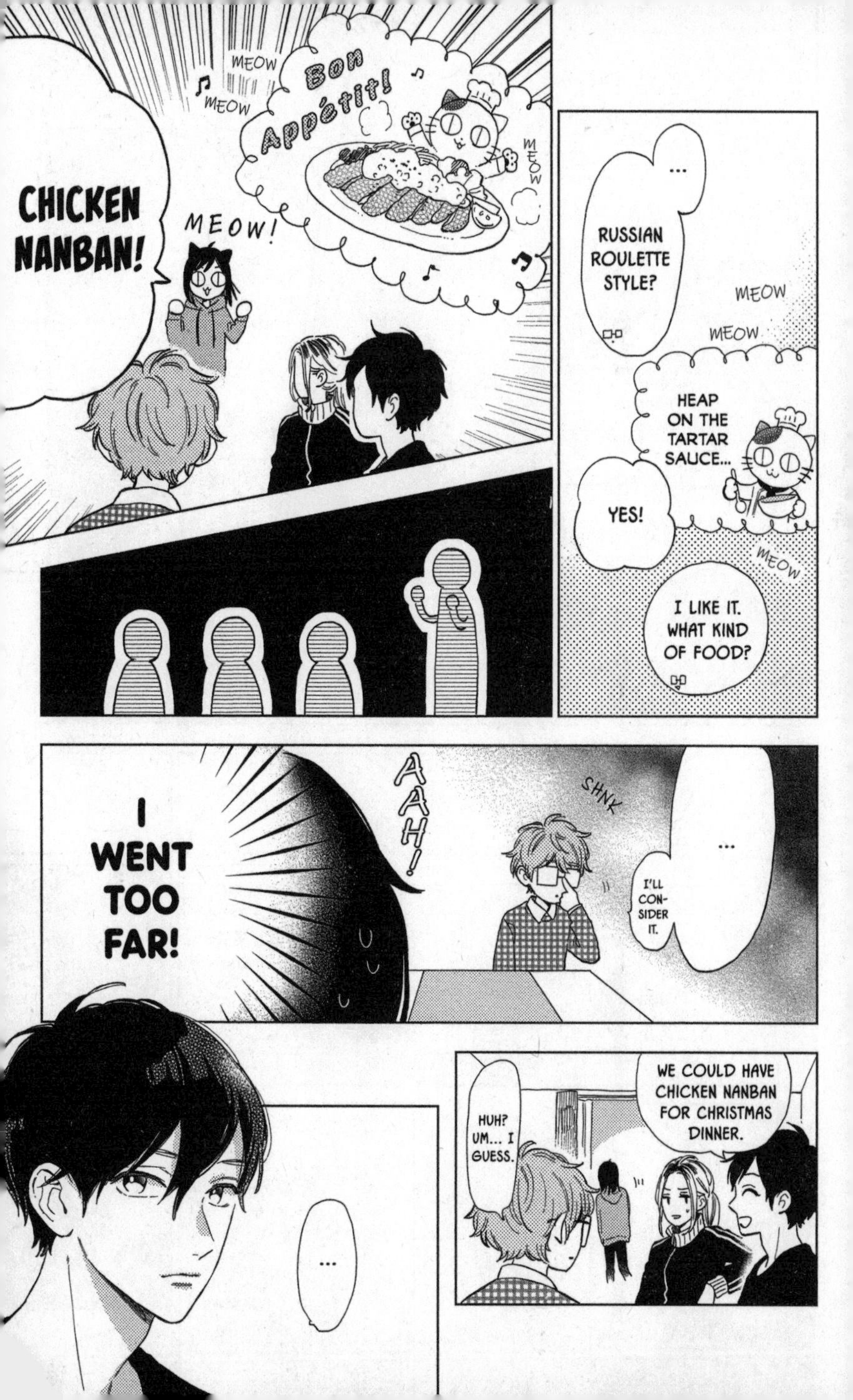
...
RUSSIAN ROULETTE STYLE?
MEOW
MEOW
HEAP ON THE TARTAR SAUCE...
YES!
MEOW
I LIKE IT. WHAT KIND OF FOOD?
MEOW
MEOW
Bon Appétit!
MEOW
MEOW
CHICKEN NANBAN!
MEOW!
...
I'LL CONSIDER IT.
SHNK
AAH!
I WENT TOO FAR!
WE COULD HAVE CHICKEN NANBAN FOR CHRISTMAS DINNER.
HUH? UM... I GUESS.
...

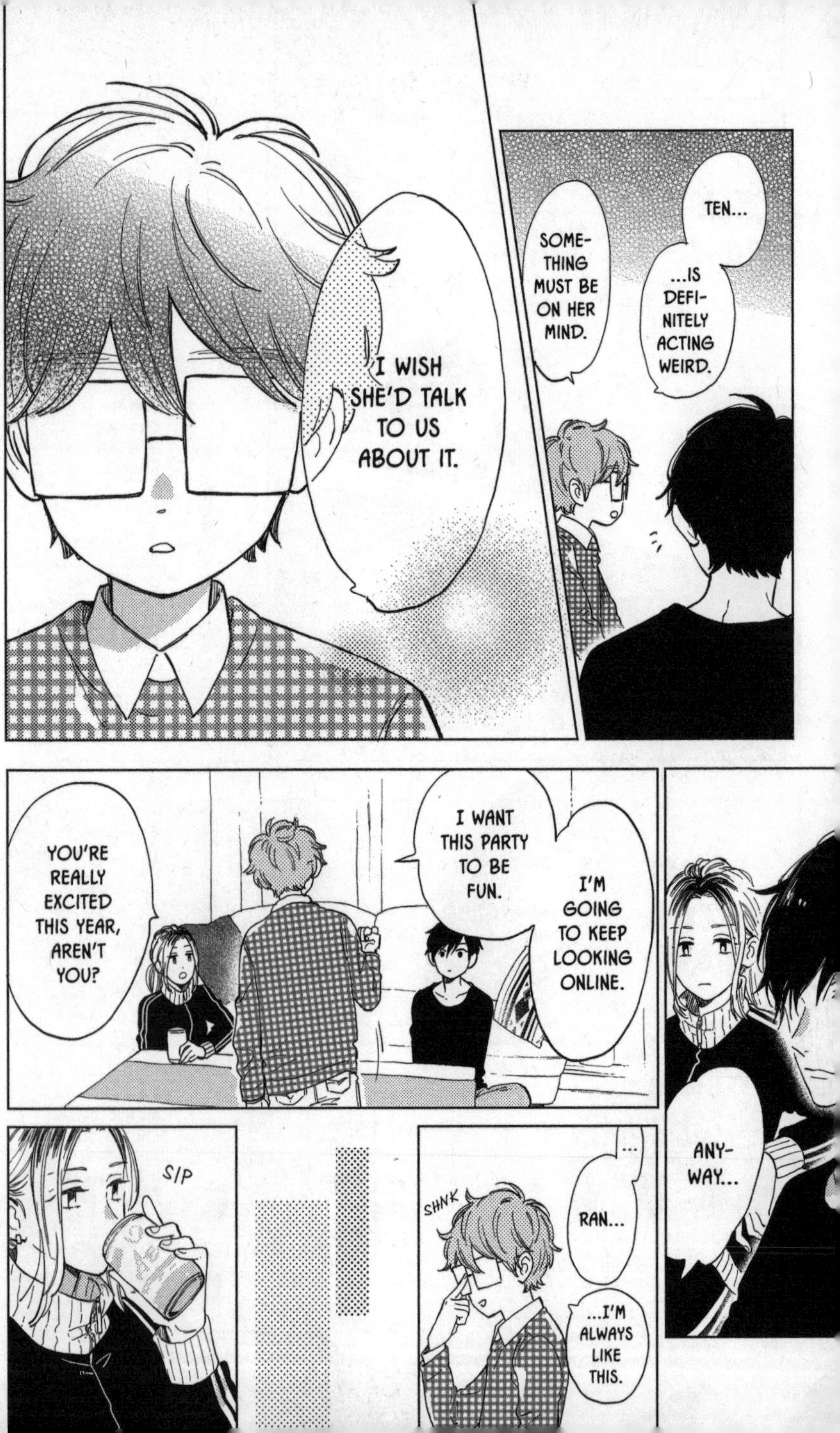
TEN...
...IS DEFINITELY ACTING WEIRD.
SOMETHING MUST BE ON HER MIND.
I WISH SHE'D TALK TO US ABOUT IT.
ANYWAY...
I WANT THIS PARTY TO BE FUN.
I'M GOING TO KEEP LOOKING ONLINE.
YOU'RE REALLY EXCITED THIS YEAR, AREN'T YOU?
...
RAN...
...I'M ALWAYS LIKE THIS.
SHNK
SIP

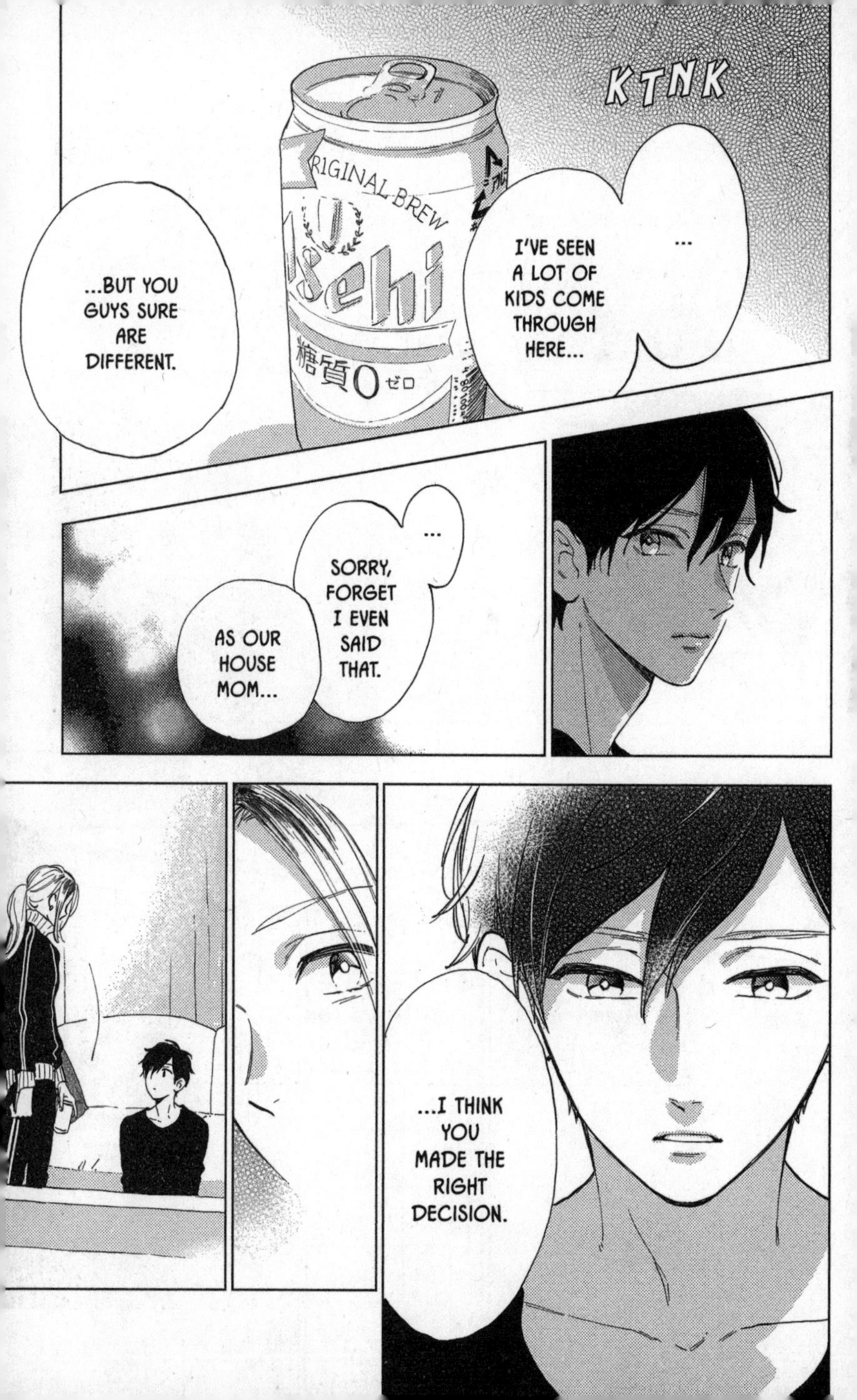
KTNK
...
I'VE SEEN A LOT OF KIDS COME THROUGH HERE...
RIGINAL BREW
糖質0 ゼロ
...BUT YOU GUYS SURE ARE DIFFERENT.
...
SORRY, FORGET I EVEN SAID THAT.
AS OUR HOUSE MOM...
...I THINK YOU MADE THE RIGHT DECISION.

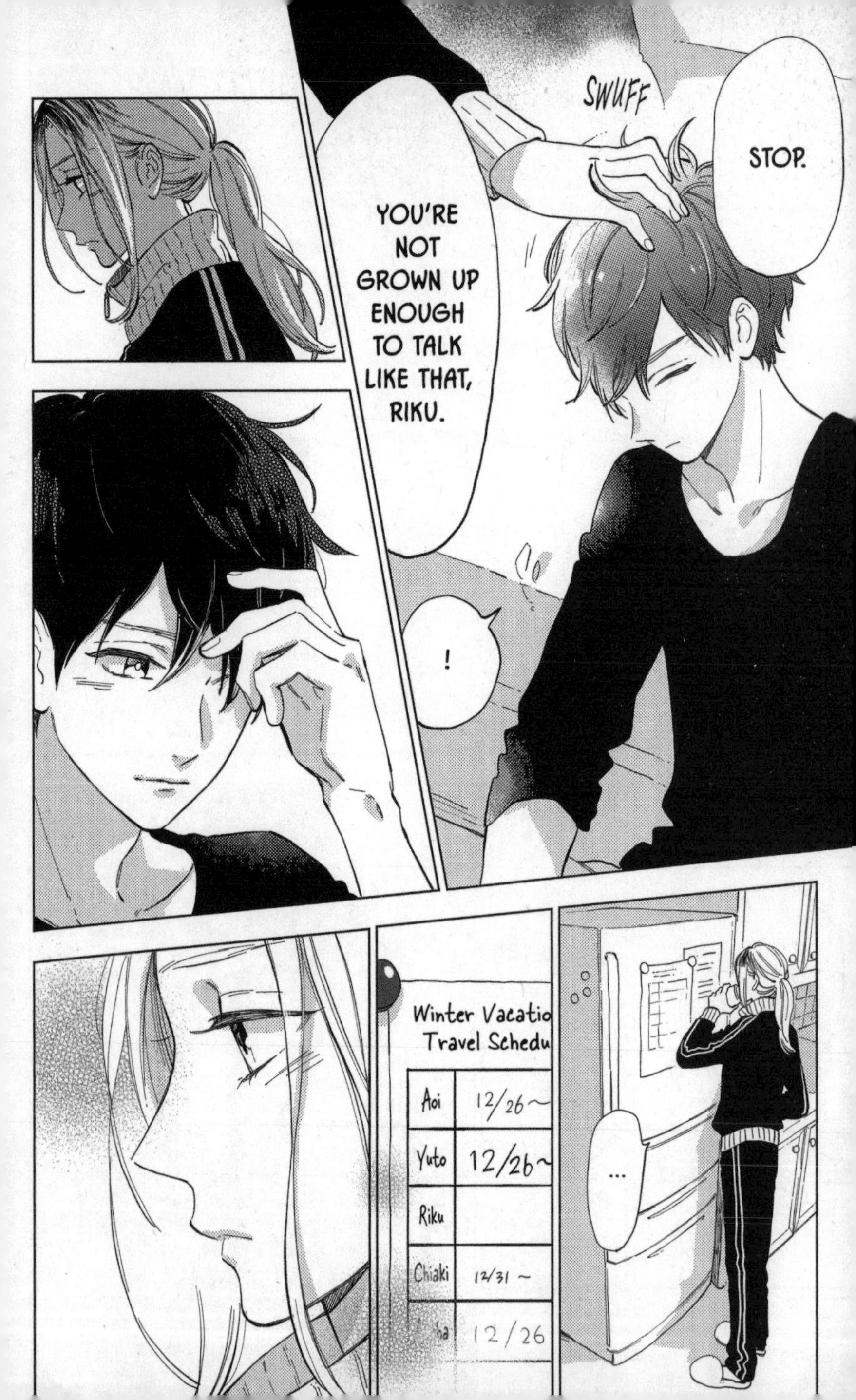
SWUFF
STOP.
YOU'RE NOT GROWN UP ENOUGH TO TALK LIKE THAT, RIKU.
!
...
Winter Vacatio
Travel Schedu
Aoi 12/26~
Yuto 12/26~
Riku
Chiaki 12/31~
12/26

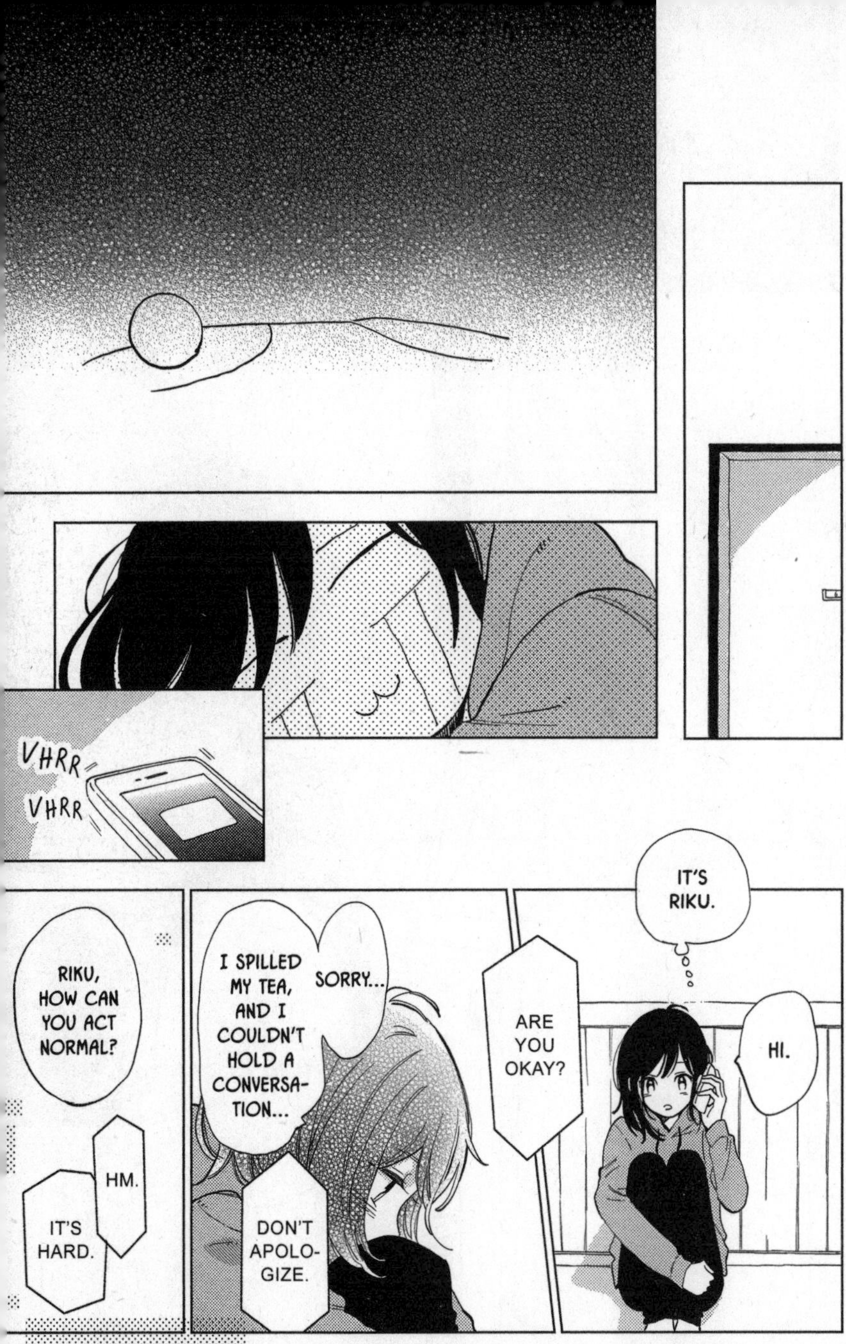
VHRR
VHRR
IT'S RIKU.
HI.
ARE YOU OKAY?
SORRY...
I SPILLED MY TEA, AND I COULDN'T HOLD A CONVERSATION...
DON'T APOLOGIZE.
RIKU, HOW CAN YOU ACT NORMAL?
HM.
IT'S HARD.

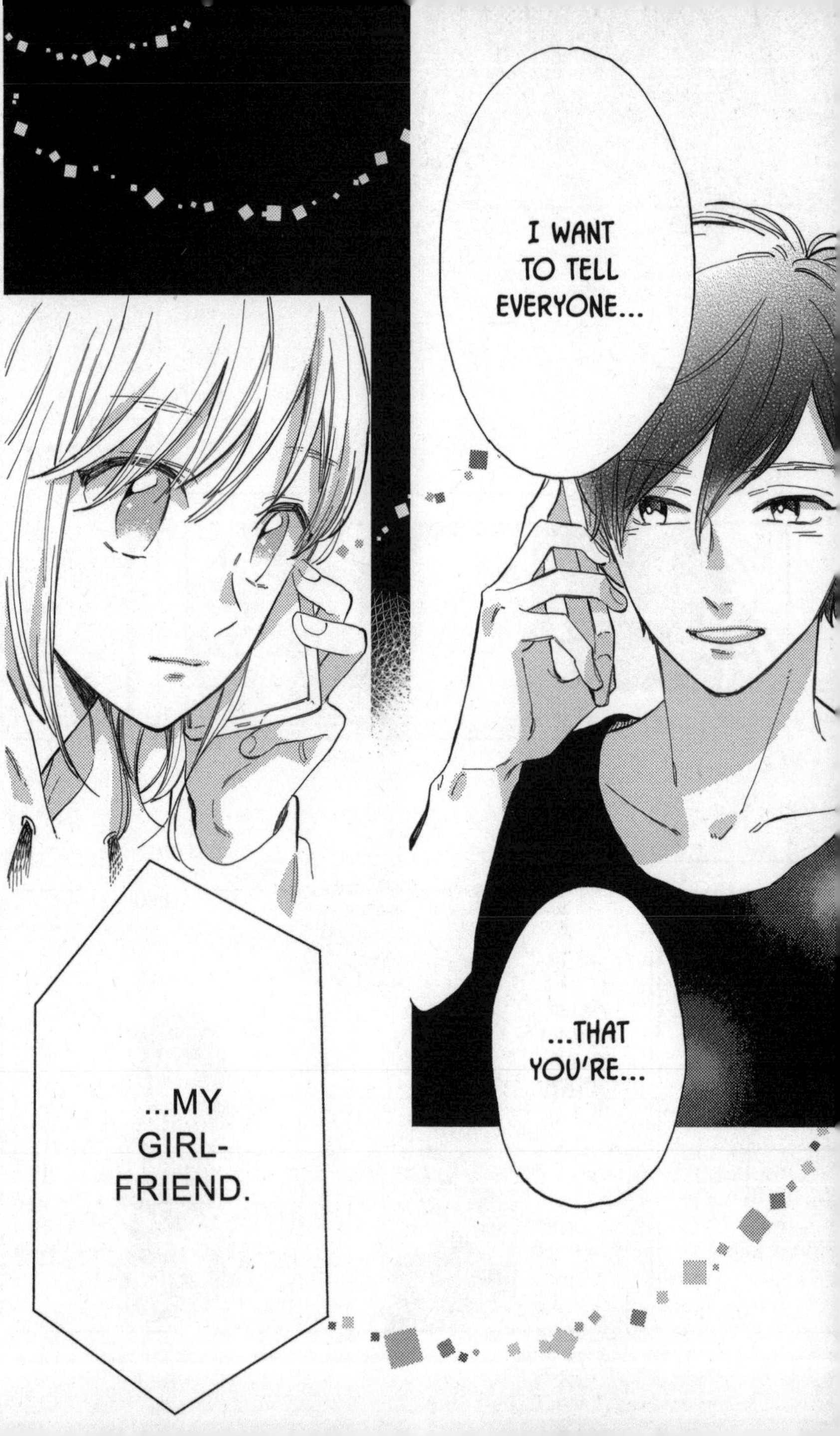
I WANT TO TELL EVERYONE...
...THAT YOU'RE...
...MY GIRL-FRIEND.

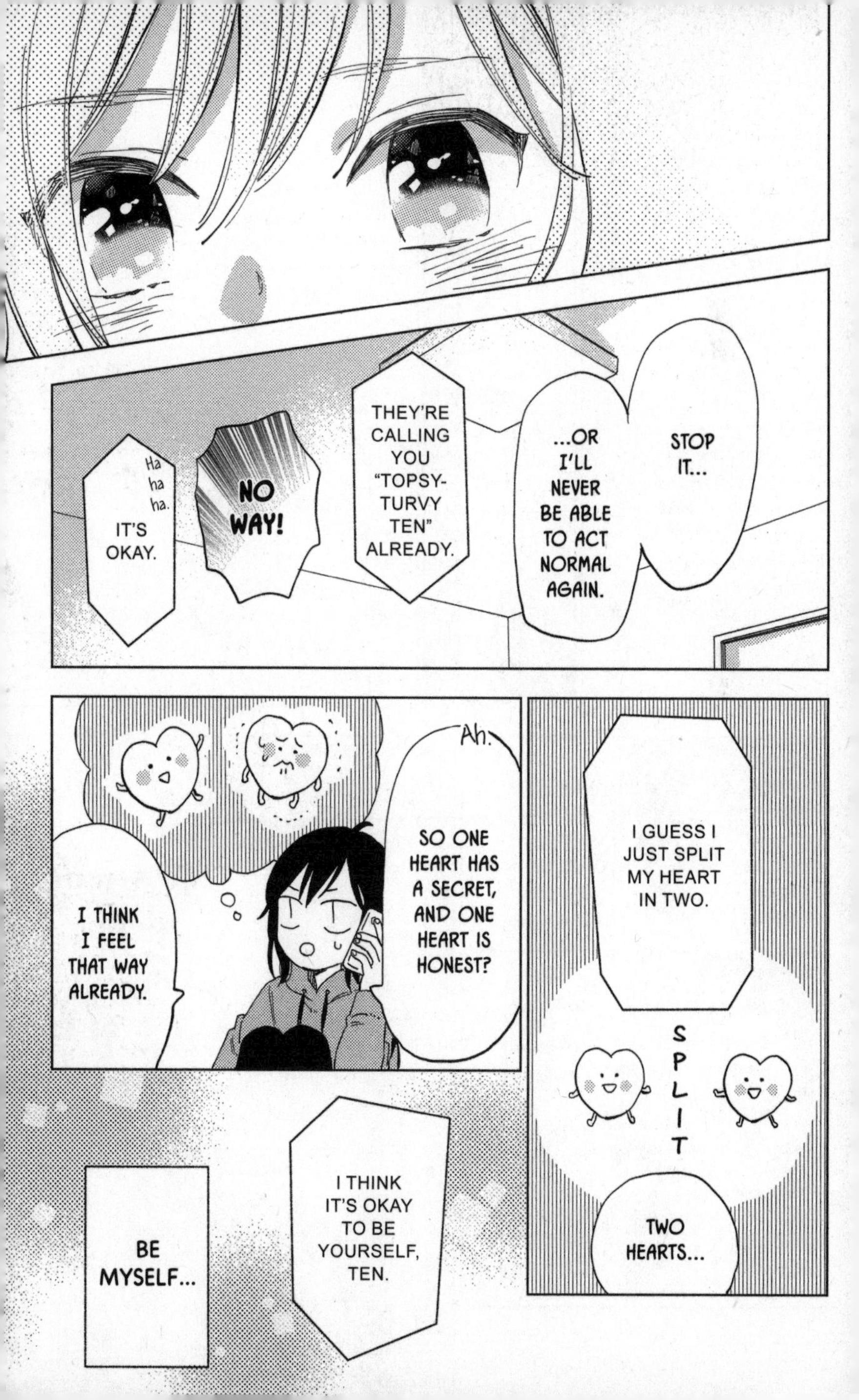
STOP IT...
...OR I'LL NEVER BE ABLE TO ACT NORMAL AGAIN.
THEY'RE CALLING YOU "TOPSY-TURVY TEN" ALREADY.
NO WAY!
Ha ha ha.
IT'S OKAY.
I GUESS I JUST SPLIT MY HEART IN TWO.
SPLIT
TWO HEARTS...
Ah.
SO ONE HEART HAS A SECRET, AND ONE HEART IS HONEST?
I THINK I FEEL THAT WAY ALREADY.
I THINK IT'S OKAY TO BE YOURSELF, TEN.
BE MYSELF...

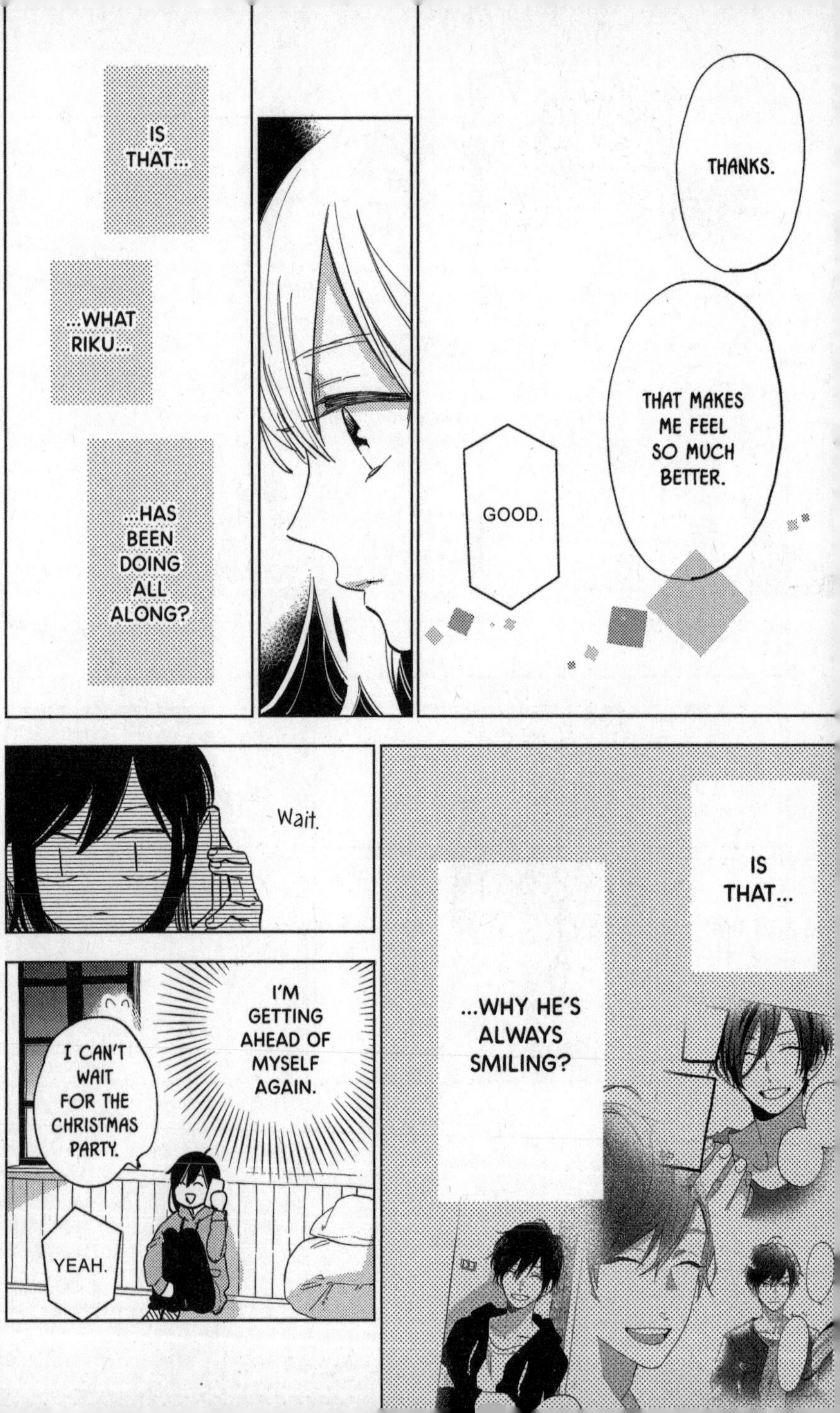
THANKS.
THAT MAKES ME FEEL SO MUCH BETTER.
GOOD.
IS THAT...
...WHAT RIKU...
...HAS BEEN DOING ALL ALONG?
IS THAT...
...WHY HE'S ALWAYS SMILING?
Wait.
I'M GETTING AHEAD OF MYSELF AGAIN.
I CAN'T WAIT FOR THE CHRISTMAS PARTY.
YEAH.

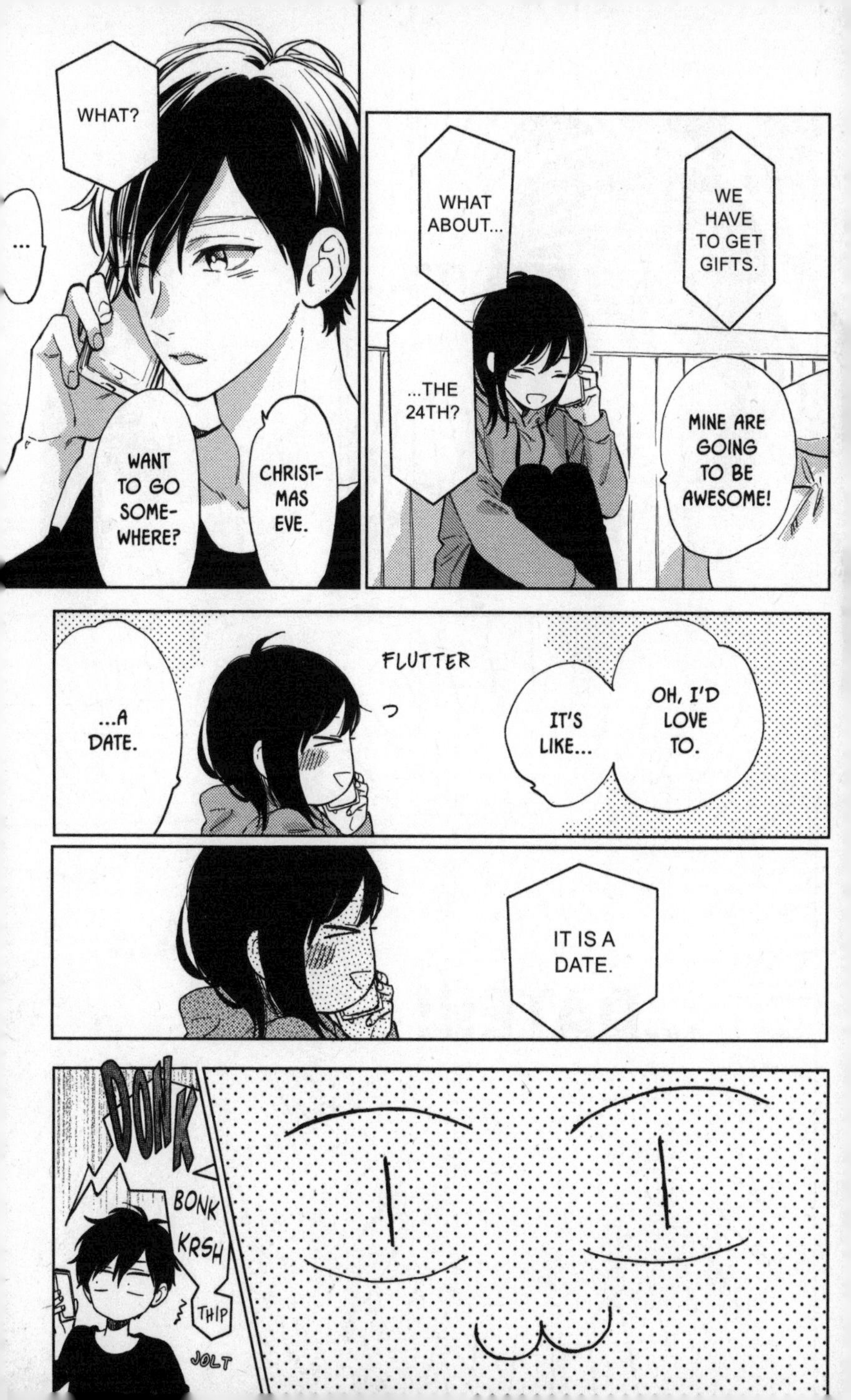
WE HAVE TO GET GIFTS.
MINE ARE GOING TO BE AWESOME!
WHAT ABOUT...
...THE 24TH?
CHRIST-MAS EVE.
WANT TO GO SOME-WHERE?
WHAT?
...
OH, I'D LOVE TO.
IT'S LIKE...
FLUTTER
...A DATE.
IT IS A DATE.
DONK
BONK
KRSH
THIP
JOLT

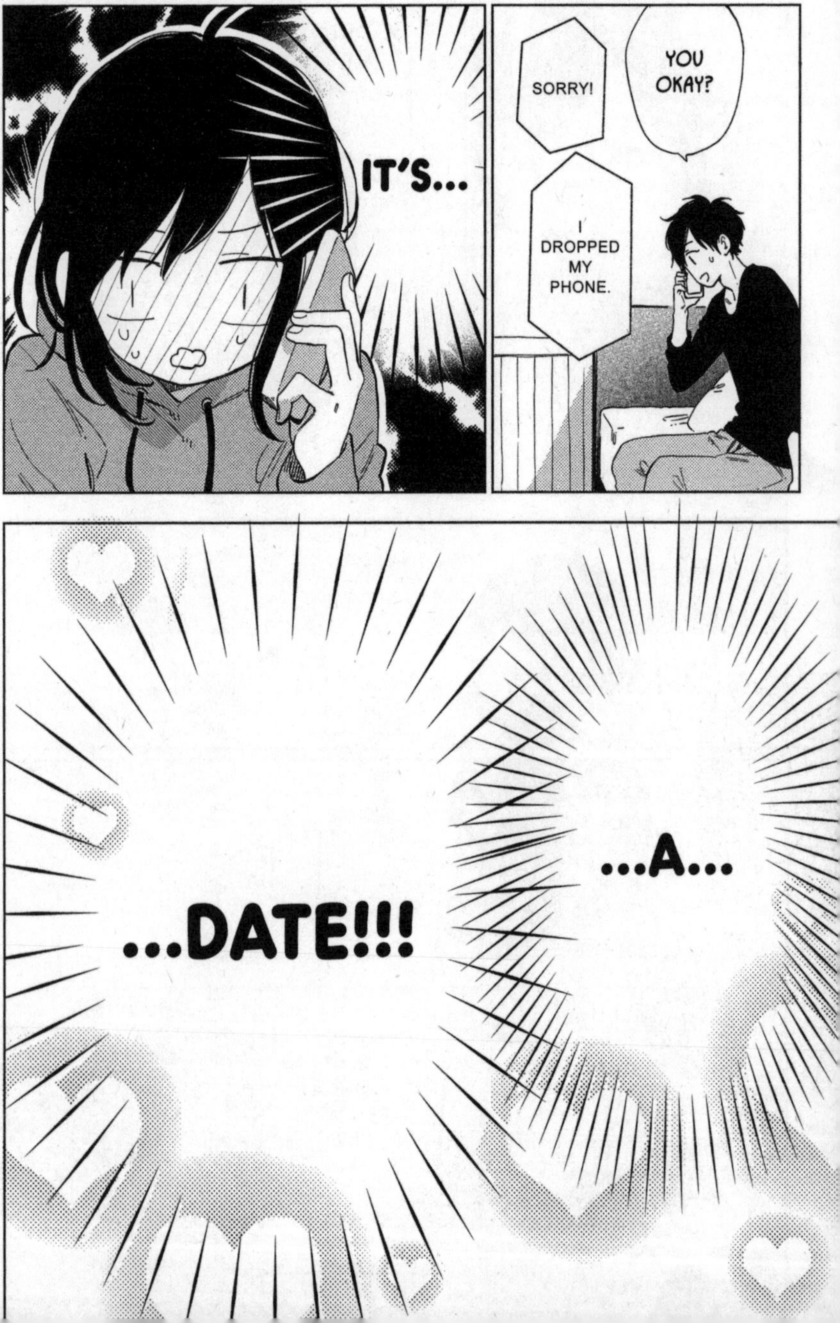
YOU OKAY?
SORRY!
I DROPPED MY PHONE.
IT'S...
...A...
...DATE!!!

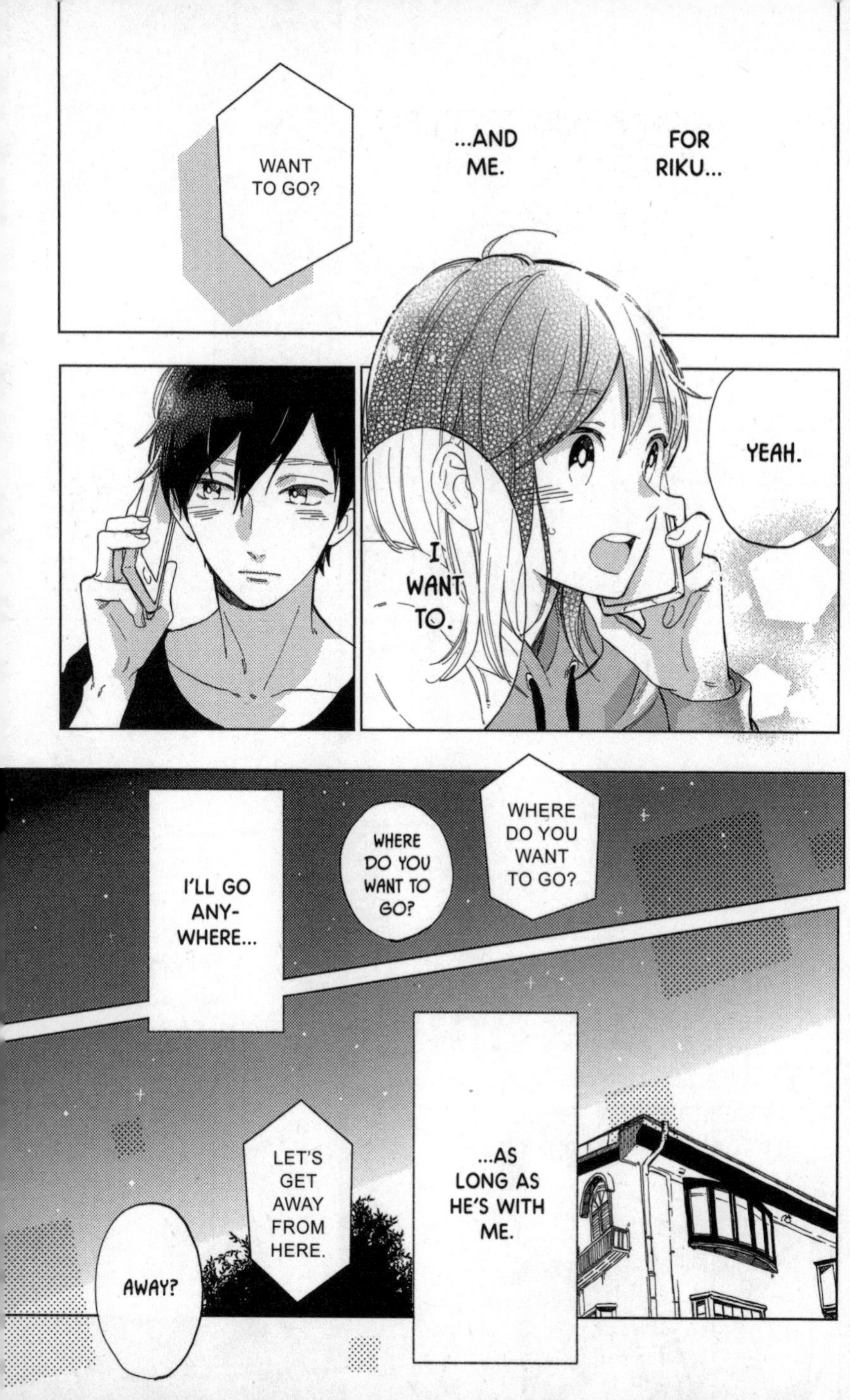
FOR RIKU...
...AND ME.
WANT TO GO?
YEAH.
I WANT TO.
WHERE DO YOU WANT TO GO?
WHERE DO YOU WANT TO GO?
I'LL GO ANY-WHERE...
...AS LONG AS HE'S WITH ME.
LET'S GET AWAY FROM HERE.
AWAY?

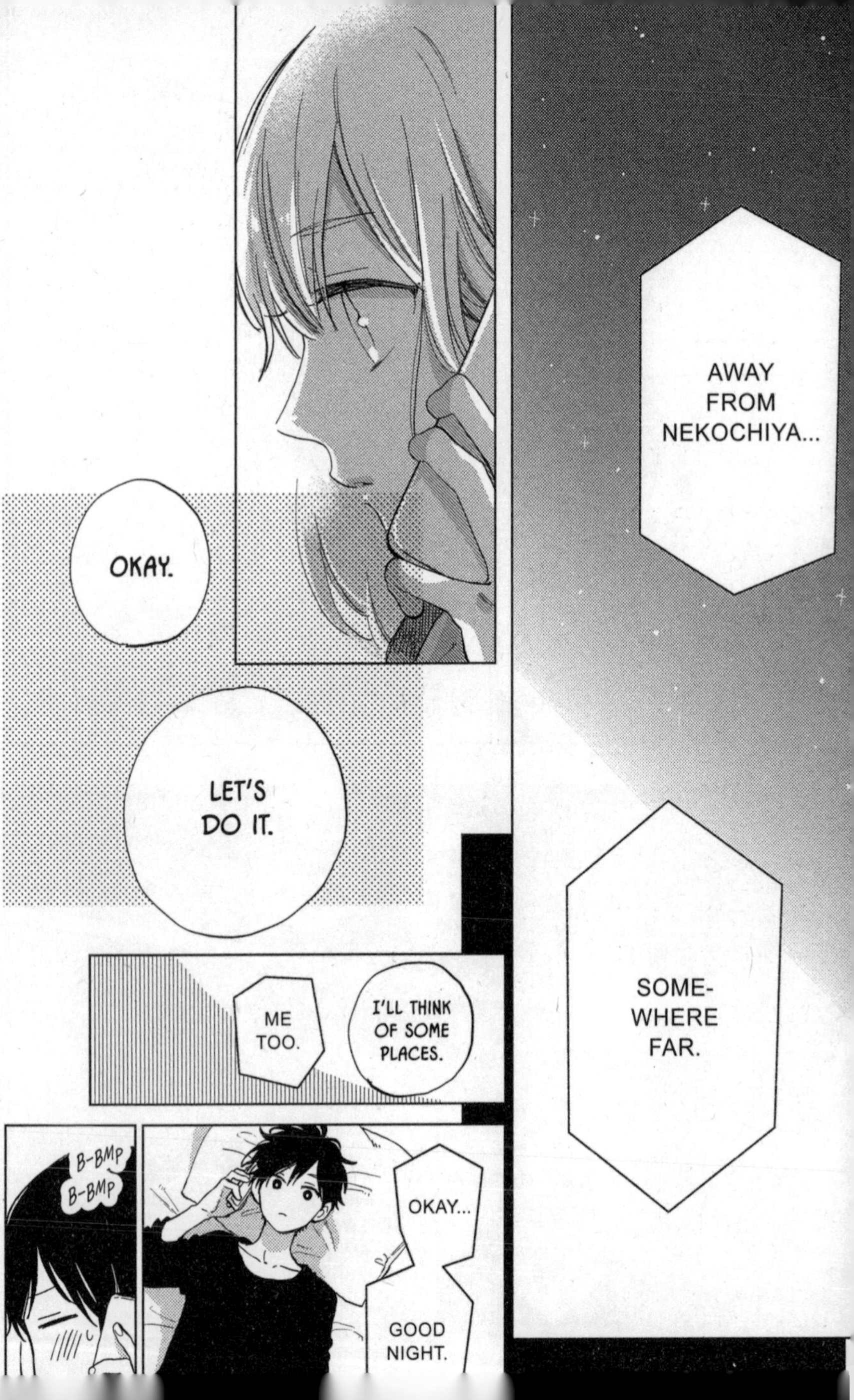
AWAY FROM NEKOCHIYA...
SOME-WHERE FAR.
OKAY.
LET'S DO IT.
I'LL THINK OF SOME PLACES.
ME TOO.
OKAY...
GOOD NIGHT.
B-BMP B-BMP

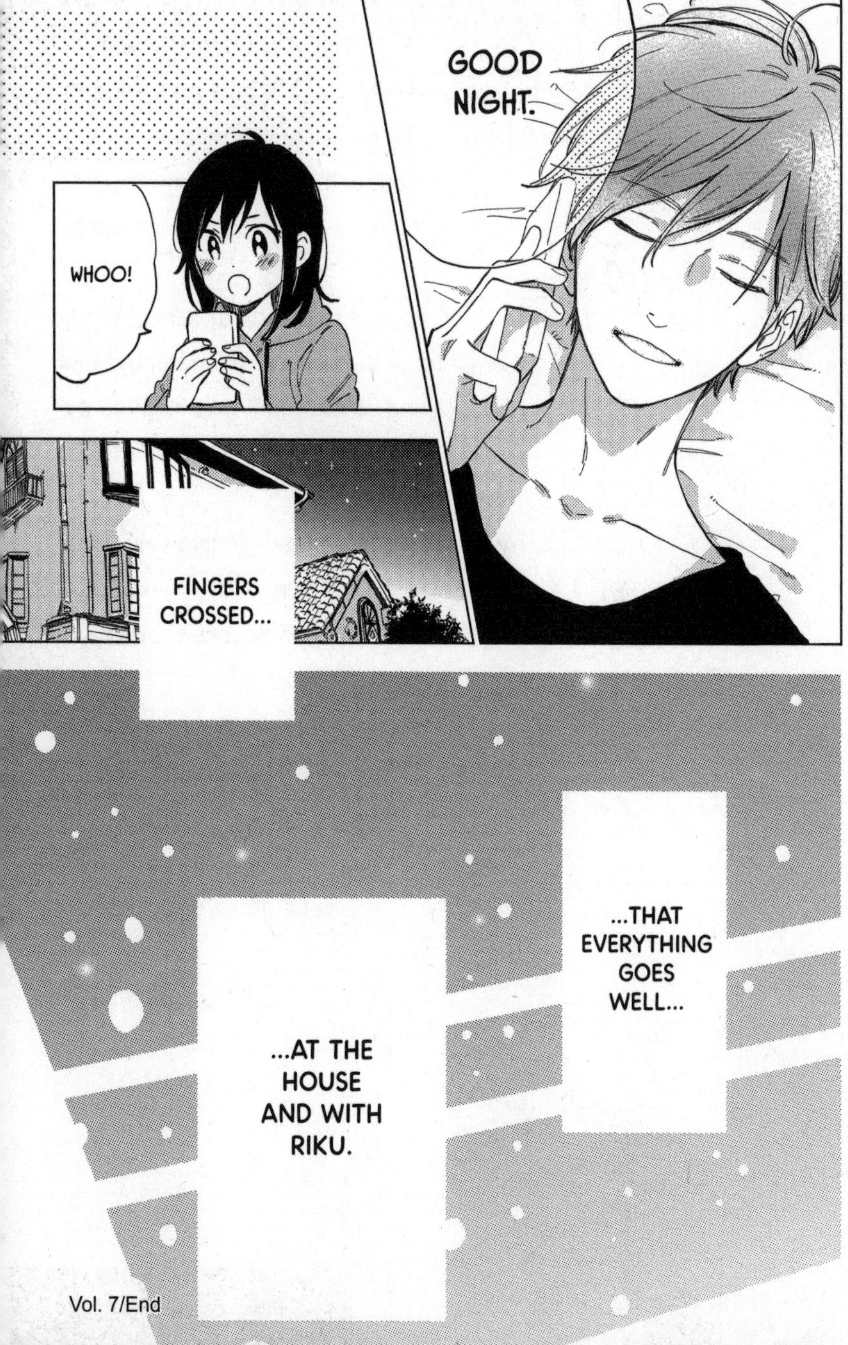
GOOD NIGHT.
WHOO!
FINGERS CROSSED...
...THAT EVERYTHING GOES WELL...
...AT THE HOUSE AND WITH RIKU.

Vol. 7/End

Hello, suu Morishita here.
Shortcake Cake volume 7 is now on sale, and
I can't help but be amazed. It's because of you
readers that we've come this far.
Thank you very much.

To give a little bit of background,
the shrine at the end of volume 6 and the
beginning of volume 7 was inspired by
the Takachiho Futagami Shrine.

Also, the karaoke place in this volume is
located in the town next to Nekochiya
and is accessible by bus.

Also, Rei is one year
older than Ten and her friends.

The next pages illustrate
a bit of Rei's school life.

—suu Morishita

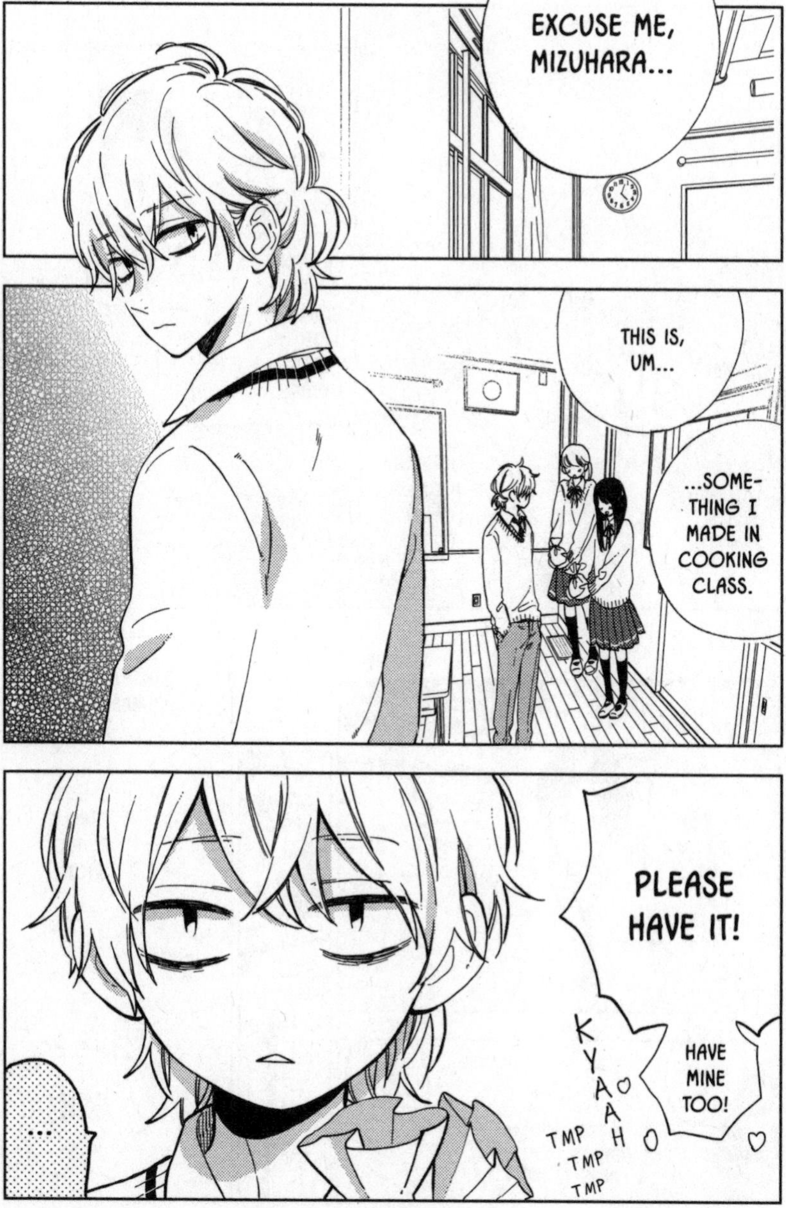
EXCUSE ME, MIZUHARA...
THIS IS, UM...
...SOME-THING I MADE IN COOKING CLASS.
PLEASE HAVE IT!
HAVE MINE TOO!
KYAAH
TMP TMP TMP
...

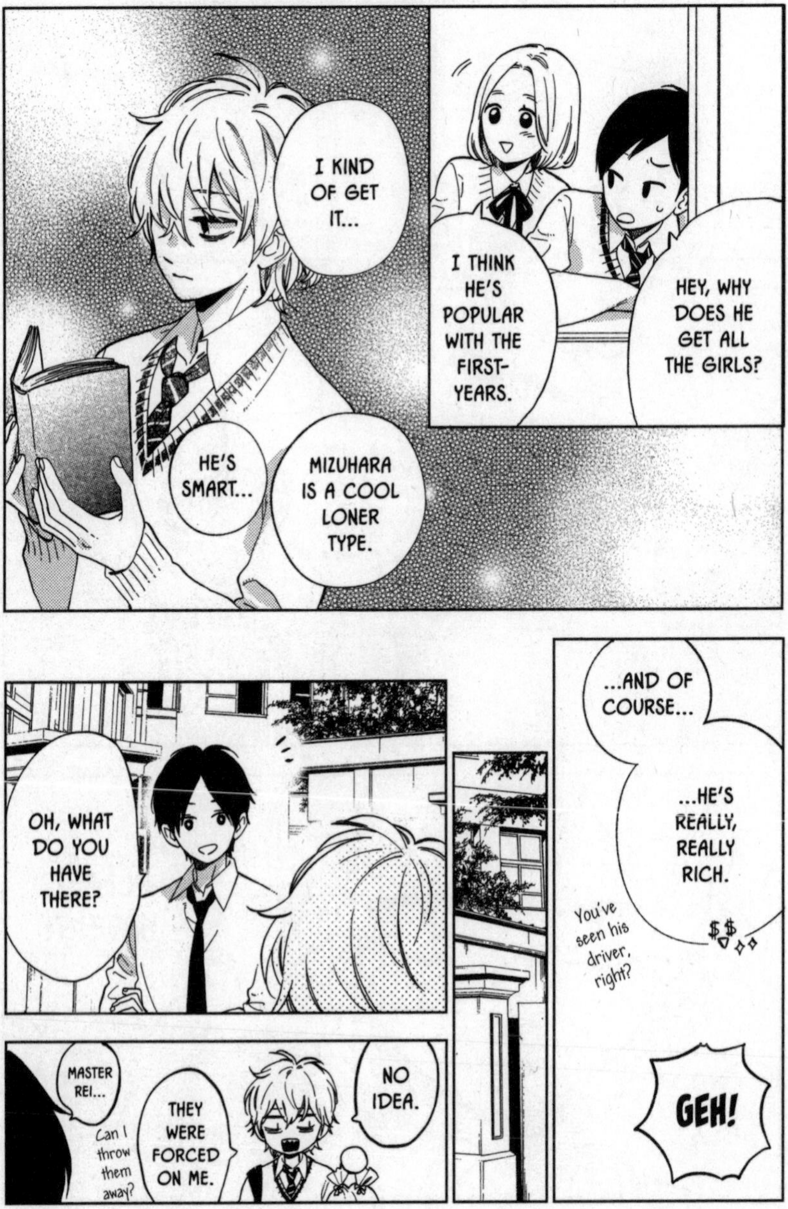
HEY, WHY DOES HE GET ALL THE GIRLS?
I THINK HE'S POPULAR WITH THE FIRST-YEARS.
I KIND OF GET IT...
MIZUHARA IS A COOL LONER TYPE.
HE'S SMART...
...AND OF COURSE...
...HE'S REALLY, REALLY RICH.
You've seen his driver, right?
GEH!
OH, WHAT DO YOU HAVE THERE?
NO IDEA.
THEY WERE FORCED ON ME.
MASTER REI...
Can I throw them away?

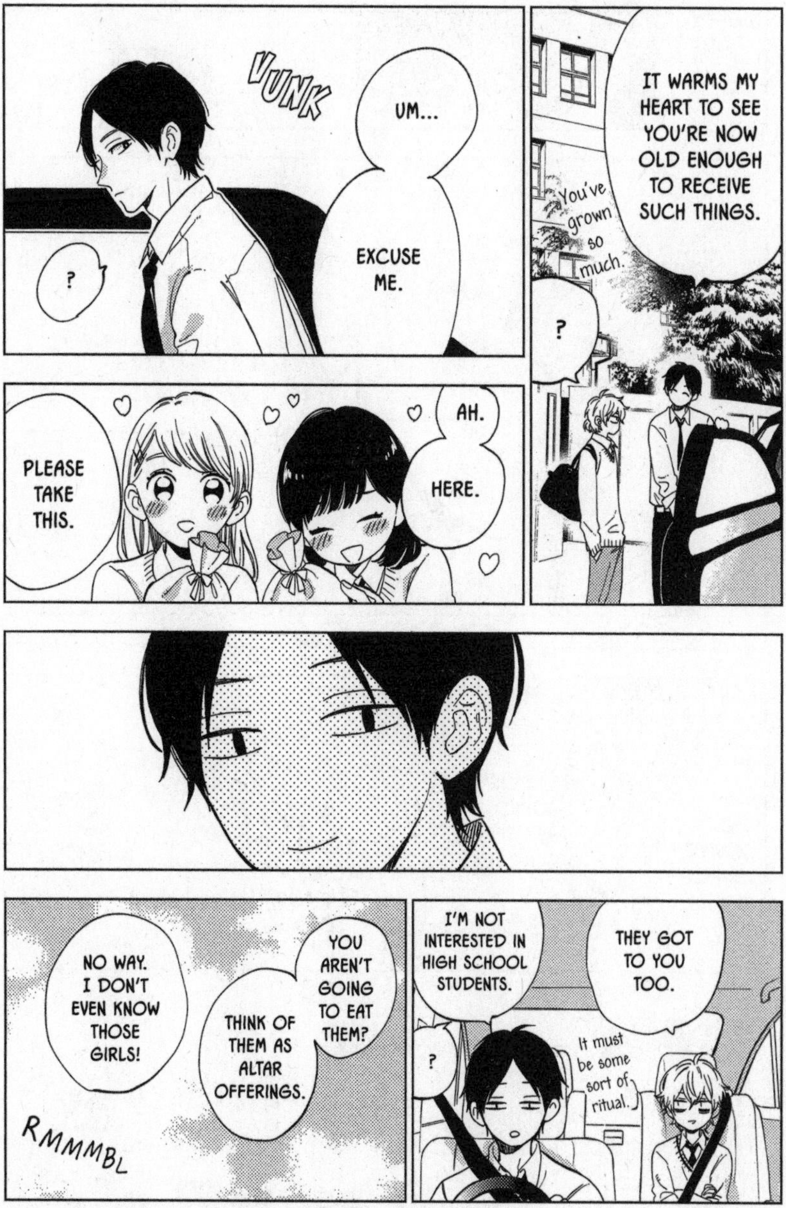
VUNK
UM... EXCUSE ME.
?
AH. HERE.
PLEASE TAKE THIS.
IT WARMS MY HEART TO SEE YOU'RE NOW OLD ENOUGH TO RECEIVE SUCH THINGS.
You've grown so much.
?
THEY GOT TO YOU TOO.
It must be some sort of ritual.
I'M NOT INTERESTED IN HIGH SCHOOL STUDENTS.
?
YOU AREN'T GOING TO EAT THEM?
THINK OF THEM AS ALTAR OFFERINGS.
NO WAY. I DON'T EVEN KNOW THOSE GIRLS!
RMMMBL

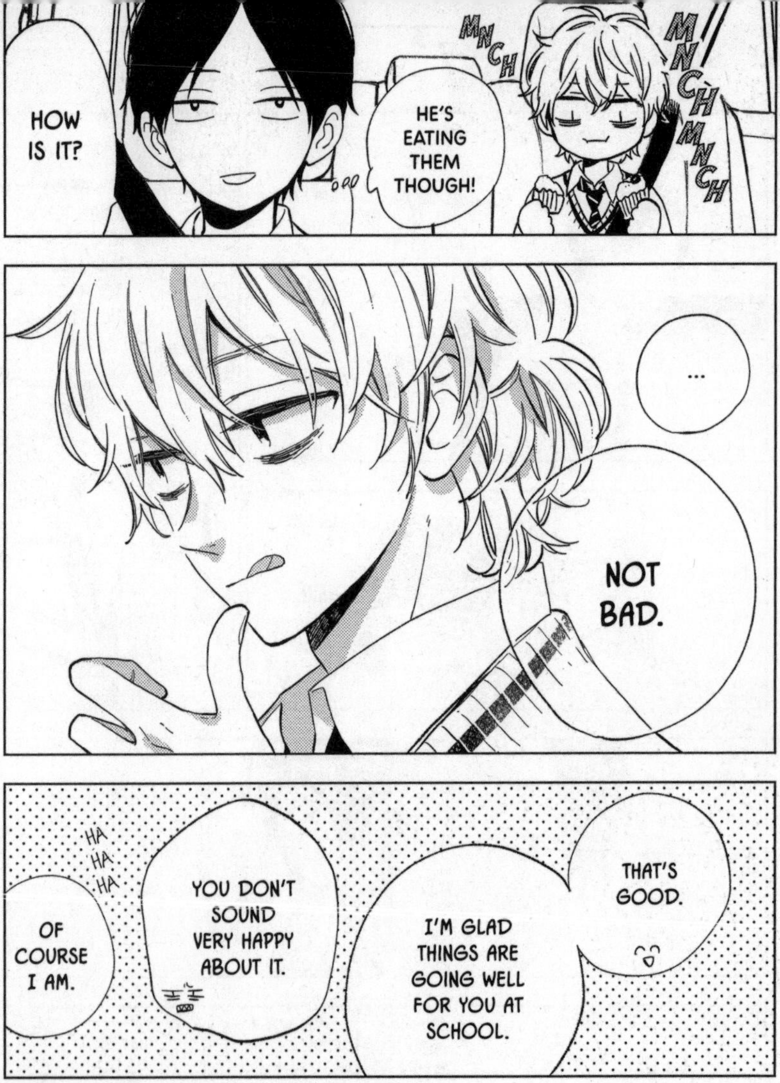
MNCH MNCH MNCH
HE'S EATING THEM THOUGH!
MNCH
HOW IS IT?
...
NOT BAD.
THAT'S GOOD.
I'M GLAD THINGS ARE GOING WELL FOR YOU AT SCHOOL.
YOU DON'T SOUND VERY HAPPY ABOUT IT.
HA HA HA
OF COURSE I AM.

SPECIAL THANKS

- Editor J
- the editorial department
- Kawatani (designer)
- Nao Hamaguchi (assistant)
- Kame-chan (assistant's helper)

& YOU!!

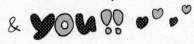

Instagram → morishita.suu

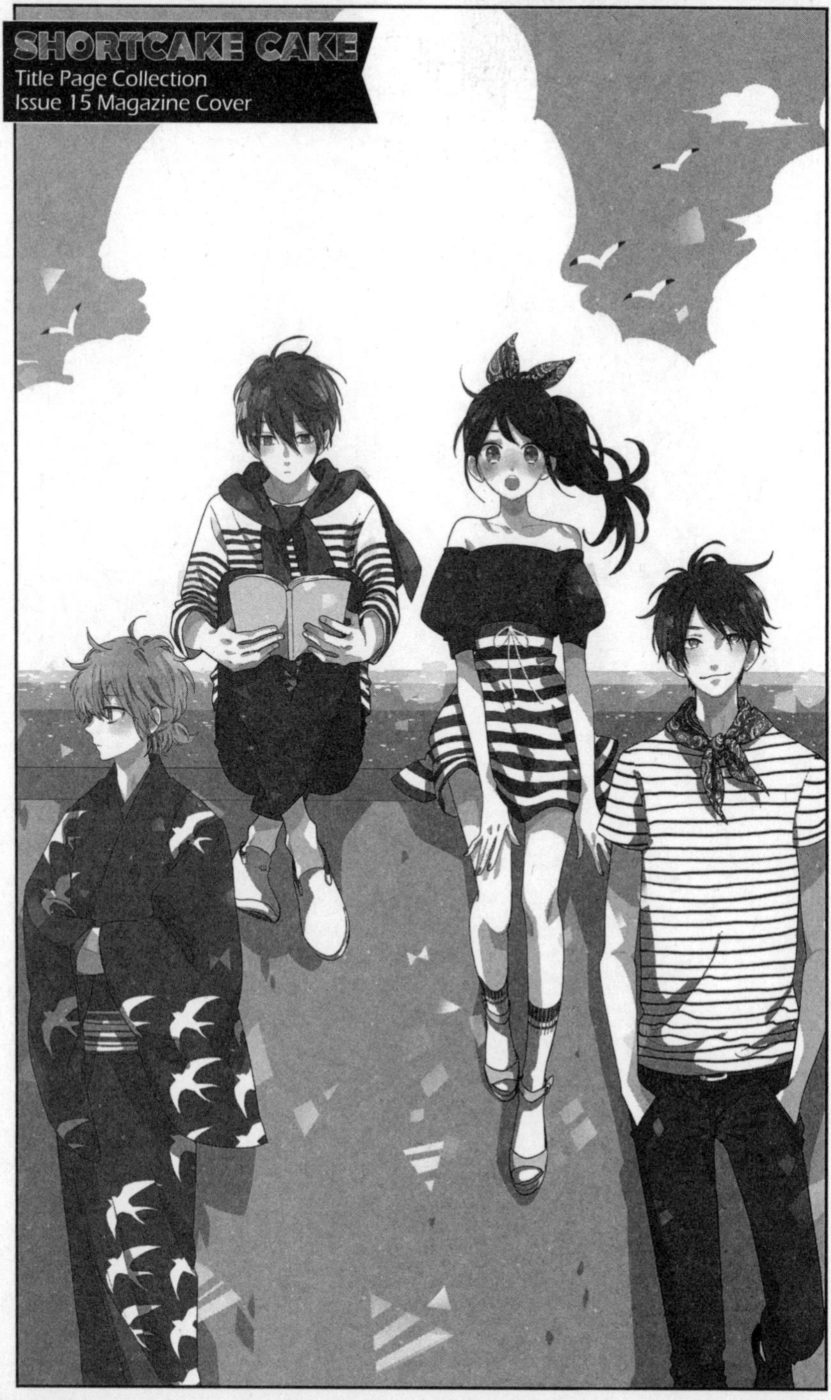
SHORTCAKE CAKE
Title Page Collection
Issue 15 Magazine Cover

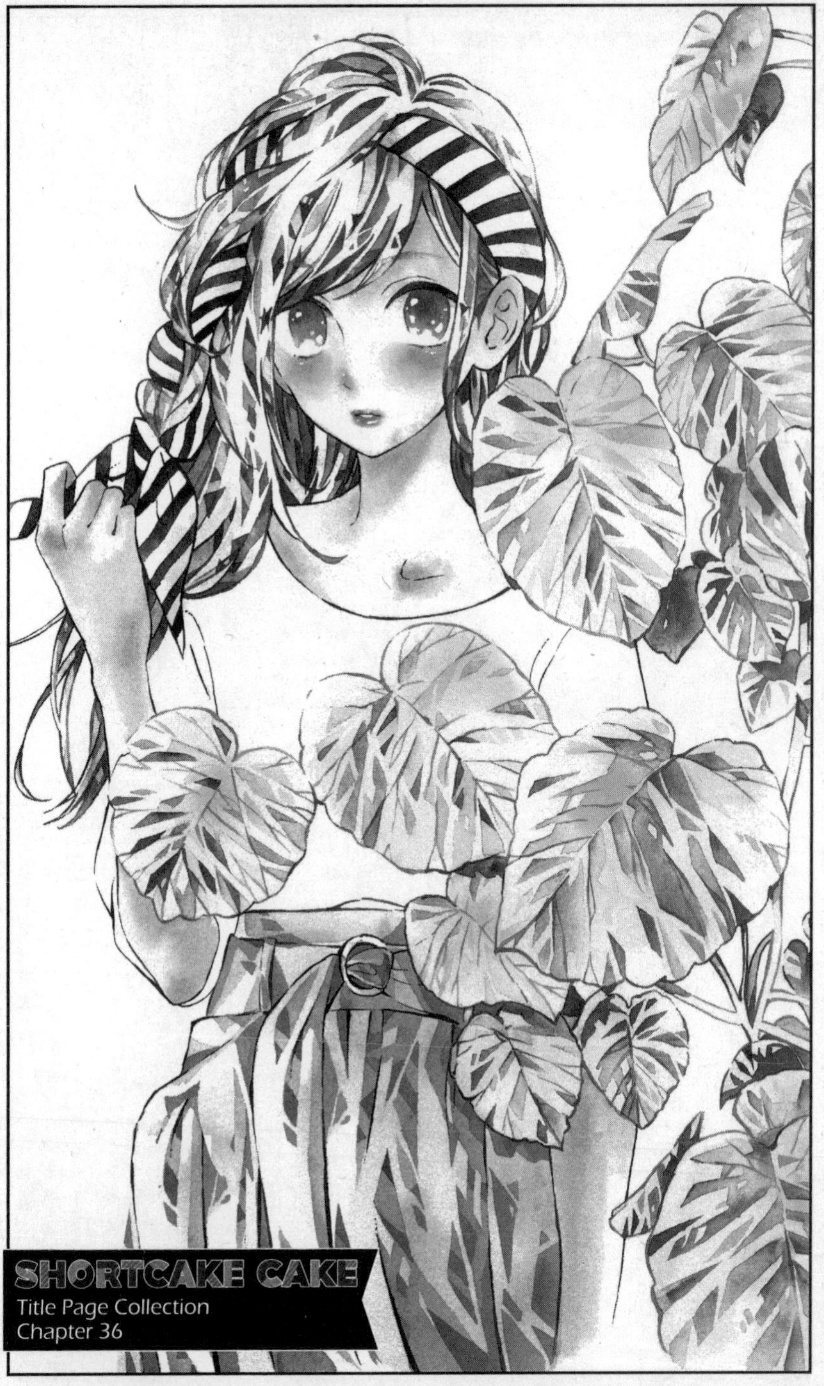

SHORTCAKE CAKE
Title Page Collection
Chapter 36

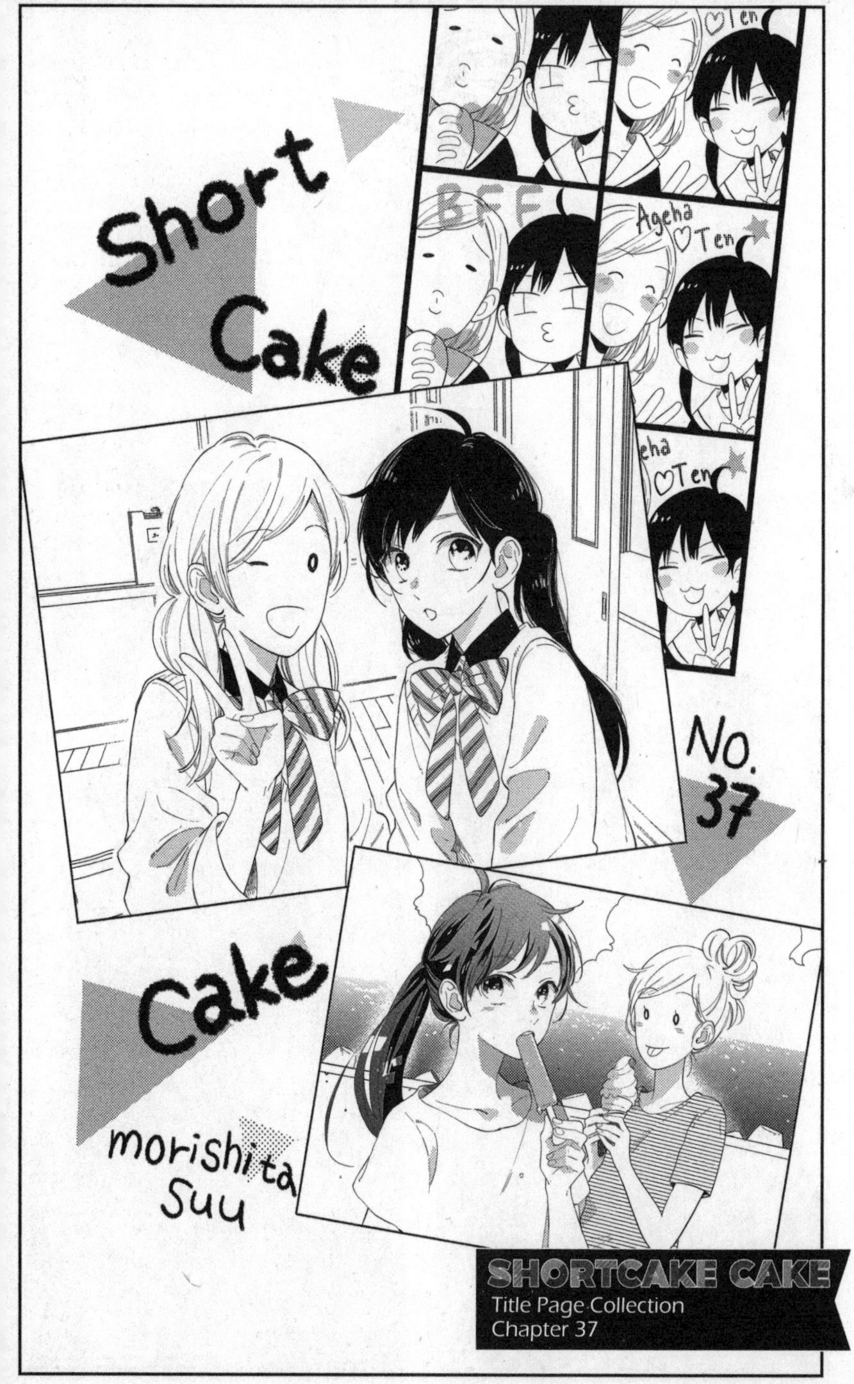
Short Cake
No. 37
Cake
morishita Suu
♡Ten
BFF
Ageha ♡Ten
♡Ten

SHORTCAKE CAKE
Title Page Collection
Chapter 37

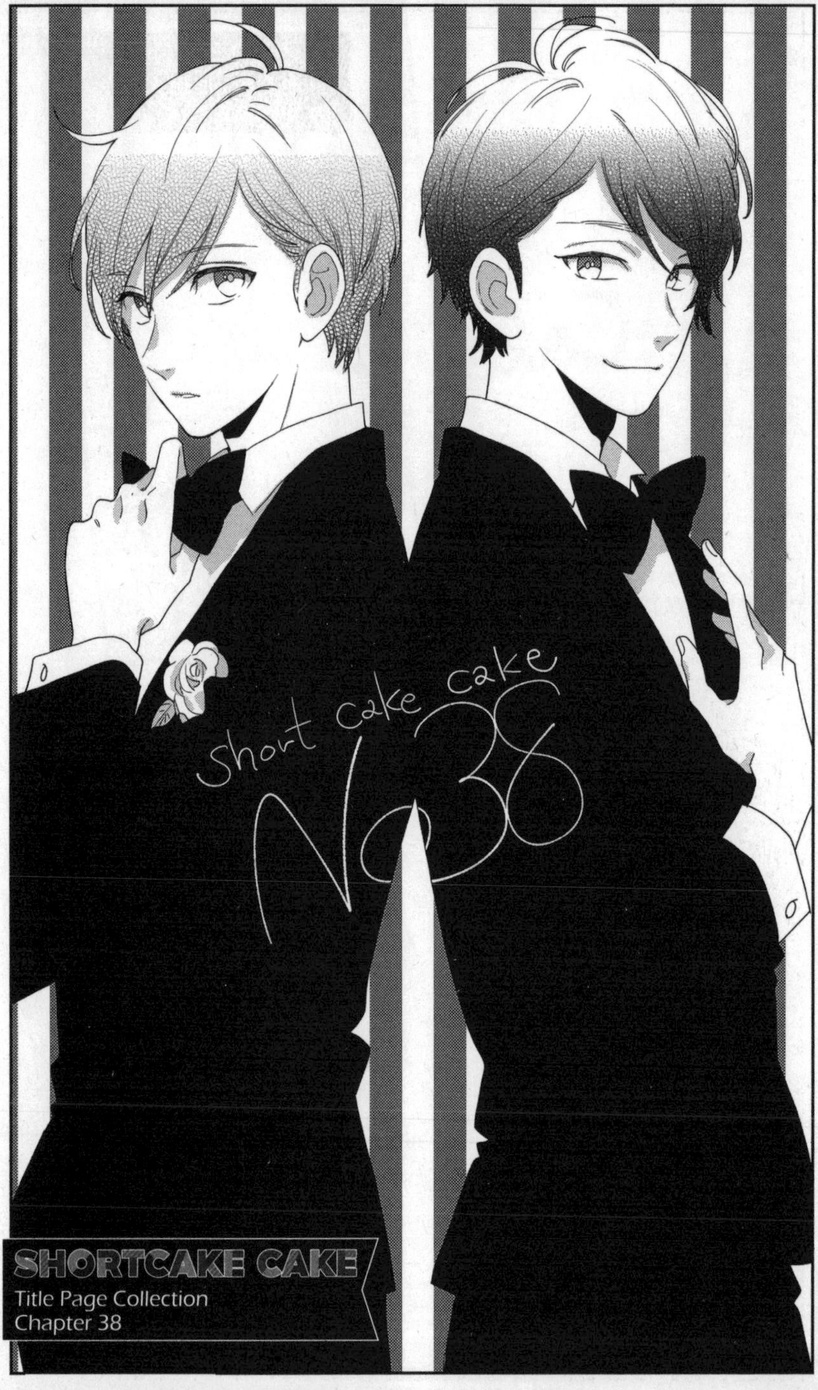
short cake cake
No.38
SHORTCAKE CAKE
Title Page Collection
Chapter 38

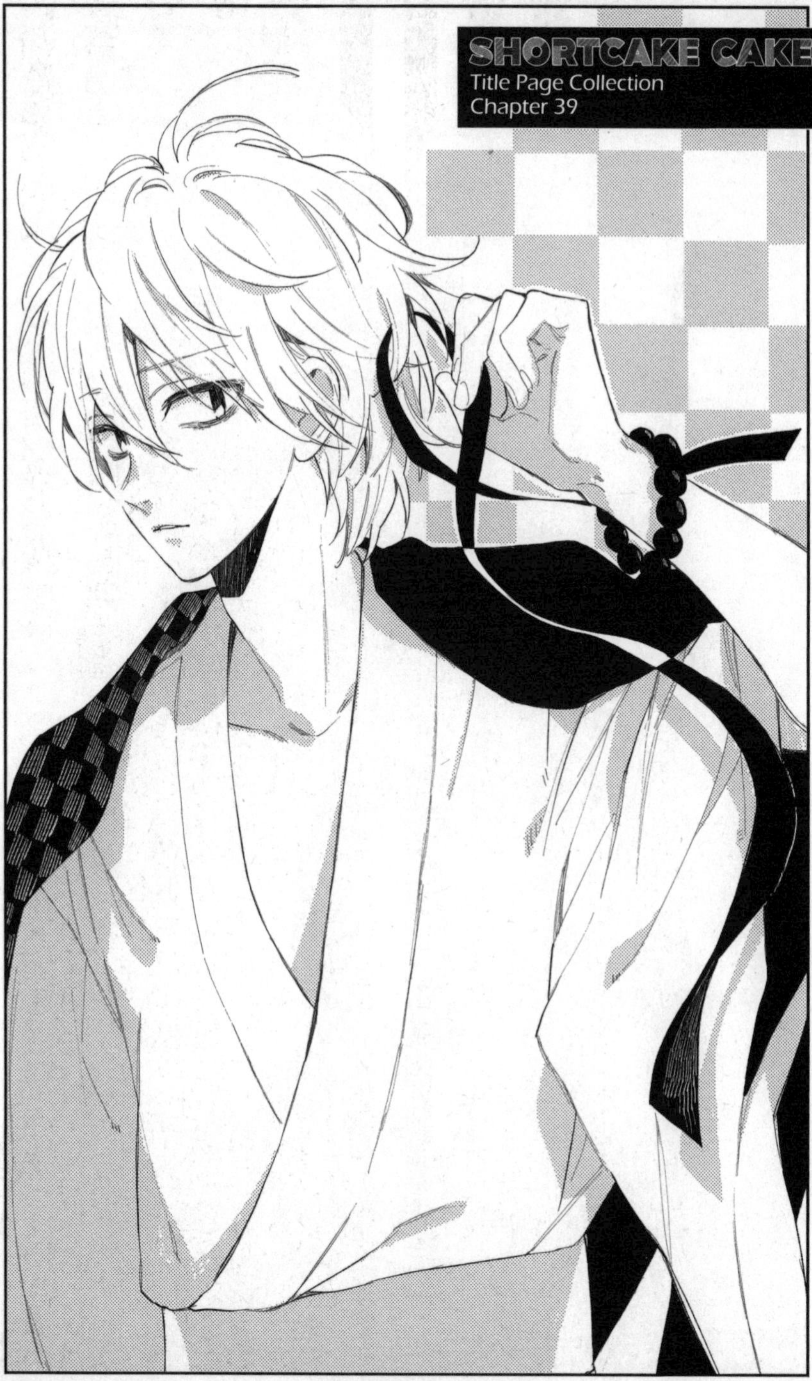

SHORTCAKE CAKE
Title Page Collection
Chapter 39

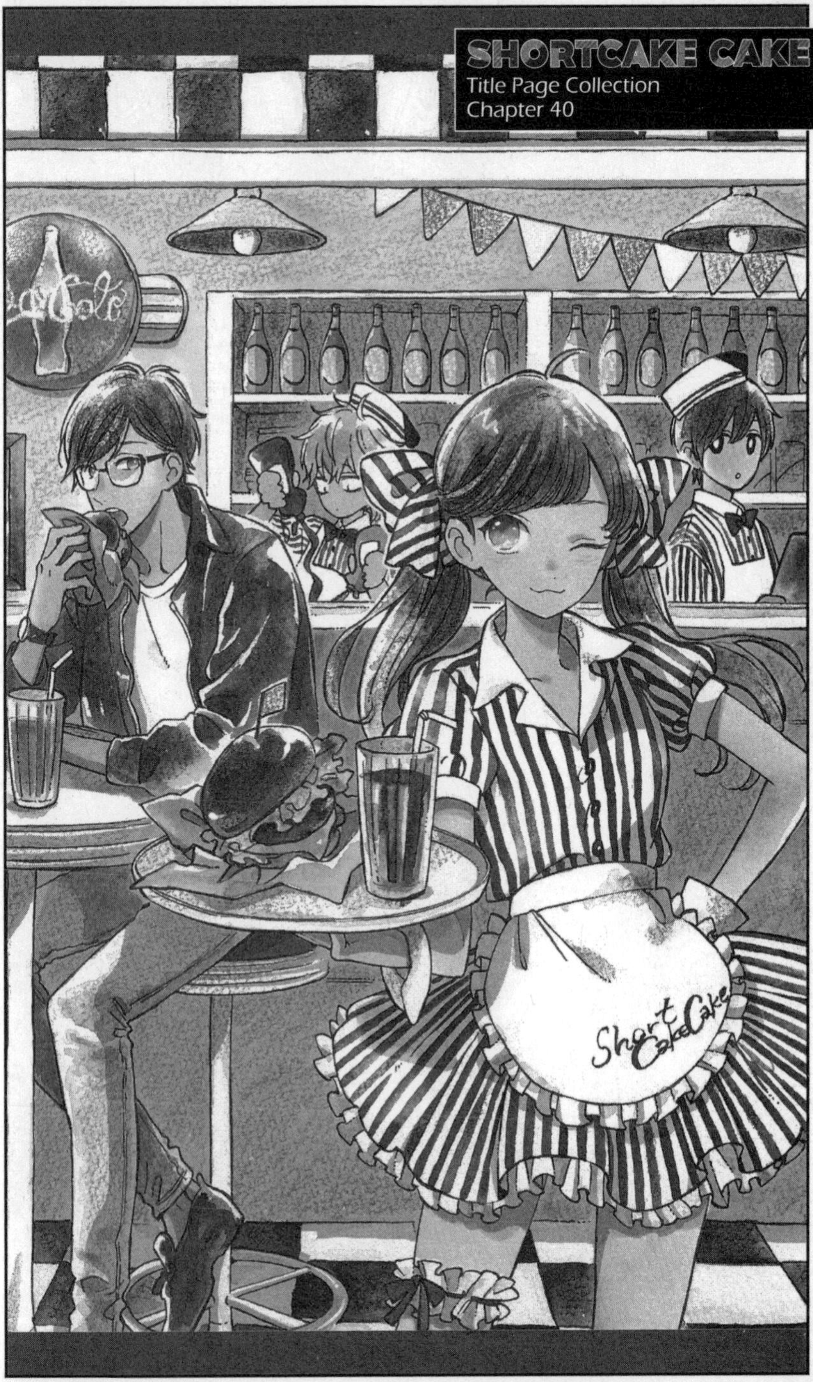
SHORTCAKE CAKE
Title Page Collection
Chapter 40
Short Cake Cake

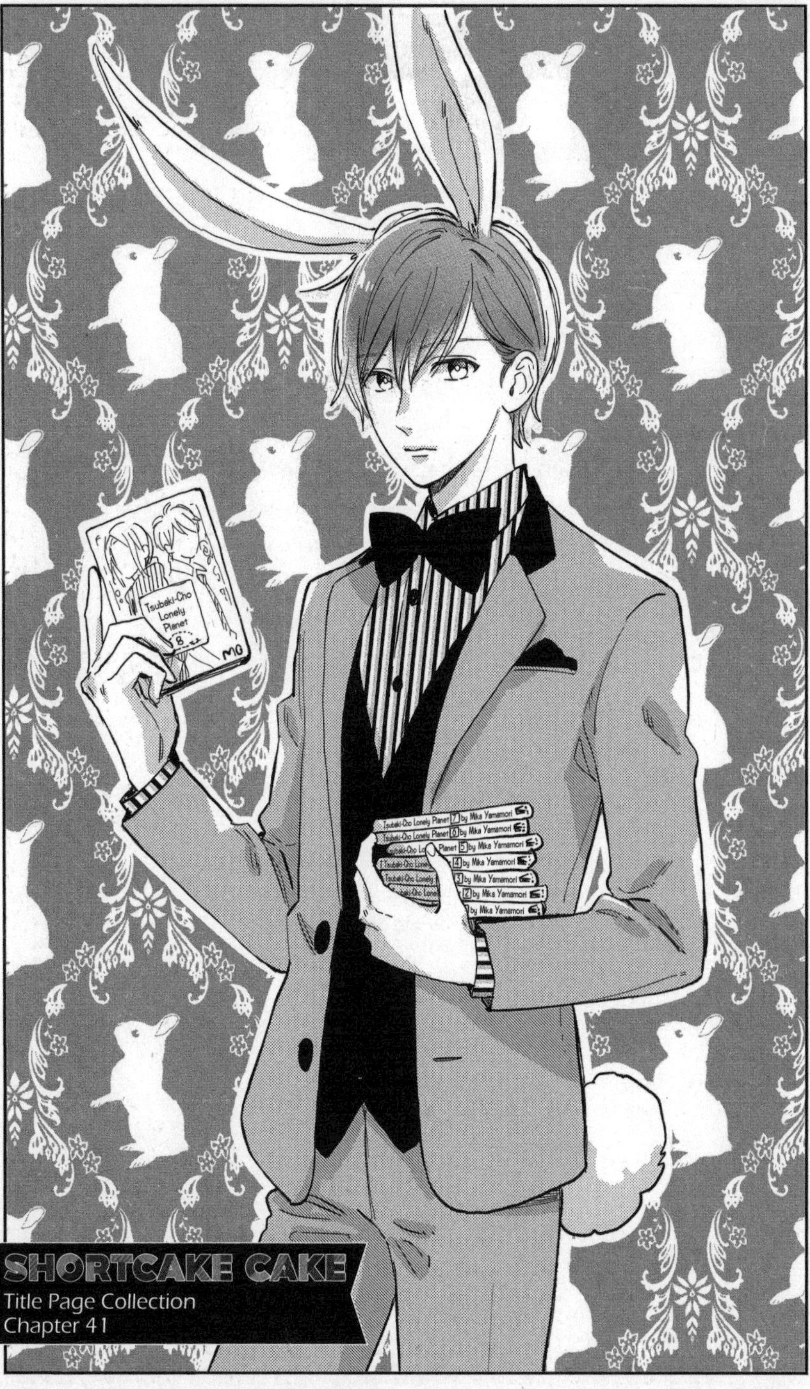
Tsubaki-Cho
Lonely
Planet
8
Tsubaki-Cho Lonely Planet 7 by Mika Yamamori
Tsubaki-Cho Lonely Planet 6 by Mika Yamamori
5 by Mika Yamamori
4 by Mika Yamamori
3 by Mika Yamamori
2 by Mika Yamamori
by Mika Yamamori

SHORTCAKE CAKE
Title Page Collection
Chapter 41

Thank you for purchasing volume 7! (^—^)
I'm spending this New Year's in Miyazaki. It's going
to be my first time back in a while, and I'm dying to
eat the fried chicken *nanban* at Ogura! And after
this, I do hope you'll read volume 8 too!

—suu Morishita

suu Morishita is a creator duo.
The story is by Makiro, and the art is by
Nachiyan. In 2010 they debuted with the
one-shot "Anote Konote." Their works include
Hibi Chouchou and *Shortcake Cake*.

VOLUME 7
SHOJO BEAT EDITION

STORY + ART BY **suu Morishita**

TRANSLATION **Emi Louie-Nishikawa**
TOUCH-UP ART + LETTERING **Inori Fukuda Trant**
DESIGN **Shawn Carrico**
EDITOR **Nancy Thistlethwaite**

SHORTCAKE CAKE © 2015 by Suu Morishita
All rights reserved.
First published in Japan in 2015 by SHUEISHA Inc., Tokyo.
English translation rights arranged by SHUEISHA Inc.

The stories, characters and incidents mentioned
in this publication are entirely fictional.

Printed in the U.S.A.

Published by VIZ Media, LLC
P.O. Box 77010
San Francisco, CA 94107

10 9 8 7 6 5 4 3 2 1
First printing, February 2020

 **MEDIA**
viz.com

shojobeat.com

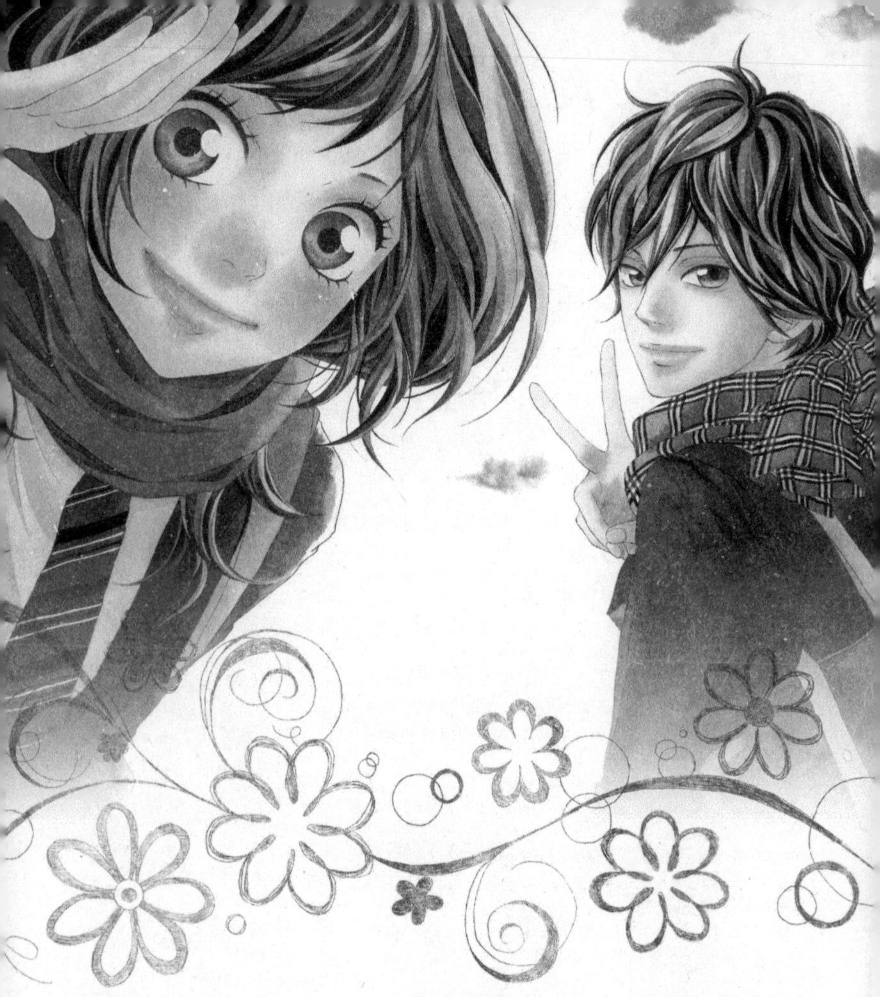

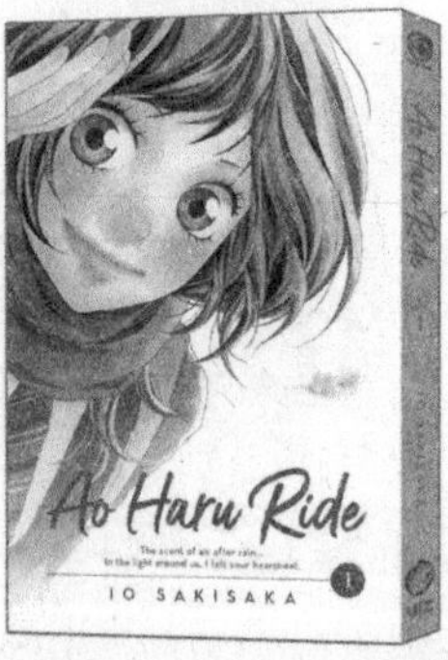

Ao Haru Ride
IO SAKISAKA

DAYTIME SHOOTING STAR

Story & Art by
Mika Yamamori

Small town girl Suzume moves to Tokyo and finds her heart caught between two men!

After arriving in Tokyo to live with her uncle, Suzume collapses in a nearby park when she remembers once seeing a shooting star during the day. A handsome stranger brings her to her new home and tells her they'll meet again. Suzume starts her first day at her new high school sitting next to a boy who blushes furiously at her touch. And her homeroom teacher is none other than the handsome stranger!

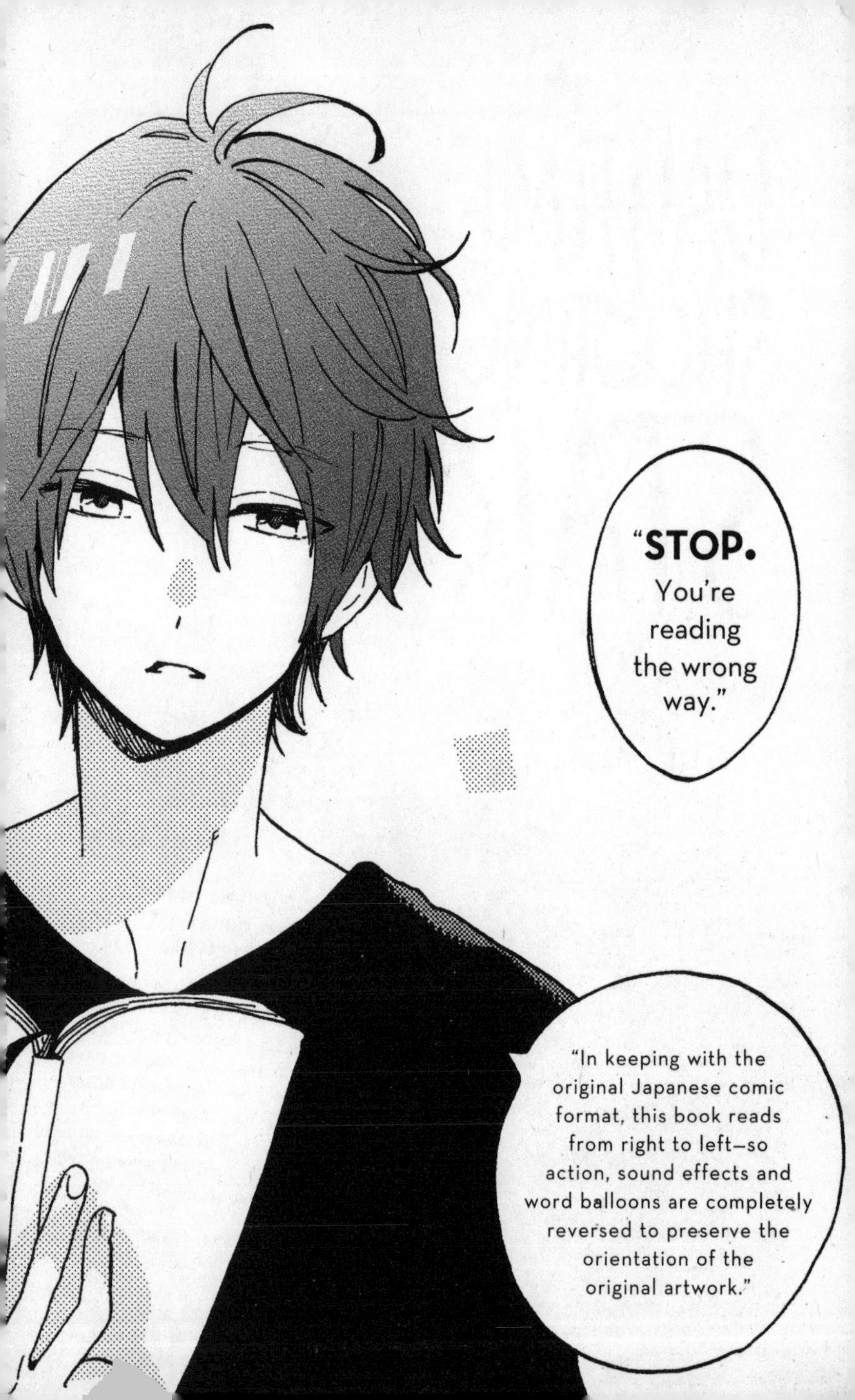
"STOP. You're reading the wrong way."
"In keeping with the original Japanese comic format, this book reads from right to left—so action, sound effects and word balloons are completely reversed to preserve the orientation of the original artwork."